WAR

A HISTORY
IN 100 BATTLES

RICHARD OVERY

**WILLIAM
COLLINS**

William Collins
An imprint of HarperCollins*Publishers*
1 London Bridge Street
London SE1 9GF
www.WilliamCollinsBooks.com

First published in Great Britain as *A History of War in 100 Battles*
by William Collins in 2014

This William Collins paperback edition published 2016

1

A catalogue record for this book is available from the British Library

ISBN 978-0-00-745251-4

Typeset in Dante MT Std by
Palimpsest Book Production Ltd, Falkirk, Stirlingshire

Printed and bound in Great Britain by Clays Ltd, St Ives plc

CONTENTS

LOCATION OF BATTLES

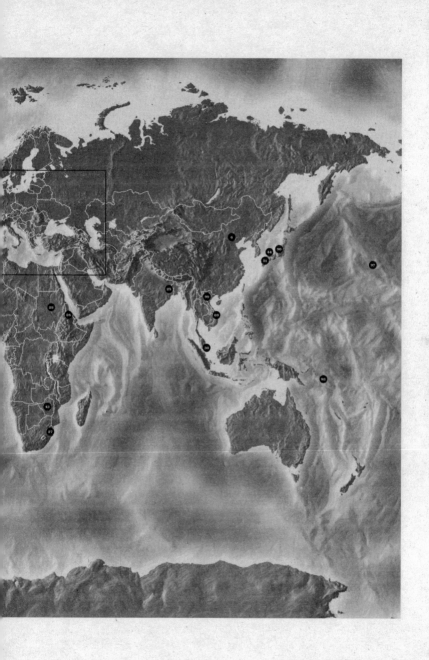

LOCATION OF BATTLES

PREFACE

Choosing just 100 battles from recorded human history is a challenge. Not just because it is necessary to cover a period of almost 6,000 years, but because men have fought each other almost continuously for millennia. Any century of battles has to be arbitrary. Anyone who knows anything about the history of war may be disappointed at what has had to be omitted, but each of the battles described here has something memorable about it. Between them, they tell us something about how the nature of armed combat has changed over time, and also how some things have remained the same, whatever changes in technology, organization or ideas separate one era from another.

It is an old adage that you can win a battle but lose a war. The battles featured here almost always resulted in victory for one side or another, but the victor did not necessarily win the war. Some battles are decisive in that broader historical sense, others are not. The further back in time we go, the more likely it is that an enemy could be finished off in one blow. The wars of the modern age, between major states, involved repeated battles until one side was battered into submission. Some of the great generals of the recent past – Napoleon, Robert E. Lee, Erich von Manstein – were on the losing side but are remembered nonetheless for their generalship. Some on the winning side have all but disappeared from the history books or from public memory.

In many of the battles featured here, the issue is not victory or defeat, but what the battle can tell us about the history of warfare itself. New weapons, new tactics and new ways of organizing armed forces can have a sudden impact on the outcome of a battle. But so, too, can leadership, a clever deception or raw courage. A history of battles through the ages shows that it is not just technical novelty that can make the difference, but the exercise of operational skill and imagination in planning, or qualities displayed on the field of battle itself, many of which are perennial. That is why the book has been divided up into a number of clear themes, which apply equally to the battles of the ancient world as they do to the battles of today.

Many of the descriptions here rely, of course, on contemporary accounts that are contradictory, confusing or plain wrong. Many battles have passed into legend. This means that some of the descriptions are best guesses by historians using all the evidence that is currently available. Tempting though it is to choose the most dramatic account, narratives of battle have to be treated with caution. Even the most modern battles – Stalingrad is a good example – are not free of embellishment or simplification or propaganda. This is perhaps inherent in the nature of the beast. Battles are remembered differently by victor and vanquished, and few people who are in the heart and heat of battle really know what is going on around them.

One remarkable thing about battles is the extent to which they have been recorded as art, from Greek friezes and Roman columns to the monumental paintings of the Napoleonic age or the modernist record of the two world wars. As a result, it proves much easier to illustrate the long history of combat than other aspects of the distant past. Where contemporary art is lacking, later generations have rendered great battles of the past with imagination and power. Each of the 100 battles featured here has been brought to life by the addition of some form of an image.

Imagination is important for the reader, too. No description, however rich, can capture the clamour of battle, the shrieks of the dead and dying, the squeal of horses, the thunder of guns, the smell of fear and the strange, eerie calmness that descends on the bloodstained landscape after the fighting is done. If these cannot be properly conveyed, they should not be forgotten. Battles are not computer games but pieces of living history – messy, bloody and real. That, at least, has not changed in 6,000 years.

Richard Overy
London and Exeter, 2013

INTRODUCTION
THE TRUTH OF BATTLE

A Japanese soldier, writing in his wartime diary during the Pacific War, confessed that, for all the horrors he confronted daily, the one beautiful thing about fighting 'is the "truth" that only war can possess'. He was writing not principally about war, but about battle – the truth that soldiers face when they are actually in combat. It is a raw, unmediated truth, for the end point of conflict can be death, injury or surrender for those in combat on either side. No other human activity makes these demands, for they lie at the extremity of human endeavour: kill or be killed, survive or perish, conquer or be conquered. The moment of truth is compelling because there is no obstruction from the outside world between you and the possibility of death. It is a truth that can seldom be veiled because it is there to see in the harsh aftermath of a field or sea littered with corpses, in the silence of the dead and the screams of the dying, the triumphant victors often as battered, exhausted and depleted as those they have defeated. It is a truth that men, and it is almost always men, have faced from the earliest recorded battles in the civilizations of the ancient Near East to the conflicts of the contemporary world.

There is, of course, a distinction between wartime and battle. Wartime describes a state of conflict between two polities, whether tribes, city-states, nations or empires, which continues temporally even when no fighting is going on, and which can be ended by negotiation or truce rather than battle. Many wars drag on for decades, punctuated by numerous battles, some more significant than others. The modern world wars did not last for decades, but their truly global scope, in three dimensions, produced hundreds of individual battles from only a few of which it would be possible to predict the outcome of the entire conflict. Battles are certainly about achieving victory, however hollow it might prove, in defined space and defined time on land or sea (and for the last half-century only, in the air), but they do not necessarily win wars. They have their own distinct historical character as particular events rather than as states of conflict. Simply put, battles involve large bodies of armed men whose principal purpose is to overwhelm the body of armed men opposed to them by killing them, capturing them or forcing them to abandon the field. The reasons why they find themselves on the battlefield are always the product of a particular historical moment. But any study of a hundred battles over recorded history shows that the outcome is almost always decided by the same mix of general characteristics: leadership, raw courage, deception, innovation or, time and again, a moment of good fortune – the legendary cavalry topping the crest of the hill. This time span also makes it clear that there is no optimum battle plan towards which humankind has been gravitating. Though strategists search for the military equivalent of the philosopher's stone to explain victory in battle, clever tactics, stratagems and novelties, morale or luck have always won battles, even if the technology available has become infinitely more sophisticated. Using battle to study the history of war is a reminder that, at the basic level of armed men pitted against armed men, warfare has changed much less over time than might be expected. This is why so many great commanders have avidly read accounts of battles fought long ago.

It is tempting to assume that fighting is something humans are predisposed towards, either psychologically or biologically, but the archaeological record shows that there have been long periods when human populations exhibited very little or no evidence of violence. Studies of the prehistoric populations of the southwest United States across a 5,000-year period have found no evidence of warfare whatsoever – neither skeletons with tell-tale cuts or broken skulls, or arrowheads lodged in them, nor evidence of stockade defences around the first small villages or settlements. Even after the population became more sedentary and cultural distinctions more marked, the archaeological evidence suggests that there was no organized violence for a further half a millennium. Only with a sharp change in environmental conditions and rising population levels from around 1100 to 1300 CE does evidence of warfare suddenly emerge in the burial record, with the skeletal remains of massacred groups or skulls broken open by weapons.

A rather different pattern emerges in the archaeology of northeast America. Here, evidence from around 5000 BCE of bone damage, weapon traces in skeletons and defensive ramparts shows that warfare seems to have been endemic, only to die out once settled communities were constructed. There are only scant traces of violence for the next 2,000 years; then, at some point after the turn of the first millennium CE, violence suddenly manifests itself on a large scale, evident in the discovery of a pit in South Dakota containing the skeletons of almost 500 massacred men, women and children. Clearly there are important environmental, social or cultural explanations for why humans choose to fight rather than collaborate, or find non-violent resolutions of conflict. The manifestations of violence in prehistoric communities across the Old World are similarly ambiguous. Evidence in pre-state Egypt shows that people were killed using arrows or spears; at Gebel Sahaba in Egyptian Nubia, more than 40 per cent of the burials in a cemetery dated to 12000 BCE have multiple injuries from weapons. In a Stone Age cave in Germany, the severed skulls of thirty-four men, women and children have been discovered, each head broken in by stone axes. In Europe, there is evidence of violence well before settled agricultural communities, which suggests that early nomadic cultures were as likely to be violent as the later, more sedentary ones. Yet here, too, can be found long periods in the archaeological record that show few if any signs of organized conflict or mass homicides.

The fact that violence between human communities over the past 20,000 years has been sporadic and at times uncommon suggests that warfare must have historical explanations rather than evolutionary ones. The early evidence of violence says little about whether these conflicts were battles as they are understood today, or mere raids for slaves and booty, ambushes to prevent encroachments on food or water sources, or ritualized acts of limited or mock violence like that still evident among tribal communities in early twentieth-century New Guinea. The idea of battle as a way of organizing violence in a disciplined way with a particular aim and a specific enemy is, according to the historical record, common only to particular cultures and across particular global regions. A study of the 2,000 years from the second millennium BCE to around 500 CE – the period when battles entered the historical record – has shown that battles were rare in most civilizations and that they were concentrated geographically in a swathe of territory from Mediterranean Europe through the Near East to Southern Asia. Out of 288 conflicts worthy of the name 'battle', 94 per cent occurred in this region, including 73 battles in civil wars. China records only two major battles over the same time span. The idea of a battle as a distinct event with its own choreography and rules seems to have been an invention of pharaonic Egypt. It was widely imitated in the Near and Middle East, and taken up with enthusiasm by the ancient Greeks and the Romans.

This is the form of battle that is familiar today and clearly it came to be widely imitated in the millennia that followed. That is not to say that all battles are equal. The exact ways in which battles have been organized and conducted over the past 2,000 years closely reflect specific cultures and prevailing historical conditions, for which anthropology is as useful as history. There have been periods when efforts were made to avoid battle, even when large armies were available. Late medieval Europe saw infrequent battles if deterrence, threats or political cunning could avoid them; eighteenth-century Europe saw a preference for manoeuvre warfare, in which armies were moved around as if on some giant chessboard with the aim to checkmate an opponent rather than force a real fight. Early modern warfare in Southeast Asia was limited by the desire to avoid battle while finding ways of seizing slaves or workers, though this did not exclude occasional conflicts of extreme violence. The refusal to accept battle, even when two armies are only miles apart, as Octavian did at Actium to frustrate Mark Antony, is highly ritualized and relies on what is regarded as culturally acceptable to both sides. Different cultures have evidently defined battle differently, from the sacred ritual surrounding Greek warfare to the utilitarian view of battle in modern warfare.

The one common denominator for all the battles identified from the historical record is the dependence on state or sub-state forms of organization that are capable of raising an army, seeing to its provisioning, and imposing sufficient levels of discipline (with the incentive of loot or the threat of punishment) to ensure that the rank and file remain in place long enough to fight. The capacity to raise an army does not mean a settled and powerful civilization. American Indian tribes could collaborate sufficiently to bring an army of warriors together long enough to achieve what was needed; the Mongol tribal units integrated by Genghis Khan into a completely militarized society represented a loose federation, but it was organized enough to divide men into divisions, battalions and platoons and to provide camels, oxen and carts to move the arrows and the few provisions that the steppe soldiers needed. The other requirement was money, and warfare played a central part in the creation of complex coinage and taxation systems – the cost of warfare was likely to exceed what could be supplied by the potential field force or navy on its own behalf. As battles became more complex with the addition of elaborate equipment and the need for large supplies of ammunition, food or weapons, Western societies came to dominate global warfare, though not exclusively so. They developed states and industrial economies capable of raising the technological and organizational threshold of conflict and applying more managerial values to the battlefield. The result since the eighteenth century was the onset of widespread asymmetric warfare between the West and the rest, though the odds could sometimes be overcome if traditional communities gained access to the new weaponry or if they could surprise their opponent. Increasingly, the only way to conduct modern battle was to borrow the Western way of war, as the Japanese navy demonstrated to devastating effect at Pearl Harbor. Even in this case, old and new mingled together as the *bushido* values of the Japanese military made surrender impossible, leaving some soldiers fighting to the death in the Pacific War armed only with swords.

If the cultural differences between battles in different eras and regions make it impossible to generalize about the historical circumstances that explain battle, some explanation is needed for the explosion in the number of battles fought over the last 1,500 years. The eighteenth-century English clergyman Thomas Malthus famously described the problems caused by overpopulation, which result in wars, disease and famine, all of which bring population back to levels the local environment can support. Population growth in the prehistoric age necessitated a search for additional resources, such as pasture, game or raw materials. If this coincides with adverse climate change, as seems to have been the case among the prehistoric native populations of the southwestern United States, then communities are compelled to violent competition for new resources. It would be wrong, however, to see this solely as a prehistoric solution. Changes in population levels in the vast Eurasian steppes partly explain the surges of violent migration and raiding from central Asia for hundreds of years in the first millennium CE. One of the excuses given centuries later for Hitler's wars of aggression was the German search for *Lebensraum* ('Living Space') so that territory and resources could match population size. When Japan found access to additional resources for her overcrowded islands blocked off by the international economic crisis, the solution was invasion of China and, eventually, the seizure of resources and territory in Southeast Asia.

This suggests crude biological or material imperatives that are all too often overlooked or denied when describing human history, but which clearly act at certain historical moments as a driver towards conflict. There is, of course, an important difference between human and animal populations when faced with food shortages, climate change and competition for resources. Human beings are conscious of what they do. War is clearly the product of growing social and political organization, and the evolution of ideologies or cultures that see conflict as justified by defining the enemy 'other', whether it is the Persian Empire, the barbarians of the great migrations or the infidels and pagans defined by the mass religions. In the period from the early medieval world, when battles occur almost ceaselessly, religion runs as a clear thread through hundreds of them. When the Sudanese Mahdist forces attacked the British expeditionary force at Omdurman in 1898, they cried out 'Fight the infidel for the cause of God!' as they rushed towards the British machine guns. Not all religions have preached virtuous battle, but those that have – in particular Christianity and Islam in all their different guises – see some form of holy war, whether *jihad* or crusade, as a divine injunction. The political religions of the last century, fascism and communism, preached simply a secular version of holy war, justified by national struggle or the class war. Ideologies, religious or otherwise, were (and still are) capable of exerting an exceptional psychological pressure to accept self-sacrifice for the sake of a cause defined as noble or sacred.

Finally, there is war as a product of hubris. As more organized states or tribal federations emerged, there arose patterns of leadership that conferred upon kings, emperors and tribal chieftains exceptional power to demand fealty and compel service. The result was the emergence of warrior aristocracies whose members combined tough military service with land ownership or other symbols of distinction. In Europe and Asia, these warrior aristocracies dominated for several thousand years; even when larger and more settled political systems emerged, the aristocracies were expected to provide military leadership, rally their own peasants as military levies, and lead them into battle. This was the Prussian model of aristocracy, but it was not exclusively Prussian and can be found in state and sub-state units for thousands of years. Kings and their warrior elites did not need population pressure or religious idealism to fight, though these might have contributed, but fought over rival dynastic ambitions, claims to land through marriage or contract, the pursuit of wealth and empire for its own sake, or simply because that is what warrior elites did. Battle was the reason for their existence. In Frederick the Great's Silesian wars in the 1740s, sixty noble generals were killed on the field of battle to ensure that Silesia was seized and held to satisfy Frederick's lust for territory.

All these explanations played some part in the thousands of battles that have been fought across recorded history, even if each has its own particular historical explanation. Nevertheless, what is striking about any history spanning those 4,000 years are the common characteristics that emerge about the nature of battle itself. John Keegan, in his book *The Face of Battle*, put together a medieval, early modern and modern battle to illustrate how men 'control their fears, staunch their wounds, go to their deaths'. But the same approach could cover all the battles in history, if there were as full a record from their participants as there has been for the past millennium. Even though battles are fought in a particular historical context and with changing military technologies, it is still possible to acknowledge their common features, and to understand what the face of battle meant for societies as far apart as the early city-states of the Near East and the developed, industrially armed states of the present. The experience of the volunteers, conscripts, levies, slaves or mercenaries who found themselves in battle on land or at sea is a daunting one. They inhabited briefly a special kind of community, cut off temporarily from the rest of the world, in which nothing mattered at that moment except prevailing over the enemy and avoiding their own death – the 'truth of battle'.

The hardest thing to understand is the willingness to fight when, as the English philosopher Thomas Hobbes understood more than 300 years ago, the rational thing to do is to run away. On every account we have from the participants, battle is a deeply traumatizing experience with exceptional levels of risk and danger and the ever-present prospect of death, or, what was often worse, a serious wound that would leave you helpless and in agony on the battlefield, later to be battered or speared or bayoneted to death if your side lost, or untreated and likely to die if they won. For most of recorded history, there was no agreed protection for those who were wounded or taken prisoner, and although prisoner-taking could be one of the benefits of battle, particularly if the prisoners could be made to fight for their captors or used as slaves, there are numerous accounts of mass slaughter, mutilation and torture. The power of the victor over the vanquished is absolute, arbitrary and, at the end of an exhausting and dangerous contest, likely to be brutal. Even the emergence of the Red Cross in the 1860s and the Geneva Conventions covering prisoners-of-war in the twentieth century have not affected the savage fighting in civil wars, nor, in the Second World War, the neglect or killing of millions of prisoners.

For most of those on ancient or modern battlefields, the willingness to fight is dictated by the options available. Social pressure, demands for sacrifice, harsh discipline, respect for comrades – often drawn from the same area or tribe – and temporary loyalty to a cause or a person combine to prevent mass desertion. Most accounts of battle from the ordinary soldier show that the event itself is dominated by a psychological commitment to combat once the point of no return has been reached. After weeks of marching and camping, actual battle can be exhilarating as men are overtaken by waves of pent-up adrenalin. Unsurprisingly, fear also exists widely in battle, yet fear does not debilitate those who fight. William Wharton, an American novelist who served at the front line in Europe in 1944, found that he was 'scared more than most people', but he controlled his fear because of his companions: 'I discover the difference between being scared and being a coward is having other people find out.' Small-group loyalty has almost certainly been the key to combat in battle because most soldiers and sailors see only a miniature part of the conflict in which they are involved, fighting side-by-side with the few men around them, the battlefield hidden by dust (in early battles), smoke (in later conflicts) or the accident of geography. In hand-to-hand fighting, found in battles across the whole historical span, there is little sense of any order or shape to the battle: the enemy in front of you has to be killed or maimed or he will kill you. At that moment, religious enthusiasm, loyalty to the king or the national ideal become meaningless. Battle is really a description of thousands of small fights for survival, which merge into the single contest once historians give them some narrative shape to explain who won and who lost.

For a large part of 4,000 years of recorded conflict, men have fought because of what they were promised or hoped to find when the enemy, whether on a battlefield or in a siege, is defeated. Looting – whether for treasure, slaves or sex – runs through the accounts of thousands of battles. The huge Ottoman army gathered by Sultan Mehmet II to besiege Constantinople in 1453 may have been attracted to the idea of *jihad* against the bastion of Orthodox Christianity, but as one observer noted of the repeated and fruitless attempts to storm the city, the soldiers 'ran towards certain death for booty'. When the city was taken, Mehmet allowed only a day of looting instead of the three customarily allowed under Islamic law, but the eyewitness accounts render a squalid picture of Ottoman soldiers on the rampage, taking anything portable, tying together groups of inhabitants to be dragged off to slavery, raping both women and young boys. Soldiers were often not paid regularly for their service before the last few hundred years (though mercenaries would only fight if they thought they would profit from it with cash, salaries or loot), so they would take any perquisites of war they could find. At Poltava in 1709, Russian troops stripped their Swedish enemies naked on the battlefield, dead and wounded, and took away the boots and tunics as their just deserts. In much classical and early warfare, stripping the dead could provide a moment of good luck, as officers and commanders often took their cash or jewels with them in case they were appropriated in their absence. The capture of the Turkish commander's ship at Lepanto in

1576 revealed his entire fortune in chests below decks, and the coins and jewellery were distributed among the incredulous marines and sailors who found it.

The possibility of booty was immediate before the professionalization of the military and its support organizations in the nineteenth century. For much of the previous 3,500 years covered by the battles in this book, armies were complex social units, accompanied by women and children, often in large numbers, and a motley crew of retainers, servants and labourers bringing the supplies and guarding any treasure. Wives commonly accompanied the march and awaited the outcome in the baggage train. Other women were brought along, voluntarily or otherwise, to service the sexual needs of the men. Hundreds of women would be employed preparing food, moving supplies, mending uniforms or helping to dig trenches. Ottoman armies numbered by chroniclers in the hundreds of thousands usually contained a whole community of followers, wives and concubines; the core of fighting men was only a smaller fraction of the whole. In Europe, the large train of women had been gradually suppressed by the seventeenth century, partly to allow armies to become more mobile but also on moral grounds. Women came to be excluded from military occupations and were left behind in the garrison towns. Those women who accompanied the army were widely regarded as prostitutes. This explains the savage killing of hundreds of women after the Battle of Naseby in the English Civil War. Puritan soldiers punished the women for their immorality, even though a number of them were the wives of Royalist officers. As women came to be excluded from military life, so battles became a male domain, occasionally invaded by a handful of women who wanted to serve as soldiers (an estimated 30 to 50 in the French Revolutionary Wars, 400 in the American Civil War). In the modern age, the identification of battle as an expression of male identity was a central feature of much pacifist writing by women, most famously in Virginia Woolf's 1938 critique of posturing manhood, *The Three Guineas*. Since the First World War, women have once again come to form an important auxiliary arm to the regular forces, but now they are uniformed and organized, and bear no resemblance to the vast baggage-trains of earlier times.

In addition to the prospect of booty, soldiers have also been sustained, or alarmed, by religious symbols, superstitions, visions and omens. There are obvious reasons why appeals to the supernatural were important. Belief in a god or gods or the power of the sacred was common to almost all armies throughout history. Since victory was never certain, soldiers and their commanders searched for some sign that they enjoyed divine protection; indications that the opposite might be the case did not necessarily stop soldiers fighting, but it could be deeply demoralizing. The ancient Greek historian Herodotus described arguments in Athens over how to interpret the Delphic Oracle when the priestess predicted that an enemy from the east would bring inevitable woe to the city – 'from the topmost roofs trickles black blood' – but that all-seeing Zeus 'gives a wooden wall' for 'divine Salamis'. The pronouncement was difficult to interpret, though it was widely regarded as a signal of impending doom. But the Athenian Themistocles insisted that the wooden wall meant ships, and that the city should spend its accumulated wealth on procuring a new fleet. His view prevailed and the Persian fleet was destroyed at Salamis a few months later. In the later siege of Constantinople, when the fearful Greek population of the city awaited the Ottoman onslaught, there was an eclipse of the full moon that left just a thin lunar crescent, symbol of their Islamic enemy. The inhabitants saw this as a profound omen of the city's collapse; the Ottoman army rejoiced at such a clear indication of divine favour and a few days later the city was in their hands. Battles were fought by soldiers blessed by priests, buoyed up by favourable auguries and omens, or certain that death in a sacred cause would ensure a life hereafter.

The conditions of most battlefields were such that superstitious expectation offered a thin ray of hope that somehow, amidst the sheer arbitrariness of combat, you might survive where others perished. The context of fighting across the ages has been universally grim. Soldiers often fought after a long march, already exhausted, with bleeding or blistered feet. They were at the mercy of the weather, and mud, rain or snow made a tough assignment tougher still. Dirt, insects, infection and hunger added to a soldier's routine woes. The anti-hero in Erich Maria Remarque's *All Quiet on the Western Front* complains that his experience of war is only 'despair, death, fear... an abyss of suffering'. The searing stories of the retreat of Napoleon's *Grande Armée* from Russia in 1812 show what price ordinary soldiers paid for their leaders' grand ambitions, as well as the civilians unlucky enough to be in the path of a desperate army. In battle, the physical demands are hard for anyone who has not experienced it to grasp. After the Battle of Blenheim in 1704, the defeated Comte de Mérode recorded that he had fought continuously for thirty hours, despite suffering an injured and swollen knee, had had no sleep, no food, and just one swig of water. This could be a soldier's tale from any battle. 'Why,' asks William Wharton, 'do humans, especially military humans, want to do things the hard way?' Soldiering before the age of aircraft and long-range artillery was an inefficient way of utilizing manpower that too often had soldiers fighting in a daze of exhaustion, at the end of their tether, bleeding from unnoticed wounds, and all because of what their commanders asked of them. Small wonder that time and again in battle accounts, from swigs of rum before a naval engagement to the half pint of brandy served to Napoleon's soldiers just before Austerlitz, alcohol is used to revive flagging spirits, to dull sharp fears or to combat the freezing climate.

Heat was just as debilitating as cold and a great many of the 100 battles recorded here were fought in searing temperatures and dry conditions that quickly turned the battlefield into a fog of churned-up dust or sand. The critical resource in all kinds of weather, more important for soldiers than any weapon, was water. It is what every wounded soldier asks for first. A shrewd commander makes sure that the army is camped near a supply of fresh water or that water can be ferried to the battlefield. Richard the Lionheart only won the battle at Arsuf because Crusader ships plied along the coast leading to Jaffa with barrels of water for the exhausted, sweaty Europeans in his army.

Even then, men died of heat exhaustion on the way. It is hard to imagine having to fight amidst all the clamour and gore of the battlefield for hours on end with no prospect of water to assuage the debilitating effects of dehydration. American army recruits in the Second World War did 'water hikes' to prepare them for the reality of battle, marching 100 kilometres (60 miles) over two days in warm weather with just a 1-litre (2-pint) canteen to last the whole time. 'My mouth starts sticking to itself,' wrote William Wharton, 'my tongue to the top of my mouth, my teeth to my lips, my lips to each other.'

There comes a moment in most battles whose outcome is decided in a day or so of combat when one side or the other senses victory and the other senses defeat. Since most soldiers can see little more of the battlefield than what is immediately around them and are given almost no information in the midst of a battle, the way that sense is communicated comes either from the exhortations of commanders if victory seems likely, or the flight of leaders who realize that they have lost. The effect when a commander flees – as at Bannockburn in 1314 when Edward II turned tail – can be immediately damaging. Flight or surrender is a fast-moving infection. Once it is evident, the willingness to continue fighting evaporates with a startling speed. One of the strangest phenomena in battle is the moment when soldiers, who only minutes before are firing muskets or hacking away at the enemy, realize that they have to save themselves. Of course, surrender was often not an option, and there are numerous accounts of battles ancient and modern in which a unit of soldiers or horsemen is annihilated where it stands, surrounded by a sea of enemies. What that moment of certain death means, when men are observed fighting with a frenetic energy against all the odds, self-evidently cannot be known. But where it is possible to flee, at the exact moment when confidence in the outcome collapses, soldiers do so, sometimes in good order, but in a great many battles in complete panic. They are then pursued, hunted down and butchered. Napoleon's Imperial Guard at Waterloo hurled themselves into the fray with determination, but shortly after, as Wellington's lines moved forward, they could be seen on their knees weeping and calling for mercy. Soldiers in flight experience a psychological transformation now that their only concern is to save themselves rather than to protect the group.

For ordinary soldiers, the comprehension that they have won a battle can take time to sink in, partly because a large battlefield is a messy and incoherent whole, in which fighting might continue for longer in one small part while overall victory is assured. The Battle of Austerlitz was essentially won by Napoleon by mid-day, but the fighting did not finish at one end of the field for another four hours. Even commanders often have only a hazy view of how a battle is going. They have relied until recently on primitive forms of communication once battle is joined. Very few armies imitated the Mongols, whose commanders would seek high ground in order to signal with coloured flags to their units about their movement on the battlefield. Navies were better adapted to complex signalling, but even here a naval mêlée could easily mask the overall balance of the battle. Otherwise, even with the advent of radio, it could be difficult to direct embattled units or to be confident that plans were being fulfilled. Victory slowly emerged from the literal fog of war only when the enemy abandoned the field, surrendered, or was surrounded and killed.

Victory in battle is clearly likely to be exhilarating and soldiers and sailors indulge that victory in a variety of ways, though time and again they are evidently too exhausted, too damaged and too thirsty to do anything more than occupy the ground. Organized pursuit of a broken enemy, even if strategically sensible, is risky with exhausted men and in many famous cases failed to materialize. The aftermath of battle can be anti-climactic for the winners, particularly the wounded, who die later in droves after battles ancient or modern, their thankless task achieved at an awful cost. Nor is there any guarantee that once the fight is over, there will be food and water available. The Swedish victors at Breitenfeld had to wait until the following morning before they were given anything to eat or drink. The soldiers who survive know what they have done and will use it to weave their own personal narratives, heroic or otherwise. In earlier battles they were often rewarded at once to avert potential disaffection or mutiny and to maintain discipline among men now liberated from the tension of combat.

However exhilarating victory might be, at least for a bittersweet moment, battles seldom decided a war, and victory in one battle could quickly be tarnished by defeat in the next. Beaten soldiers or sailors returned home understanding the nature of their failure, even if glad to have survived. Japanese soldiers were encouraged to kill themselves rather than remain alive and dishonoured. One young conscript in the 1930s recorded in his diary that he was given a knife by his mother so that he could ritually disembowel himself if he was captured. The homecoming could be a mixed blessing even for the victors. The sailors who helped to defeat the Spanish Armada in 1588 were delivered to ports in England a few weeks later with no pay and no means of finding food or shelter save begging. Winning a battle could also be costly for the fortunate commander. The Roman general Flavius Aetius, who defeated Attila the Hun, was battered to death by his jealous emperor in person when he returned to Rome. The victor of Ain Jalut, where the Mongols were finally stopped in their tracks on their way to Egypt, was murdered by jealous officers on his way home. Battle is an event in its own right, with its own history and outcome, but what is made of the battle depends on the wider historical context, political as much as military. Winning in this sense really is only half the battle.

In some cases, battles have been used to serve as symbols or myths to endorse a particular political order or to encourage a shared cultural identity, and have soon assumed a historically abstract character, important for what they might mean for future generations and often surrounded by embellishments that turn the account from historical reality into a comfortable legend. For most ancient and early medieval battles, historians rely on accounts that are literary representations of what might have happened, largely devoid of detail and usually written long after the event. The eleventh-century epic French poem *Chanson de Roland* was based loosely on a battle that took place at Roncesvalles three centuries before, but its purpose by then was to enshrine notions of Christian nobility in French culture. The famous battle on the ice at Lake Peipus in 1242, where Alexander Nevsky drove back the German invader, was distorted by centuries of myth-making, and in the twentieth century it was adopted as a central motif of Soviet propaganda against the fascist enemy in the Second World War. The Battle of Britain and the Battle of the Somme have become central epic accounts in the search for a British identity, symbols of endurance and courage. Other battles are appropriated as foundation moments – the Battle of the Volturno River in 1860 cemented the unification of Italy; Marengo paved the way for Napoleon's empire; Actium in 31 BCE became the founding battle of the Augustan age and the triumph of Octavian. There is also a history of how battles have been remembered once they are transformed over time into legend, distinct from the history of the battles themselves.

'Battle' as the key element of warfare for at least the past 4,000 years may nevertheless be dying out. The American belief that there is now a fundamental 'Revolution in Military Affairs' (RMA) – prompted by the new possibilities opened up by cyberwar and precise drone strikes – might make battle in a conventional sense obsolete. The exploitation of the 'cognitive domain' suggests that enemies could be subject to psychological pressures and threats that produce disorientation and uncertainty sufficient to obviate the need for actual killing. Perhaps the world is about to enter on one of those long periods of tranquillity detected by archaeologists when they examine the hidden record of prehistoric violence. Or then again, perhaps not.

CHAPTER 1
LEADERSHIP

In our current age, 'leadership' is taught as a classroom subject, as if everyone could become a leader if they paid enough attention and did their homework. The history of warfare through the ages should be enough to disabuse us of this illusion. The quality of leadership has varied widely in battle. The fact of command does not turn an indifferent officer into a true leader, any more than a leadership seminar today can turn someone into a leader of tomorrow. Indeed, it is possible for a leader to emerge quite independent of the formal military structures, as the success of Spartacus as leader of the slave rebellion against Rome, or the victory of the iconic Che Guevara in the Cuban Revolution, have both demonstrated. Successful military leaders are usually defined by their successes, but in many conflicts this means success on the battlefield, once, twice or many times, rather than success in war. Napoleon Bonaparte and Erich von Manstein are two such figures whose qualities of leadership are not in doubt, with an impressive list of battle successes, but both faced historical forces that doomed their efforts to eventual failure.

What, then, defines leadership in battle if it is not ultimate strategic or political triumph? This is a difficult question to answer because the nature of battlefield leadership has changed considerably through time. When rulers and generals led their men in person, leadership was based partly on the bravery and fighting skill they displayed as an example to their men. When a leader fell or was killed, the effect on those fighting around him could be disastrous, as it was in the medieval battle of Legnano when the German king, Frederick Barbarossa, fell from his horse in the fighting and disappeared from view. Leaders who ran risks were respected; those who sat prudently on a nearby hill or in their tent relied on lesser commanders to win the loyalty of their troops and sustain their will to fight. In modern wars, the leaders seldom shared the dangers of battle and could be remote from the action. Their skill lay in working out the operational strategy that would secure victory, and their qualities were managerial as well as physical. Even then, knowledge that the leader was there, in contact, was still important. When Napoleon retired hurriedly from the disastrous campaign in Russia in 1812, he doomed his remaining, hopeless troops.

The most distinguished battlefield leaders have been those who combined a grasp of operational reality, a willingness to be imaginative with new technology and tactics, a courage and confidence communicated to those around them, and a willingness to share the dangers of combat. When Alexander the Great went calmly to his tent to sleep on the night before the Battle of Gaugamela, his nervous officers were uncertain how to react. Alexander assured them that victory was certain and, according to the ancient accounts, slept soundly. The overwhelming majority of battles through recorded history suggest that soldiers and sailors fought on the day for their leader rather than for any great ideal, whether religious, political or national. This explains how fighters from very different ethnic or cultural or national communities, often pressed involuntarily into service, could still fight side-by-side against the common foe. The battlefield was a community all of its own in which leaders of whatever kind played a decisive part in holding that community together.

It is obvious in any history of battles that leadership is not a universal quality among military leaders, and many of those on the losing side were poor planners, with little grasp of the battlefield, were overconfident or arrogant in their assessment of the enemy, or were simply lacking in the necessary courage and optimism their forces needed. Such leaders can be found in many of the battles selected here. On the other hand, it was possible to have two leaders of evident quality pitted against each other, where only one could win. The Battle of Hastings perhaps comes closest to that model. It would be difficult to fault Harold for what went wrong that day and no-one would consider it a historical anomaly had he won the field rather than William. This is a reminder that even leadership was seldom enough on its own, which is why innovation, deception, raw courage or good fortune were there to supplement it.

1. BATTLE OF GAUGAMELA

1 October 331 BCE

In October 331 BCE, Alexander the Great destroyed in a single day the power of the largest empire in the Middle East, that of the Persian ruler Darius III. Success had followed Alexander since he took the throne of Macedonia in 336 BCE, but victory over Persia and its allies sealed his legendary reputation as a military genius at the tender age of twenty-five.

Alexander succeeded to the throne following the murder of his father, Philip. Within five years, he had confronted the Persian Empire and its wide network of satrapies (provinces) in Anatolia, the coastal communities along the eastern Mediterranean littoral and in Egypt. He seems to have been an instinctive battlefield commander, though aware of the lessons to be drawn from triumphs of the past and the strategic practices of his father. In 333 BCE, he inflicted a heavy defeat on the Persian emperor at the narrow coastal plain around Issus in northern Syria, but failed to capture him. Alexander had ambitions to become master not only of Western Asia and Greece, but of the entire area that the wealthy warrior empire of Persia had ruled for centuries. In 331 BCE, he set out from Egypt to track Darius down somewhere in present-day Iraq, determined it seems to inflict a decisive defeat on the Persians. According to classical historians, he went armed with news from the oracle at Siwah in Egypt's Western Desert that he might be the son of Zeus, chief of the Greek gods. This certainly might explain the remarkable confidence that Alexander displayed in the final showdown against a Persian army at least four times larger than his own.

The Macedonian force was still large – 40,000 foot soldiers and 7,000 cavalry – and its movement across hundreds of miles of territory was an organizational feat in its own right. Alexander crossed from Egypt to Syria, where he lingered for some weeks, waiting to hear if Darius was preparing his own army for combat. When news reached him in mid-July of the Persian emperor's whereabouts, Alexander led his army towards the River Euphrates, intent on his showdown. On the opposite side there were 3,000 of Darius's cavalry under the command of Mazaeus, but they withdrew southwards, scorching the earth as they went. This was to force Alexander to take the longer northern route past the Armenian mountains then down into the valley of the Tigris, where Darius was already preparing his battlefield near the village of Gaugamela. Stakes and snares were set to halt a cavalry charge; the ground was flattened to enable the 200 Persian chariots armed with sharp scythes to run straight and fast at the ranks of the enemy. Ancient authors talked of one million men in the Persian army, but the number is likely to have been perhaps 200,000, of whom 30,000 were cavalry drawn from all over the empire. Fifteen Indian elephants were to guard the centre of the Persian line.

Alexander captured Persians sent to reconnoitre his force and learned exactly where Darius was. On 29 September, he ordered his army to march off in battle order for a possible night attack on the enemy; sensing their fear as they sighted the 100,000 camp fires of the enemy host, Alexander called a halt on the heights overlooking the 'Camel's Hump', the hill from which Gaugamela took its name. He spent the day exhorting his troops and inspecting the prepared battleground. In the evening he made a sacrifice in honour of Fear, to propitiate the emotion. Then he worked out his battle plan in detail with his commanders, compensating for the strength of the enemy by unconventional means.

On the following morning, 1 October, Alexander woke late, well rested and confident of the outcome – a mood that was intended to inspire confidence in his men. His complex battle-line was drawn up: on the left, a large body of horse and shield-bearers under Parmenion; in the centre, 10,000 of the highly-trained Foot Companions in a phalanx armed with the formidable two-handed 6-metre (20-foot) *sarissa* spears, flanked by 3,000 shield-bearers (light infantry); and sloping to the right, creating an angled front, Alexander with his cavalry, fronted by archers and slingers. On each wing a 'flap' of cavalry was attached, among whom were concealed heavily-armed infantry, which could fall back to protect the rest from encirclement. Behind these were 20,000 reserve infantry, which could be moved forwards to create a large protected oblong.

Managing such a complex battlefield was difficult, as information could only be sent by messenger or trumpet, and thick dust was thrown up by the horses wheeling around on the sandy earth. Alexander's strategy carried risks should any of the units misunderstand their orders or fail to hold fast. Darius had a simpler plan: to send forward his much larger bodies of cavalry, to decimate the Foot Companions with the scythed chariots, and to scare off the Greek cavalry with the elephants. Around mid-day, Alexander's army moved onto the prepared battlefield in tight order. What happened next relies on accounts whose authors had a vested interest in painting Alexander's achievements in glowing colours, but the main shape of the battle seems clear. Alexander moved his cavalry forwards but to the right to tempt the Persian left to follow him, thus exposing the centre and opening up a gap in the Persian line. On rougher ground, the Persian Scythian cavalry charged at Alexander, but were caught up among foot soldiers and archers. Darius released the chariots, but they were subjected to an accurate volley of arrows and sling-shots; those that reached the Macedonian lines were let through, then slaughtered by the soldiers behind. The rest of Alexander's line was subject to heavy cavalry attack, and might well have collapsed, but Alexander, looking for the gap caused in the Persian centre, wheeled round and charged directly at Darius and his entourage, avoiding the elephants. The Macedonian Foot Companions with their fearsome sarissas and their cry of 'alalalalai' surged forwards and Darius, sensing his extreme danger, fled from the scene.

The flight of the emperor seems to have infected much of the rest of the Persian army, which melted away to the south and east. Large numbers of horsemen had succeeded in cutting past Parmenion and rampaged forward to seize Alexander's baggage camp, where, to their surprise, they met the 20,000 reserves, who overwhelmed and destroyed them. Alexander rode off after Darius but his rearguard fought a ferocious defence and by the time the battlefield could be left behind and the hunt begun, Darius was already far away, fleeing to the mountains and the safety of the city of Ecbatana (Hamadan). The Persian emperor had overestimated the power of sheer numbers and fought a predictable battle; Alexander, by contrast, had made the most of his limited numbers, using them to unhinge the enemy at a crucial moment by careful exploitation of combined-arms tactics. Victory at Gaugamela brought him a reputation in the classical world to match the mythic stories of Achilles or of Hercules. Alexander moved on to Babylon and then the Persian capital at Susa. In so doing, he became, it has been estimated, the richest man in the known world.

2. BATTLE OF CANNAE
2 August 216 BCE

The Battle of Cannae is one of the most famous battles of all time. The catastrophic defeat of the Roman army by Hannibal's smaller force has been regularly invoked to describe a particularly dramatic or heavy defeat. The myth that surrounded Hannibal as a general who carried victory with him wherever he went has lived down the ages. Hannibal's own presence at Cannae and his operational genius explain an outcome that might well have gone another way.

The North African empire of Carthage dominated present-day Libya, Tunisia, Algeria and areas of conquest as far as Spain. The rising might of Rome in the third century BCE challenged Carthaginian ambitions and led to a series of Punic Wars between the two rival powers. In the second of these, at some point in 218 BCE, Hannibal persuaded the Carthaginian senate to let him set off on an epic journey across Spain, present-day France and over the Alps into Italy. What his ultimate objective was remains unclear, but he took with him an invasion force of probably 100,000 men, many of them Spanish mercenaries, and a huge train of supplies and animals, including his famous elephants. The journey itself undermined the scale of his ambitions. By the time the Alps were reached, he was down to 50,000 men; after crossing the mountains in autumn snow, he arrived in the northern Po Valley with only 20,000 foot soldiers and 6,000 cavalry to invade the Roman heartland. Bolstered by Gauls who joined his cause, Hannibal meted out heavy defeats on the Roman armies sent north to intercept him. As he moved south, Rome was gripped by panic. Hannibal's military reputation inflated the threat out of all proportion. Lacking a secure base, living off the land, and not entirely sure of his Gallic allies, Hannibal chose to inflict on Rome what damage he could while himself avoiding defeat.

In 216 BCE, Hannibal moved into Apulia in south-central Italy and in June that year set up his camp at the hilltop city of Cannae, guarding the route to the rich grain-lands of the south. The Romans had begun to create a force to eliminate the threat from the invader. Four new legions were raised, bringing the Romans' strength to around 40,000 men with 40,000 allied soldiers, but only a small number of experienced cavalry. The two Roman consuls for 216 BCE, Gaius Terentius Varro and Lucius Aemilius Paullus, led the new army south to meet Hannibal, whose forces they probably outnumbered by two to one. At the beginning of August, the Roman army arrived at the flat plain in front of

Cannae. As was customary, the consuls took turns to command on alternate days; Varro was the more audacious and on 2 August 216 BCE he led his force, spread out over nearly a mile, onto the plain to do battle. Accounts of the battle suggest that the infantry were packed between fifty and seventy ranks thick. The Roman cavalry were on one wing and the allied cavalry on the other, with a river protecting one flank. Roman battlefield strategy was to smash the enemy by sheer weight of numbers.

At Cannae, Hannibal showed his exceptional grasp of the battlefield. He formed his infantry into a shallow force, weaker in the centre, with his veteran Libyans on both flanks. On one wing were Numidian cavalry, on the other Spanish and Gallic, 10,000 experienced horsemen who greatly outnumbered the 6,000 Roman horses. His infantry were ordered to form a bulge outwards with the object of enticing the Roman legions into the arc, which would then bend inwards, giving the wings the chance to encircle and annihilate the enemy while the cavalry defeated the enemy horsemen and turned to attack the Roman army from the rear. It was a textbook operation and functioned like clockwork. The Romans pressed forward into the yielding arc, only to find themselves surrounded as the Libyan infantry advanced on the flanks. The Carthaginian cavalry swept aside Rome's horsemen and plunged into the Roman rear. Cannae was a massacre, the worst defeat the Roman army ever suffered. An estimated 50,000 died that day; others were taken prisoner. Only 14,500 survived out of an army of 80,000. Hannibal lost 6,000, two-thirds of them Gauls. No effort was made to bury so many dead, which included Paullus and eighty Roman senators. The gold rings and ornaments were collected from the dead and sent to Carthage to show the extent of the victory and to demonstrate the need for reinforcements.

Hannibal could perhaps have marched on Rome and brought the empire to its knees. The disaster at Cannae left the city briefly defenceless, though new legions were immediately raised. The Senate ordered that there should be no weeping, and buried two Greeks and two Gauls alive to propitiate the gods. But Hannibal perhaps sensed that his depleted force was not large enough to march the 500 kilometres

(300 miles) to Rome and to invest the city. Carthage was too busy fighting in Sicily, Spain and Sardinia to send help, so Hannibal undertook limited campaigns in southern Italy for a further fourteen years, too dangerous an opponent for the Romans to challenge again. To scare the citizens, he took 2,000 cavalry up to the gates of the city in 212 BCE, but could not risk a siege.

When Hannibal's brother Hasdrubal came to join him in 207 BCE by the same awkward route over the Alps, his forces were devastated near present-day Rimini and Hasdrubal was killed. Carthage was undermined on every front except in the south of Italy, where Hannibal was isolated. In 202 BCE, he finally left Italy for good to return to Carthage. A battlefield genius, he did not know how to win the war.

3. BATTLE OF ACTIUM
2 September 31 BCE

The victory won at Actium off the coast of Greece by Julius Caesar's adopted son, Gaius Julius Caesar Octavianus (better known as Octavian, and soon to become Augustus) marked a decisive end to the long period of savage civil wars that had plagued Republican Rome from the middle years of the first century BCE. The battle was fought between the two most powerful men in the Roman Republic: Octavian, ruler of the western half of the Roman territories; and Marcus Antonius (better known as Mark Antony), ruler of the eastern region. Octavian had little reputation as a commander or soldier, but from an early age he had understood how to balance the arts of politics and war. Mark Antony was out-thought by a leader whose political intelligence and strategic calculation opened the way to a new imperial age.

After the assassination of Julius Caesar in 44 BCE, there followed an uneasy decade as Caesar's supporters fought against the defenders of Republican Rome and rival claimants to his mantle. Octavian became the dominant figure in Italy because he was more clear-sighted and unscrupulous than his competitors. Though he had no constitutional basis for his claim to rule, he was backed by soldiers loyal to the legacy of the great Caesar, and had enough money to buy the loyalty of others. He collaborated with Antony for much of the decade, and relied on Antony's military help against the armies raised by Caesar's assassins. But by 34 BCE, when Antony married the Egyptian queen Cleopatra in a theatrical ceremony in Alexandria, Octavian could see the possibility that Mark Antony might soon want control of the whole Roman sphere and not just the east. By 32 BCE, their rivalry was overt. One-third of the Senate in Rome supported Mark Antony and fled to join his army, which was gathering in Turkey; Octavian had been busy recruiting supporters in Italy, raising taxes for a military expedition, buying the loyalty of his own troops and spreading hostile propaganda against his rival. Ambition turned both heads as the two men contemplated the prospect of ruling the whole Roman world.

In the second half of the year, Antony brought an army of around 100,000 soldiers and 12,000 cavalry to Greece, supported by 500 ships, many of them huge triremes capable of carrying large numbers of soldiers and catapults to be used while ramming and boarding enemy vessels. The object was to prepare for an invasion of Italy, or to lure Octavian into a land battle, which Antony was confident of winning. The fleet was scattered along the coastal ports, but around 250 ships were concentrated in the Gulf of Ambracia, a bay on the west coast of Greece protected by a narrow strait near the town of Actium. They included sixty vessels supplied by Cleopatra, who had accompanied her new consort to witness his triumphant return to Rome. Octavian knew that he had time on his side and decided to blockade Antony. His own fleet, commanded by the very effective Marcus Vipsanius Agrippa, preyed on Antony's supply routes. Octavian moved his army of around 80,000 legionaries and 12,000 horsemen to Greece and set up camp well to the north in order to avoid a land battle, while the fleet of Antony and Cleopatra remained bottled up at Actium, unwilling to risk a major sea battle against the larger naval forces waiting beyond the Gulf.

In this trial of wills, Octavian understood that Antony's expeditionary force could only decline in fighting power as it struggled to find food and fodder locally and to cope with camp diseases. There were defections to Octavian as morale declined. Antony's decision to base himself at Actium had been a mistake, but Octavian exploited this misjudgement to the full by avoiding a pitched battle and relying on attrition. Unable to bring his strength to bear against an evasive enemy, Antony decided that his only option was to try to break out of the Gulf and fight his way through Agrippa's blockade. He concealed his intention from his already demoralized army and when a strong northwest wind arrived on 2 September 31 BCE, Antony ordered his fleet, now reduced to no more than 170 vessels, out of the Gulf and into the open sea.

The four-hour battle that followed was directed by Octavian, who was aboard a small brigantine (suffering, it has been suggested, from sea-sickness), but fought by his admiral, Agrippa. The long delay and the strategy of blockade both played to Octavian's advantage. Antony's ships did not seek battle, but were equipped with sails and masts for a break-out. The decks of his ships were cluttered with stores and 20,000 marines, who were embarked with the fleet. His oarsmen were hungry and disease-ridden and no match now for Agrippa's 400 faster and lighter ships, but they were forced to fight rather than flee. As Antony's three squadrons came out of the gulf they formed into a crescent, with a fourth squadron of Cleopatra's sixty ships behind them, prepared with full sail and carrying the treasure needed to fund the war. Agrippa was ready for them. His right squadron engaged with Mark Antony's left at once, coming to close quarters and using marines to devastate and board the enemy vessels.

As Mark Antony's right tried to manoeuvre around Agrippa's fleet, the latter moved his ships further north to envelop the enemy, until the two wings became separated from the rest of the battle. As the centre opened up, Cleopatra seized her moment to sail between the two fighting wings out into the open sea. Mark Antony and some of his vessels on the right then followed them, but sensing that his flagship was too slow, he transferred to a lighter and faster vessel and caught up with Cleopatra, leaving his fleet and his army to their fate.

That fate was harsh indeed. At least two-thirds of the fleet was captured after several hours of fierce fighting and perhaps 10,000 men killed, some of them, according to ancient accounts, 'mangled by sea monsters'. Much of the army came over to Octavian and those who fled the scene surrendered not long after in Macedonia. The victory at Actium owed something to the mistakes of Antony and Cleopatra, but much to the strategic understanding of Octavian, who, though he lacked the hero's touch, understood that a battle could be won by patient waiting and the fruits of calculated attrition. The following year, Octavian pursued Antony and Cleopatra to Egypt, captured Alexandria and shared its treasures with his army. Mark Antony stabbed himself and perished in Cleopatra's arms; she died nine days later once it was clear no deal could be struck with Octavian, reputedly from the bites of twin asps. Gaius Octavianus returned in triumph to Rome in 29 BCE and was declared 'Augustus' by the Senate two years later, de facto ruler of the Roman Empire. A holiday was proclaimed to mark the victory in Egypt, still celebrated in Italy two millennia later as 'Ferragosto'.

4. BATTLE OF THE MILVIAN BRIDGE

28 October 312

The battle between two rival emperors outside the gates of Rome in 312 CE was memorable not so much for what happened on the battlefield between two opponents steeped in Roman fighting traditions, but because Constantine, who had come to capture Rome, was supposed not long before the battle to have had a vision of the Christian cross in the sky with the inscription 'by this win', and a dream in which Jesus told him to use the symbol of Christ (the Greek letters 'chi-rho'). It is claimed that Constantine, buoyed up by this apparition, led his army to a certain victory over the pagan Maxentius and opened the way to Europe's Christian age. At the Milvian Bridge, God was on the side of the victor. Constantine was a leader on a divine mission.

The Roman Empire in the early fourth century was ruled by a 'tetrarchy' of four emperors, each ruling over a defined imperial territory. At York in 306, Constantine was declared ruler of the northern provinces of the empire, which covered present-day Britain, France (Gaul), Belgium and western Germany. That same year, the young Maxentius usurped the imperial title in Rome. A year later, one of the four emperors, Galerius, attempted to overthrow the usurper, but without success. Then in 312, Constantine, a popular ruler in contrast to the brutal and untrustworthy Maxentius, marched across the Alps at Susa to try his luck at capturing Rome, still regarded as the centre of the empire. His army captured Turin and Milan, won a battle at Brescia, then laid siege to Verona, where it defeated Maxentius's leading general as he tried to flee. From a small force, Constantine's army was augmented by deserters from Maxentius's cause. He marched south towards Rome, mustering an estimated 50,000 men.

To oppose him, Maxentius had perhaps 100,000 men to call on, though many were less well-trained than those of his opponent, raised from levies forced on a reluctant population. He gathered stores of wheat and supplies to withstand a siege, as he had done successfully with Galerius. To hold up Constantine's advance, he ordered the destruction of the wide stone Milvian Bridge across the Tiber, which lay on the path of his enemy's army. But at the last moment he changed his mind and decided that his forces were large enough to secure a land victory. A new pontoon bridge was constructed, and Maxentius led his large army across it to Saxa Rubra. At the core were the famous Praetorian Guards (the elite imperial bodyguard), and on the flanks were the new heavy cavalry modelled on the Persian example. Opposed to them was a conventional force of Roman infantry supported to either side by experienced horsemen. Constantine's forces, so it is said, were told to paint the 'chi-rho' sign on their shields to show that they were protected by the new Christian God. They marched into battle inspired by Constantine's vision and the certainty of victory.

Victory was in fact far from certain, since Maxentius had the much larger force, but Constantine, in imitation of Alexander the Great, led his seasoned cavalry in a determined charge against the horsemen on the flanks of Maxentius's army. Little is known in detail about the battle, and what is recorded comes from a later account by the Christian bishop Eusebius, based on conversations with Constantine, and cannot be regarded as reliable. However, the outcome is known with certainty. Constantine's cavalry smashed their opponents and drove them back to the Tiber. The infantry lines of Maxentius were exposed to flank attacks and the line caved in. Panicking soldiers fled to the pontoon bridge or tried to cross the river, while the Praetorian Guard held its ground and was cut down rank by rank where it stood. Whether the pontoon bridge collapsed or the unruly crowd surging across it pushed others into the water, the fleeing Maxentius ended up drowned in the Tiber, weighed down by his armour. His body was dredged out and decapitated, and his head displayed on a lance as Constantine marched on into the city.

The extent to which Constantine's army fought and won because of his vision is open to debate. His forces won notable military successes in northern Italy without the aid of divine inspiration, but with an astute and experienced commander to guide them. It is not clear how Constantine himself interpreted his vision, since he had previously claimed to see visions of pagan gods, particularly Apollo. After his capture of Rome, which left him as unchallenged ruler of the western part of the empire, he admitted to many subsequent visions of Jesus. Modern accounts suggest a possible atmospheric phenomenon which Constantine interpreted as he wished, but since he claimed to have had visions often, he may have been the victim of hallucinations caused, experts now think, by a particular form of migraine. Whatever the truth, Constantine knew how to use the vision to his advantage; in this case it must have reinforced the confidence of his men in a leader who had already proved his qualities on numerous occasions. There are times in battle when a perceptive leader can see how the supernatural might help, as Alexander had at Gaugamela.

The Battle of the Milvian Bridge became a reference point for the establishment of Christianity in the Western Roman Empire. A year after the battle, Constantine published an edict of religious toleration at Milan and, although only a small percentage of the Roman population was yet Christian, the victory at the bridge and the support of Constantine for Christianity worked rapidly to spread the religion, with its now protected status, across the Western Empire. The legends surrounding the Milvian Bridge were what counted, not the truth of a battle that was just one of many internecine conflicts in the fading years of Roman imperial rule, won by a man who had been happily pagan only years before.

5. BATTLE OF HASTINGS
14 October 1066

The most famous battle in all English history is undoubtedly the bloody day-long struggle between the Anglo-Saxon forces of the English king, Harold II, and the invading army of William, Duke of Normandy. It has been known for centuries as the Battle of Hastings, but it was fought on a narrow slope leading up to what is now the small Sussex town of Battle, halfway between Pevensey and Hastings, a short distance from the English Channel. With around 7,000 men apiece, William and Harold battled for the future history of England.

The cause of the battle was the straightforward prospect of ruling a prosperous and fertile country. English territory was divided between areas of Viking and Anglo-Saxon settlement, and for several centuries had been the object of the ambitions of Scandinavian rulers. The throne of England was an unstable inheritance, and when King Edward, known as the Confessor, died on 5 January 1066 without an heir, there were a number of claimants to the English throne. The English earls elected Harold Godwinson, Earl of Wessex (in southwest England), who had no direct blood ties to the royal line, but was a tough and successful warrior. In the space of less than a year, he faced two separate invasions by claimants who did have royal blood, and believed that the throne belonged to them. In September 1066, the king of Norway, Harald Hardrada ('hard ruler'), invaded northeast England with a large Viking army, determined to wrest control of the kingdom; less than a month later, a Norman army under William landed in the south, driven by the same ambition.

Politics in early medieval England was decided by the sword. William had been promised the throne of England not only by Edward the Confessor, but, or so the Normans claimed, by Harold Godwinson himself. An ambitious and violent soldier, descended from Viking settlers, Duke William had already subjugated much of the area around his duchy of Normandy. In the summer of 1066, he summoned his own levies and those of his allies and vassals to mount an invasion of England. He had 700 boats built in a short space of time, but he still needed favourable winds. His army of 2,500 horsemen (with 2,000 horses), 1,000 archers and 3,000 infantry was forced to sit on the coast for 45 days before the wind finally changed. At dawn on 28 September, the army disembarked on the coast at Pevensey and awaited the English. The strength of William's invasion force lay in the body of heavily armoured cavalry, by then commonly used in battles in France but rare in England, and also the archers, whose longbows and crossbows could rain arrows down on the enemy infantry. Almost all his men were trained soldiers rather than conscripted militia, with experience in using the bows, javelins and swords with which they were armed.

Harold was on the other side of England. On 20 September at Fulford, near York, an army of 10,000 Vikings under Harald Hardrada and

Harold's brother, Tostig Godwinson, annihilated a force of perhaps 6,000 under earls Edwin and Morcar. Collecting levies from the south, Harold rode north from London, moving so quickly that his 5,000 men found the Viking invaders unprepared on both sides of the River Derwent, near a small village at Stamford Bridge. Charging the forces on one side of the river, the English soldiers slaughtered them all before crossing the narrow bridge and falling on the rest of the invasion force. Some 7,000 corpses littered the battlefield. Only 24 out of the 500 ships that had carried the Vikings to England were needed to take the survivors home.

Harold's victory ended any prospect in the near future of Scandinavian intervention in English affairs. If Hardrada's invasion had been his only problem, the battle would be hailed as the start of a different English history. But messengers told Harold that another enemy awaited him in Sussex, ravaging the countryside, burning villages and towns and seizing their goods. He rode south with his tired and battered army and arrived at London on 6 October, where he was joined by other levies and his brothers Gyrth and Leofwine. Harold had at his command a mixed army of Anglo-Saxon nobility, their 'housecarles' or professional soldiers, and the trained militia, the *fyrd*. He was joined by a number of Danish mercenaries, or *lithsmen*. The housecarles and nobility wore long protective mail coats or 'hauberks' and carried spears, daggers and the deadly double-handed battleaxes that could cleave a man and horse in two. The *fyrd* were more lightly armed, and wore only thick leather jerkins. The principal tactic of Harold's army was the shield wall, composed of lines of housecarles with heavy shields, forming a solid barrier of the toughest soldiery against which enemy attacks were designed to be broken by sheer physical power and the courage of the defending fighters.

Harold moved south, arriving opposite William's army on 13 October, and camped near the shallow Caldbec Hill. His army left their horses and proceeded early on the morning of 14 October to take up position at the top of a long but shallow slope, protected on both sides by swampy ground, where Harold set up a solid shield wall some ten or twelve men deep and perhaps 7,000-strong in total.

Although he had successfully used a cavalry charge at Stamford Bridge, Harold chose to fight without cavalry and with very few archers. The shield wall, in contrast, was a primitive tactic to choose against William and left very little flexibility. The Norman army was drawn up in the early morning in a way that made the most of the mixed force William had brought with him. There were three sections: Flemish allies on the right, a Breton force on the left, and 3,500 cavalry and heavy infantry in the centre led by William. Throughout the day the Norman duke displayed a shrewd tactical judgement, making the most of his cavalry and his archers, probing to find a way to wear down the shield wall. Occasionally, as the legend of Hastings has it, his cavalry made feints as if to retreat, tempting Harold's soldiers to run after them, only for the Anglo-Saxons to suddenly be surrounded and cut down.

Battle was joined at around 9 a.m. Since the Normans were attacking up a slope, Harold had some advantages. His spearmen could throw more powerfully downwards, while William's archers had to fire uphill, and his cavalry were forced to charge against the gradient. Most medieval battles were over in a couple of hours, but Hastings, contested by two battle-hardened and professional forces, lasted the whole day, at a terrible cost to both sides. At one point, the ferocity of the English stand broke the left flank of William's force and threatened a more general retreat, rather than a ruse to lure the enemy into pursuit. Accounts of the battle have William removing his helmet to show he had not been slain and shouting to his men to hold firm and rally. They did so, just as a large group of English militia chased after them, thinking the whole army was in flight. The Anglo-Saxons were surrounded on a hillock and, despite a desperate effort to save themselves, each one was bludgeoned or speared to death where he stood.

William then opted for attrition. Small groups of horsemen and heavy infantry attacked, taking casualties but also eating into the shield wall. Hour after hour of gory combat left all the men exhausted, desperate with thirst, and covered in wounds, great and small. The corpses were so many that it proved hard at times to fight on the slope made slippery with their blood. After six hours of slaughter,

William could see that attrition was taking a greater toll of the enemy. He ordered a charge against the shield wall by all his surviving army. The Anglo-Saxon line gave way, and small groups of housecarles rallied round their lords as the Norman wave washed over them. Harold and his brothers were killed, the king so mutilated by the hacking Norman swords that his body could only be identified later by his mistress.

There was no concept of surrender and Harold's surviving men could be butchered where they were found. Some 4,000 of the Anglo-Saxon army died at Hastings, 2,000 of William's men. William marched north to London, where he was crowned king in Westminster Abbey. England became a Norman province, united under one monarch. It is easy to be sentimental about Harold's defeat, but he, like William, was just one of a long line of warrior noblemen, with Norse blood in their veins, who fought to the death for land and wealth. What made William different was his sharp military mind, shown in his ability to 'manage' the battlefield in an age of primitive combat. Crude though the fighting was, William's victory rested on solid military understanding and bold leadership.

6. BATTLE OF ZHONGDU
1215

There are few military leaders in world history with a more elevated reputation than the Mongol tribesman Temüjin, better known to history as Genghis Khan, or Chingghis Khan. Conqueror of half of Asia, his name became a byword for military ruthlessness and competence. No ambition was more vaunted or, in the end, more successful than his conquest of the vast northern Chinese Empire of the Jurchen Jin in the first decades of the thirteenth century. Few battles are more symbolic of the shift in the Asian power balance than the fight in 1214–15 to capture the Jin capital of Zhongdu on a site near present-day Beijing.

Temüjin left few records and many of those who knew him well were illiterate. He was an outcast from his Mongol tribe following the death of his high-ranking father, and was said to have learned how to judge others and exploit their differences from his mother, Hoelun. He overcame the disadvantages of his youth and became a successful Mongol prince and warlord, his exploits and his political cunning attracting Mongol warriors to his side. Since the tribal rivalries of the Mongolian plain were a constant source of jealous friction and political uncertainty, there seems little doubt that Temüjin's own astuteness, ruthlessness and shrewd judgement, as much as his success in almost constant fighting, explain his emergence as the dominant figure over the Mongol peoples. By 1206, he had become at last Genghis Khan, ruler of the Mongols, the name by which he is commonly remembered.

In 1211, he embarked on the conquest of northern China, then ruled by the Jurchen Jin dynasty, which had captured the region from the Song some years before. His army probably totalled about 120,000, though the exact figures are not known. Mongol society was organized for military operations, since all men between the ages of fourteen and sixty were liable to serve when required. They learned to ride and to fire the powerful composite bows of the steppe horsemen from an early age; large hunting trips were used as surrogates for military training. Genghis Khan insisted on tough discipline, executing anyone who abandoned the fight or began to plunder before the order was given. The Mongol army was organized into units based on a decimal system: 10,000 men made a division, or *tümen*; each division was divided into units of 1,000, those into hundreds and the core unit was one of ten men. They were adept at ambushes and feints, and retained exceptional mobility.

The standard Mongol military practices, however, could not easily be deployed against large cities unless the garrison was foolish enough to sally out to fight. The conquest of Jin China required siege equipment, so Genghis recruited Chinese experts to supplement his large cavalry army. Much of the frontier area was conquered in rapid and devastating raids, but Genghis knew it was necessary to seize the Jin capital at Zhongdu to complete the conquest. The vast capital, surrounded by 15 kilometres (10 miles) of walls, 12 metres (40 feet) high, protected by 900 towers and a triple moat, was larger than any city the Mongols had captured. It was defended by an estimated 36,000 men, including 20,000 inside the walls and 4,000 stationed in each of four subsidiary towns where stores were kept, connected to Zhongdu by underground tunnels. Genghis and his army arrived outside the walls early in 1214. Two attempts to storm the city were beaten off. On the first occasion, it seems likely that the Chinese let some of the attackers break through a gate, only to set fire to the street behind them, trapping the Mongols and slaughtering them. Genghis knew when to stop. A truce was called and the Chinese emperor paid over a Jin princess, 500 boys and girls, 3,000 horses and 10,000 *liang* of gold to get the Mongols to leave.

Genghis almost certainly planned to return and when he heard in July that the emperor Xuanzong had decided to abandon Zhongdu as his capital and move it further south to Kaifeng, he took this as a sign of treachery and sent a large army of Mongols, Khitans and renegade Chinese to blockade the city. Blockade was not a usual Mongol strategy, but in this case it did what Genghis wanted. Xuanzong sent two large relief armies with supplies to break the blockade, but the first was surprised by a Mongol raid and its leader, the drunken Li Ying, was captured along with 1,000 wagons. The second suffered the same fate, ambushed at the River Yongding and destroyed by a much smaller Mongol force. The situation in Zhongdu became critical. One story has it that due to the shortage of stone or metal shot for the cannon in the city (among the first recorded uses of artillery with gunpowder if true), the ammunition was substituted with balls made of melted-down gold and silver. Genghis waited for the defenders and the population to starve. Cannibalism was later reported among both the besieged and the besiegers. The whole Mongol army now invested the city, preventing further supplies for the stricken capital. In late spring, the Jin commanders abandoned the city, Wanyen Fuxing choosing to commit suicide, while the army commander Mojan Chinchung smuggled himself at night through the Mongol lines, only later to be executed by the emperor in Kaifeng.

In June, the abandoned garrison opened the gates and surrendered. Although Genghis had wanted to prevent the usual bloodbath, his angry and impatient soldiers looted the city (this was their only source of payment for military duty) and butchered thousands of the inhabitants, though not as mercilessly as in later sieges – at Urgench in 1220, the entire population would be decapitated and pyramids built of their heads. The capital, with its vast walls, was now a Mongol city, signalling the rapid decline of Jin rule. By 1234, the rest of Jin China was subject to the Mongols. Genghis Khan proved himself a shrewd commander, whether fighting on an open plain or besieging vast cities. According to his published *Bilik* (*Maxims*), he saw warfare as the finest of activities: 'A man's greatest pleasure is to defeat his enemies, to drive them before him, to take from them that which they possessed.' Warfare was the breath of life for Genghis Khan, a fact that helps to explain his remorseless pursuit of battle and the single-minded quality of his leadership.

7. BATTLE OF BANNOCKBURN
23–24 June 1314

The famous battle in June 1314 at the small river of Bannock Burn, near Stirling in Scotland, was fought between two leaders whose presence on the day made all the difference between victory and defeat. The English army, large and well-trained, should have defeated a Scottish force less than half its size, but its commander-in-chief, King Edward II, chose to flee the field. His opponent, Robert Bruce, who had declared himself King of Scotland in 1306, knew he was at a disadvantage fighting his powerful neighbour in open battle, but he stayed, rallied his men and won a victory that opened the way to full Scottish independence fourteen years later, with a treaty that acknowledged Robert as Scotland's true king.

The battle came at the end of a long period of almost twenty years of violence between the two kingdoms following the death of the last heir to the Scottish throne in 1290. By the early fourteenth century, the English king, Edward I – 'the Hammer of the Scots' – had forced Scotland to submit to English government, but in 1306 Robert Bruce, Earl of Carrick, supported by defiant Scottish noblemen, was chosen as the new King of Scotland and crowned at Scone. He was almost immediately defeated by Edward I. Legend has it that he hid in a cave, where he watched a spider struggling to climb its gossamer thread until it finally reached its goal; this, so it is said, inspired Bruce to return to the fight for a free Scotland. Whether the story is true or not, Bruce was a remarkable military commander and over the seven years that followed Edward I's death in 1307, he succeeded in retaking many of the English strongholds, including Edinburgh Castle. In the summer of 1313, Bruce's brother, Edward, agreed with the English commander of Stirling Castle, Sir Philip Mowbray, that if no English army had come to rescue him after exactly one year, the castle would be surrendered to the Scots. This was a challenge the new English king, Edward II, could not ignore. He gathered together a large army, numbering an estimated 18,000 cavalry, archers and foot soldiers, and marched north to restore English rule.

The English army arrived near Berwick-upon-Tweed on 10 June 1314. Edward was an unpopular king, famous for his male favourites, and five of the eight English earls failed to join him. He nevertheless mustered an impressive military force, led by around 2,500 heavily armed and armoured knights, whose giant warhorses, the destriers, acted like tanks on a modern battlefield. Bruce summoned his supporters to the forest of Tor Wood, close by Stirling Castle; they included perhaps 1,000 men from Argyll and the Scottish islands under Angus Óg MacDonald, and a further 6–7,000 foot soldiers. Bruce had only 500 light cavalry under Sir Robert Keith, Marischal of Scotland, and a body of archers. The Scottish army generally avoided pitched battles against a larger enemy, but on this occasion Bruce, warmly supported by his other commanders and his men, decided that a stand had to be made. The battle tactic of the Scots was simple and thoroughly rehearsed. In front of where Bruce expected the battle to take place, the soldiers dug deep pits almost half a metre in diameter, close together and concealed with grass and twigs. Behind the traps, the army relied on the shield ring or 'schiltron', 500 men formed in a tight circle, several deep, with long 16-foot (5-metre) iron-tipped spears pointing outwards and upwards to ward off attacking horsemen. These human fortresses were carefully constructed, the outer ring kneeling, the ring behind with spears at chest height, both designed to stop oncoming horses.

The problem for the Scots was the sheer number of the enemy. On 23 June, one day before Stirling Castle was to be surrendered, Edward moved his vast force north from Falkirk. They arrived at the small river, Bannock Burn, where the Scottish army had been drawn up for battle on New Park, a slope of land beyond the river, which dominated the road to Stirling. The Park had forest behind, through which the Scots could escape, and swampy ground to both the south and east, making a flanking attack by the English difficult. Bruce's army might nevertheless have succumbed to a frontal assault. Instead the English attacked in the order they arrived, without waiting to assemble a full field of battle. The vanguard under the Earl of Gloucester, seeing what they mistakenly thought was a Scots army withdrawing from an encounter, charged across the pits and swamp. Among those who succeeded in getting across was the young Sir Henry de Bohun. He made straight for Bruce, who was clearly marked out by his golden coronet. Bruce in turn charged on his small grey horse at de Bohun, dodged the lance, and in a deft movement split open de Bohun's skull with his axe. The vanguard hesitated and withdrew. Another 300 horsemen under Sir Robert Clifford attempted to break through to Stirling Castle, but they were obstructed by a schiltron led by the Earl of Moray. After a vicious engagement, the English again fell back. As dusk fell, Edward ordered his army to set camp.

There was now a marked contrast between the two forces. Bruce's single-handed combat had inspired his men, who were now eager for the battle. Edward had misjudged the day and among his commanders there was a despondent expectation that their king lacked the flair or will for the contest. A Scottish knight, fighting with Edward, defected to Bruce that night with news that the English were demoralized by what had happened and the king uncertain of his support. On the morning of 24 June, Edward decided to avoid a fight and to move on to Stirling. The way was blocked by the Scots, who marched in formation down New Park to obstruct the only way through. Edward's commander, the Earl of Gloucester, again preferred battle and charged at the first schiltron before the army was ready. He was among the first unseated and killed. Edward had to turn his army to face the Scots, and as he did so, the other schiltrons entered the fray. The English archers found it difficult to concentrate their fire, and feared by this time hitting their own knights in the back. Bruce ordered Keith to take his 500 horses and disperse the archers while the English knights were locked in combat. He did so effectively, pursuing them into the marshland. The schiltrons held, partly because the swampy ground hemmed in the English and made it difficult to deploy the foot soldiers behind. Then suddenly, at the height of the battle, Bruce led the islanders of Angus Óg MacDonald in a famous charge down the slope towards the English, screaming and waving their iron axes. Edward fled the field of battle to avoid capture, leaving a leaderless army which, scenting disaster, finally turned and ran, whereupon they were hunted down or drowned in the marshy ground. Bannock Burn was awash with the corpses of horses and men, many of them the noblemen who had rallied to Edward's cause. Bruce and his commanders survived. No accurate account of the numbers killed on either side can be made.

The battle proved decisive. Edward returned several times but was unable to overturn the rule of King Robert Bruce, now firmly ensconced as Scotland's monarch. Edward II was murdered by his opponents in 1327, and the following year Edward III reached agreement with King Robert confirming Scotland's independence. The

Battle of Bannockburn could so nearly have been an English triumph; but Edward II could not inspire or command his army with the same energy, sympathy and tactical imagination displayed by Robert Bruce.

8. BATTLE OF MOHÁCS
29 August 1526

The role of leadership was an important one at the battle on the plain of Mohács that destroyed the Hungarian king and nobility and opened the way to centuries of Ottoman domination of south-central Europe. But it was a role shared by two very different men: the first was the Ottoman Sultan, Suleiman I, scion of the Osmans, later known as the 'Magnificent'; the second was his grand vizier, Ibrahim Pasha, a young Greek whom Suleiman had met when he was governor of Magnesia. Ibrahim became his close companion and adviser, eating at the sultan's table, even sharing his tent. The victory over the Hungarians was celebrated as Suleiman's triumph, but it was sealed by the two men who fought side-by-side that day.

The conflict between Hungary and the Ottoman Empire went back many years, but by the early sixteenth century, Ottoman encroachment had become more insistent. In 1521, Belgrade fell to the sultan and regular raids were carried out further north towards the Danube. Suleiman's reputation as a military leader to be reckoned with was secured by the capture of the island of Rhodes in 1522, but he then rested on his laurels. In 1525, the elite janissary guard staged a violent protest against the failure to make war again (for they relied on booty to supplement their meagre pay). Suleiman quelled the rebellion, distributed 200,000 ducats to his troops, and sounded the drum of conquest on 1 December 1525, summoning his people to war. He could have moved east against Persia but decided to return to Hungary; he knew that the kingdom was divided politically and that little help was to be expected from the other Christian monarchies of Europe, occupied with the crisis of the Reformation. He was impelled as Sultan to expand the territory of Islam as a step towards achieving a universal monarchy; for him, expansion against the infidel Christians was a sacred obligation.

On 23 April 1526, Suleiman and Ibrahim left Constantinople with 100,000 men and 300 guns. It took almost three months before the cavalcade reached Belgrade. Torrential rain had swollen all the rivers, but Ibrahim pushed ahead to make sure they were bridged. Ibrahim was also trusted to sweep aside the few Hungarian troops still found on the road to the Danube. The fortress of Peterwardein was stormed and the garrison of 500 decapitated on Ibrahim's orders. The Hungarian forces in the path of the Ottoman army, led by Pál Tömöri, the martial Archbishop of Kalosca, retreated back to the Hungarian plain. Here a waterlogged steppe 10 kilometres (6 miles) wide reached south from the small village of Mohács, ending in a line of tree-covered hills. It was there, on the edge of the plain nearest the village, that the Hungarian King Louis and the cream of Hungarian nobility set up their camp. The final number in the Hungarian force is open to conjecture, but is generally thought to be between 25,000 and 30,000, though reinforcements were arriving from Bohemia, Croatia and Transylvania, totalling perhaps 30,000 more.

As Suleiman's army drew up among the hills and woods on the far side of the plain of Mohács, the Hungarian nobles pressured the king to fight the battle there and then rather than wait for help. They were confident that the heavy cavalry, armoured man and horse from head to toe, would be able to smash the advancing Turks by a combination of sheer weight and their fiery élan.

The Hungarian tactic was unsophisticated. Suleiman by contrast thought out how best to be certain of victory. The general of the *akinci*, the light troops and skirmishers, advised the sultan to let his front line bend inwards as the Hungarian heavy cavalry attacked. This would allow strong forces on either side of the curved line to attack the Hungarians on both flanks and eventually to encircle them. Estimates suggest that there were perhaps 45,000 fighting troops with the sultan, both cavalry and foot soldiers, and an unknown number of guns, a balance less uneven than the later Christian accounts suggested. Both armies took time to reach battle stations and the Hungarians, determined to take the offensive, finally charged the Ottoman line in the middle of the afternoon, commanded by the redoubtable Archbishop Tömöri in his golden armour.

The battle details vary among contemporary accounts, but the general picture confirms that the Ottoman plan worked almost like clockwork. The Hungarian cavalry charged the first line, commanded by Ibrahim Pasha himself. The Turkish account of the battle, written by the contemporary historian Kemal Pashazade, attributed the victory to the prowess of the vizier, 'whose lance was like the beak of the falcon in vigour and whose sword, thirsty for blood, was like the claws of the lion of bravery'. Embroidered though the account was, Ibrahim organized the fall-back that created the fatal crescent shape. When King Louis and the reserve saw the Turkish line bend, they eagerly attacked across the plain, expecting victory. They arrived just as the first Hungarian charge, which almost reached Suleiman himself, was spent. The Ottoman cannon opened a murderous fire while the Hungarian horsemen were assailed from both flanks by the light infantry and cavalry clustered around them. The doomed army fought, according to the accounts, bravely but vainly. By evening it was destroyed. Among the slain were three archbishops, five bishops, 500 Hungarian nobles and the king himself, drowned when he tried to escape across the marshy ground. His body was found a month later buried in the mud.

The defeat was comprehensive. Ottoman soldiers took no prisoners, as a result more than 20,000 Hungarians died that day, tearing the heart out of the Hungarian nation. Ibrahim's generalship so impressed Suleiman, who had also bravely stood his ground while lances and arrows struck his breastplate, that he presented his vizier with a heron's feather covered with diamonds as a token of his esteem. On 31 August, Suleiman noted only the following in his diary: 'The

Sultan seated on a throne of gold receives the salutations of the viziers and officers; massacre of two thousand prisoners. Rain falls in torrents.' The Ottomans proceeded to the Hungarian capital of Buda. Suleiman had not intended it to be sacked, since the citizens had prudently sent him the keys to the city as a sign of supplication, but his troops were eager for booty and hard to control. Buda and Pest, the twin towns of the Hungarian capital, were both burned down and their treasure ransacked. Hungary was left temporarily to its own ruined devices, but three years later southern Hungary came under indirect Ottoman authority. Once again, Ibrahim and Suleiman proved an irresistible partnership, whose leadership inspired and disciplined an army that was otherwise motley, hard to control and greedy for loot.

9. SIEGE OF VIENNA
12 September 1683

The battle that took place outside the Austrian capital of Vienna on 12 September 1683 marked a turning point in the history of European warfare. The victory by a Christian 'Holy League' composed of Poles, Germans and Austrians against a huge Ottoman army marked the end of the centuries-long expansion of Ottoman Turkish power in southeastern Europe and saved central European Christianity. After Vienna, the Ottoman sultanate did not inflict serious defeat on Western enemies again, and the Turkish Empire began a long decline.

The Ottomans had long harboured ambitions to capture Vienna and dominate the trade routes of eastern Europe. Buda, in Hungary, was an Ottoman city and to the south the Ottomans ruled as far as present-day Bosnia and Croatia. A restless frontier between the Austrian Habsburg and Ottoman empires ran through northern Hungary. The Ottoman sultan, Mehmed IV, decided on the advice of his grand vizier,

Kara Mustafa Pasha, that it was time to launch a major campaign against the Habsburgs and to extend Ottoman suzerainty over the whole area of central Europe. Plans were made to strengthen roads, repair bridges and gather together a large army from among the vassal states of the empire. On 6 August 1682, war was declared on Austria, but the late season postponed the advance of the Ottoman army until the following March. The Habsburgs had plenty of time to prepare defences and seek allies. Emperor Leopold I reached an agreement with the King of Poland-Lithuania, John III Sobieski, for mutual aid in the defence of Christian Europe. This was to prove an inspired choice.

In the early summer, the huge Ottoman army, followed by herds of cattle, flocks of sheep, wagon trains of supplies and thousands of camp followers, moved north from Thrace, reaching Belgrade in May (where the sultan stayed to await results). The army was commanded by the grand vizier himself, who moved northwards to encircle Vienna by 14 July 1683. Leopold and 80,000 Viennese fled westward to Linz to avoid Ottoman conquest, leaving Count Ernst Rüdiger von Starhemberg with 16,000 soldiers and militia and 370 cannon to defend Vienna against the siege. For two months, the defenders endured disease, hunger and the constant threat that Turkish engineers would succeed in mining under the walls and blowing a gap in the defences. Kara Mustafa Pasha did nothing to rush the capture of Vienna. Short of heavy artillery, and confident that there was no prospect of relief, he waited until his miners had breached the walls. This long delay allowed the Christian Holy League to mobilize its forces, prepare the campaign and march to the relief of the city.

The League was made up of 47,000 Germans and Austrians and an army of 37,000 Poles and Lithuanians. King John III Sobieski was the key figure holding the force together. He was a remarkable commander, with a string of earlier victories against Tatars and Ottomans to his credit. He had been responsible for reforming the Polish army to create a modern force. He understood Ottoman military doctrine, having been an envoy in Istanbul, and he could speak all the major Western languages (plus Tatar and Turkish), a big advantage in a multi-national force. On 6 September, his army crossed the Danube and met up with Imperial forces under Charles of Lorraine, but two days later Ottoman miners succeeded in breaching the defensive walls. The Ottoman army was poised to enter the city.

The 85,000 Holy League troops moved into position on the Kahlenberg hills above Vienna and on 12 September they prepared for battle. There has always been some confusion over the exact size of the Ottoman force. The hard core of 20,000 warrior janissaries were supported by as many as 100,000 allied and vassal soldiers, but many were poorly armed or clothed, while the 40,000 Tatars were unreliable. The battle started at 4 a.m. with a spoiling attack by Ottoman forces, which was repulsed by the Austrians and Germans. During the morning, Kara Mustafa Pasha was determined to complete the capture of Vienna. He divided his forces between the city and the threat to the Ottoman rear, a crucial miscalculation. For twelve exhausting hours, the German–Polish infantry launched attacks against the two Ottoman flanks, while at the city walls Ottoman engineers prepared a final explosion to breach the fortifications. Ottoman troops were kept back in readiness to occupy Vienna, but an Austrian miner detected the Turkish explosive and defused it.

Ottoman strategy exposed the army to profound danger. At 5 p.m., John Sobieski gathered the combined cavalry of the relief force together on the hills above the battle. Judging the moment to be right after hours of infantry attrition, he launched the largest cavalry charge in history. Some 20,000 horsemen, including 3,000 of Sobieski's famed 'winged hussars', swept down from the hills. The Ottoman forces, exhausted after fighting all day on the plain and on the walls of Vienna, collapsed in a matter of minutes in the face of this cavalry onslaught. By 5.30 p.m., Sobieski was standing in Kara Mustafa's magnificent tent. The Turkish armies broke and fled, leaving 15,000 dead and wounded, 5,000 prisoners and the loss of all the Turkish artillery and great quantities of treasure. The Holy League had casualties estimated at 4,500. The victory ended any prospect of an Ottoman central Europe.

John Sobieski famously remarked 'We came, we saw, God

conquered'. Pope Innocent XI declared the feast of the Holy Name of Mary to be celebrated on 12 September throughout Catholic Christendom in commemoration. The Ottoman forces failed to return, and over the next decades Turkish rule was driven back in Hungary and Transylvania. The Habsburg–Ottoman war was finally ended with the Treaty of Karlowitz in 1699. On 25 December 1683 in Belgrade, Kara Mustafa Pasha was ritually strangled with a silk rope. John III Sobieski died in 1696, Poland's most famous king and military commander.

10. BATTLE OF VALMY
20 September 1792

The Battle of Valmy is commonly regarded as the battle that saved the French Revolution. Three years after the overthrow of France's absolute monarchy in summer 1789, large Austrian and Prussian armies were advancing on Paris to eradicate the revolutionary regime and restore the old social order. The Prussians were met by an army of French levies raised, they were told, to save the new nation and the liberty of its people. In truth the battle was little more than a modest exchange of fire, but the Prussians withdrew and Paris was saved. The revolution entered its more radical phase, and four months later the French king, Louis XVI, was executed.

The horror stories spread abroad by émigré Frenchmen of the violence and depravity of the revolutionary leaders and the mobs they led fuelled the ambition of the crowned heads of Europe to try to extinguish the new system before its seditious infection touched them, too. An army of around 30,000 was gathered together by the Prussian King, Frederick William II, under the command of the Duke of Brunswick, widely regarded as one of the finest commanders in

Europe. Alongside some 32,000 Austrians to the north and the south, the Prussian army moved forwards through Luxembourg and eastern France in August and early September, capturing one city after another to reach and cross the River Meuse. In Paris, the fright of invasion sped up the search for counter-revolutionary suspects and the subsequent September Massacres accounted for more than 1,000 grisly deaths, among them priests, aristocrats and a much larger number of common prisoners who were an easy target, but largely guiltless.

The main French force, commanded by General Charles-François Dumouriez, arrived to the west of the river to occupy a ridge of hills and strongpoints. Dumouriez told the minister of war that he would defend to the death, like the Spartans at Thermopylae, but the first strongpoints soon fell to determined Prussian and Austrian attack. Dumouriez retreated south, where he was joined by 10,600 men under General Pierre de Beurnonville and 16,000 troops brought from Metz by General François-Christophe Kellermann. Brunswick was confident that his well-trained Prussians would sweep aside what he regarded as a revolutionary rabble, but his 30,000 soldiers were now faced by as many as 36,000 French, with 28,000 in reserve some distance away, a half-and-half mixture of veterans from the armed forces of the king and new National Guard levies raised to defend the revolution. Although discipline was lax, and the reliability of former royal officers unpredictable, it was commitment to the new national cause, rather than military spit-and-polish, that shaped the force, just as it had encouraged Washington's irregulars in America a decade before.

The Prussian king, travelling with Brunswick, insisted that the French would continue to retreat and encouraged him to move forward to cut off their line of escape and destroy them. On the night of 19 September, the Prussians prepared to march. At 6 a.m., the advance guard moved forward through thick rain and fog until, to their consternation, they were shelled by Kellermann's invisible artillery, drawn up on the slopes of Mont Yron, around which Dumouriez had placed his guns and long lines of infantry, a total front-line force of 36,000 men. The artillery was manned by the old regular army and was regarded as among the most proficient in Europe. The Prussians continued to move forward, more hesitantly now until they had captured the first French guns at the inn of La Lune, where the king and his staff could also shelter. Brunswick then drew up his army in battle array opposite the hills and the village of Valmy, the artillery lined up in front of the 34,000 soldiers he had brought this far. What he lacked was a clear operational plan.

Only when the fog lifted at noon could the Prussians see, not a revolutionary mob, but line upon line of uniformed and disciplined soldiers, well-established at the summit of an awkward slope. He ordered his infantry to form columns and advance against the French line. It was at this moment that Kellermann rose to his role as commander of the revolutionary troops. He stood up in the saddle, placed his hat with its red-white-and-blue cockade on the end of his sword, and, raising it on high, called out 'Vive la Nation!' It was the first battle-cry of a new age of national wars. His troops echoed back with cries of 'Vive la Nation!' and 'Vive la France!' and prepared to fight the Prussians singing the new revolutionary anthem, *La Marseillaise*. This was war for a modern cause, not to satisfy dynastic ambition.

The story of Kellermann's rallying call may have become embellished in the telling, but all witnesses recall it. Whether it was this that perturbed Brunswick, or simply the growing evidence that he was greatly outnumbered by men who could, after all, fight effectively, he hurriedly recalled the columns. An artillery duel continued until dusk when torrential rain brought the desultory conflict to an end. Though no real battle had occurred (300 French casualties, 184 Prussian), Valmy was treated as the first major victory of the revolution. The next day, the monarchy was abolished and the First French Republic proclaimed. Brunswick and Frederick William prudently withdrew back to the Rhineland, leaving the French free to deploy an impressive total of around 450,000 men for adventures in Savoy and Belgium. There were to be more than twenty years of war before the disruptive effects of the new revolutionary order were tempered by defeat and the restoration of a monarchy. The Prussian Carl von Clausewitz, in his reflections *On War*, saw the revolutionary victory as the start of a new age, in which war became the business of the whole body of citizens: 'nothing,' he wrote, 'now impeded the vigour with which war could be waged.' Kellermann could not know that his flamboyant gesture, enough to turn the cautious Prussians back, would open the way to total war.

11. BATTLE OF TRAFALGAR
21 October 1805

Any visitor to London standing in Trafalgar Square and gazing up at the tall column at its centre may well wonder why the British named such a prominent landmark after a small southern Spanish cape, lapped by the cool Atlantic on the Costa de la Luz. The column supports the slender statue of Admiral Horatio Nelson, almost certainly Britain's most famous sailor, whose smaller fleet defeated a large Franco-Spanish naval force in a bitter day-long engagement in 1805, at the height of the Napoleonic Wars. Even more remarkable for a battle in which leadership played a critical part, Nelson himself was mortally wounded early in the fight and died before it was over.

The battle was in many ways accidental. In the summer of 1805, Napoleon planned the invasion of England across the Channel from Boulogne and Calais. A large army gathered there, but by August it still lacked the naval superiority necessary to give invasion any chance of success. An alliance with Spain earlier in the year might have given Napoleon the large naval force that he needed, but the British naval blockade kept the Franco-Spanish forces divided. When Napoleon ordered Vice Admiral Pierre Villeneuve to gather a fleet together from the scattered units, the best that could be achieved was the safety of the Spanish port of Ferrol and, later, Cádiz. Napoleon flew into a rage at the apparent timidity of his naval commander – 'What a navy! What an admiral! What useless sacrifices!' – but the truth was that French and Spanish ships were not fully prepared for combat, many lacking trained men, or in some cases even men who had been to sea. Villeneuve knew that command of the British fleet sent to prevent an invasion force from gathering had been given to Nelson, victor at the battles of the Nile in 1798 and Copenhagen in 1801. Nelson's reputation preceded him: a shrewd tactician and a brave and aggressive admiral. Unsurprisingly, Villeneuve, and the even less enthusiastic Spanish commander, Admiral Federico Gravina, were reluctant to risk a major battle. When a frustrated Napoleon finally abandoned the invasion, he ordered the combined Franco-Spanish fleet to leave Cádiz for Naples, where it could support the French army preparing for war against a new anti-French Coalition. The Spanish commanders objected to risking a fight and even Villeneuve's own subordinates hoped that battle could be avoided. The French commander finally persuaded the fleet to leave by arguing that Nelson had only twenty-two ships to the Franco-Spanish force of thirty-three. With a poor wind the ships straggled out of port on 19 October, where Nelson's advance guard spotted them.

Battle was still not inevitable. Villeneuve was supposed to be heading for Naples, already knowing that he was to be sacked and humiliated by his emperor. The ships made an untidy line towards the Straits of Gibraltar, forcing Nelson to pursue them. He had planned a classic operation in which the long Franco-Spanish line would be pierced by two columns of ships that would then encircle the enemy and destroy them in a 'pell-mell' battle. The French attempt to flee to the Mediterranean might mean no such operation was possible. Despite the poor winds, the Franco-Spanish fleet passed Cabo Trafalgar and could see the possibility of safety. All at once, in mid-morning, Villeneuve decided to throw caution to the wind. He ordered the fleet to turn, prepare battle stations and engage with the oncoming British. The manoeuvre was carried out in no particular order and the ships eventually emerged in small groups rather than an ordered line, the northernmost squadron under Rear-Admiral Pierre Dumanoir out of touch with the main area of the battle that followed.

Nelson was delighted with the prospect of battle, but puzzled by the unusual Franco-Spanish battle order. He ordered his two columns to form, one under his command, one under Vice Admiral Cuthbert Collingwood. He ordered an unusually long signal to be hoisted, since immortalized in the Nelson saga: 'England expects that every man will do his duty.' The signal provoked roaring cheers from the ships around him. Battle stations were prepared and at 11.30 a.m. the first British ships sailed for the enemy line. Nelson in *Victory* finally let the *Téméraire* enter the fray ahead of him; Collingwood's *Royal Sovereign* led the assault further to the west against the end of the enemy line. The British fleet boasted 2,148 guns, including the heavy carronades designed to rake the enemy deck and smash the masts, against 2,568 of the enemy; there were 30,000 sailors and marines in the Franco-Spanish fleet, 17,000 in Nelson's. But the British ships had commanders with greater experience, gun crews who understood the terrible demands of an artillery duel at sea, and a confidence that the enemy did not possess. When Nelson finally spotted Villeneuve's flagship *Bucentaure*, he changed the direction of his charge and under heavy fire from the French ships, steered straight for his opposite number.

The ferocious battle between *Victory* and the French ships *Bucentaure*, *Redoubtable* and *Neptune* symbolized the whole afternoon of battle and illustrated the impact that Nelson's courage and determination could have on the rest of his fleet. After taking terrible damage, Nelson pierced the French line and began his own cannonades against the enemy. His conspicuous uniform and his refusal to shelter made him an obvious target for enemy sharpshooters in the French rigging and at 1.25 p.m., he was shot through the shoulder. The bullet pierced his lung and crippled his spine. Nelson died three hours later in the ship's primitive hospital. The fleet did not know this and fought as he had required them. By the time he died, some fifteen French and Spanish ships had already been captured as prizes, including Villeneuve's flagship, which he surrendered shortly before Nelson's death. British gunnery was lethal, particularly at close range, while marines and sailors stayed as far as possible below decks to avoid high casualties. British captains revelled in the ship-on-ship combat that now developed and not a single British ship surrendered, despite exceptional levels of damage, which left one vessel, the *Bellisle*, with no masts or bowsprit and no longer able to fire a gun. On both sides, masts and rigging crashed to the deck or into the sea. Thunderous cannonades destroyed the sides and decks, while fire directed at decks maimed and killed thousands on board, including the captain of the British ship *Mars*, whose head was blown off by a shot. In many cases the French or Spanish ships that surrendered had suffered no worse damage than the British ships to which they submitted.

The battle was, as Nelson had hoped, 'pell-mell', but it was not a walkover. French and Spanish commanders, though in some cases unhappy about having to fight, gave as good as they got; all except Rear Admiral Dumanoir, whose ten ships took little part in the battle. Had they done so, the outcome might have been different. Some turned back to engage in the fight later in the afternoon, but Dumanoir and four vessels steered on towards Cádiz. They were captured a few days later by another British squadron. By 5.45 p.m., the battle was over, ended spectacularly by the explosion of the French *Achille* as it was devoured by fire. Collingwood succeeded Nelson as commander and could count nineteen enemy ships captured for the surrender of not a single British vessel. Franco-Spanish losses were 6,953 dead and wounded, while the British suffered just 449 dead, including Nelson, and 1,241 wounded. Most of the nineteen captured ships were lost on passage to Gibraltar in a storm (two escaped). Other French and Spanish ships sank or were captured in the next few days; of the thirty-three combined Franco-Spanish ships, twenty-three were lost and the rest badly damaged.

Napoleon raged at news of the defeat, but Villeneuve was now safely a British prisoner.

Trafalgar did not bring the war with Napoleon any closer to a conclusion. French shipyards turned out more vessels to replace those lost, but the balance of power at sea remained with the Royal Navy, an outcome that only in the long run contributed to the eventual collapse of the French Empire. Nelson became the most famous British hero of the nineteenth century, and in 1843 his completed granite column finally gazed out over the capital, its metal friezes fashioned from melted-down French guns captured at Trafalgar.

12. BATTLE OF AUSTERLITZ
2 December 1805

There is perhaps no finer example of Napoleon's remarkable military genius than the comprehensive defeat he imposed on a numerically superior Russian–Austrian force near the small Austrian town of Austerlitz at the height of the war between France and its allies and the Third Coalition of Britain, Russia and Austria. Napoleon was not diffident about his military reputation. In 1804, he had had himself crowned emperor in what was until then a new revolutionary and republican state; he had little respect for his enemies and great confidence in his capacity to out-think and out-fight them. This confidence was infectious. On the eve of Austerlitz, 1 December 1805, he was almost captured as he went with his guards to reconnoitre. On his return to camp, his troops spontaneously lit straw torches to light his way and struck up a strident chorus of 'Vive l'Empereur!' With the cries echoing around him, Napoleon was heard to mutter 'it has been the finest evening of my life'. The following day, the first anniversary of his coronation, was a remarkable triumph for Napoleon and his enthusiastic soldiers.

The victory at Austerlitz came at an opportune moment. Napoleon's Grande Armée was campaigning in cold winter weather far from France, deep in central Europe, and with the prospect, despite earlier victories, that Prussia might join the war and send a large army southwards. In late October, the British had contributed the decisive naval victory at Trafalgar to the Coalition's efforts. A large Russian army, personally led into Europe by Tsar Alexander I, was supported by a smaller Austrian force, both approaching from the east. Napoleon needed to be sure that battle would be joined and won; he dispersed his forces to lure the Tsar into thinking that he was weaker than he really was. The bait was swallowed, and although some advisers wanted the Tsar to wait until even more reinforcements were available, he was impatient to impose his mark on European history by vanquishing the undefeated emperor of France. Once it was evident that battle was what the Coalition wanted, Napoleon drew up his main force at a battlefield of his own choosing and summoned the distant armies of Marshal Bernadotte and Marshal Davout to join him. The French would eventually have a mixed French and Italian force of 73,000 (not all of whom would see action) and 139 guns against a Coalition force of 85,700 with 278 guns spread across two or three fronts.

The site of the battle played an important part in the final outcome. Napoleon chose a narrow plain, the Plain of Turas, positioned between two small branches of a river, with a hilly plateau, the Pratzen, to his right and a good field for cavalry action in front. His inspiration lay not only in choosing a suitable field, but in anticipating what his enemy would do. He expected the Russians and Austrians to try to outflank him by occupying the Pratzen as a base from which to turn the French line by attacking the right wing from the rear. To do this, the Russian army would be stretched out along the few miles of the plateau, itself exposed to a possible counter-thrust, which the French would mount from the plain, cutting the enemy army in two and destroying it. This is exactly what the Russian generals Mikhail Kutuzov and Franz von Weyrother decided to do, though Kutuzov was aware of the risks involved. Expecting the Coalition armies to outnumber Napoleon by perhaps two to one, the object was to keep the French front line occupied by a limited threat, while the rest of the army crept along the plateau and behind the enemy. It was not a poor plan, though it depended on Napoleon not realizing the danger until too late. In fact, Napoleon planned the battle to take exactly this form; holding the front line, keeping a weaker but sufficient force on the right wing, at the end of the plateau, and sending the bulk of his army up the slopes of the plateau to shatter the enemy from the flank.

No battle goes exactly to plan, but in this case Napoleon understood his enemy so well that had he had spies at the Coalition headquarters, set up at the small town of Austerlitz, they could hardly have informed him better. During the night of 1 December, some 56,000 Coalition infantry and a large body of cannon made as secret an advance as they could across the Pratzen plateau. Their objective was to be in position the following morning to attack the French right through the villages of Telnitz and Sokolnitz, then cross onto the Turas Plain where the main French force could be rolled up from behind. The plan went wrong from the start. The cavalry under Prince Lichtenstein had misunderstood its orders and was at the front of the columns moving across the plateau instead of behind it on the cavalry plain. The effort to reverse the movement of men and horses slowed up the advance and meant that early the following morning there were fewer Russians to storm the French right than intended. Somehow, the French and Italians of Davout's right wing, still waiting for reinforcements on the march to the battle, held up a force five times their size. This was the most risky element of Napoleon's plan, for if the front here cracked quickly, the enemy might indeed take his forces from the rear. The French defenders and the Russian attackers took heavy casualties and the villages changed hands many times, but the line did not break.

Napoleon's main army was poised to attack the plateau. Heavy mists meant that the move into position was invisible to the Coalition columns, while the higher plateau was bathed in sunshine, making the enemy entirely visible to the French below. Around 29,000 French troops commanded by Marshal Jean-de-Dieu Soult suddenly appeared out of the mist, to the consternation of the enemy. The delay caused by the movement of Coalition cavalry meant that more Russians were on the plateau than expected and there were fierce contests to control the heights. But Kutuzov, already wounded, could see what was happening and tried to rescue an imminent disaster. The Russian Imperial Guard, held in reserve near Austerlitz, were sent to drive the French back, but despite savage hand-to-hand fighting, some of it close to where Napoleon, now on the plateau, was directing the battle, the Guard was decimated. At the front line, French cavalry and infantry held back and then repulsed the smaller Russian cavalry forces under Prince Pyotr Bagration, who, seeing the disaster unfolding, retreated in good order. For the 35,000 Russians crammed into the far end of the plateau and still unable to penetrate the French right wing, there was little hope. The battle was effectively won by mid-day, but the fighting on the ridge and in the villages continued; Kutuzov's order to retreat took four hours to reach the drunken commander, General Frederick Buxhouden, who by mid-morning was too intoxicated to understand anything. The Russians began retreating while bombarded by French cannon and attacked from the rear. Thousands tried to cross the frozen Satschen Lake, hauling cannon across, until the ice broke. Several hundred drowned, the guns were lost and thousands more dragged themselves, frozen and exhausted, onto the muddy banks, to be slaughtered or captured by the French.

This was a classic victory and Napoleon savoured the moment. Tsar Alexander burst into tears when the disaster was over. The Coalition remnants retreated, but the French army was too exhausted by the contest to pursue them. The Coalition losses have been estimated at 27,000 dead, wounded and captured, though precise Russian figures are lacking; French losses were 1,305 dead, 6,940 wounded and 573 prisoners. This was Napoleon's finest battle, a testament to his strategic intuition and charismatic example.

13. BATTLE OF MAIPÚ
5 April 1818

'This battle,' announced General José de San Martín to his troops shortly before the fight at Maipú, 'is going to decide the fate of all America.' This was a grandiose claim for a battle involving no more than a few thousand men in the remote Latin American territory of Chile, but San Martín – 'the Liberator' – was about to defeat the last attempt by the Spanish Empire to retain its grip on the country. Defeat would mean the re-imposition of Spanish rule; victory would send a message to Madrid that Latin America was going to free itself entirely from European rule, just as the United States had done some forty years earlier.

The outcome of the battle rested almost entirely on the organizational and strategic qualities of the commander of the army of liberation (known formally as the Army of the Andes), which San Martín had brought to Chile more than two years before with 5,000 soldiers and horsemen and 9,000 pack animals. He was an unusual liberator. Born to a Spanish family in a remote part of what is now Argentina, San Martín was sent back to Spain where he became a colonel of cavalry in the Spanish army, fighting in north Africa and then against Napoleon in the Peninsular War. He was strongly influenced by enlightenment ideas, but remained a political conservative in favour of monarchy. The crisis caused by Napoleon's invasion and the overthrow of the Spanish crown encouraged San Martín to return to the country of his birth in 1812, two years after a revolt in Buenos Aires against rule from Spain. He formed a lasting commitment to the cause of political independence for the states and provinces of South America. San Martín joined the fledgling Argentine army as a colonel of grenadiers and spent the next two years imposing on a ramshackle military organization the principles of discipline, loyalty and sound training. He was a commanding personality: upright, honest, efficient and committed entirely to his conception of a 'Continental Plan' to free all America from colonial oppression.

San Martín's tough stance on military reform and his growing reputation provoked plots and jealous rivalries. Yet nothing stopped his plan to create a new Army of the Andes in Mendoza, capital of Cuyo province, within striking distance across the mountain chain from the Spanish colony of Chile, struggling for its independence under General Bernardo O'Higgins, son of an Irish-Spanish official. In February 1817, San Martín brought his army of men, better trained and equipped than any rival force, across the high passes of the Andes, along narrow defiles and in bitter cold. Arriving on the other side, his army immediately inflicted a heavy defeat on the Spanish Chilean army at Chacabuco, killing 600 for the loss of only 12 men.

The Spanish retreated south, while San Martín entered the capital, Santiago, and established Chilean rule. The Spanish forces in the far south were neglected. Reinforcements arrived by sea under General Manuel Osorio and in spring 1818, 4,600 troops moved north to try to restore Spanish rule. O'Higgins's army was caught and beaten as it tried to retreat, and the Spanish now bore down on Santiago, intent on a savage retribution for the insurrectionary insolence of the Chileans.

San Martín's greatest victory came on a clear April day near the town of Maipú, north of the River Maipo on the approaches to Santiago. He drew up his mixed force of around 5,400 cavalry and infantry (many of them freed black slaves), with cavalry on the extreme right, infantry at the centre and left and a reserve of horse behind them. His favourite battlefield tactic was to imitate Alexander the Great, swinging the cavalry on his right in an oblique attack against the enemy left while part of his reserve came round to attack the rear. After charging several times, the grenadiers broke the Spanish left, but the right held firm against San Martín's infantry, inflicting heavy losses. He ordered three battalions of the reserve to charge the Spanish regiments and they, too, collapsed in confusion. Osorio fled from the battle.

Surrounded on all sides, the Spanish soldiers fought bravely in the face of heavy fire from the twenty-one Chilean cannon and relentless pressure from the enemy infantry. As resistance crumbled, they were massacred where they stood or taken prisoner. Little effort was made to prevent the foot soldiers in the army of liberation from exacting revenge on an army identified with years of local atrocities against the 'patriots' fighting for independence. Of the Spanish army, 2,000 were killed and more than 2,000 taken prisoner. The Army of the Andes suffered an estimated 1,000 casualties.

San Martín's achievement was not simply to out-fight the Spanish army and free Chile from colonial rule. It lay above all in his decision to create a force from the ground up capable of fighting like a European army. With few weapons and fewer clothes, the handful of fighters he had found in Mendoza were transformed, with new uniforms, guns forged in an arsenal created by a Chilean armourer, and gunpowder produced from local saltpetre. Training was strict and discipline harsh, but San Martín earned the confidence of his army by example. His only weakness was hesitancy when faced with the unpredictable and devious world of Latin American politics. His desire to free America as a whole was an ideal that could inspire temporary loyalty but not a permanent trust. Four years after Maipú, he resigned in disillusionment from command of the army and government of Peru (only half of which he had succeeded in liberating), the victim of malign gossip and political hostility. He sailed to Europe as an exile in 1824 and died in Boulogne in 1850. Before his death, Chile had woken up to its debt to his military talent and offered him the rank and pay of a Chilean general, while the rest of independent Latin America came to see him as their hero too.

14. BATTLE OF VOLTURNO
1–2 October 1860

Probably no military leader was so admired and lionized in his own day as the commander of the famous 'Thousand' redshirts, Giuseppe Garibaldi. His inspirational leadership was acclaimed by those volunteers who flocked to his call to create a united Italy, but feared and vilified by politicians and monarchists who understood the revolutionary potential of Garibaldi's 'people's army'. The story of the expedition of the Thousand to free Sicily and southern Italy from the rule of their authoritarian Bourbon monarchy is one packed with drama, but nothing was more dramatic than the first and only major defensive battle fought by the *Garibaldini* along the south bank of the River Volturno, north of Naples.

The campaign that ended with Volturno had begun on 11 May 1860, when the *Piemonte* and *Lombardo*, two ships appropriated by Garibaldi in Genoa, arrived at the Sicilian port of Marsala with 1,217 patriots, revolutionaries and students on board. His force faced a Bourbon army numbering 140,000, of whom 25,000 were in Sicily. The odds meant little to Garibaldi. Supported by a flood of volunteers and Sicilians hostile to Bourbon rule, the Thousand had turned by August into a motley force of 20,000. Among them were British and Hungarian veterans keen to support the aspirations for a united Italy and hostile to those great powers, principally the Austrian and Russian empires, which sought to shore up conservative monarchy. The Bourbon king, Francis II, had mixed loyalty from his Neapolitan army, many of whom threw in their lot with Garibaldi over the course of the year. Sicily was overrun and on 19 August, Garibaldi crossed to the mainland at Melito in two old steamers, *Torino* and *Franklin*, the latter flying an American flag. He brought 4,200 with him to start a campaign against 17,200 Neapolitan soldiers and 32 cannon.

The expedition was not approved by any of the European powers except Britain. Even the northern Italians, now unified under Victor Emmanuel II thanks to the help of the French army, were wary of Garibaldi and hoped that his ships might run aground or sink. Instead, the numbers flocking to join the *Garibaldini* grew rapidly, though out of the 50,000 in the south no more than half constituted a real fighting force. The Neapolitan army was quickly cleared from Calabria and Garibaldi marched on Naples, the Bourbon capital. As enemy soldiers surrendered, so the rifles and cannon fell into the hands of what was now called the Army of the South, organized like a regular army in divisions and brigades, but reliant for its supply on what it could capture or the money and equipment sent by romantic supporters of Italian freedom. As the *Garibaldini* moved north, Victor Emmanuel moved his army south through central Italy in the hope that he could prevent Garibaldi from provoking republican revolution. Francis II was caught between the two, but it was the irregulars of Garibaldi who defeated him and made unification possible.

Francis abandoned Naples and moved a little further north to the strongly fortified centres at Capua and Gaeta, where he determined to make a stand. He still commanded 50,000 men with 42 cannon and a body of cavalry, but only half were sent to the front line established along the River Volturno under the command of Marshal Giosuè Ritucci. Garibaldi's army began to arrive on the south side of the river, and thinking there would be the same uncontested advances seen in Calabria and much of Sicily, István Türr, Garibaldi's Hungarian commander, launched premature attacks towards Capua. Here and at Caiazzo the *Garibaldini* were driven back with heavy losses. Francis and Ritucci decided their army was now in a strong enough state to mount a general offensive. The Neapolitan plan was to attack across the river from three different directions, one division from the north-west and two from different points to the east, in the hope that they could surround and annihilate Garibaldi's army. Garibaldi and his senior commander, Giuseppe Sirtori, were forced to spread out their defensive system to avoid being outflanked. What followed were three different contests that eventually merged into a single battle.

Both sides fought, according to observers, with a ferocity and desperation that had been lacking in many of the earlier engagements. Much rose and fell on the outcome. The end of Bourbon rule was certain in the event of a defeat, but a victory for Francis would destroy the momentum for unification and postpone it, perhaps for years. The attack began at dawn on 1 October with a frontal assault on the two major outposts of the *Garibaldini* at Sant'Angelo and the village of Santa Maria. Good progress was made at first and Garibaldi, who exposed himself time and again to the greatest danger, hurried to Sant'Angelo to try to stem the tide. He was surrounded by the enemy, but rescued almost at once by a group of his own men. He rallied some of the retreating units and with banners flying and sword in hand, if the later images are to be believed, Garibaldi led the counter-attack, smashing the Neapolitan lines. He then rushed to Santa Maria where Giacomo Medici was leading a desperate defence against deter-mined enemy assaults. Again Garibaldi saved the day. He ordered the reserve under Türr to come by train the few miles to the village. Led by the ferocious charge of the Hungarian Hussars, they drove the Bourbon army back to the walls of Capua.

The other axes of advance also went the way of the Neapolitans to begin with. Two columns from the east swept towards Caserta, the main city and road junction. On the right of the line of *Garibaldini*, a division commanded by Nino Bixio first absorbed the attack, then drove the enemy back in disorder. The central column was more successful and soon reached and occupied Caserta Vecchia. After hours of fighting, the exhausted Neapolitans, unaware of the defeats else-where, slept in and around the small town. Sirtori ordered those units that had seen the least fighting to assemble during the night for an attack on the unwary Neapolitans. Early in the morning they woke to gunfire and the sound of the approaching enemy. The 3,000 men were surrounded and either killed or captured. The battle was over. Garibaldi and his thousands had made possible the creation of a new Italy, for the death or injury of 1,634 of his men against the 1,128 casualties and 2,160 prisoners suffered by his enemy.

Garibaldi was essential to the victory, not only for his capacity to out-think the professional officers he opposed, but for his courageous and conspicuous presence at all points of a wide and dangerous battle-field. Nevertheless, Victor Emmanuel refused on his arrival to review the *Garibaldini*, unable to embrace the idea that patriotic irregulars and foreign volunteers alone could have secured victory. Disillusioned, Garibaldi abandoned his army and departed for his home at Caprera carrying, it is alleged, a year's supply of macaroni. 'You have done much,' he told his men, 'with scant means in a short time' – a fitting epitaph for an unpredictable adventure against seemingly invincible odds, and a modest assessment of his own charismatic contribution.

15. BATTLE FOR WARSAW
13–20 August 1920

There are few more obvious examples of the importance of leadership in the history of modern war than the story of Marshal Józef Piłsudski's rout of the Red Army before the gates of Warsaw in the summer of 1920. What made the battle all the more extraordinary was the curious blend of old and new. There were pitched engagements between cavalry units with lance and sabre; the progress of the Red cavalry was marked by a level of violence towards the troops and populations in its path that resembled the Thirty Years War of the seventeenth century; but there were primitive tanks, armoured trains and a handful of aircraft to show that this was also a conflict of the twentieth.

Piłsudski was a remarkable individual. Born in 1867 in a Poland divided between Russia, Prussia and Austria, he spent thirty years campaigning for Polish independence as a clandestine terrorist. Before the war, he organized a Polish armed force with 20,000 volunteers, known as the Legion. When war broke out that summer, the Austrian army recruited the Legion to fight against Russia and when the war ended, these experienced legionaries formed the core of a new Polish army under Piłsudski's command. Their job was to build a new Polish state with their commander as its first president. The victorious Allies were willing to recognize Poland's right at last to independence, but they had no means to help the infant state in case of any threat. Germany was temporarily immobilized by defeat, but revolutionary Russia, struggling under Lenin to defeat its many anti-communist enemies, was an unknown quantity.

The Bolshevik leaders in Moscow had grandiose ambitions. The gradual defeat of the White armies in the Russian Civil War paved the way for a revolutionary crusade into Europe. In February 1920, Lenin ordered a war against Poland as the first stage in the possible 'liberation' of the workers and peasants of eastern and central Europe. There was talk of sweeping through to Germany and Italy; world revolution seemed within the grasp of the new Red Army. The Soviet troops were commanded by a spirited commander, Mikhail Tukhachevsky, a young Russian soldier who had been a prisoner-of-war for most of the First World War but who was nevertheless trusted by the Red Army commander, Leon Trotsky, to organize and lead whole armies. By chance, both Tukhachevsky and Piłsudski were avid readers of Napoleon; it was the Pole, however, who drew the better lessons.

In April, the new Polish army, a hotch-potch of units from the Great War and volunteer patriots, undertook a pre-emptive strike against the Red Army in Ukraine and Belorussia. It failed to achieve anything decisive, and in May a Russian counter-offensive pushed the Poles back rapidly. Two large army groups were formed: one in the north striking from Belorussia; one in the south made up of cavalry, the Konarmia, under the swashbuckling horseman, Semyon Budionny, which swept like a Tatar horde against the Poles, driving them back towards Lvov, though suffering heavy losses in the process. On 29 May, Budionny's Cossacks met the Polish 1st Krechowiecki Lancers and an old-fashioned encounter took place between a champion chosen from each side. The two men rode at each other, but the Polish lancer was quicker, slashing his opponent open from the neck to the waist. The Cossacks turned and fled.

In the north, an even more terrifying army of horsemen was formed under Gaia Bzhishkian, nicknamed Gai Khan because of his reputation for exceptional savagery. His army, known as the Konkorpus III, was composed of Circassian cavalry from the Caucasus, more used to sabres than rifles. By July, the Red Army had crossed the River Bug and was bearing down on Warsaw, spearheaded by Gai's terrifying vanguard. Confidence rose in Moscow. A provisional communist government was formed; Lenin expected Tukhachevsky to enter the Polish capital in early August 1920 and declare a communist Poland.

Polish forces were short of equipment – even boots and uniforms – and spent much of the summer retreating in haste before the apparently unstoppable Red Army, whose reputation for rape, pillage and slaughter preceded them; Polish villagers fled west, while Polish soldiers lost the will to defend themselves. On 8 August, the Russian armies were ordered to seize Warsaw, 30 kilometres (20 miles) from the Russian lines. There were around 68,000 Poles facing two Russian army groups of between 100,000 and 130,000. Both sides were exhausted and short of materiel after the long summer's fighting, but the Polish position seemed hopeless. Warsaw was filled with a mood of panic. On 5 August, Piłsudski locked himself away in a room in the Belvedere Palace in the capital to think out a way to snatch victory from the jaws of imminent defeat.

His solution was exceptionally daring. He planned to leave weaker forces in front of Warsaw under the overall command of General Józef Haller, while using the armies of the southern Polish wing to swing north to strike the Russian armies an unexpected and annihilating blow in the flank and rear. If it worked, victory was possible; if it failed, Warsaw would be taken anyway. Having organized the defence of Warsaw, Piłsudski headed south where he reviewed all his troops, instilling in them at last a belief in the possibility that the Russian onrush could be halted. This tall, tough, rough-hewn man, with dark bushy brows and a large military moustache, was an inspiration to the dispirited soldiers around him and he posed the chief obstacle between Tukhachevsky and a quick victory.

The Russian armies began the assault on Warsaw on 13 August. There were problems with the Red Army, too. The long supply line back to Belorussia left units short of ammunition and reserves; most soldiers were barefoot, fighting in rags or a jumble of borrowed clothing. They were bullied by political commissars and sustained only by the promise of loot and women. Tukhachevsky had expected to be supported by the Konarmia in the south, but Budionny's advance had stalled from exhaustion, and the Moscow representative on the southern front, the young Joseph Stalin, refused to release any forces to help against Warsaw. In addition, Gai's army of horsemen were sent west to bypass Warsaw and reach the German frontier, leaving Russian armies short of cavalry. Gai's force cut a swathe of terror through the Polish countryside and was at the German frontier within days, but they were not available for the decisive battle. The Poles were, nevertheless, heavily outnumbered. Piłsudski had received poor intelligence on the whereabouts of the main Russian forces and had not realized that so many were deployed in the north. The 5th Polish Army under General Władisław Sikorski fought a bitter three-day battle for the line of the River Wkra, yielding, then counter-attacking against the main Russian force. The Poles found a new heart and their defence against the encirclement and capture of Warsaw made Piłsudski's plan all the more likely to work.

On 16 August, a day earlier than planned, the Polish armies from the southern wing rolled forwards against the Russian flank. The main Russian weight was in the north, so Piłsudski's forces made rapid progress. His 53,000 infantry and 4,000 cavalry reached the Warsaw battle by 17 August and the following day crashed into the side and rear of the attacking Russian force. The Russian 16th Army disintegrated in panic. Tukhachevsky knew little of what was happening because radio communications had been jammed by the Poles. He ordered a new front to be formed, unaware that his armies were now in full retreat, trying to avoid the trap set by the oncoming Polish army in their rear. By 20 August, he finally realized the situation and ordered a general retreat, but it was too late. The Red Army moved east in complete disorder, intercepted by Polish forces moving at right angles to them every few miles. The Poles reached the German and Lithuanian border, wheeled east and pursued the Red Army past Minsk and almost to Kiev. Gai's savage horsemen, cut off and harried by the Poles, escaped into East Prussia, where they were disarmed and interned by German troops, who had been warily watching his progress. On 15 October, Lenin's government was forced to seek an armistice.

The Battle for Warsaw depended for its outcome entirely on the success of Piłsudski's operational inspiration and bold leadership. An ability to act opportunistically, even in the face of uncertain risks, had strong echoes of Napoleon at his best. Victory did not depend on the modern armoury of aircraft, tanks and radio, but relied a great deal on the simplicity and speed of the Polish counter-strike, and on the patriotic fervour of the embattled Polish divisions; this meant literally a matter of life or death for them and for a new national Poland. Nineteen years later when it was the German turn to attack, the armoury of *Blitzkrieg* condemned the Poles to the rapid loss of Warsaw and showed what a modern war of manoeuvre could achieve. Piłsudski became Poland's hero and died in 1935, four years before the new war; Tukhachevsky was eventually arrested and executed on Stalin's orders in June 1937, a long revenge for the failure at Warsaw.

16. THIRD BATTLE OF KHARKOV
19 February – 15 March 1943

German Field Marshal Erich von Manstein titled his memoirs, published in 1955, *Lost Victories*. This was not an ironic title, for Manstein believed that with the right supreme commander, Germany might not have lost the war nor have squandered the successes he had managed to achieve for Hitler. Both during and after the war, his enemies agreed that Manstein was the finest operational commander the German army possessed. Those qualities were displayed on numerous occasions, but no battle displayed them quite as fully as the sudden German counter-offensive in February 1943 after months of retreating, when Manstein's panzer armies recaptured the Russian city of Kharkov and won back a large swathe of southern Russian territory against a surprised Red Army. This was perhaps the most poignant of those 'lost victories', for within months the German army was again in full retreat, never again to win a clear-cut battle.

Manstein was a tough, resolute, perceptive commander who flourished on manoeuvre warfare. He took risks, but won dividends. Best known for his contribution to the operational plan that destroyed the Franco-British front in 1940, Manstein had a professional confidence in what he did that contrasted sharply with his inexperienced supreme commander. Both men found it difficult to give way once they had arrived at a decision. The leadership that Manstein displayed in what came to be called the Third Battle of Kharkov (the city had changed hands twice in the 1941–42 campaigns) was not simply that he understood the nature of the crisis facing his Army Group South after the retreat from Stalingrad and how it might be reversed, but in the fact that he had to argue his case against a sceptical and obstructive supreme commander.

A crisis loomed in late January 1943, as large Soviet forces from the Voronezh Front pushed into a gap that had opened up between Army Group Centre and Army Group Don (renamed South on 12 February). If successful, the Red Army might advance to the Black Sea and encircle the defending German armies in the south. Though Manstein asked for more reinforcements from static sections of the German-Soviet front further north, none arrived. The Red Army recaptured Kursk and Belgorod and by mid-February was pushing into the Ukrainian capital of Kharkov. The commander of the SS panzer divisions holding the city disobeyed Hitler's orders to hold fast and slipped out of the noose. He was sacked and replaced by General Werner Kempf, a successful tank commander.

In his memoirs, Manstein recalled that grim though his position looked, he could see the germ of an idea to reverse the situation. Both armies were exhausted, with many Soviet divisions down to only a few thousand men and limited numbers of tanks; German divisions, too, were fighting with a fraction of the tanks and armour they needed, but there were still panzer units available to him in the 1st and 4th Panzer Armies and the Army Detachment Kempf further north. The 4th Air Fleet, under General Wolfram von Richthofen, was also strengthened with up to 1,000 aircraft for the operation. Manstein's idea was to use the available armour to attack the long flank of the Soviet advance from north and south, then push on to retake the Kharkov area. The critical issue was to persuade Hitler that his plan would work. On 17 February, Hitler arrived at Manstein's southern headquarters at Zaporozhe on the River Dnepr, in southern Ukraine. For three days they argued about Manstein's plan and the future of the southern front. Hitler feared the coming of the rainy season, the *rasputitsa*, which might halt the whole plan; he wanted Kharkov recaptured first on grounds of prestige; he almost certainly wanted his view to prevail over Manstein's for political reasons. After two days, Hitler finally agreed that the 'defensive-offensive' Manstein proposed could take place, though he insisted that Kharkov should be retaken. The morning of his flight back to his headquarters, a unit of Soviet tanks moved up the road towards the airport, and Hitler was flown off just 30 kilometres (20 miles) away from the nearest Russians.

The tanks near Zaporozhe stopped because they ran out of fuel. This was the furthest the Soviet offensive came. On 19 February, Manstein's plan went into operation. The extended Soviet armies, short of supplies and taking heavy losses, crumbled in a matter of days, pushed back by the 4th Panzer Army northwards towards Kharkov or into the German net. By 2 March, the German units counted 23,000 Soviet dead, 615 captured tanks and 9,000 prisoners. The next blow was struck north towards Kharkov itself. Manstein wanted the SS panzer divisions under the command of Lieutenant General Paul 'Papa' Hausser (nicknamed as father of the Waffen-SS) to drive west of Kharkov and encircle it from the north. He did not want to risk a second Stalingrad in the ruined streets of the city. But Hausser ignored the instructions and sent his three SS panzer divisions, *Totenkopf*, *Das Reich* and *Leibstandarte Adolf Hitler*, directly into the city from three directions. Manstein thought he had done it to find favour with Hitler, but his Stalingrad fear proved misplaced and by 14 March the last pockets of Soviet resistance in the city were snuffed out. Hitler visited Manstein's headquarters again on 10 March with victory in the battle assured. When he returned to Berlin, Hitler characteristically gave the impression that he had been the author of the success. Goebbels, the Nazi propaganda chief, noted in his diary: 'the Führer is very happy that he has succeeded in closing the front again'.

The battle was a triumph for Manstein's sense of where and when to strike to maximize the impact even of weakened forces and the defensive-offensive, risky though it was if the rains had started early, probably postponed the Soviet victory on the Eastern Front by anything from six months to a year. It was his last 'lost victory'. The subsequent Battle of Kursk was lost despite Manstein, who had urged an earlier start before the Russians were dug in, but this time found Hitler adamantly against the idea. Time and again, Manstein recommended that Hitler should appoint a commander-in-chief in the East to ease his burden as supreme commander. He suggested it in February 1943 and again in September. In March 1944, Hitler had finally had enough and Manstein was sacked. Western commanders were keen to learn after the war was over how Manstein had succeeded at all, given the obstacles presented by Hitler, and he proved more than willing to oblige. Implicit in all he wrote is the belief that the war might have gone very differently under his high command. More recently, his record has been sullied by evidence of his endorsement of or indifference towards the many atrocities committed in the regions under his command in the East.

CHAPTER 2
AGAINST THE ODDS

To fight against the odds can mean many different things. It can simply represent a battlefield triumph of a much smaller force over one much greater in size. There are many examples through history where sheer numerical or material advantage has not been enough to secure victory. Against the odds can also describe a battle fought successfully against a famous military juggernaut, whose defeat few would have predicted. When the Mongols were defeated at Ain Jalut by a Mamluk force, few observers would have thought the outcome likely. The Battle of Carrhae was fought against a large, well-organized Roman army by horsemen with military traditions from the Asian steppelands, and most contemporaries would have bet on a Roman victory. The Norse Vikings, who ravaged northern Europe in the early medieval world, carried a terrifying reputation before them, yet at Edington in southern England and Clontarf near Dublin, their conquests were halted in their tracks.

Against the odds has yet another sense as well. There can be many factors that stack the odds against one side or the other, whether it is material advantage, reputation, topography or betrayal. In most cases, the side with the odds stacked heavily against them, for whatever reason, loses the battle. But in other cases the menace of overwhelming odds can evoke a response – better planning, greater determination or outstanding courage – to compensate for adversity. Few would have imagined that the small garrison at Rorke's Drift could hold out against a Zulu army, but the embattled men found reserves of desperate bravery to help them to do so. Soldiers or sailors with nothing to lose can evidently, under the right conditions, find the means to obstruct an enemy confident of victory. Indeed, high odds in your favour may even be an inhibiting factor if they induce overconfidence, careless operational thinking or a lack of the necessary psychological pressure to push that advantage home.

An imbalance of resources or men can be misleading, since there are cases where sheer numbers manifestly fail to give the advantage. The vast numbers facing the British-Egyptian expeditionary force in the Sudan in 1898 were overcome by fire discipline and machine guns. Fidel Castro's revolutionary fighters on Cuba in 1958 had none of the sophisticated weaponry available to Cuba's dictator, Fulgencio Batista, but they prevailed in large part because the government forces they faced suffered from a loss of morale in the face of widespread popular hostility to the regime and the crumbling confidence of the dictator himself.

Technical or moral factors can play an important, even decisive, part in tilting the balance back when, on paper, forces seem unevenly matched. This phenomenon is common in the development of asymmetric warfare during the course of the twentieth century, in which a notionally powerful state finds itself unable to bring that power to bear effectively against an elusive or determined enemy. This imbalance was evident in the struggles to liberate areas from colonial rule or post-colonial dictatorship. French failure in Algeria and Vietnam in the 1950s, for example, was not a product of military weakness in any formal sense, but a result of popular hostility to colonialism and growing uncertainty among the French people about whether empire was any longer worth the military cost of defending it. The United States has enjoyed the world's largest military budget for decades, but that has not made it any easier to project that power in Vietnam or Somalia, or in the 'war on terror' in Afghanistan. Here, too, the odds against smaller and less sophisticated forces can be compensated for by a variety of factors that inhibit the full exercise of power by the dominant state. It is possible to be too powerful as well as too weak. Nuclear weapons might well have transformed the war in Vietnam but they were unusable given the prevailing political situation; drone strikes are supposed to wear down the resistance of Al Qaeda but they have failed to halt the terrorism and invite wide condemnation. The 4,000-year history of battles shows that an apparently weaker or outnumbered force can, under the right circumstances, achieve much against the odds.

17. THERMOPYLAE AND SALAMIS
August 480 BCE

The Greek victory over the vast invading army and navy of the Persian emperor Xerxes in the late summer of 480 BCE is one of the great legends of the classical world. The famous 300 Spartans at Thermopylae, led by their king, Leonidas, has for centuries been a model for courage and discipline seldom exceeded in the modern age – and is now the subject of a blockbuster film. Though this was a battle lost, it was a costly victory for the Persians, and almost immediately following it, the huge Persian fleet, three times the size of the combined Greek vessels, was shattered at the great naval battle of Salamis. Greek independence was saved and Persia finally pushed back into Asia.

The odds were stacked overwhelmingly in the Persians' favour, for Xerxes could mobilize the soldiers and ships of his many vassal states. The Greek chronicler Herodotus, writing some forty or fifty years after the battles, numbered the Persian army at 1,700,000. Modern calculations suggest 180,000, including camp followers, and perhaps 130,000 soldiers, marines and sailors in a fleet that Herodotus numbered at 1,207 vessels, a figure more readily accepted today than his statistics on the army. The Greek alliance – those city-states in the peninsula not yet vassals of Persia – could muster only a fraction of this manpower, though in general they were more heavily armed and armoured than Persian soldiers. The

Greeks depended on a navy that was for the most part newly built. The Athenian leader Themistocles had persuaded the citizens to use rich new supplies of silver, discovered at the mines of Laurium, 60 kilometres (40 miles) from Athens, in 483 BCE, to fund the building of a large fleet of trireme ships to guard against a Persian invasion. Athens had around 200 triremes by the time Xerxes began the invasion three years later; the rest of Greece supplied perhaps 170–80 ships.

Xerxes's strategy was simple. He would march his huge army into Greece, supported and supplied on the seaward flanks by his fleet, until he had defeated any city-state not sensible enough to send him the gifts of water and earth indicating submission. Unlike the failed invasion at Marathon ten years earlier, Xerxes bridged the Hellespont at the modern Turkish Straits so that his army could march overland to its objective. The Greeks met in council at Corinth in 481 BCE to decide their strategy. The Spartans and Corinthians favoured defending at the Isthmus of Corinth to guard the Peloponnesian peninsula. Themistocles, his arguments reinforced by a brand-new fleet, argued that the Persians could easily envelop the defending Greeks by landing troops from their fleet behind them. His strategy was to find a site further north to halt the Persian army while the Greek fleet engaged the Persians and cut off the army's source of supply. With reluctance the others agreed, though the Spartan king would only take 300 men with him as they sailed north. The Persians swept into Macedonia and Thessaly in the summer of 480 BCE and marched south towards Athens. The Greek army, around 10,000 men, withdrew to the pass at Thermopylae, only 15 metres (50 feet) wide at its narrowest point, and the only road south for a large army. The Greek fleet positioned itself at Artemisium on the flank to keep the Persian ships away. A sudden gale on 26 August wrecked between 200 and 400 of the Persian ships, which were lighter and less seaworthy than Greek ships. The two fleets clashed inconclusively on 30 August, but according to Herodotus, a second gale that night scattered and destroyed more of the Persian ships.

That same day, the Persian army tried to break through at Thermopylae, only to find that the few thousand Greeks, with the

300 Spartans at their core, could hold the narrow pass with their longer spears and heavier armour, while the Persian archers could not find room to manoeuvre effectively. But on 31 August, Xerxes was told of a narrow gorge that led through the hills beside Thermopylae and dispatched his 10,000 crack troops, the 'Immortals', to navigate the path and attack the Greeks from the rear. Leonidas sent most of his forces south to escape destruction, and with just 1,400 men he came out for a final battle with the vast Persian army. They all died where they stood, fighting, according to Herodotus, with 'their hands and teeth' when their swords and spears were lost.

Themistocles received news of events at Thermopylae in the camp at Artemisium, and ordered the fleet to sail south at once. They arrived a few days later in the straits by the island of Salamis, which lay opposite Athens and the Piraeus. Xerxes's army marched through Attica, sacked Athens, and reunited with the Persian fleet at the city's port. The Greek allies argued about the next step: the Spartans, whose admiral Eurybiades commanded the fleet, wanted to withdraw once again to the Peloponnese; Themistocles pointed out that this would allow the Persians to land forces wherever they wanted and insisted on staying at Salamis to engage the enemy fleet. Themistocles won the day and the outcome at Salamis showed that his strategic thinking, as the Athenian historian Thucydides later wrote, 'displayed genius in the most unmistakable way'. Yet arguments between the Greek allies continued until, on 23 September, the Persian fleet arrived at the mouth of the narrow Salamis Strait.

The ancient accounts do not make clear why Xerxes sought a battle when the Greek fleet could have been blockaded. Modern views suggest that the Persian emperor wanted to avenge the losses to his fleet by one decisive battle that would salve his pride. On the day of Salamis, he set up a throne on Mount Aegaleus overlooking the strait to watch what he expected to be a decisive victory. The Greeks still had an estimated 360 ships. The Persian fleet, though still vastly greater, now contained only an estimated 600–800 vessels after the earlier losses. The Persians drew up the fleet in three ranks on a north-south axis in open sea, but the ships then had to turn sharply to the west to enter the narrow straits in much smaller lines, and here their numerical superiority was no longer an advantage – it was the naval equivalent of Thermopylae. The Greeks, according to the chronicles, sang a paean before they sailed, which put the stakes clearly before them: 'Forward sons of the Greeks...Now is the fight for everything.'

The details of the battle itself remain frustratingly sketchy. To encourage Xerxes to attack, Themistocles sent a messenger to the Persian camp with false news that the Greeks were intending to flee, but the lines of Greek ships, drawn up north to south across the narrow channel, instead did the equivalent of what Leonidas's Spartans had done, luring the Persian ships on, then moving out to ram and board them. The disadvantage of greater numbers soon became evident. The Persian ships crashed into each other, lost formation, and even, it seems, attacked each other in error. It is possible to picture the water full of a mess of drowning men, capsized ships, the debris of broken oars, the wounded and dying. The heavier Greek vessels were at an advantage when it came to ramming, while their more heavily armed marines could be deployed more easily on a narrow battlefront. Persian ships tried to escape and instead became entangled. The Greek marines disembarked to finish off isolated groups of Persians who had struggled to shore. Herodotus has Greek ship losses at 40, but Persian losses at 200 sunk and more captured. Whether these figures are precise or not, the Persian defeat was real enough.

According to Aeschylus, who served at Salamis, Xerxes 'shrieked aloud' at the sight of the disaster, 'rent his clothes' and ordered a retreat. Salamis was a decisive battle, entirely against the odds, and it demonstrated how sea power, properly exploited, could, in the right geographical circumstances, compensate for any weakness on land. Fortunately for the Greeks, Themistocles turned out to be a strategic genius. A smaller Persian army returned in 479 BCE, but was shattered at the Battle of Plataea, while the Persian fleet was finished off the same year at Mycale. Even more than Marathon, the victory at Salamis saved Greece and opened the way to the extraordinary flowering of classical Greek culture that followed.

18. BATTLE OF ZELA
1 August 47 BCE

Every schoolchild knows the phrase made famous by Julius Caesar: 'Veni, vidi, vici' – 'I came, I saw, I conquered'. However, the battle at which he is supposed to have uttered the immortal words is all but unknown. At the town of Zela (now Zile in modern-day northern Turkey), Caesar's legions faced a very much larger enemy on the very site where, 20 years earlier, a Roman army had been comprehensively beaten. The Battle of Zela was a much riskier venture than Caesar's brief epigram suggests, but in the end it was indeed a short, sharp victory for the Roman side.

The battle was prompted by events during the civil war that had raged between Caesar and Pompey (his erstwhile colleague in the First Triumvirate). The war ended with Pompey's defeat at Pharsalus and his subsequent murder in 48 BCE on the orders of Ptolemy XIII, one of two claimants to the throne of Egypt. Caesar arrived in Alexandria shortly after Pompey's death and began a notorious affair with Cleopatra VII, the other claimant to the throne. After summoning Roman reinforcements and allies from the garrisons of the Middle East, Caesar defeated Ptolemy, and Cleopatra became queen (as co-ruler with her younger brother Ptolemy XIV). With Egypt secure as an ally, Caesar left with just 1,000 men to settle affairs in the Roman provinces in the Middle East and Anatolia, where some of the local rulers had supported Pompey. One province in particular took his attention. While the civil war distracted Roman commanders, Pharnaces II, who had been installed by Pompey as king of the Crimea, arrived in Anatolia to claim back the kingdom of Pontus, taken from his family by the Romans a few years after the first Battle of Zela. Pharnaces defeated Caesar's local commander Gnaeus Domitius Calvinus, seized the region, castrated and enslaved all Roman citizens and murdered Roman tax collectors. This was a challenge Caesar could not allow to go unpunished.

As Caesar approached, Pharnaces tried to buy him off with the offer of his daughter and a heavy golden crown in return for the right to rule his ancestral lands, but Caesar was not to be appeased. The details of the battle that followed are scanty. The number of men on each side is at best an estimate: perhaps 20,000 with Pharnaces, while Caesar brought four badly depleted legions, one composed of local troops from neighbouring Galatia, whose ruler, Deiotarus, had been compelled to provide them as penance for supporting Pompey. It is likely that the seasoned troops with Caesar were greatly outnumbered. Pharnaces made camp on a hilltop at Zela, confident that he would repeat the victory over the Romans won by his father Mithridates in 67 BCE. Caesar was camped 8 kilometres (5 miles) away, but during the night of 31 July moved his force to the opposite side of the valley from Zela to await the probable battle. While Caesar's troops began to fortify their hilltop, Pharnaces moved to catch them unprepared.

The chief account of the battle comes from *The Alexandrian War*, written by an anonymous Roman officer. According to this source, Pharnaces massed his forces together, including a cohort of scythed chariots, and set them off down the hill to cross the valley floor and rush up the far slope towards the Romans. Caesar thought this was simply a display, since no sane commander would send his troops and horses uphill to fight a battle, but the enemy rolled on until the chariots reached the surprised Roman line. Caesar hastily assembled his legions and showers of javelins blunted the impact of the first wave of chariots. Despite the confusion and the unequal numbers, the disciplined Roman army drove the enemy back, killing and capturing a great many, until they reached and occupied the camp at Zela. Pharnaces fled back to the Crimea where he was later killed in a fight with one of his governors. Caesar, it must be assumed, had the tactical skill and inspiration lacking in the two Roman commanders already defeated in Pontus, though too little is known of the battle to be certain of how the odds were overcome, save the tactical ineptitude of the tiring charge uphill against veteran Roman legionaries.

Caesar wrote to a correspondent in Rome after the battle that he had come and seen and conquered, a phrase borrowed, so it is thought, from the Greek philosopher Democritus. The campaign against

Pharnaces completed the pacification of Asia Minor. Caesar sailed back to Italy, where he landed in September 47 BCE. Three years later he planned another major expedition to the east to punish the Parthians for the defeat of Crassus at Carrhae, hoping to take 16 legions and 10,000 archers and cavalry with him. Shortly before he was due to depart, on 15 March 44 BCE, he was stabbed to death in the Senate by a group of men alarmed by his appointment as 'Perpetual Dictator'. Though Caesar fought back, these were odds even he could not overcome.

19. BATTLE OF EDINGTON
May 878

Anyone travelling along the railway line that links Exeter to London will notice shortly after Westbury a large white horse laid out in the chalk of a shallow hillside. It is said to commemorate the site of the Battle of Edington fought between the West Saxon King Alfred and the forces of the Danish leader Guthrum, though the truth of the story is elusive. The Saxon victory has always been seen as a defining moment in English history, when the future of an Anglo-Saxon kingdom was finally saved from the apparently irresistible encroachment of the Vikings. Little is known in detail about the battle itself (or if it even took place at Edington) but it came to symbolize the end of this stage of Viking conquest, a time when all the dice had seemed loaded in their favour.

The Viking Danes arrived with the so-called 'Great Army' of pagan warriors in 865, not to raid, as they had done repeatedly, but to seize a kingdom. A decade later the Danes had conquered Northumbria, East Anglia and the central English kingdom of Mercia. They had been blocked only by the English kingdom of Wessex in southern and southwestern England. The King of the West Saxons from 871 was Alfred, who came to the throne shortly after defeating the Danes in a major battle at Ashdown in January of that year. But Danish infiltration was difficult to resist. Alfred was forced to raise money to pay off the Danish leaders, an extortion characteristic of Viking warfare and a way of achieving wealth without having to conquer it. In 874, the Great Army divided, some to go north, some to maintain their rule in Mercia, and one part, under Guthrum, to move south. In 875, this Danish army set out from Cambridge to Wareham in Dorset, supported by a Danish fleet sailing along the coast. The fleet was lost in a storm and with it a potentially large Danish army. Guthrum occupied Exeter, where Alfred surrounded him and forced him to agree to leave the West Saxon kingdom. Hostages were exchanged as a sign of good faith, but almost all the chronicles from the time indicate that the good faith of pagans was not to be trusted.

The best accounts of what followed – the *Anglo-Saxon Chronicle*, begun later in Alfred's reign, and a short account of Alfred's life written in 893 by the monk Asser – have clearly been embroidered in order to demonstrate that what followed was Alfred's noble triumph over adversity. It is evident that Guthrum moved away to the Mercian city of Gloucester, but unlikely that he felt bound by any oaths he had made. In the early weeks of 878, the Danes co-ordinated a strike against Wessex, which was designed to bring the kingdom finally into the Danish sphere. The first coup was against Alfred, who was spending Christmas at his estates in Chippenham. Guthrum led a surprise attack and Alfred was fortunate enough to flee without being caught. It was following this flight to the Isle of Athelney in the marshy Somerset Levels that Alfred is supposed to have taken refuge in a shepherd's hut, where he famously allowed the cakes to burn which he had been told to watch. The story was added later to Alfred's biography, perhaps to embellish his flight and isolation with an added sense of pathos. Reading behind the near contemporary accounts, it is evident that Alfred's position was less dangerous than the texts suggest.

Further west, the Viking leader Ubba Ragnarsson led a fleet across the channel from Wales to north Devon to try to encircle the Saxons.

His force was defeated by Ealdorman Odda of Devon and Ubba killed. At Athelney, Alfred could rely on his liegeman, Ealdorman Æthelnoth of Somerset, and the levies of Somerset soldiers. In the spring of 878, Alfred sent a summons to the men of Hampshire and Wiltshire and Dorset to assemble at a large rock known as Ecgberht's Stone in order to do battle with the threatening Danes. The sources are short in detail on what followed. Alfred's army moved to an old hill fort near the royal estate at Edington and at some point, estimated between 6 and 12 May 878, engaged what seems likely to have been just a portion of Guthrum's army, sent south from Chippenham. No source records the presence of the Danish king, nor is there any solid evidence of the numbers involved or the tactics employed. The Saxon warriors were armed with a variety of spears and swords, including the *aesc*, a long pike made of tough ash with a heavy metal blade; the Danes were armed with Viking swords, axes and spears. Whether most of the Danish army was present or only a large warband, it was smashed by the Saxons and driven back to Chippenham, suffering heavy casualties as the Saxons pursued them on horseback and cut them down.

Guthrum and an unknown fraction of his army took refuge in Chippenham. Alfred invested the town and after two weeks, running short of food and water, the Danes asked for a truce. What followed indicated that, however limited the battle itself might have been, the political aftermath was of real historical significance. The Vikings, who had seemed poised to complete their conquest of Anglo-Saxon England, had been halted, and one of the conditions insisted on by Alfred was that Guthrum accompany him to Somerset, there to be baptized into the Christian church. At Aller, a sumptuous ceremony was performed where the Danish leaders were formally admitted to the church, while a treaty later negotiated at the nearby town of Wedmore confirmed that Guthrum would settle as king in Mercia, respecting Alfred's kingdom of Wessex. By 927, the whole of England was united under an Anglo-Saxon king, Alfred's grandson Æthelstan. Ferocious, cruel and deceitful warriors, according to all the ancient accounts, the Vikings had met their match at Edington.

20. BATTLE OF CLONTARF
23 April 1014

Like many battles from the early Middle Ages, the exact events that took place on a low plain just north of Dublin on Good Friday, 1014, are shrouded in later legend and obfuscation. What is certain is that the man who claimed the kingship of all Ireland, Brian Bóruma mac Cennétig, better known in the Anglicized form Brian Boru, defeated the combined armies of Laigin (Leinster) and the Dublin Vikings. By the battle's end, Brian lay dead, but all the later annals of the Irish saw the victory as a hard-won triumph against the looming threat of conquest by what were called the 'Foreigners of the West'.

There is much to disentangle in the history of the Battle of Clúain Tarbh, or Clontarf, a place not even mentioned in some of the near contemporary annals. Ireland in the early eleventh century was a kaleidoscope of tribal, clan and regional loyalties, broken up into small kingdoms, with settled Viking communities around the coast and the main Viking centre at Dublin. Brian, overking of Dál Cais, king of Munster, who rose to power across the last third of the tenth century, had succeeded by 1011 in imposing some kind of suzerainty on the rulers of much of the island, beginning with his home province of Munster. This was a unique achievement, but the restless, bellicose nature of Irish clan politics doomed Brian to fight in defence of his claim. In 1013, the Leinstermen and the Vikings of Dublin rejected Brian's authority and embarked on a violent rebellion, pillaging and laying waste territory ruled by Brian's vassals. Brian was obliged to take up the challenge posed by the Viking king of Dublin, Sigtrygg. He gathered forces from Munster and neighbouring Mide, ruled by Máel Sechnaill, and from among the men of Connacht. They all set out for Dublin, appropriately, on St Patrick's Day.

Like the conflict between Alfred and the Danes, the subsequent battle was once seen as a decisive turning point in the struggle between the pagan Scandinavians and the Christian Irish, but the truth is certainly more complicated, since the Leinstermen were also Christians, and there were many Viking converts. The real explanation for the legend surrounding Brian's victory at Clontarf lies in the long list of Viking friends and allies summoned by Sigtrygg once he heard of Brian's advance. The year was a critical one in Viking history, for Sveinn Tjúguskegg ('Forkbeard'), king of Denmark, completed the conquest of England and had himself declared king late in 1013, only to die five weeks later and allow the English under Æthelred 'the Unready' to reclaim the throne. Sigtrygg summoned Norsemen from as far north as the Orkney Islands and as far south as Brittany in the hope that Ireland too could be conquered as a Viking kingdom. This explains the long list of 'foreign' Vikings in the Irish annals, and the fact, generally agreed in most accounts, that at the early morning high tide on 23 April 1014, a fleet of Viking ships disgorged their eager warriors onto the Irish coast between the River Tolka and the Howth Peninsula at Clontarf, a few miles north of Dublin.

It was here that a large contingent from overseas, together with men from Leinster and the Dublin Vikings, though not their king, gathered to do battle with Brian's forces, who had been raiding the surrounding area to squeeze money and food out of the local Christian communities. The only extensive account of the battle comes from the *Cocad Gáedel re Gallaib* (*The War of the Irish with the Foreigners*), but it is light on detail. Both sides fought in much the same way, with shield walls to protect the fighting men, and dependence on sheer brute force and savagery. Hardly impartial, the *Cocad* describes the Viking forces as possessing arrows that were 'terrible, piercing, fatal, murderous, poisoned', steeped in the blood of 'dragons and toads', while Brian's Irish wielded swords that were 'glittering, flashing, brilliant, handsome, straight'. There was, in truth, little difference in the weaponry available to both sides; the difference may well have come in the numbers fielded, but the size of the two armies is simply guesswork.

The rebels were probably drawn up as the annals describe, with the Vikings who had come from overseas in the front, including warriors and commanders from York, the Orkney Islands, the western Scottish coast and the Isle of Man, backed up by the Irish Vikings and finally with the men of Leinster in the rear. The medieval account has Brian's son, Murchad, leading the men of Munster into the fray, to die in the attempt, supported by some mercenary Norsemen, while the men of Mide under Máel Sechnaill and a reserve from Munster held the rear. But the battle was almost certainly a confused, blood-soaked mêlée as each side endeavoured to encircle and slaughter the other. The clash of mail and armour, the roars and cries of the fighting men and the dying, and the growing mound of gore on the battlefield can be imagined without much difficulty.

After a dozen hours of exhausting combat, Brian's army won the day. The Viking invaders found that their ships had been dispersed as the tide went out. By the time the battle ended, the tide was high again (a fact confirmed by more modern calculations), cutting off any retreat along the coast. They were pushed back into the sea where, it is to be presumed, many drowned. How many died will never be known, but at the end of a fight in which both sides suffered heavy losses, it is unlikely that quarter was ever considered.

When the fog of battle cleared it was found that Brian's son Murchad and his teenage grandson Tairdelbach had both been killed, Murchard with his legendary twin swords, hewing Vikings left and right, until one of them disembowelled him with a knife. The principal victim of the battle was Brian Bóruma himself. A man of seventy-three by the time of Clontarf (some annals have him in his eighties), he sat in a tent praying while the battle went on. A band of Danes, wandering from the fight, came across his tent and, according to the *Cocad*, Brian was killed with an axe through his head, though not before he had cut off his attacker's left leg and right foot. Brian's death did not alter the outcome. Sigtrygg remained in Dublin, but his brief ambition to use the arrival of a large fleet of Viking invaders to secure dominance of Ireland, a menace to Irish independence much greater than the threat of a local rebellion, was eliminated in the aftermath of Clontarf and its legendary defence of a fractious Irish liberty.

21. BATTLE OF LEGNANO
29 May 1176

Traditional Italian accounts of the battle between a group of northern Italian communes and the famous German emperor-soldier Frederick Barbarossa amidst the woods and vineyards near the town of Legnano in northern Lombardy always held that the Italians were greatly outnumbered by their German enemy and achieved victory only because they were spurred on by a profound Italian patriotism. Recent research now shows the reverse case: an estimated 3,000 German heavy cavalry against 10–12,000 infantry and an unknown number of horsemen. In truth, even with these odds, the two sides were unevenly matched. In late medieval warfare, it was assumed that any disciplined body of professional knights-at-arms would sweep aside a mass of citizen infantry; led by the fearsome Barbarossa, a commander of prodigious reputation, the odds would have seemed more loaded still. The victory did, indeed, defy those odds to demonstrate that motivated foot soldiers could defeat even the most heavily armed and experienced cavalry.

Italy was nominally part of the Holy Roman Empire, ruled in the late twelfth century by the German emperor Frederick I, known as 'Barbarossa' or 'Kaiser Rotbart' after his large red beard. The northern Italian city-communes sought their independence from imperial domination following the sacking of Milan by the emperor in 1161. The cities of Piedmont, Lombardy and Venetia formed the Lombard League in 1167 to give each other mutual support in the contest with Frederick. It was to disrupt and defeat this league that Barbarossa summoned an army of knights from Germany in the spring of 1176. Organized by the Archbishops of Cologne and Magdeburg, around 1,500 heavy cavalry rode with their baggage and servants south over the Alps, where they joined Frederick and his 2,000 knights at Como.

The League had been preparing to defend the town of Alessandria, further to the south, but seeing the threat from Frederick, the Italians moved north past Milan to try to force the Germans back by blocking

Barbarossa's only path south between the Olona and Ticino rivers. Reinforcements arrived from Brescia and the towns of Venetia and a camp was set up just in time at Legnano, since the German cavalry, unencumbered by infantry, could move rapidly and had already reached the town of Cairate, only 14 kilometres (9 miles) distant.

The German army consisted almost entirely of heavy cavalry – knights with lance, shield and a considerable weight of armour. Their battlefield tactic was simple: they would charge in close order to form an irresistible weight of metal and animal designed to smash through the enemy line, exposing the broken infantry to encirclement and annihilation – a medieval version of *Blitzkrieg*. Frederick was unlikely to be deterred by the sheer size of the infantry units opposed to him because 3,000 knights represented a formidable force of nature. On 29 May, he set out from Cairate towards the League army with a vanguard of 300 of his horsemen riding ahead to spot any dangers.

The League prepared its defences near the village of Borsano, a little to the north of Legnano itself. A site was chosen that gave the defenders considerable advantages: there were natural obstacles to the enemy on either side to prevent encirclement, and a mix of trees and canals in front which made it difficult for Frederick's cavalry to manoeuvre. The army was drawn up in a number of ranks – four is usually suggested – each armed with long spears, the front rank probably kneeling to maximize the damage inflicted on the oncoming horses. There are few precise descriptions of the battle, but it seems likely that the infantry were spread in the shape of a broad and shallow arc around the most important piece of equipment they had brought with them. On a heavy cart (*carroccio*) was the image of the patron saint of Milan, St Ambrose, surrounded by the communal banners. It was placed so that all the League soldiers could see it, a sacred inspiration and an indication, so it was hoped, of divine protection.

As Frederick approached, some 700 League cavalry from Brescia and Milan were sent north to scout for his whereabouts. Because of the wooded countryside, the two vanguards ran into each other unexpectedly. Frederick's 300 horsemen sensibly retreated in the face of their much larger enemy, but the League cavalry pursued them until suddenly they found themselves in front of the main force of 3,000 Germans. After a brief engagement, the League horsemen fled from the scene, riding towards Milan. Frederick and his host rode on until they reached the main lines of League soldiers and there prepared to charge. No doubt the sight of Frederick's mounted army, its armour and lances glinting in the hot sun, banners flying, must have been daunting indeed for the League foot soldiers. Some of the remaining League cavalry had dismounted and prepared to strengthen the infantry line, where they would fight with sword and axe. A test of two very different styles of fighting was to begin.

The German cavalry charged, and almost at once disaster struck. The knight carrying Barbarossa's standard fell from his horse and was trampled to death by the onrushing horses behind him, leaving the banner lying on the ground. The wave faltered and was turned back by the wall of spears bristling in front of it. For hours the German cavalry tried to find a weak point in the line, but the League ranks held sufficiently firm to prevent the breakthrough that Frederick's strategy required. The Italian soldiers were perhaps buoyed up by the sight of St Ambrose in their midst; they were certainly helped by the fact that they fought with companions from the same city, often from the same parish, which created a greater sense of solidarity and civic pride.

Gradually as the afternoon wore on, the League could sense a historic victory. Frederick's men were tiring after six hours of fighting in hot sun and heavy armour when suddenly they were hit by a flank attack carried out by the same cavalry group from Brescia and Milan that had fled from the first encounter. Regrouped and now with fresh courage, this mounted attack divided the German line. Suddenly Frederick himself, the only rallying point after the loss of the standard, had his horse killed under him and fell to the ground. Threatened now from all sides, and apparently leaderless, the cavalry broke and fled, some back to where they had come from, others across the River Ticino, where many were drowned. Those who remained died where they were or surrendered. The losses for both sides seem not to have been computed.

Barbarossa survived and fled back to Como and thence to Germany. He never again threatened the northern cities of Italy and seven years later, in the Treaty of Constance, the communes won a large measure of political independence. The battle signalled an important shift in the way medieval warfare was to develop. On their own, a body of knights, however experienced or skilled they were, could not expect their sheer power and mobility to be enough against a courageous or shrewd opponent, or one, as at Legnano, inspired by faith in their commune and their saint.

22. BATTLE OF THE RIVER SALADO
30 October 1340

Many of the battles fought between Islam and Christianity have been hailed as the decisive encounter between the two religions. Few of them can have been more decisive than the crushing defeat of the wealthy emir of Marinid Morocco, Abu al-Hasan, inflicted by King Alfonso XI of Castile and King Afonso IV of Portugal on a clear October day in 1340 in the far southwest of Spain. The Battle of Salado was blessed by the Papacy as part of a new crusade against the infidel; a relic of the True Cross was held aloft in the battle by a priest dressed in white, seated on a white mule. Abu al-Hasan put round his neck on the morning of the battle a reliquary holding a fragment of the Prophet's clothing. He was determined to smash Christian power in Spain with a major holy war, or *jihad*, after decades in which the Muslim hold on southern Spain had been slowly eroded.

Later chronicles speak of an army of 70,000 cavalry and 400,000 to 700,000 foot soldiers massed at the Moroccan port of Ceuta to cross the straits to Algeciras, a port still in Muslim hands. The best estimate today suggests perhaps a total of 60,000. The Christian kings between them could muster 22,000 horse and foot. Contemporary opinion held that in open battle the Moroccans were difficult to defeat, but open battle is exactly what Alfonso XI sought.

The battle at the River Salado was won against many odds, by not just the numbers on the battlefield. For years Alfonso had had to battle his own nobles, who accepted vassalage or rule from Castile with ill grace. He was forced to balance the threat from Morocco with the challenge from the vassal state of Granada, still under an Islamic ruler, Yusuf I; he had to win support from other rulers, notably from Aragon and Portugal, and this was a laborious and frustrating task. When the threat from the Marinid Empire of Morocco became evident in the late 1330s, Alfonso found himself almost entirely isolated. Only fear of a Muslim invasion persuaded Afonso IV of Portugal to reach an alliance with Alfonso, signed on 1 July 1340.

By this time the invasion was already under way. In 1339, one of Abu al-Hasan's sons, Abu Malik, began raiding Andalusia from his bases in Gibraltar and Algeciras. In a major skirmish in late October with Spanish knights, Abu Malik was killed. Abu al-Hasan was already preparing an expedition, but his son's death sharpened his desire for a savage revenge against the infidel. A letter claimed to have been found after the battle, allegedly from the Sultan of Babylon (probably an Egyptian title), called on the emir to 'smash their children against the wall; slit open the wombs of pregnant women; cut off the breasts, arms, noses, and feet of other women...Do not leave until you have destroyed Christendom from sea to sea.' Though probably a piece of Christian propaganda, it is at least consistent with the fiery threats made by Abu al-Hasan as he prepared his campaign.

Troops began to cross the straits in July and on 4 August 1340, Abu al-Hasan himself arrived at Algeciras. By this time Pope Benedict XII had declared a crusade and sent Alfonso the necessary banner and additional funds. Alfonso's real difficulty was money, a problem that meant little to the wealthy Marinids. He could bring with him supplies for only a few days of fighting, and in order to pay for what he needed he had to pawn the royal jewels. On 23 September, Abu al-Hasan, now joined by Yusuf I of Granada with 7,000 cavalry, began the siege of Tarifa, the only port overlooking the Straits of Gibraltar still in Christian hands. He hoped Alfonso would rise to the challenge. A few weeks later, on 29 October, the Christian army arrived at La Peña del Ciervo (The Hill of the Deer) about 8 kilometres (5 miles) from Tarifa, intent on battle. There were 1,000 knights with the Portuguese king, while Alfonso XI counted on 8,000 knights and 12,000 foot soldiers, mostly recruited from Asturias and the Basque provinces. The number of their Moroccan enemy was much lower than the hundreds of thousands suggested by Christian accounts, but was certainly greater than the crusaders. Alfonso reduced the size of his army even more by sending 1,000 knights and 4,000 foot soldiers round the Muslim lines to reinforce the 1,000 men in Tarifa. This was to prove an inspired move.

Abu al-Hasan drew back from the siege and arrayed his forces along the hills surrounding the port. On the morning of 30 October both sides received blessing from their clergy before moving out to face each other. On the Christian left was Afonso of Portugal, reinforced by 3,000 of Alfonso's men; on the Portuguese flank were the foot soldiers with lances and crossbows; on the right the bulk of Alfonso's remaining knights. The Islamic armies were drawn up with Yusuf's Granadans on the right, the emir's son Abu 'Umar on the left, in front of Tarifa, and the centre commanded by Abu al-Hasan himself. Exactly what happened in the battle is not entirely clear. The Christian right began to cross a small bridge over the River Salado where they forced back the Muslim defenders. Then the bulk of Alfonso's force smashed into the army of Abu 'Umar, driving it uphill towards the Muslim camp. At some point the 6,000 men in Tarifa stormed out and hit the enemy in the rear, causing a panic which left the emir's baggage train unprotected.

While the Castilians swarmed up to the camp in pursuit of booty, Alfonso found himself temporarily supported by only a small body of troops. Abu al-Hasan tried to wheel his army around to attack the king, but soon found himself surrounded as the Castilians charged back down the hill and the force from Tarifa hit his flank. Instead of fighting for the faith, he fled with his troops, putting his honour, as one account put it, 'under his feet'. When he arrived at Ceuta, he told his followers that he had won a great victory, but the sorry remnant of his army that returned could scarcely be concealed.

The victorious Christians pursued the enemy for 8 kilometres (5 miles), slaughtering those they overtook, leaving a field littered with bodies, though how many is uncertain. Muslim women and children, including Abu al-Hasan's wife, Fatima, were murdered when the camp was overrun and all its occupants killed. Only twelve ships were needed to take the survivors back to Morocco, which suggests either a large-scale massacre or that the Moroccan forces were much smaller than most medieval accounts claimed. Either way the defeat was decisive. Africa never again mounted a major invasion of Spain and Castile extended its domination over the peninsula. Algeciras fell to Alfonso four years later, leaving only Gibraltar as a Muslim outpost. Yusuf was lucky to escape, and Granada survived for a further 150 years. The colossal booty in gold and treasure captured at Salado helped to solve, at least temporarily, Alfonso's financial embarrassments. So great was the wealth that it temporarily forced down the value of gold and silver on the Paris exchange.

23. BATTLE OF AGINCOURT
25 October 1415

Immortalized by Shakespeare in *The Life of Henry the Fifth*, the Battle of Agincourt has retained its reputation as one of the greatest feats of arms of any English army. Yet it could so easily have ended in disaster. The armies mustered by the French king, Charles VI, despite the often tense relations between the powerful nobles who commanded them, numbered an estimated 60,000 soldiers and camp followers with a core of 12–15,000 men-at-arms – trained soldiers, armoured and heavily armed, who would do most of the fighting. The English king, Henry V, crowned in 1413 at the age of twenty-five, had a mixed force of perhaps fewer than 6,000 English, Welsh and Gascon soldiers, one-fifth of them armed and mounted men-at-arms, four-fifths of them longbowmen, with little armour. They had marched hundreds of miles on little food. On paper, the gap between the two sides was vast. 'That's a valiant flea,' Shakespeare has one of the French commanders utter, 'that dare eat his breakfast on the lip of a lion.'

Henry and his army arrived on the Normandy coast, near present-day Le Havre, in the middle of August 1415 in a vast armada of small boats. He was the leader of a bold but risky invasion for which he was completely responsible. He was related to the French royal family and wanted to mark his assumption of the English throne by claiming France as his kingdom too, and the French people as his subjects. Having experienced English depredations on many occasions in what eventually became known as the Hundred Years War, the French king wanted to negotiate, even to make concessions. But Henry was eager to exercise his claim, which meant invasion. The story goes that the French court sent him a box of tennis balls with the implication that he should confine himself to harmless games; whether true or not, Henry now became determined on war at all costs, little understanding just how limited were his military means compared with the vast resources and experience of the French.

Everything went wrong for the English army. It began by investing the small city of Harfleur on the Norman coast, which refused to submit and had to be subjected to a destructive siege. The besieging army was short of food and soon ravaged by dysentery. Some 2,000 of an already small force died or had to be shipped home. The town garrison suffered even more and on 22 September Harfleur was surrendered. Henry had initially imagined a triumphant march on Paris, but with his army now down to barely half its initial strength and many of the troops ill, his commanders would consent to nothing more than a forced march to the English enclave at Calais, whence they could return home. With the guns and siege equipment left behind at Harfleur, the king set out to cross the River Somme and on to Calais.

By this time, the French had amassed a huge army and when the English approached their chosen ford across the river, they found it guarded by 6,000 men under Marshal Boucicaut. With men forced to march up to 30 kilometres (20 miles) a day and rapidly running out of food, the king gambled on finding a crossing further south. As luck would have it, two small crossings were still unguarded, though their causeways were destroyed. On 19 October, the army reached the east bank of the Somme and began a forced march towards Calais. The French army, commanded by the Dukes of Bourbon and Orléans, shadowed them and on 20 October sent a challenge to engage in battle. Since the French could easily block the route to Calais, Henry accepted.

No attack came, and the English continued north. But at the small town of Blangy, still far short of their destination, scouts spotted vast columns of French troops, like 'an innumerable host of locusts' crossing to block their path. In almost continuous rain, which churned the ground into treacherous mud, the two armies approached each other. On the eve of St Crispin's Day, the English stopped at the village of Maisoncelle, while the French halted some distance to the north, flanked on each side by a thick wood. The French army had numerous knights, but only a small number of archers armed with crossbows. Mounted knights were on the flanks, supported by the French guns. Behind was a motley rabble of footmen and servants. In the centre were two dense rows of dismounted men-at-arms. The French commanders were no doubt overconfident that their large host would soon dispatch Henry's force, which was outnumbered by more than two to one, so that little thought was given to the nature of the battlefield. Henry, on the other hand, had to gamble everything on the way he set out his forces. He divided the dismounted men-at-arms into three groups, four deep, divided by parties of longbowmen, and with more archers on each side in a curved flanking position, so that arrows could be rained down both from the front and the side. The longbow could be shot with deadly effect from 300 metres (1,000 feet). To protect the archers, Henry ordered them to fix pointed wooden stakes, which he had made them cut and carry days beforehand. They were now to be set at an angle to impale oncoming horsemen. Though tired and hungry, his troops rallied to Henry's confident faith that God would favour them.

The French strategy proved to be disastrous. Drawn up in tight ranks with a narrowing slope in front of them, bordered by two woods, they had little room for manoeuvre, while the knights jostled and argued to find a place in the front rank on the mud-soaked field. They stood where they were for three hours waiting for the English to attack. At 11 a.m., Henry decided his tired and hungry men could wait no longer. He marched them forward to within 300 metres (1,000 feet) of the enemy, the stakes were fixed and then the order went out to the archers, 'Nestroque!' ('Now strike!'). The famous scene of the dark cloud of arrows, spectacularly replicated in the 1944 film *Henry V*, was almost certainly the truth. Stung by the deadly rain, the French moved forward. Their ill-conceived deployment soon became apparent. The gun crews became ensnared with the horsemen, who plunged through the heavy mud, only to become impaled on the stakes and tormented with the arrows. The men-at-arms on foot found themselves struggling through piles of armoured figures on the ground and dead or dying horses. Knights who turned back became hopelessly entangled with those coming forward; hampered by heavy armour and clinging mud, the front line was pushed over by those behind. Hundreds suffocated in the scrum. Like the Persian ships at Salamis, an abundance of numbers was no advantage in a constricted space. The archers alternated between their deadly salvos and murderous forays against knights who could not easily move or escape and who were axed or stabbed to death where they stood or lay. As the French dead piled up, two or three high, those behind were forced to fight at a growing disadvantage against the smaller numbers of English men-at-arms who still had the space to move. Seeing the massacre, the third line of mounted French hesitated to move forward. English soldiers and archers pulled the wounded or immobilized enemy into their own ranks, disarmed them and kept those whose value was evident in order to ransom them after the battle.

It was at this point that Henry ordered his men to kill the prisoners in cold blood. He was uncertain about what the rest of the French army would do, and worried lest the numerous prisoners seize arms and attack from the rear. His men obeyed reluctantly, since they were destroying a source of future wealth for them all. The prisoners were stabbed or battered to death, or had their throats slit.

The third line never attacked. The disaster was clear for all to see and the French king's herald arrived to concede the battle. Henry wanted a name for it; the herald told him the nearby castle was called Agincourt, and the battle has carried the title ever since. The three hours of combat were gory and uncompromising. Though weak and hungry, Henry's troops were tough and brutal, neither giving nor expecting quarter. The remaining wounded were killed off or brought in to the English camp for ransom. The bodies were stripped of anything the troops could carry, leaving a muddy field littered with blood-soaked, naked corpses, including much of the flower of the French aristocracy. Figures of the French dead vary, though around 7,000 is generally accepted. Some 5,800 were finally placed in three large pits and covered over. The rest were collected for burial by their families or servants. For the French, the battle was a catastrophic defeat against an enemy that they had underrated and for whose defeat they had made inadequate preparations. Nevertheless, the English army executed a model operation given their small numbers. English casualties have been estimated at little more than 500 dead and wounded. Henry returned to a triumphant welcome in London and a legendary place in British history books.

24. SIEGE OF BELGRADE
4–22 July 1456

The sound of a bell ringing out from Catholic churches at noon every day is a familiar reminder of the Church's presence. Modern Europeans have largely forgotten why it happens. The bell is tolled on the order of the first Spanish pope, Callixtus III, to mark the victory of the Hungarian king, John Hunyadi, over the Ottoman sultan Mehmet II at the siege of Belgrade in the summer of 1456. Following the fall of Constantinople to the Ottomans three years before, the onward march of Islam against the Christian West seemed unstoppable. When the Ottoman army of 30,000 or more arrived to besiege Belgrade, a key city on the road to Christian central Europe, it seemed unlikely that Hunyadi's 4,000 regular soldiers could stop him. But against all the odds, an improvised force of Hungarians, Belgrade militia and crusading peasants rallied outside the city and inflicted a heavy defeat on a sultan still basking in the glory of his success at Constantinople. The bell still rings today to celebrate the salvation of Christendom from the onrush of Islam.

The capture of Constantinople in May 1453 was a shock to Christian Europe, though little had been done to aid the city. Mehmet II began to ponder the possibility of adding Rome to his conquests. The pope warned his Christian flock that Mehmet would not rest until he had 'imposed the law of the false prophet upon the whole world'. One of the Ottoman sultan's many expansive titles was indeed 'world conqueror'. The long road to Rome for the sultan led through the Balkans. In 1454, the Serbian kingdom of George Branković was raided, and the following year a full-scale invasion captured southern Serbia and Kosovo. Although George signed a treaty with Mehmet to respect what remained of his kingdom, the sultan returned in 1456 with an army estimated at between 30,000 and 60,000, together with 300 cannon (many which had been used to destroy the walls of Constantinople) and 200 galleys plying along the rivers Sava and Danube. The object of the campaign was the strategic city of Belgrade (Nándorfehérvár in Hungarian) whose capture would open the way to Hungary and the Christian West. He positioned his army and camp on the headland by the city, and at the end of June 1456, began bombarding the walls.

There were two men intent on halting the Islamic tide. The first was János Hunyadi, a nobleman soldier from Transylvania, who had fought against the Ottomans for twenty years and in 1453 became Captain General of Hungary. Disliked by other Hungarian noblemen for his success, he was left alone to organize a response to the vast Ottoman forces approaching Belgrade. He sent his son László and his brother-in-law Mihály Szilágyi to reinforce the Belgrade garrison, bringing the number up to somewhere between 5,000 and 7,000 men. Meanwhile, Hunyadi recruited soldiers and militia from across central Europe, though the exact number is not known.

The second man was an elderly Franciscan friar, Giovanni da Capistrano, a fiery preacher and member of the Italian Inquisition, who was sent by the Papacy to raise a crusade. He managed to create a people's crusade among the peasantry. Many of his followers carried little more than farm implements – a scythe or a pitchfork. They moved towards Belgrade under Capistrano's command. Estimates suggest that Hunyadi and Capistrano between them mustered 40,000 irregular and modestly armed fighters, though the real state and size of the army is open to conjecture.

The siege began on 4 July. Like the siege of Constantinople, the Ottomans hoped to make breaches in the walls large enough to allow the attacking troops to push through into the city. Belgrade was modelled on Byzantine and Arab castles and was among the best fortified positions in Europe. The stout walls guarded three lines of defence, with the inner castle the toughest part of the structure. Hunyadi understood Mehmet's methods well; he had visited the Ottoman camp in 1453 during the earlier siege, where it was said that a Hungarian had given the sultan advice on how to make the bombardment more effective. The walls of Belgrade withstood a great deal, but by the time Hunyadi arrived downriver with a fleet of 200 assorted vessels, the first breaches were opening up. His ships scattered the Ottoman river blockade, capturing and sinking more than twenty galleys, and he was able to bring supplies, food and thousands more men into the city. A week later, Mehmet judged that the time had come to take the city by assault.

On the night of 21 July, thousands of the elite janissaries forced their way through breaches in one of the walls and into the port area and the upper town. While veteran troops with Szilágyi held off furious attacks on the remaining outer walls, Hunyadi ordered his men to throw pieces of wood and other material covered with tar into the streets and there to set fire to them. Soon a sheet of flame separated the janissaries from the rest of the troops behind. The trapped men were slaughtered and the rest of the Ottoman attackers withdrew.

What followed next is not entirely clear, but a number of Capistrano's crusading peasants sallied out and attacked the Ottoman camp. The friar, though now seventy years of age, led 2,000 of them across the River Sava and into the rear of the Ottoman lines. Seeing the raid grow in size, Hunyadi had little alternative but to order a general attack. His men charged the Ottoman line of cannon and then fell on the main body. So surprised were the Ottomans at the audacity of the assault that they broke. The remaining janissaries defending Mehmet were beaten back and the sultan was hit by an arrow in the thigh. Hunyadi managed to get the scattered garrison back together and ordered them to stay in the fortress and expect a return of the Ottoman army. But Mehmet had had enough. His army returned to Constantinople through Serbia, ravaging the countryside as it went.

The victory at Belgrade was unexpected, for the advantage had lain with Mehmet, but the victory proved to be a hollow one. Bubonic plague broke out in the Christian camp and Hunyadi died on 11 August, Capistrano on 23 October (later to be canonized). The Ottomans returned three years later and although Belgrade was held by the Hungarians until 1521, the rest of Serbia fell to a fresh campaign in summer 1459, to remain a vassal of the Ottoman sultans until the nineteenth century. The victory did, nonetheless, slow the Ottoman advance through Europe, which had seemed irresistible on account of the size, wealth and cruel fighting traditions of the sultanate. Not for nothing did Callixtus order the bells to be rung.

25. BATTLE OF PLASSEY
22–23 June 1757

Perhaps the most significant battle to take place on Indian soil in the modern age was the encounter near the Bengali village of Plassey (more properly Palasi) between the huge army of the Nawab of Bengal, Siraj-ud-daula, and a small force of European and Indian troops commanded by Colonel Robert Clive of the British East India Company. On paper it looked as though Clive's forces would be annihilated. Clever deployment and guileful diplomacy between them secured a victory by a force of 784 European soldiers and 2,100 Indian soldiers, or 'sepoys', against a Bengali army estimated at approximately 50,000.

The background to the final encounter at Palasi (the 'place of the Palas trees') was complex in the extreme. The Indian Mughal Empire was in the throes of dissolution, and European powers vied for the rich trade that access to Indian markets allowed. They established local trading companies and bribed and flattered local rulers to allow them to carry on a commerce that made many French, Dutch and British families rich. In Bengal, the three European states competed with each other to win the support of the nawab (king), who in turn played one off against another to extort what he could from the deals he made. In 1756, Nawab Alivardi Khan died and was succeeded by his rapacious and temperamental great-nephew, Siraj-ud-daula, who, barely twenty, had already established an unenviable reputation for debauchery and vice and was little liked by much of Bengal's elite.

The new nawab resented the British presence and feared their long-term ambitions. In May 1756, he launched war against the East India Company, sacking its settlement at Kasimbazar and then marching on Calcutta, where the British traders were based. The city was captured by a large army and looted, while the European prisoners were forced into a small airless prison, known in British army slang as the 'Black Hole', where 123 out of 146 of them suffocated to death during the night. The atrocity became one of the reasons why the Company brought together an expeditionary force at Madras to sail north, recapture Calcutta and re-establish British trade. The expedition was led by Colonel Robert Clive, supported by a small fleet of ships under command of Vice Admiral Charles Watson. By December 1756, they had arrived in Bengal and within weeks had retaken Calcutta using only 500 British troops and the threat of naval bombardment. In February 1757, Clive, supported by Watson, inflicted a heavy reverse on the nawab's large army, which forced the Indian ruler to seek a temporary armistice. Meanwhile, war had broken out in Europe between Britain and France, and Clive used this pretext to attack and capture the main French trading base at Chandernagore.

The arrival of a British force reignited the nawab's growing hatred for the East India Company, while the French were happy to support him following their defeat. Clive was adept at manipulating the factions at the Bengali court in Murshidabad and promised alliances with wealthy merchants and soldiers if they came over to his side, but it was a risky business in a world where betrayal of trust and pursuit of self-interest assumed Machiavellian proportions. The nawab finally decided to make one last attempt to oust the British before his own political position became too tenuous. In June 1757, Clive led his 784 British troops and 2,100 sepoys, supported by 12 guns and a large stock of supplies, towards the nawab's army of around 35,000 infantry, 15,000 cavalry and 53 guns (under the command of French artillerymen) which had gathered near the village of Muncarra.

Clive was anxious about the risk of confronting such a large force, but the disparity was reduced not only by the greater discipline and training of the British troops, but by the fact that two-thirds of the nawab's army, under command of two conspirators, Mir Jafar and Rai Durlabh, were unlikely to take part in the fight. Clive could not be sure of this, but on 22 June, he finally risked a showdown and moved his small force to occupy a large orchard of mango trees and the small buildings of the village of Palasi, 5 kilometres (3 miles) from the nawab's camp. That evening both sides moved into position. Clive placed his artillery so that it could engage the French guns in front of him. His forces were dispersed in such a way that they could take the offensive when the moment came. The nawab's colourful army, accompanied by scarlet-coated elephants and camels, and thousands of horsemen with glittering sabres, prepared for battle – 'a pompous and formidable appearance' according to one of Clive's collaborators.

The battle began at 8 a.m. and after four hours of artillery duel, which mortally wounded Siraj-ud-daula's only reliable general, Mir Madan, a monsoon storm hit the battlefield. The British powder was kept dry under tarpaulins, but the French powder was soaked, and their guns fell silent. When the rain stopped, the Bengali force pulled back to the shelter of a redoubt, but became the victim of a determined British offensive which by 5 p.m. had broken the resistance of those of the nawab's forces still fighting for him. Siraj-ud-daula fled north to his capital, packed what treasure he could and continued north. He was discovered and surrendered to the conspirators, who had him hacked to death and paraded through the streets of Murshidabad on the back of an elephant. The battle at Palasi resulted in the death of an estimated 500 Indian soldiers, but fewer than 20 from Clive's diminutive force. Many of the Bengali soldiers held back; they did not want to fight for a ruler widely despised, and with little prospect of loot.

Though small in losses, the battle had momentous consequences. Clive put Mir Jafar on the throne of Bengal while the East India Company was reinstated as the chief trading power. Clive was rewarded with £234,000 worth of treasure, though the unfortunate Watson died at Calcutta a few weeks after the battle. By the 1760s, victory at Palasi had opened the way to British imperial domination not just of Bengal, but eventually of the whole Indian sub-continent.

26. BATTLE OF LEUTHEN
5 December 1757

If Frederick the Great of Prussia needed a battle to complete his impressive *curriculum vitae*, then Leuthen was certainly it. The battle was fought against all kinds of odds, not least the prospect of a winter confrontation at a time when most armies had abandoned combat for winter quarters. The most impressive odds against Frederick lay with his Austrian enemy. After a number of major victories they had seized back much of Silesia, conquered by Frederick several wars before, in 1740–41. The Austrian army, reinforced by Imperial troops from the smaller German states, outnumbered Frederick's 39,000 men and 170 guns with an army of 66,000 horse and foot with 210 cannon, a disparity that ought to have made a decisive difference given the way eighteenth-century battles were fought, line against line until the weaker gave way. Frederick risked all on a radical battlefield manoeuvre that succeeded in reducing the odds to a more than even bet, and it is for this reason that Leuthen was remembered long afterwards as Frederick's apogee.

The renewed struggle for control of Silesia was part of what became known as the Seven Years War (1756–63). It was in reality a series of different wars between the European powers, which merged into a single conflict. At its heart was the desire of Austria, France and Russia to hold down the emergent state of Prussia under its bellicose monarch, Frederick II. During 1757, the Austrian army, together with its allies, drove Prussian forces back towards the Prussian heartland in northern Germany. Commanded by Prince Charles of Lorraine, who had learned much about Prussian tactics since his defeat at Hohenfriedberg in 1745, and the Habsburg field marshal Leopold Daun, the Austrians set out to achieve a decisive victory over Frederick before the end of the year. On 4 December 1757, they set up camp on either side of the Silesian town of Leuthen (Lutynia in present-day Poland) and awaited the Prussians.

Rousing his camp at 4 a.m., Frederick led the vanguard forward, followed by columns of infantry flanked by large numbers of cavalrymen, the troops singing hymns as they marched. An enemy outpost was destroyed and Frederick captured several hundred men. When he arrived to view the Austrian camp he saw that it stretched almost 8 kilometres (5 miles) in width, with the left flank unsupported by any natural barriers. Along most of the length of the Austrian line was a shallow ridge that could shield the Prussian army from view. Frederick took a gamble that he could exploit the ridge's shallow cover to move most of his army in an oblique manoeuvre across the Austrian front in order to make a powerful attack on the exposed enemy flank, so compensating for his lack of numbers. To deceive the enemy as to his intentions, Frederick sent a small force of cavalry and infantry to threaten the other wing of the Austrian army. It was the stronger end of the line, commanded by the Italian cavalry general Andrea Lucchesi, where Daun and Charles were also positioned. All three took the bait, Lucchesi insisting on reinforcements as the Prussians approached with a deliberate languor.

Frederick compelled the rest of his army to form into two long snaking columns and march along the face of the enemy, concealed by the landscape. This was an exceptionally complex manoeuvre, requiring a high level of marching discipline to prevent the units from becoming entangled. When Charles and Daun detected the rightwards movement of the Prussian force, they took it for a retreat in the face of overwhelming odds. While the Prussian feint continued to absorb Austrian attention, the rest of the Prussian army arrived in good order at the far left of the enemy line, wheeled left and then, supported by heavy guns and lines of infantry 50 metres apart, sent in three crack infantry battalions to begin the process of unhinging the whole Austrian line. The main attack came at 1 p.m., with only a few hours of daylight left. The Hungarian commander on the Habsburg left flank, General Franz Nádasti, could see Prussian movement along his front and called to Charles for reinforcement, but the Austrian high command ignored him, still sure that an attack would be mounted against their sector. The Prussians stormed forward and the less reliable German Imperial troops panicked and turned, 2,000 of them falling prisoner. The Prussian cavalry under Hans von Ziethen drove off the Austrian horse and completed the rout of the infantry. The oblique attack began as a resounding success.

Nádasti withdrew towards Leuthen in disarray and Charles and Daun at last realized that they had been tricked. The Austrian line was ordered to swing at right angles to face the onrushing Prussians on either side of Leuthen. The result was a chaos of disorganized units, muddled orders and confused men, forced to march three or four miles to confront an enemy already in command of the field. Resistance in Leuthen was fierce but as dusk fell the town was cleared. Lucchesi brought up his fresh cavalry from the right wing and charged forward against the Prussian infantry, not realizing that Prussian cavalry, under Lieutenant General Wilhelm von Driesen, was positioned on his right flank. As they galloped forward, they were hit from the side by the onrushing Prussian horses. The shock was sufficient. Lucchesi was killed and his cavalry forced back into the ranks of the defending Austrian foot soldiers. The ensuing panic took root across the remaining Austrian line and the whole front collapsed, fleeing in disorder towards the Silesian capital of Breslau. Frederick pursued the stragglers at the head of a small force gathered from among his exhausted men. Heavy snow began to fall and the pursuit was halted. The reformed infantry lines began to sing the hymn 'Now Thank We All Our God' and the song rolled out over the mass of soldiers, to be known henceforth as the 'Leuthen Chorale'.

Losses on both sides were high from the savage hand-to-hand fighting. Prussian casualties were 6,000; Austrian and Imperial losses were 10,000 dead and wounded and 12,000 prisoners. The risky battlefield plan tipped the odds and flank encirclement became a speciality of the Prussian and later German armies, and was imitated by Napoleon. The battle opened the way to Prussian reconquest of Silesia but the cost for Prussia, smaller, poorer and less populous than its enemies, was substantial. Frederick had to sustain four more years of bruising conflict, always against the odds, until the Habsburg empress, Maria Theresa, finally abandoned the attempt to defeat her German rival.

27. RORKE'S DRIFT
22–23 January 1879

Among the many fables and legends that surround the remarkable survival of a small handful of British soldiers in the mission house at Rorke's Drift during the Zulu Wars in southern Africa, one unassailable truth stands out: this was a victory, if victory it was, quite in defiance of the odds. A total of around 100 fit men, supported by a small number of invalids, held at bay all night an estimated 4–6,000 Zulu warriors. Even more extraordinary, all but 17 of the tiny garrison lived to tell the tale.

The battle should never have been fought at all. It came in the early weeks of a war between a British army in southern Africa commanded by Lord Frederic Chelmsford and the Zulu kingdom ruled by the powerful Cetshwayo (Cetawayo). The war was the result of growing imperial pressure from London to secure the demobilization of the large Zulu army and to force the Zulus to acknowledge British suzerainty. Zulu leaders would have preferred to keep the kingdom and reach a peaceful accord with British representatives, but British officials in Africa were determined on a war to reduce what they saw as a permanent threat to European settlement in the region. An ultimatum was sent to Cetshwayo on 11 November 1878 calling on him to demobilize his army and accept a British resident for Zululand as a way of ensuring that the army was not later reassembled. As the British knew, this was unacceptable to Cetshwayo, for the military system was a central element in the maintenance of Zulu rule. The British sought war, and when the ultimatum was not immediately accepted, Chelmsford was ordered to begin hostilities.

The British had 17,000 men and 20 artillery pieces. Zulu fighting quality was rated as poor against a disciplined force, and Chelmsford divided his troops into three columns, each sent across the border from the British colony of Natal into Zululand from a different direction. The British forces were supported by black auxiliaries that were in general less well-armed than white troops, who carried the

Martini-Henry breech-loading rifle, a fast-firing infantry weapon first adopted in 1871. The Zulu army that gathered at the capital, Ondini (Ulundi), in early January 1879 numbered perhaps 20,000 men, armed with shields, the *assegai* spear, the 'knobkerrie' club and numerous older rifles, which they fired inexpertly. According to Zulu military practice, the army was divided into the shape of a buffalo: the main force in the centre (or chest) with two wings (or horns) that encircled the enemy right and left and then closed back towards the centre. A reserve force (the loins) was held behind the chest in case it was needed. This battlefield system had brought the Zulu army regular victories in open ground, but was less useful against a well-fortified position.

On 11 January, one of Chelmsford's three columns, commanded by Colonel Richard Glyn, set out from Rorke's Drift, a small mission house and store on the banks of the Buffalo River. They crossed the river and set up camp at Isandlwana Hill some miles inside Zulu territory, a position invitingly in the open. A small garrison was left at Rorke's Drift to guard the stores, under the command of Lieutenant Gonville Bromhead. On 22 January, while Chelmsford was 16–19 kilometres (10–12 miles) from Isandlwana to reconnoitre the area with the main column, the Zulu commander, Chief Ntshingwayo, attacked the camp (which was defended by 1,000 troops) with perhaps 10,000 warriors in 'buffalo' formation. The camp was destroyed and all but a handful of the defenders were slaughtered and ritually mutilated.

News of the massacre arrived at Rorke's Drift by the afternoon and frantic efforts were made to construct proper defences there, including walls built with bags of mealie, the local grain, and a fortification of biscuit tins. Two buildings, one of which was a makeshift hospital, were rapidly turned into an improvised fortress. As it became clear that a massive Zulu army was closing on the station, some of the British officers made good their escape, while 100 colonial militia camped nearby disappeared into the bush. Bromhead was joined by Lieutenant John Chard, an engineer in charge of the floating bridges over the river. They expected to be killed in turn, but rather than flee and be caught in the open they chose to stay and fight with their tiny detachment of fit men and a small quantity of ammunition.

Cetshwayo had not expected his army to carry on as far as Rorke's Drift. Most warriors returned laden with plunder to bring news of their victory. But Prince Dabulamanzi, one of the king's brothers, and a commander of the reserve 'loins' force, was frustrated at missing out at Isandlwana. Perhaps as many as 5,000 of his men swarmed on towards the Buffalo River where Dabulamanzi ordered them to take the post at Rorke's Drift. The first wave attacked at around 5 p.m. and was driven off by concentrated rifle fire. The whole army could have swamped the post with ease, but the Zulu army attacked in smaller waves on each side of the buildings, withdrawing after suffering from the heavy British fire, to be replaced by new units. Dabulamanzi, who was sheltering behind nearby trees, could not direct the battle clearly. As dusk fell, the Zulus continued their assault, making it more difficult for the defenders to pick out the enemy. The hospital was set ablaze, providing improvised lighting to allow more accurate rifle fire, but by now there was regular hand-to-hand fighting, bayonet against *assegai*, as the Zulu soldiers reached the perimeter of the crude defences.

The few defenders in the hospital held up with bullets and bayonets the Zulus who broke in; but they were forced to retreat back through the flimsy partition walls from room to room. Those who were caught, including some of the patients who could not easily escape, were stabbed and beaten to death; the rest scurried across the yard between the two buildings and behind the biscuit-box barricade. The stone-walled *kraal* (enclosure) was stormed, but an interior wall and a redoubt of mealie bags some 6 metres (20 feet) high held the attackers at bay. A relief force from a nearby settlement was spotted by Zulu scouts, which may well explain why the assault on the remaining buildings petered out after 9.30 p.m., to be replaced by intermittent rifle fire from both sides. But the relief force, seeing the flames from some distance away, assumed the mission house had been captured and returned whence they had come. The Zulu losses had been high and they were reluctant to fight at nighttime. In the early dawn the tired defenders, down to their last box of bullets, saw the enemy forces marching away. Dabulamanzi arrived back to join the main Zulu army the next day, 23 January, to a derisory chorus for his failure with thousands of warriors to capture a small mission post.

In the morning, Chelmsford and his men arrived. They buried 351 Zulu dead lying around the buildings at Rorke's Drift, but the troops, after seeing the slaughter and mutilation of the corpses at Isandlwana, were hard to control. An estimated 500 wounded and exhausted Zulus found in the surrounding countryside were bayoneted or clubbed to death. It was, one eyewitness recalled, 'as deliberate a bit of butchery as I ever saw'. The defenders at Rorke's Drift were liberally decorated with honours, including seven Victoria Crosses for non-officers. One of the recipients, Private Henry Hook, who had stubbornly defended the hospital as long as he could, ended his working life as the cloak-room attendant at the Reading Room of the British Museum Library. Chelmsford used Rorke's Drift as cover for his incompetence at losing the camp at Isandlwana. The campaign was won after a tough struggle and Cetshwayo lost his kingdom. Rorke's Drift lived on as an imperial legend, to be immortalized decades later in the film *Zulu*. Whatever mistakes the cinema version made, the courage and ingenuity of a small handful of British soldiers and officials has never been in question.

28. BATTLE OF ADWA
1 March 1896

By the mid-1890s the empire of Ethiopia, ruled over by the Lion of Judah, the emperor Menelik, was the only region of Africa not dominated by Europeans. It was a unique state, committed to an ancient form of Christianity, ruled over by a quarrelsome elite of kings and governors (Ras) who each ruled their own principality or province under the eye of the emperor. The European states misunderstood Ethiopia, assuming that it was just another barbarous African kingdom ripe for the European 'civilizing mission'. In 1895, an Italian force commanded by General Oreste Baratieri, governor of the Italian colony of Eritrea, invaded and occupied the Ethiopian province of Tigray. Italian imperialists itched to add Ethiopia to the tiny Italian empire. No-one considered it likely that Menelik would be able to organize resistance against a modern army, equipped with the tools of modern war. Against all expectations the Ethiopian emperor not only raised a disciplined army, but imposed on Italy's invaders a humiliating defeat, the single most important reverse against the remorseless tide of nineteenth-century European imperialism.

Italian confidence was boosted by Menelik's apparent failure to react to the occupation of Tigray. The appearance was deceptive. In September 1895, Menelik summoned the nation to war; but the slow pace of communication and the large area of the empire meant that months passed before the men assembled in answer to the summons. By tradition all males had an obligation to answer the emperor's call, bringing with them shield, lance, sword and, if they had one, a rifle. Menelik left his capital, Addis Ababa, in October, a royal procession that wound its way slowly across the mountainous terrain towards Tigray, gathering as it went an army of more than 100,000 men, most on foot, but with numbers of fierce horsemen, the Oromo cavalry, alongside. The Ethiopians had artillery, bought from European suppliers, and a surprisingly large number of rifles. The army was commanded in regional units by the Ras. Tactics relied on the sheer mass of soldiers, but the Ethiopian commanders also displayed a shrewd grasp of operational realities. The Italian army underestimated Ethiopian capability and did so at its peril.

The arrival of the vast Ethiopian army was a shock to the Italians posted as a vanguard to await developments. Expecting at most a few thousand, the 2,000 Italian and local *askari* troops atop the small plateau of Amba Alage watched 40,000 soldiers approach led by Ras Makonnen. They were overwhelmed and most of them slaughtered.

The Italian fort at Mekele was then besieged and forced to surrender on 20 January 1896. Menelik continued his march, reclaiming much of Tigray and threatening Eritrea. He camped on one side of a large plateau at Gundapta and waited for the Italians to come to negotiate their withdrawal from Ethiopian territory. Despite the recent setbacks, Baratieri rejected any compromise and brought most of his 16,000 soldiers, the majority of them *askaris*, to a camp at Sauria, on the eastern edge of the Gundapta plateau, in order to protect Eritrea. The standoff frustrated the Italian prime minister and arch-imperialist, Francesco Crispi. He decided to replace Baratieri, but in the interim sent him a final telegram prodding him urgently to take action. At almost the same time, Menelik moved his camp across the mountains west of Gundapta, to the small town of Adwa (Adowa). The Italians interpreted this as a retreat and Baratieri at last planned an offensive.

Confident that Italian firepower would keep the Ethiopians at bay, Baratieri divided his force in four. Two columns commanded by Generals Matteo Albertone and Vittorio Dabormida were to occupy the main passes between Gundapta and Adwa, while a third brigade under General Giuseppe Arimondi would hold the mountainside between them. A fourth brigade was held in reserve. Baratieri hoped that Menelik would be provoked to fight and his army destroyed by Italian guns, but he was less confident than his commanders, who eagerly expected a decisive Italian victory. The plan went disastrously wrong from the start. During the night of 25 March 1896, the *askaris* hurried ahead and then waited at the passes for the slower elements of the brigade to catch up. When Albertone arrived, reluctant to let the local troops tell him his job, he insisted that the pass was much further on. As dawn broke the advance guard of his brigade had in fact descended to Adwa, where it ran directly into Menelik's camp. Alerted by gunfire, the whole Ethiopian army assembled for battle. The Italian vanguard was destroyed, its few survivors running back in panic through the Italian lines. Albertone formed a line on a shallow hill but his force was soon embattled by 40,000 Ethiopians, who surged forward against the guns. Ethiopian sharpshooters were told to kill the white officers in order to leave the *askaris* leaderless; out of 610 officers in the Italian force, only 258 survived. Soon Ethiopian soldiers were working up the slopes surrounding Albertone, firing on all sides.

Baratieri saw at once what had gone wrong and ordered Dabormida to move forward from the second pass to stand at Albertone's right, supporting his withdrawal. Instead Dabormida took the wrong fork on the path down and ended up far from Albertone, in the valley of Mariam Shavitu, surrounded by slopes on three sides. Menelik saw the mistake and sent 15,000 men into the gap between the two Italian brigades. At this point, General Arimondi finally arrived at the passes and was told to hold them to enable the Italian force to retreat. At 10.30 a.m. on 26 March, with most of his force dead or captured, Albertone ordered the withdrawal. He was wounded and caught, but those still able to flee scrambled up to the passes and through Arimondi's brigade, ignoring all orders to stop and fight. Now there was no hope. The *askaris* fled through the passes to the Gundapta plain, some north towards Eritrea. Ethiopian soldiers now swarmed over the hillsides, charging the few soldiers and artillerymen still in the fight. Crazed by thirst, hunger and fear, the whole force broke and was pursued through the passes and onto the flat plateau where Oromo cavalry cut hundreds of them down. Far away, cut off from the main battle, the Dabormida brigade stood its ground, surrounded by Ethiopian soldiers. At 3.30 p.m., the remnants charged at the circling enemy and Dabormida, revolver in hand, was killed where he stood, a forlorn Italian Custer.

The level of casualties on both sides was never calculated precisely. Some years later an Italian investigation team found the skeletal remains of 3,643 men, but hundreds remained unaccounted for. The Ethiopians who, the Italians said, 'despised death', embraced it in large but unknowable numbers, and almost certainly suffered considerably more dead than the enemy. On the field of battle, the Italian dead and wounded were stripped naked by soldiers keen for some semblance of booty. Some, though not all, of the Italians, dead, wounded or captured, were castrated. Condemned in Europe as a barbarous practice, it was a symbol for Ethiopians of their 'unmanning' of a fallen enemy, a practice that had its roots in a traditional Ethiopian reading of the Old Testament. Adwa shocked Italian opinion. Baratieri was court-martialled, while Crispi was forced to resign. Menelik insisted on a peace treaty and following its signature in October 1896, the hundreds of Italian prisoners were allowed to go home. Adwa remained a symbol of a broader African wish for independence from European rule, a victory against the loaded odds of European imperialism.

29. BATTLE OF OMDURMAN
2 September 1898

One of the commanders of the Sudanese army at the Battle of Omdurman, Ibrahim al-Khalil, had the habit of taking two horses with him into battle. The first was always called 'Aim', the second one 'End'. If Aim was hurt, he would switch to End so he could carry on fighting. On the fateful early morning when between 50,000 and 60,000 men of the Mahdist leader, Khalifa 'Abdullahi, advanced on a mixed British–Egyptian expeditionary force with only half the number of troops, Ibrahim led the army in a massed charge against the enemy encampment. Aim was hit by shellfire and collapsed; Ibrahim jumped onto the ill-named End and was killed by machine-gun fire a few minutes later. Thirteen years earlier, the Mahdist army had swarmed into Khartoum and famously killed General Gordon. At Omdurman, mere numbers no longer sufficed to ensure a Mahdist victory.

The expedition to Omdurman was only loosely connected with the British desire to avenge Gordon's death. For years after the fall of Khartoum to the Sudanese army of the self-proclaimed Mahdi, the Islamic religious reformer Muhammad Ahmad, the British allowed the new Islamic state to survive. The Mahdi died in 1885 and his place was taken by one of his closest advisers, Khalifa 'Abdullahi, who used a reign of terror to impose his own domination over the regions of Sudan and to enforce the strict Islamic code favoured by the Mahdi himself. As the state began to disintegrate in the late 1890s, the British once again became concerned about the region's security, and the threat to British-occupied Egypt, while the British public was fed on horror stories of rape, torture and slavery which only European rule could expunge. In January 1898, the commander, or *sirdar*, of the Egyptian army, Colonel Horatio Herbert Kitchener, was sent with a force of 8,000 British and 17,000 Egyptian and Sudanese troops for the long trek to the Mahdist capital at Omdurman, on the opposite side of the River Nile from Khartoum, charged with the unpredictable task of overthrowing the Khalifa.

The risks were considerable since disease and the dangers of river navigation were bound to eat into the small number of European soldiers dispatched for the campaign. Kitchener understood these dangers and insisted on making sure that communication by rail and telegraph would be constructed all the way south into the Sudan; he also tried to discipline his troops to drink only filtered water to prevent dysentery. The long journey for men who had in many cases never seen service in the tropics was fraught with difficulty, with temperatures rising at times to 48°C (118°F), and men and animals covered with a thick, dark dust thrown up by the march of men and horses over the sandy ground. Not until August 1898 did they arrive at the approach to Omdurman knowing that the Khalifa was gathering a large army to challenge them. The Mahdist leader chose to meet them on a broad plain north of the city with the Karari (Kerreri) hills to the north and the Jebel Surgham hills to the south, both high enough to allow his armies to gather out of sight of the enemy. The Sudanese commanders arrived with their men organized in units called *rub's*, each of which comprised 800–1,200 men, most armed with swords and spears, the privileged *jihadiya* with firearms. After arguing whether it was better to attack by night or by day, the Khalifa finally insisted on an early morning attack. Prayers were said and the standards –

Green, Dark Green and Black – were allocated to the main divisions of the Mahdist army. On 1 September, the forces moved into position.

Kitchener arrived at Karari with enough time to build a defensive perimeter of stakes, thorn bushes and shallow trenches (known in North Africa as a *zariba*). He was supported by ten gunboats on the Nile, armed with thirty small artillery pieces and twenty-four Maxim machine guns. The land forces had forty-four guns and twenty machine guns. These were positioned to do maximum damage to any onrushing enemy. The army stayed on watch the night of 1 September expecting an attack at any moment, but not until early morning did scouts detect the whole Mahdist army on the march. Around 6.45 a.m., the first waves of *rub's*, dressed all in white, wailing loudly and firing at random, ran across the barren plain towards the British *zariba*. A mix of artillery fire, accurate rifle fire and the machine guns ripped the attacking forces apart. Most died or were wounded at more than 1,000 metres from their goal, brought down by the long-range British Lee-Metford rifle. A few intrepid *jihadiya* got within 50 metres (160 feet) of the British line before their suicidal run was ended. A second wave attempted to attack from a different direction, but the onrushing soldiers were mown down in their turn. The plain was strewn with the dead and dying. Sudanese cavalry and infantry on the left wing under the Green Standard then attacked the British cavalry and the Camel Corps perched on the Karara hills at Abu Zariba, driving them north but unable to destroy them because of intense fire from two of the gunboats.

It was at this point that Kitchener sent off the 21st Lancers to round the Jebel Surgham hills to try to cut off any Mahdist retreat to Omdurman. Unknown to the British, Osman Digna and 2,000 soldiers were concealed behind the ridge in a small depression. The cavalry rode right into the trap. Their number included the young Winston Churchill, who would later write a two-volume account of the campaign in Sudan called *The River War*. Attacked on all sides, the lancers fought back, eventually dismounting and using their carbines to drive off the enemy, for the loss of one officer and twenty men. Meanwhile the remaining Black Standard and Green Standard warriors drove forward to meet the advancing British and Egyptian forces, suffering the same withering fire. The large contingent to the Mahdist far left under the young Shaykh al Din arrived too late to prevent the decimation of the Black Standard army under Amir Ya'qub, whose 12,000 men were slaughtered by the British battalions that were now on the move across the plain. When the final wave of horsemen and infantry attacked from the Karara hills, the forward British units, reinforced from the *zariba*, inflicted the same punishment. Some of the *rub's'* remaining soldiers rushed at the enemy unarmed, embracing death in their fight with the infidel.

By 11.00 a.m. the contest was over. The wounded Mahdists were shot or bayoneted as the British and Egyptian soldiers advanced, since it was argued that they continued to fire or slash with their swords even when immobilized by injury. An estimated 10,800 Mahdists were killed, 16,000 wounded. Kitchener's losses were 47 dead and 434 wounded, testament to the efficiency of new forms of defensive fire-power against which a mere mass of soldiers was helpless. Omdurman was occupied under a joint Anglo-Egyptian condominium, which lasted until 1956. One of the cavalrymen present on the day of the battle was the young Captain Douglas Haig. Eighteen years later he was ordering his own troops to run the gauntlet of artillery and machine guns across open ground in the first days of Battle of the Somme.

30. FALL OF SINGAPORE
8 December 1941 – 15 February 1942

The greatest and most humiliating defeat of British Commonwealth forces during the Second World War came with the loss of Malaya and Singapore in the first weeks of the Japanese Pacific campaign. More than 130,000 men surrendered on 15 February, facing a Japanese army of around 35,000. The odds against the Japanese commander, General Tomoyuki Yamashita, were on paper considerable, but they were overcome in a battle in which the experienced Japanese armed forces exploited their formidable tactical skills to overcome the much larger numbers they confronted.

Singapore was a British island colony at the foot of the Malay Peninsula. It was at the heart of plans to defend the eastern Empire and Australasia against any likely threat. In the 1930s, a new naval base was constructed with formidable guns pointing out at sea. The island, with its population of almost one million Malays and Chinese, was expected to hold out against a siege for at least 180 days. Almost no thought had been given to an attack from the Malayan mainland across the Strait of Johore and the northern coast of the island remained unfortified. When it became clear in November 1941 that a clash with Japan was likely in the very near future, British plans were to defend Malaya on the northern border with Thailand, or even to cross into Thai territory if necessary. On 2 December 1941, two major warships, the *Prince of Wales* and the *Repulse*, arrived in Singapore Harbour to strengthen the British Empire position. On 6 December, a Japanese convoy was spotted along the coast of the Gulf of Siam. Unlike the American forces at Pearl Harbor on 7 December, the commanders at Singapore expected trouble.

The convoy was carrying Yamashita's 25th Japanese Army and its supplies. Japanese aircraft were now based in neutral Thailand, within striking distance of Singapore, which was bombed on 8 December. The first Japanese forces landed on the coast of northern Malaya the same day. The Japanese army had a good deal of experience from the four-year war in China, while the British Empire forces, mainly drawn from the Indian army but with large contingents of British and Australian troops, had never fought the Japanese. The assumption was that they would not fight as effectively as European troops or troops led by white officers. When the governor of Singapore was told the news of invasion he retorted: 'Well, I suppose you'll shove the little men off.' The 'little men' numbered at first little more than a division. After several days Yamashita had 26,000 men ashore, supported by a limited amount of artillery and a few tanks. Within days the position in northern Malaya was overrun. The *Prince of Wales* and *Repulse*, setting out unwisely from Singapore, were both sunk on 10 December. The RAF in Malaya and Singapore, armed with obsolete aircraft, were shot out of the skies by the more modern 'Zero' fighters.

At the start of the campaign, there were more than 80,000 British Empire forces supported by more artillery pieces than the Japanese and with generous supplies of ammunition. Yamashita relied on the battlefield skills of his infantry, who infiltrated at night, surrounded and isolated groups of enemy soldiers, created effective ambushes, and for much of the time took no prisoners. In hostile jungle terrain both sides faced problems, but the Japanese soldiers showed a determination and stamina not matched by the enemy. By the end of January, the British army commander, Lieutenant General Arthur Percival, had to acknowledge defeat on the Malay Peninsula and ordered a withdrawal on the night of 30–31 January to the island of Singapore. Losses had been heavy, thanks to poor communication and the collapse of British air power. But Yamashita's forces, with few reinforcements, had travelled 800 kilometres (500 miles) in 55 days, fighting all the way and increasingly short of ammunition. The British Empire garrison, on the other hand, was sent more than 20,000 additional men in January and February. Losses of 19,123 in the fighting in Malaya left a garrison on Singapore island of somewhere around 130,000, supported by artillery and 56 Hurricane fighters brought in by sea.

Yamashita had been so successful that Percival assumed he must have at least 150,000 men and 300 tanks, making the odds appear in *his* favour and encouraging the climate of demoralization. He estimated that the northeast of the island was the most likely point for a Japanese attack, when in fact Yamashita chose the northwest. Dummy installations were used to confuse the enemy, while Japanese preparations to throw the 5th and 18th Japanese Divisions across the

Strait were concealed as much as possible. Percival put his largest force in the northeast and the smaller Australian 22nd Brigade, already mauled from the long retreat down Malaya, along a wide stretch of coast in the northwest. Here on the night of 8–9 February, shadowy landing craft emerged from the gloom. Some were hit by machine-gun fire, but the orders to the artillery were not sent because communications had been cut by earlier Japanese shelling. The same tactics were used by Japanese soldiers to cut through and surround isolated enemy units, using bayonets when ammunition ran low. The Australian front broke and scattered units stumbled back to the line of the River Jurong in the centre of the island. Further east the Japanese Imperial Guards Division commanded by Lieutenant General Takumo Nishimura stole ashore and drove back the Australian 27th Brigade.

As resistance on the island crumbled, Winston Churchill sent a telegram to Percival calling for a fight to the death; commanders and officers, he wrote, 'should die with their troops'. In reality, the mixed Empire force fell back in confusion on the perimeter of Singapore City. Percival co-ordinated operations poorly, communications were rudimentary, and a growing belief that the Japanese were simply unstoppable further contributed to a crisis of morale. On the dockside, deserters struggled to get on the few remaining vessels hurriedly leaving Singapore. Percival's chief commanders recommended surrender as Japanese aircraft bombarded the civilian population. Yamashita's force was in reality stretched thin and short of supplies of all kinds, but Percival finally accepted that he could not organize a proper defence and in the late afternoon of 15 February he met Yamashita to discuss terms. Bizarrely, the two men shook hands before Yamashita insisted on complete capitulation. The Japanese officers were astonished at what they found. Around 130,000 British Empire troops came into captivity, the largest number in British history. They had been out fought at every level by a force only a fraction of their number. The military ethos that permeated the Japanese army could not brook surrender but, despite Churchill's exhortation, the British one could.

31. BATTLE OF SANTA CLARA
28 December 1958 – 1 January 1959

The final decisive battle in the revolutionary war waged in Cuba by Fidel Castro's 26th July Movement was fought by a group of around 300–350 guerrilla fighters commanded by the Argentinian former medical student, Ernesto 'Che' Guevara, against an estimated 3,900 soldiers of the Cuban army and police force who were supported by ten tanks, an armoured train and B-26 bombers based in and around the town of Santa Clara in the centre of the island. The odds were overwhelmingly in favour of the army, but the revolutionary fighters were armed with great confidence that justice was on their side, while the men defending the crumbling regime of the dictator Fulgencio Batista were demoralized by the prospect of fighting against a revolution that now seemed on the brink of victory.

The road from hunted fugitive in the mountains of Cuba – following the landing of Castro's rebel group in 1956 – to guerrilla leader poised to complete the revolution was a long and hard one for Che Guevara. By the summer of 1958, the revolutionary movement had grown larger and had won the tacit support of much of the poor rural population, but the 10,000-strong Cuban army remained a major obstacle. In August 1958, Guevara led one of three major guerrilla units to the central area of the island, Las Villas. It was a challenging and arduous trek, with few horses, beset by swarms of mosquitoes, many of the guerrilla fighters barefoot and trying to carry heavy equipment through wet, swampy ground. Guevara's force arrived dispirited, 'an army of shadows' as he later described them. On 16 October, they finally reached the sanctuary of the Trinidad-Sancti Spíritus mountains and could rest. Over the next month, they attacked key communication points across the centre of the island, forcing small army or police garrisons to surrender. By December, they had succeeded in cutting major road and rail links. After capturing the small port of Caibarién, the column marched past the rail junction at Camajuaní on the way to Santa Clara, where Batista's army was gathered under the command of Colonel Joaquin Casillas Lumpuy. The rebels arrived outside the town on 29 December 1958.

Guevara, his arm in a sling after a fall in the capture of Caibarién, wearing his iconic black beret and an open-necked shirt, divided his small band into two groups. One was sent to intercept an armoured train laden with military supplies and men on its way to help Lumpuy. The attack was directed by the twenty-three-year-old Roberto Rodriguez ('El Vaquerito'), commander of what Guevara called the Suicide Squad, chosen for dangerous missions and dedicated to the revolutionary cause. Fierce fighting around the Capiro Hills above the stationary train resulted in the death of an unknown number of guerrillas, including the eighteen-year-old Captain Gabriel Gil, who had been chosen to lead the assault, but the army commanders decided the train would be safer nearer to the barracks, and it set off along the rail route into Santa Clara. In the town itself, Guevara had set up his headquarters in the university and here he found tractors belonging to the School of Agriculture. The tractors were used to tear up the rail tracks so that the train would have to halt. The front carriages were derailed and the guerrillas attacked it with small arms fire and Molotov cocktails ('an arm of extraordinary value', wrote Guevara in his handbook on guerrilla warfare). After several hours sealed up in carriages made unbearably hot by the fires, the train commanders surrendered. Some of the 350 soldiers fraternized openly with the guerrillas. According to Guevara's account, his band suddenly possessed twenty-two armoured cars, anti-aircraft guns, machine guns and 'fabulous quantities of ammunition (fabulous, that is, to us)'.

These new weapons certainly helped the second column in the city, commanded by Rolando Cubela, to capture key points in the northern quarters. The urban battle was quite different from the usual hit-and-run attacks the men had carried out in the Cuban countryside, but the group adjusted well to a prolonged fight, sheltered by buildings and primitive barricades built by sympathetic townspeople. On 30 December, a fierce gun battle raged around the police station, which was finally captured the following day, although 'El Vaquerito' died during the assault. The guerrillas laid siege to the army barracks of the Leoncio Vidal Regiment and the 31st Regiment of Rural Guard, which between them housed some 2,900 men. The army had tanks and air support, but the garrisons were demoralized and poorly led. The 31st Regiment surrendered and attention was then turned to the Grand Hotel. The guerrillas cleared all but the upper floor, from which snipers continued to fire until the rest of the town had been captured. The guerrillas, now with the open support of many of the towns-people, surrounded the Leoncio Vidal barracks and called on Casillas to surrender. On the morning of 1 January news arrived that Batista and his entourage had fled Cuba, leaving the garrison with little choice but to give up. A force almost ten times larger than Che Guevara's original unit finally abandoned the struggle. Casillas and the police chief Cornelio Rojas were shot by the revolutionaries the following day. How many others died on the two sides has not been recorded.

The Battle of Santa Clara has gone down in Cuban mythology as the fight that ended the Batista dictatorship. It contributed to the popularity of Guevara himself, who was hailed as a military genius for winning the largest open battle between the rebels and the government. The fall of the regime was more complicated than this, since by late 1958 the loyalty of the army was in doubt and much of the island could no longer be defended against local guerrilla initiatives. Much rested on the ability of the large armed force in Santa Clara to halt the decline and impose a punishing defeat on Guevara, but the Cuban regular army was full of disillusioned men, unwilling to die for Batista. The dictator was already getting ready to run.

This moral contrast was all-important, for the revolutionaries had no real military background, though they quickly learned how to make a Molotov cocktail, to lay explosives on a rail track, or to fire the weapons they captured. Guevara was by most accounts a stern and puritanical commander. He would not allow gambling or alcohol among his recruits and expected undeviating commitment to the cause. 'The chiefs,' he later wrote in his handbook, 'must constantly offer the example of a pure and devoted life,' while their men must display 'valour, capacity and a spirit of sacrifice'. When he found that one of his troops had fallen asleep, having lost his gun, he sent the soldier back to the front line unarmed and told him to find another one. Guevara next saw the man a few moments before he died in the rough hospital set up for the injured, his new gun beside him. 'It seemed to me,' wrote Guevara, 'that he was pleased to have proved his courage.' The victory against the odds owed a good deal to the self-confidence of Guevara and his small band of followers that in the end numbers did not matter as much as the rightness of the cause.

CHAPTER 3
INNOVATION

A good case can be made for the proposition that innovation in war, whether technological, tactical or organizational, has been continuously evolving over the last few thousand years in a straight line from the stone axes and spear-tips of prehistoric man to today's nuclear weapons and electronic battlefield. But this would be a misleading judgement of the way in which the practical nature of fighting has changed over the past 4,000 years. For most of that period the battlefield was dominated by foot soldiers carrying shields, spears, swords and axes and by horsemen wielding lances, sabres, axes and broadswords. In some cases both foot and horse used bows and arrows. There were tactical changes and variations in the balance between foot and horse; armour as a protection fluctuated in extent and quality. But a Bronze Age warrior and a medieval spearman would have recognized each other without difficulty.

Much the same can be said of the first 3,000 years of naval warfare. Ships using oarsmen and sails, carrying missiles and marines, characterized the battlefield at sea until the coming of cannon. Even with added firepower, naval battles could be decided by more skilful seamanship and aggression, while boarding the enemy vessel continued long into the gunpowder age. Tactical differences fluctuated over time, while small changes in the height or length of fighting ships, or the number of oarsmen, could make a significant difference, as was the case at Lepanto and Actium. Major naval engagements were less common than battles on land and were usually designed to prevent a ground invasion – the Spanish Armada or Trafalgar are obvious examples – or to enable ships to supply a shore-based army.

The major technical changes came with gunpowder, developed first in Asia then taken up and exploited rapidly in the Western world. Musket fire and cannon shot did not change the shape of a battlefield a great deal – it still depended on cavalry and infantry in combination driving one or other combatant from the field – nor did it render the lance, sabre and spear (in the form of a long bayonet) redundant. The major changes in technology are those of the very modern age – all metal warships, tanks, aircraft, radio, radar, submarines, nuclear weapons and rockets. These were all the products of new science-based industry and they have defined battle on land, at sea and in the air only over the course of the last century. Today's electronic battlefield is only a quarter-century old. Even today, much of the irregular warfare conducted in insurgencies and civil wars uses a simpler technology and relies on tactics of surprise and terror to counterbalance the advantages enjoyed by powerful adversaries. These are battlefield strategies with a long pedigree.

Innovation in the way armies and navies are organized has also changed remarkably little over time, and was driven chiefly by the increased size of armed forces. The armies of Genghis Khan were based on divisions of 10,000 men organized in a decimal system right down to a unit of ten. Roman armies were a model of unit organization. Even battles fought between less organizationally sophisticated armies relied on careful disposition of the soldiers. The Anglo-Saxon shield wall, the ranks of medieval archers or Genghis Khan's steppe horsemen all needed careful training for the moment they would be tested, even if they were peasants or labourers in everyday life. Conscription and regular military practice are features of all ages of battle.

The tactics of the battlefield have also remained remarkably constant over thousands of years. Commanders imitate the practice of others or devise their own ways of coping with unorthodox threats. The variations in the way forces are deployed on land or at sea did not develop in a linear way, but relied on a constant search for some form of tactical advantage, which often required not innovation but imagination and cunning. In the battles described here, a tactical breakthrough – as at Carrhae or Lepanto – can have decisive effects. But it is generally the case that one side tries to outmanoeuvre the other, an aim that has resulted in the constant repetition of battlefield patterns from the ancient world to today. Encirclement, flank attack, oblique formation, column or line, are not the tools of the modern battlefield commander but are as old as battle. When General Longstreet at Gettysburg tried to persuade Lee to allow a wide flanking attack on the Union line, he had Alexander the Great, Hannibal and Attila the Hun as his supporters. None of this is to suggest that innovation is not significant, since it has decisively changed the modern battlefield, but simply a reminder that novelty in tactics, organization or the exploitation of weaponry is not a monopoly of the recent Western way of war.

32. BATTLE OF LEUCTRA

6 July 371 BCE

When King Cleombrotus of Sparta marched along the Peloponnesian coast towards the town of Leuctra at the head of 10,000 Spartan and allied hoplites, the heavily armed infantry of Greek warfare, he must have been confident of victory. Sparta, with its rigorous military training and ethos of tough combat, had dominated the Greek world for a generation. Prudent city-states threw in their lot with Sparta and provided a good proportion of the men marching behind the Spartan king. To defeat a Spartan host of this size would require either special courage or a novel battle plan. The commander who opposed Cleombrotus was the Theban soldier

Epaminondas, and he possessed both. On a plain outside Leuctra, Sparta's fearsome reputation was about to be blunted by a startling battlefield innovation.

The Spartans were marching to punish the city of Thebes for its efforts to dominate a cluster of cities in Boeotia, in central Greece. The Thebans were adept horsemen, in territory not well adapted to horse warfare. Together with some 6,500 hoplites raised from Thebes and their reluctant Boeotian allies, Epaminondas had 1,500 cavalry and 1,000 lightly armed peltasts, or skirmishers. The Theban hoplites had at their core the famous 'Sacred Band' of 300 selected men, who trained and fought in pairs and were also lovers, so it was said, in order to cement the soldierly bond between them. They were led by Pelopidas, the key commander on the Theban side. Cleombrotus had with him 1,000 cavalry and 1,000 peltasts (the figures may be conjecture, but they give a sense of scale), but he relied on his powerful hoplite phalanx with its 400 royal guard, armed with breastplate, helmet and the deadly hoplite spear, the *hoplon*. When his force arrived on the plain near Leuctra he drew them up in conventional linear form, with a strong right wing containing the king and his guard, his weaker allies on the left and a force of cavalry and skirmishers in front. His phalanxes were twelve rows deep.

Epaminondas was already in position on higher ground. The Theban commander drew up his army in defiance of convention. On his left wing he created a narrow phalanx fifty rows deep, with an extraordinary weight of attack. At the centre and right he placed much shallower units, each one staggered back from the one in front in echelon formation. The cavalry was probably to the front, together with the peltasts. This was a risky strategy. If the Spartans could hold back the massive Theban phalanx, their left wing could sweep through the Theban right and encircle the enemy. Epaminondas perhaps gambled that the shock of his novel tactic would disorient the more numerous Spartans before they could adapt to the new battlefield situation. He also wanted to bring his best troops to battle first, leaving his unreliable Boeotian allies in the weaker echelons to the right.

Whether that was the true motive for his novel formation, rather than a stroke of military genius, as some historians have argued, remains speculation.

The ancient sources, on which the account of the subsequent battle is based, differ considerably in detail. Only Xenophon, who was in Sparta at the time and is almost certainly the most reliable guide, described the use that Epaminondas made of the Theban cavalry. The battle opened, according to Xenophon, with a cavalry engagement that in some ways proved as decisive as the hoplite struggle that followed. The clash of horsemen produced an immediate panic among the Spartan cavalry, who rode back in confusion into their own hoplite ranks, breaking up the tight and disciplined formation typical of Spartan warfare. Before the Spartans had a chance to regroup, the powerful Theban phalanx was pushing forward, with the Sacred Band at the front. Bloody hand-to-hand combat convulsed the Spartan right wing, while the left wing, uncertain of how to respond and composed of less reliable allies, found it difficult to engage with the weaker Theban front because of its staggered formation. By the time the left wing moved forward, the right wing was collapsing, exposing the whole Spartan force to encirclement.

The Theban strategy was fully justified by the results. Cleombrotus and most of his royal guard were slaughtered and the Spartans retreated, leaving at least 1,000 dead on the field (4,000 according to a later account). The remaining Spartan commanders requested a truce so that the dead and wounded could be carried away. The Thebans, rather than pursue the beaten enemy and risk a confrontation with Spartan reinforcements in the Peloponnese peninsula, withheld the *coup de grâce*, but the reputation of Sparta for invincibility was destroyed and the Thebans went on to wage victorious but more destructive battles at Cynoscephelae in 364 BCE, in which Pelopidas was hacked to death, and Mantinea two years later, where Epaminondas died from a spear thrust. His strategy survived him. A young Macedonian, Philip, was almost certainly present at the time of Leuctra and was impressed by the Theban ploy. When he became King of Macedonia, Philip used the tactic to devastating effect, while his son Alexander the Great defeated the Persian Empire with a polished version of the oblique attack. Millennia later, Frederick II, King of Prussia, understood the significance of a battlefield innovation that was capable of evaporating Sparta's aura of invincibility, and used it to his own advantage at the Battle of Leuthen in 1757.

33. BATTLE OF CARRHAE

53 BCE

The English expression 'parting shot' derives from 'Parthian shot', a term used to describe the deadly tactical practice of the mounted archers of the Parthian Empire, who could swivel on their horses and fire an arrow while riding away from their enemy. This skill was used to catastrophic effect against a large Roman army led by Marcus Crassus, famous for his ruthless suppression of the Spartacus revolt. In the context of the ancient world, where military innovation was slow to evolve, the Parthians made the most of their unorthodox military equipment and fluid battle tactics against a Roman army used to fighting and winning on its own terms. What followed on the arid plains of what is now southeast Turkey was probably the worst defeat suffered by a Roman army throughout the entire period of Roman domination of the Mediterranean basin and Middle East.

There is no general agreement about why Crassus was there in the first place. The Parthian Empire, stretching across modern Iran and Iraq, was founded in the late third century BCE by invaders from northeast Persia, and its powerful warrior caste successfully kept the menacing Roman Empire at bay roughly along the line of the River Euphrates. Crassus was a member of the First Triumvirate, ruling the empire together with Julius Caesar and Gnaeus Pompey. Their rule was divided up territorially and Crassus claimed Syria, where he arrived in 54 BCE, intent either on adding to his already legendary wealth or securing military victories against a new enemy to enhance his own political stock in Rome. His son Publius, who had been campaigning in Gaul with Caesar, was keen to raise his own reputation and obtained permission to travel with 1,000 Gallic horsemen to join his father in the campaign planned against distant Parthia.

The Parthian king, Orodes II, knew well in advance of the arrival and probable intention of the invading Roman army, but he needed to be sure that Crassus would not join up with other local kings in an anti-Parthian alliance. The King of Armenia, Artavasdes II, not only offered Crassus large bodies of men, including 6,000 cavalry, but also advised him to attack the Parthians by moving through the mountains in southern Armenia, where infantry were better able to fight and the Parthian cavalry would be at a disadvantage. Crassus refused both offers (though the 6,000 horsemen joined his army), perhaps because he thought the size of the army he had gathered – around 40,000 legionaries, 4,000 cavalry and 4,000 light infantry – would easily overcome a force of desert horsemen. In spring 53 BCE, he set off with his army from northern Syria to attack Parthia directly and seize the major city of Seleucia. He knew almost nothing about his enemy or his whereabouts.

Orodes had not been idle. He moved a large army to Armenia to intimidate the king and prevent Armenian forces from linking with Crassus. He left his lieutenant Surena as commanding general (*spahbod*) of 9,000 light horsemen and 1,000 heavily armoured cavalry, or cataphracts (no more than a quarter the strength of the approaching Roman army), with orders to harass and hold up the Roman approach. The light horsemen were armed with a powerful composite bow made of laminated wood and sinew, which they fired as they rode. The impact of the arrows from close range was considerable. There remains dispute about whether they could penetrate Roman body armour effectively, though the barbed arrows could inflict serious wounds on exposed arms, legs and faces. The real innovation on the Parthian side was the cataphract, a warrior covered with scale armour of bronze and steel plates protecting most of the rider's body, as well as the horse. They each carried a long heavy lance, or *kontos*, twice the length of the Roman javelins. The Roman legionaries were armed with the standard short sword, spear and shield, but had nothing that would allow them to come to grips with their mobile opponents, forerunners of the knights who later dominated medieval warfare.

The novel warfare practised by the Parthians proved enough to compensate for the great gulf in size between the two sides. Crassus relied for his route on an Arab guide, Ariamnes, but he was in the pay of Orodes and led Crassus into a trap across largely waterless desert, where the Parthian horsemen would be in their element. They passed the small town of Carrhae, which was already garrisoned by Roman soldiers, crossed a minor stream (where it is alleged that Crassus would not allow his thirsty troops to drink) and finally saw and heard the Parthian enemy ahead of them. Loud drums beat out a constant rhythm while the horsemen kicked up clouds of sandy dust around them. The cataphracts advanced with blankets shrouding their armour. Crassus was uncertain how to meet this odd formation. After trying a conventional line, he opted for a large square, with the cohorts each protected by a small squadron of Roman cavalry. It turned out that this was the worst formation he could have chosen.

At some point towards mid-day the Parthians attacked. The cataphracts threw off their covering, revealing armour, according to one ancient account, 'blazing like fire' in the hot sun. Surena sent his horsemen first, galloping at speed around the whole Roman square, firing arrows at will because the Roman soldiers were so closely packed together. Crassus first sent his light infantry to try to drive them off, but they were deluged with arrows and hurried back to the shelter of the square. Frustrated at being unable to get at an enemy who had already inflicted heavy casualties on his soldiers, Crassus sent his son Publius with 1,300 cavalry, 500 archers and 4,000 infantry to eliminate the threat from the enemy bowmen. Publius rashly followed where the Parthian horses fled only to discover, at some distance from the main army, that the cataphracts were drawn up in a solid phalanx waiting to charge. The heavily armoured cavalry crashed into the

Roman force, while the lighter horsemen kept up a volley of arrows, replenished throughout the battle by a large reserve of missiles carried by 1,000 camels. All but 500 of the force were slaughtered. Badly injured, Publius ordered his shield-bearer to kill him, while his Gallic horsemen fought to a blood-soaked standstill.

The extent of the disaster was brought home to Crassus when he saw a Parthian lance carrying the severed head of his son. His Roman legionaries tried to keep close order as they were subjected to repeated charges from the cataphracts trying to break the Roman line, and a relentless wave of arrows began to eat away at Roman strength. Only when night fell did the killing stop, with few of the Parthians slain but thousands of injured, dying and dead legionaries piled on the sandy soil. Crassus ordered a retreat back to Carrhae, leaving, it was estimated, 4,000 wounded to be killed by the Parthians. The surviving army began to break up and move back to Syria. Crassus was invited to parley with Surena, but an altercation between the delegations ended with the murder of Crassus and his senior officers. Molten gold, it was claimed, was poured down the throat of his corpse as mocking retribution for his greed. The vast Roman army lost 20,000 dead and 10,000 captured. Later Roman accounts blamed Crassus for military incompetence, for which there was some justification, but the problem for Rome was the unconventional tactics they confronted. With the Romans unable to conquer Parthia, the Euphrates remained their unstable frontier.

34. BATTLE OF AIN JALUT
3 September 1260

The Battle of Ain Jalut, fought in the Jezreel Valley in southeast Galilee, in present-day Israel, signalled the end of the threat posed by the great Mongol khans to the Middle East and Europe. It also marked the start of a remarkable age of military innovation. During the encounter, small cannon, which used explosives developed first in China and possibly diffused to the Arab world from Mongol sources, were deployed for the first time in the recorded account of a battle. They did not win the battle – artillery would become important only centuries later – but they defined a moment of transition to a type of warfare that would culminate in the giant guns of the twentieth century, long after the Mongol threat was no more than a fading folk memory.

Beginning with the conquests of Genghis Khan across Asia, the Mongol overlords had ambitions to dominate the whole of the known world. For decades, the march of Mongol armies west and south from their Asian heartland had seemed unstoppable. In 1251, Möngke Khan, Genghis Khan's grandson, became Great Khan. His ambition was to complete the imperial conquest of the Christian and Islamic worlds and establish a Mongol world empire. He assembled a vast army, supplied by many of the vassal states that the Mongols had already conquered, and put it under the command of another grandson of Genghis Khan, Hülegü Khan. In 1256, after five years of preparation, the Mongol army moved out from its stronghold in Persia to complete the conquest of the world.

The huge force swept aside Islamic states in its path and destroyed Baghdad, the heart of Islam and the seat of the Abbasid Caliphate, which had ruled from there for 500 years. The population was slaughtered and the cultural and architectural treasures of the city destroyed. Next, Hülegü moved on to capture Damascus, seat of the Muslim Ayyubid dynasty. He planned to move south through Palestine to destroy the last remaining Islamic power in the Middle East, the Mamluk Sultanate of Egypt. This would open the way to Mongol domination of North Africa and the Mediterranean. In 1260, Hülegü sent envoys to Cairo to demand that the sultanate surrender or suffer the consequences. 'Resist,' wrote Hülegü, 'and you will suffer the most terrible catastrophes.' The Mamluk Sultan Qutuz replied by murdering the envoys and displaying their heads on the gates of Cairo. This was a declaration of war.

Just as Hülegü prepared to move south, news arrived that Möngke

Khan had died. Hülegü hurried eastwards with much of his army in the hope that he could claim the Great Khanate for himself. The remains of his army, an estimated 10–20,000 men, was placed under the command of a Christian Turk, Kitbuqa Noyan. The army moved south through Palestine, crossing the River Jordan in late August 1260. Qutuz formed an alliance with another Mamluk leader, Baibars, and moved northwards with an army of approximately the same size, 20,000 horsemen and archers. When news arrived of Kitbuqa's approach, Qutuz advanced to meet him at the spring of Ain Jalut, in the Jezreel Valley.

The Egyptians had the advantage that they knew the terrain well. It was decided that Baibar's army would stand and face the Mongols, but engage only in small punitive sallies, provoking the Mongols, but not risking the whole Mamluk force. The rest of Qutuz's army hid in the highlands around the valley, unobserved by the Mongols, and waited for Baibars to bait the enemy enough to provoke an advance into the valley. The Mongol army responded angrily to the failure of Baibars to stand and fight and finally, believing that the weaker Mamluk force was retreating, Kitbuqa ordered the whole Mongol army to pursue the enemy into the valley ahead. The trap was sprung. The Mongol army found itself the object of fierce attack from Mamluk soldiers and cavalry hidden in the trees on the valley sides, and an easy target for the many Egyptian archers. The Mamluks used small explosive hand cannons (*midfa*) for the first time in battle, designed to frighten enemy horses and horsemen, though not capable of inflicting serious damage. The Mongol forces nevertheless fought a desperate hand-to-hand battle to escape and almost succeeded until Qutuz, at the head of his own elite unit, rushed into the battle to rally the Mamluks. Qutuz was heard to shout out 'Oh my Islam!' to urge his followers to the defence of the faith. The tide turned in his favour, and while some Mongol troops fled, Kitbuqa fought to the end until he and thousands of his men were slaughtered.

It was a historic victory. Although Hülegü planned to avenge Ain Jalut on his return to Persia in 1262, the Mongol Empire was splitting up and his own lands were threatened by the Muslim Khanate in Russia.

A second small expedition sent against the Mamluks was driven back. The Mamluk victory marked the end of Mongol expansion, broke the spell of Mongol invincibility and preserved the Islamic world.

The triumph did Qutuz little good. He was murdered on his way back to Cairo by emirs almost certainly in the pay of Baibars, who feared that Qutuz would not honour his pledge to grant Syria to him in the event of a Mamluk victory. Baibars became the new sultan. Under his rule, the Mongols were expelled from Syria and the remaining Christian crusaders from Palestine, and Islamic rule placed on a firmer foundation. The decisive battle had been won through a simple act of battlefield deception, but the use of small cannon had a much greater implication. From this meagre start began the long evolution of gunpowder weapons that made the battlefield a more lethal environment and threatened the immunity of fortified cities. Qutuz could never have realized how rapidly this modest innovation would change the nature of battle.

35. BATTLE OF CRÉCY
26 August 1346

The Battle of Crécy was an exceptional medieval battle. The risks of actual combat were high for monarchs and the nobles and knights they took with them to war, so in many cases in the High Middle Ages, battle was not actually joined. Raids, skirmishes and sieges were common, but a full-scale battle between two major armies was a relative rarity. Crécy, so it is estimated, pitted an estimated 10–14,000 Anglo-Welsh men-at-arms and archers against perhaps 20,000 French and mercenary forces, at least 12,000 of them mounted and armoured men-at-arms. What made the battle so remarkable was that this smaller force inflicted a devastating defeat on the 'flower of Christendom' fighting for the French king, Philip VI. The army of the English king

Edward III won the battle as a result of a simple cluster of operational and tactical innovations, which turned a kingdom regarded as militarily mediocre into Europe's most dangerous battlefield opponent.

England and France were old enemies. The campaign which ended with the English triumph at Crécy was part of a long-drawn-out struggle between the French and English crowns over lands in France. In 1346, Edward III planned a major operation to stake his claim to the French throne. After raising a great deal of money, men and supplies, and requisitioning, it is estimated, up to 1,000 vessels, his vast armada landed, with complete surprise, at St-Vaast-la-Hougue on the Normandy coast. This combined arms assault on France was the first major innovation: no army of this size, complete with thousands of horses, had ever engaged in an amphibious operation of this size and complexity – a remote ancestor of D-Day, 600 years later. Not much is known about Edward's motives, but historians now suggest that he had planned to lure Philip to battle on ground of his choosing and that the area of Ponthieu south of Calais (which was technically English territory), in which the forest and village of Crécy were situated, was his intended destination. This was a high-risk strategy, and for six weeks the English army forced its way along a 30-kilometre (20-mile) wide corridor towards the Seine and then the Somme, devastating everything in its path and risking retaliation. This was a challenge to the honour of France that Philip could not ignore and he summoned his military nobility, allies and paid mercenaries to march on the impertinent English and offer them battle.

Edward's army reached its destination, having broken across the River Somme on 24 August. After marching through the Crécy forest, they arrived at the slope at the top of the Vallée des Clercs, where Edward positioned his forces to block the northwards advance of Philip's vast army. The English had many advantages from their ability to choose the place and time of engagement, but the critical factor was the way in which Edward disposed his forces. The various early accounts of the battle are inconsistent, but it seems clear that Edward divided his army into three divisions, probably one behind the other, with the king's son, the Black Prince, leading the vanguard so that, according to legend, he could 'win his spurs'. The long wagon train that had accompanied the army was drawn into a tight circle like an improvised fortress, with the pack animals and horses inside, protected by archers and cannon. Most accounts agree that the English long-bowmen, the key to the new English battlefield tactics, were positioned in triangles facing the oncoming French, probably on each wing of the English men-at-arms, as well as in front. Pits and trenches were dug to hamper the French cavalry, but once the archers had done their damage, Edward's military elite abandoned their horses in favour of fighting on foot. This was a tactical arrangement tried a number of times before, but Crécy saw its triumphant fulfilment.

Edward was fortunate that Philip VI had little room for manoeuvre in every sense. Recent study of the topography of the battle has demonstrated that the French had to advance on a narrow and difficult front to get at the English, an outcome almost certainly planned by Edward and his commanders. On other occasions, Philip might have mustered his forces while avoiding open combat, but on this occasion the savage passage of the English through northern France had been a calculated challenge. He pursued the English and arrived at Crécy late on the afternoon of 26 August. Some of his senior advisers cautioned delay until the morning rather than fighting in the twilight; others, it seems, were impatient to get at the English and felt any delay would dishonour them. Philip hesitated, but before a clear decision could be taken, numerous French cavalry moved forward towards the English lines, eager to take up the challenge. The decision was taken out of the king's hands. He ordered the sacred banner of France, the *Oriflamme*, to be raised, indicating that no quarter was to be given. Edward responded by raising the Dragon banner, which meant the same. Few prisoners were taken at Crécy.

Philip expected his mercenary Genoese crossbowmen to open the battle. They hurried forward, hampered by the crowd of French horsemen. The crossbow was a formidable weapon with a range of up to 400 metres (1,300 feet) and a heavy, lethal bolt; but it could only be fired intermittently, after laborious reloading. Some accounts have a shower of rain just before the Genoese advanced, which would have damaged their bowstrings. Whatever the truth, the crossbow was outdone by the simple English longbow, with a rapid rate of fire, three times that of a crossbow, and a deadly impact at 300 metres (1,000 feet). The Genoese had been sent forward without their shields. After the first hail of arrows they panicked and fell back among the advancing French cavalry.

The nature of the narrow approach maximized the damage the English archers could inflict and made it impossible for Philip to use his greater numbers to his advantage. As the first divisions of French horsemen moved forward, they were mown down by the missiles. The English men-at-arms then joined the mêlée, taking advantage of the French confusion and pushing back the enemy until, so it now seems, those behind were crushed to death by the retreating knights. The ebb and flow of the battle has differing accounts, but there is no doubt about the outcome. Over 1,500 of the French elite lay dead on the field for the loss of 300 English knights. Philip fought bravely on some accounts and was wounded, but he was eventually led from the field to avoid his capture. The most famous knight in Europe, John of Luxembourg, King of Bohemia, though now blind, tied his horse together with those of his retainers and plunged into the fray. He and his companions were all found dead the following day on the battle-field. This news perhaps shocked Europe more than the battle itself.

Reports and newsletters swiftly travelled to Europe's major cities. Crécy was seen at the time as a stunning victory for an upstart king against the very flower of Europe. Edward moved on to besiege Calais, which fell the following year. Philip tried to salvage his reputation by blaming others. The real explanation for French defeat lay in the new English way of warfare. The defensive longbow, properly exploited, together with the deployment of armoured men on foot, unhinged the traditional domination of battlefield cavalry. The battle demonstrated that quite simple tactical innovations could transform, if temporarily, the art of war.

36. BATTLE OF LEPANTO
7 October 1571

It is hard to imagine a more extraordinary battle scene than the carnage at the decisive clash between the Muslim and Christian fleets in the narrow strait dividing mainland Greece from the Peloponnesian peninsula. Grand paintings made to celebrate the Christian victory give some sense of the tumult and the innumerable dead. More than 450 ships rowed by tens of thousands of oarsmen, most of them slaves, crashed together in the narrow seas. What the paintings fail to show is the slender but probably decisive advantage enjoyed by the Christian fleet: large, heavily gunned 'galleasses', bristling with cannon and men armed with light muskets (the 'arquebus'), whose raking fire broke up the Ottoman line, were an innovation that stunned the enemy vessels and left more than eighty of their number at the bottom of the sea.

The battle came about as a result of the increasingly desperate efforts of the Spanish emperor and the Papacy to hold back the moving tide of conquest of the Muslim Ottoman emperor, Selim II. In 1571, the Turks seized Cyprus from the Venetians with an orgy of cruel violence, massacring 20,000 inhabitants in Nicosia and seizing 2,000 young captives for sexual slavery. The cautious Venetians, whose whole empire in Greece and Dalmatia now seemed open to Ottoman ambitions, finally joined with Spain, Genoa and the Papal States in a Holy League to free the Christian world from the looming threat to Italy, and to frustrate the Ottoman boast that St Peter's in Rome would soon become a mosque. King Philip II of Spain, who later sent the Armada to conquer Protestant England, gave command of the fleets of the Holy League to Don Juan de Austria, the title given to his brother Gerónimo, the illegitimate son of the Habsburg emperor, Charles V. It proved an inspired choice. Don Juan (Don John in English) was an able commander, a skilful diplomat between the differing forces assembled under his flag, and an inspiration to the thousands serving under him.

The seizure of Cyprus was completed with a long siege of the Venetian fortified town of Famagusta. After the garrison negotiated surrender, the Venetian commander had his ears and nose cut off, was exhibited in chains on all fours and was finally flayed alive, his skin then stuffed with straw and paraded as a Turkish trophy. The commander of the Turkish fleet, Admiral Ali Pasha, next took his force, which numbered in the end 251 galleys, galliots and smaller vessels, to the advance Ottoman naval base at Lepanto, on the southern coast of mainland Greece. He had with him perhaps 50,000 men, militia, archers, slaves and the better armed elite janissaries. It was late autumn and Ali was uncertain whether he would winter there unmolested. Sultan Selim sent him a messenger to say that if the fleet of the Holy League appeared, he was to seek battle.

Unknown to Ali Pasha, Don John had succeeded in assembling a large fleet, eventually some 208 vessels, including 154 galleys, 38 smaller vessels or 'lanterns', and six new ships put together in the dockyards at Venice. These giant galleasses carried 40 guns apiece, 30-pound guns on the deck, 50-pounders down below. The regular galleys carried perhaps four or five guns. The object was to send them out ahead of the main fleet, with 500 men aboard armed with the standard musket or 'arquebus', to smother the enemy decks with fire. Don John also ordered galleys to remove the large prow used for ramming an enemy ship, so that the forward guns could fire directly down at the Turkish waterline. It has been estimated that the Holy League had 1,334 guns to the Ottomans' 741. Concentrated gunfire in Mediterranean warfare was a novelty and its effects were devastating.

There were risks for Don John in seeking battle. To lose would again open the West to Ottoman conquest, but the autumn weather was treacherous, holding his fleet in harbour on 5 October after its arrival in Greece, with the wind against them. The fog, however, helped to shield the Christian fleet's approach. On the morning of Sunday, 7 October, Mass was said aboard the whole Christian fleet. As if in answer to Christian prayers, the wind suddenly changed direction, swelling their sails but forcing the enemy fleet to row. Then silently the whole body of Christian ships moved into the strait, suddenly sighting the vast Ottoman fleet, arranged in its traditional long crescent so that it could envelop and destroy the enemy. The right wing was commanded by the Turkish admiral Mehmet Scirocco, the left by a notorious corsair, the savage and disfigured Italian renegade, Uluch Ali (Occhiali).

Don John had drawn up a battle plan that deviated from the conventional approach. He divided his forces into three contingents, with the galleasses out in front, and a reserve force behind. This gave the whole Christian line more flexibility, as long as it held. The northern wing was commanded by the Venetian Marcantonio Quirini, the southern by Gianandrea Doria from Genoa. Don John and his flagship *Real* led the centre. In the morning sunlight the two fleets slowly crept towards each other, the Turks noisy with coarse shouts and music, the Christian vessels menacingly quiet. Suddenly as the Turkish galleys approached, the galleasses opened up. The deadly salvos quickly broke up the Turkish line while the fire from the massed musketeers wreaked havoc among the lightly dressed Ottoman soldiers. Then the other Christian galleys began their cannonade; freed from the oblique angle required with a large fixed prow, their guns sank galley after galley of the enemy.

Don John soon found himself engaged with the flagship of his enemy, the substantial *Sultana*, flying a large pennant dedicated to Allah, whose name was embroidered in gold 28,900 times. The two ships crashed together and Don John's crew swept aboard. In the savage fighting Admiral Ali was shot through the forehead. A galley slave, one of the thousands released by Don John to fight the Muslim enemy, hacked off Ali's head and displayed it on a pike. The *Sultana* was seized along with a remarkable hoard of gold. The flag of Allah was hauled down and later taken to Spain as a trophy. On the left wing, the Venetians had at first faced encirclement, but superior gunfire and the help of Christian galley slaves, who slipped their shackles to attack their enslavers, turned the tide. Scirocco was killed and his head, too, displayed on a lance to his demoralized followers. The battle in the centre and north swung firmly towards Don John. In the south, Uluch Ali tricked the Genoese admiral by sailing south as a feint. As the Christian line stretched, it lost contact with the centre and Uluch Ali swiftly took his light corsair galliots through the gap and attacked ships in the rear belonging to the Knights of Malta. He seized their flagship and made off westwards trying to avoid the rest of the Christian fleet, which was now free to engage him. He had to abandon the flagship prize and in the end only eight of his ships managed to escape. The rest were sunk or beached. By 4 p.m., a historic victory had been won. Uluch Ali fled back to Constantinople where he reported the disaster to an incandescent Selim.

Accounts of the battle convey its messy and sanguinary character, the sea full of the dead or dying, the decks awash with blood, freed galley slaves murdering their Ottoman tormentors with zeal. Christian losses are put at between 7,000 and 8,000, with a further 4,000 dying of their wounds. Ottoman dead are estimated to be at least 26,000, with 3,500 taken captive and 12,000 slaves freed. The vast Ottoman fleet was reduced to around 40 ships; of the rest, 127 were captured and 84 sunk or burnt. The Holy League lost perhaps 33 vessels, but these could be more than replaced with those they had captured. The gunships had done their work. The Ottoman menace had not entirely receded, but it was held at bay for seventy years and Christians in Europe could get back to the familiar task of fighting each other.

37. THE SPANISH ARMADA
1–9 August 1588

The defeat of the Spanish Armada in the late summer of 1588 has remained one of the most famous dates in English history. It is always called the Spanish Armada, as if that were the name of the battle. The Armada was in reality the Spanish word for the huge fleet of ships, now thought to have numbered 130, which set out from the port of Corunna in July 1588 to invade England. The critical battle in a week of naval skirmishes came on 8 August off the French coast at Gravelines, when the English fleet inflicted what turned out to be a decisive defeat on the only major attempt to invade England throughout all the centuries since 1066.

Invasion of England was the brainchild of King Philip II of Spain (nicknamed 'Philip the Prudent'), who had briefly been consort to the Tudor queen Mary I before her death in 1558. He was sincerely committed to eradicating Protestantism as a force in Europe, and the English, who supported the Protestant rebellion in the Spanish Netherlands and preyed incessantly on the rich Spanish trade with Latin America, came to be seen as the main threat to Spanish Catholic interests in Europe. The Armada was gathered together to bring pressure to bear on the English to overthrow Queen Elizabeth and to halt English intervention in the Low Countries. This was to be achieved either by the mere threat of invasion or, if the large Spanish army in the Netherlands commanded by the Duke of Parma could be ferried across the English Channel, by actual invasion and occupation for as long as it took to get the English to agree to Philip's terms.

The Armada began to take shape in 1587 as a stream of ships and supplies came from all over Europe, at great expense, to provide the necessary resources. The original commander, the Marquis of Santa Cruz, died before he could take the fleet out, to be succeeded by the Andalusian nobleman, the Duke of Medina Sidonia. He was a reluctant commander, partly because he could see that the fleet, for all its size, was probably not equal to the task. The supplies wasted or rotted as the months passed and many of the ships were suitable only for Mediterranean sailing, not for the harsher Atlantic. The whole enterprise depended on good communication with the Duke of Parma, who had a personal antipathy to the new fleet commander, but above all on finding an effective deep-water port where the Armada could anchor while the Spanish army was prepared, embarked and convoyed across the Channel.

The ships finally left Corunna on 21 July 1588 in a better state than they had been, but still divided between a core of royal galleons designed for ocean combat, and a host of smaller vessels that were not. There were also four galleasses, which had proved their worth at Lepanto a decade earlier, but were difficult to manoeuvre on the open sea with their great banks of oars. Against them was ranged the English fleet commanded by Lord Howard of Effingham, the Lord High Admiral. There were at least 230 ships available, though they were divided into detachments to safeguard the coast from Cornwall to Essex.

The English had similar problems securing manpower and supplies from a parsimonious monarch, but also important advantages. The English ships were far more manoeuvrable than those of the enemy, being for the most part narrower and longer, without top-heavy castles fore and aft. They were manned by sailors with a great deal of experience, much of it in privateering against Spanish ships. The guns were designed for rapid reloading, and though generally smaller than many of the Spanish guns, they could be fired more regularly. Nor were English decks cluttered with soldiers and their equipment, unlike the Armada, which carried 24,000 men on board. These soldiers had no experience of sea-fighting and although they could prime Spanish cannon for a first volley, they had no training in moving and reloading them. The Armada had been hastily put together with cannon from across Europe, which meant problems in finding the right ammunition. Spanish shot was cast quickly in 1587–88 and contained many impurities, making it prone to break up either in the cannon or as it was fired.

The English did not fully understand the technical advantages they held, but these advantages proved decisive. On 1 August the Armada, keeping very close formation so that the more vulnerable ships could be protected by the larger galleons and galleasses, was met by a portion of the English fleet under Howard off Lizard Point in Cornwall. It was then that Sir Francis Drake, half-admiral, half-pirate, was supposed to have finished his game of bowls before attending to the Spanish. The story is almost certainly apocryphal, but Drake ('El Draque' to the Spanish) was a formidable opponent, greedy for riches, ruthless and an excellent seaman. The English fleet was nevertheless cautious in its approach because the Armada looked worryingly large. Throughout the days that followed, the English were generally helped by a favourable wind, which allowed their vessels to remain behind the Armada, threatening its rearguard. What the English had to avoid was a close encounter, because the Spanish ships were used to grappling and boarding an enemy, not to long-range gun battles. Further skirmishes occurred off Portland Bill and the Isle of Wight, but as the Armada continued to its uncertain rendezvous with Parma, the English held back. 'We pluck their feathers by little and little,' wrote Howard.

Medina Sidonia and his commanders were confused by the English tactics and anxious about what would happen when they arrived off the Flanders shoals and sandbanks to try to shield Parma's embarking army. There had been no reply to any of Medina Sidonia's letters to Parma, but when news finally arrived on 7 August, it was evident that the Spanish army of the Netherlands was in no state to stage a cross-Channel invasion. The Spanish fleet anchored off Calais, unable to find a port and worried by the risk of beaching on the shallows. On the night of 7–8 August, the English prepared eight fire ships from among their older vessels and sent them towards the anchored Spanish. The captains immediately cut their cables and anchors and dispersed into the night. Not one Spanish vessel was ignited but the tight formation was at last broken up. At 7 a.m. on 8 August, the English fleet, now organized into four squadrons, closed with the scattered enemy north of Gravelines. At some point Howard and his admirals had realized that the Spanish were not prepared for a gun duel. He ordered attack in line astern, a tactic used thereafter up to Trafalgar and beyond. They brought their ships within 100 metres (330 feet) of the Spanish and pounded them with shot that holed many below the waterline. There was little response, though Drake's *Revenge* was badly damaged as he engaged Medina Sidonia's flagship. The battle raged all day until the Spanish fleet began a full retreat into the North Sea, abandoning any attempt to collect the invasion army.

The scale of the victory took some time to understand, since only two galleons had been sunk, though many were holed. Some 600 Spaniards were killed compared with a mere 20 on the English side, and the loss of not a single English vessel. The Armada was doomed, for its large number of weaker Mediterranean ships proved no match for the weather on the long trip home around Scotland and Ireland. Only 66 ships returned, most of them damaged, and 20,000 out of the 30,000 on board perished – killed, starved, drowned or dead from disease. The English sailors were little better off, short of food and racked with epidemics. Many were left to die in the street on their return to port and Howard was forced to pay half their wages from his own pocket. But soon the result was understood, and on 30 August the City of London, with as much pomp and circumstance as it could manage, celebrated victory at St Paul's Cathedral. Medina Sidonia arrived back in Spain seriously ill and was never forgiven. King Philip blamed his sins and those of his people for the fact that God had abandoned the Armada to its fate, but in reality the outcome rested on small but significant material differences between the two navies.

38. BATTLE OF BREITENFELD
7 September 1631

Historians are generally agreed that some kind of military revolution took place in the conduct of war during the seventeenth century and one name that stands out above all others in implementing it is Gustav Adolf II, king of Sweden, best known in the Latin form as Gustavus Adolphus. At the Battle of Breitenfeld, north of Leipzig in Saxony, his army had the opportunity to show what his reforms could achieve in one of the major battles of the Thirty Years War, a conflict that raked its way back and forth across the German lands from the 1620s to the 1640s. So effective were his tactical innovations that by the end of five hours of exhausting fighting against well over

30,000 troops of the Habsburg Holy Roman Emperor, Ferdinand II, only half of his men had actually seen combat.

This outcome was possible because Gustavus Adolphus had implemented a number of major changes in the way Swedish forces were conscripted, trained and deployed in the decade before Breitenfeld. The reforms were certainly not entirely original, owing much to the sixteenth-century Dutch military reformer, Prince Maurice of Orange. Gustavus Adolphus took ideas where he could and made them into a system. His Articles of War, read out in 1621, placed great emphasis on military discipline to make sure his army fought as a unit and avoided behaviour likely to undermine that unity. Swearing, drunkenness and desertion were severely punished – indeed, there were forty military offences for which the punishment was death. His men were trained in musketry and the use of the pike, while cavalry was restored as a truly offensive arm, working in combination with the foot soldiers. His most significant innovation came in the way forces were to be laid out on the battlefield. Gustavus rejected the idea of a phalanx in favour of a long line of brigade-strength units, supported on the wings by cavalry and each with its own mobile artillery. To fight effectively in defence and on the offensive, his army had to drill hard to ensure that movement on the battlefield did not turn into a confusion of men and horses. So important was regular rehearsal thought to be that on the very eve of Breitenfeld the men were ordered to practise their manoeuvres.

The Swedish army was also a conscript army, to which all Swedish communities were required to supply a given number of conscripts. This was essential to supply enough men from a small population to match Gustavus's large ambitions, though it was eventually to leave some villages almost entirely devoid of men. It was this army, made up predominantly of peasant recruits, that intervened in the Thirty Years War to safeguard Sweden's interests in the Baltic trade and to protect the coastal territory along what are now the Baltic States. As a Protestant state, Sweden was opposed to the imperialistic ambitions of the Habsburg emperor and his Catholic allies, though this did not stop Catholic France from giving him a substantial five-year subsidy to keep the emperor busy fighting in the east. In 1630, Gustavus landed in northern Germany with an army of perhaps 50,000 men. He could find few Protestant princes willing to support him, except for the Duke of Brandenburg, but when the Imperial army, led by the Austrian commander Johann Tserclaes von Tilly, undertook an invasion of Saxony, the Swedish army moved south to support the Saxon elector, Johann Georg, whose efforts to remain neutral in the war had finally broken down. Tilly's forces began the systematic spoliation of Saxon territory in late August 1631. On 2 September, the elector signed an alliance with Gustavus and three days later their two armies, 24,000 veteran Swedes and 18,000 inexperienced Saxon levies, met up some miles north of the Saxon city of Leipzig, which Tilly had just captured.

The Imperial army moved north from Leipzig and on 7 September (17 September in the Gregorian calendar) drew up on a field of Tilly's choosing near the village of Breitenfeld. The site was mainly flat with shallow undulations, ideal for the Imperial army to deploy the 23,000 infantry in the conventional *tercio* formation (thick squares of pikemen and musketeers, thirty men deep) and also ideal for the 12,000 cavalry under the command of Count Gottfried zu Pappenheim, drawn up on either wing. The Swedes and Saxons arrayed themselves in two independent formations facing the enemy. The Saxons on the left were organized in a thick pyramid of pikemen and musketeers, with no reserve, but supported on each side by horsemen, a deployment similar to the larger Imperial force. The Swedish line was unconventional. Their units were spread out in a long line in brigade formation, with a second line of reserves behind. Each brigade was supported by its own mobile battery of nine or twelve guns with the heavy artillery in front. The lines of musketeers were six deep, the pikemen five deep. On each wing was a mix of cavalry and musketeers, with gaps between the infantry to allow the cavalry room to charge through and to retire when the charge was done. Each time they returned, the musketeers let off the next fusillade, giving the enemy no breathing space. The object was to use the arms in combination, increasing both defensive and offensive power.

It may have been the novelty of the Swedish organization that prompted Tilly to destroy the Saxons first. Beginning in early afternoon, the cavalry on his left under Pappenheim assaulted the Swedish right, while the *tercios* lumbered forward and then turned right towards the Saxons. Tilly hoped to outflank the Swedes on both wings and crush the centre like a nutcracker. Pappenheim immediately discovered the strength of the new Swedish tactics. As he tried to outflank the line, Gustavus stretched it further with the reserves. The Imperial horse found that wherever they went they were met by a wall of musket and artillery fire, interspersed with violent sallies by the Swedish cavalry. On the other wing, however, the Saxons folded up; their cavalry was routed and the pyramid crushed. Johann Georg fled with his battered remnants from the field. What followed was decisive. Tilly ordered his *tercios* to turn and crush the exposed Swedish flank, but as they did so, the Swedish commander there, Field Marshal Gustav Horn, rapidly wheeled his entire force at right angles so that his 4,000 men now faced the 20,000 Imperial troops trying to manoeuvre into position. Firing with all his cannon and muskets, Horn ordered his foot and horse to charge the enemy. The *tercios* were clumsy on the move and were not yet ready to meet an assault; their numbers proved a handicap as they crushed together, unable to use their pikes effectively. Horn brought up reserves as planned from the second line and Gustavus sent reinforcements. The Swedish right had now routed Pappenheim and swung round to seize the Imperial guns, which were then fired on the disordered *tercios*. They fled in panic, and the elderly Tilly, wounded in the fray, joined the flight.

The battle was an overwhelming vindication of the new tactics of the line developed by Gustavus Adolphus. There were 7,600 Imperial dead, 6,000 prisoners and a further 3,000 who surrendered when the Swedes caught up with them at Leipzig. Tilly lost an estimated two-thirds of his entire army. Swedish casualties amounted to 2,100. Emperor Ferdinand was so alarmed when news reached him that he contemplated flight from Vienna to Graz, or even Italy, but the Swedes did not invade his capital, making instead for Bavaria and the Rhineland to rest and replenish supplies. In hostile territory, the Swedes proved less disciplined than their king's instructions suggested, committing regular atrocities against the local population. Gustavus and Tilly did not long survive their memorable duel. Tilly died of tetanus in April 1632 after he had been hit by a cannon ball. Gustavus Adolphus was killed at the Battle of Lützen in November 1632, shot in the shoulder, then in the back, and finally as he lay bloody and covered in mud, shot in the head. His flexible, combined-arms line survived for a while, but like all innovations, it was overtaken by the inevitable evolution of both battle tactics and technology.

39. BATTLE OF NASEBY
14 June 1645

The English Civil War between King Charles I and the forces of the English Parliament was in its third year when Parliament finally approved the creation of what was called the New Model Army, set up in an attempt to revive its flagging military fortunes. In truth there was not much that was new about it in terms of the tactics, technology or organization involved. The innovation was in the name. Instead of three separate Parliamentary armies, none of which could inflict a decisive defeat on royal forces, the New Model Army was given new leaders, a unitary organization and a fresh spirit.

The decision to create a new army arose from the strategic stagnation on the Parliamentary side caused by the division of its forces and the many political and religious arguments that weakened its cause. Charles and his German generals, Prince Rupert and Prince Maurice, were beginning to achieve a military advantage. In December 1644, the cumbersome twenty-five-strong Parliamentary 'Committee of Both Kingdoms', which managed the war effort, agreed to establish a New

Model Army which would unite the three separate armies in the field and create a solid force of 22,000 men (6,600 cavalry, 14,400 foot and 1,000 dragoons, or horse infantry), all to be raised from the Parliamentary counties in the east and south of England. To give the army some professional leadership, a Self-Denying Ordinance was introduced into Parliament, preventing Members of Parliament from also holding army command. The army was formally constituted on 27 January 1645, under the command of two men who had proved themselves able and resourceful officers: Sir Thomas Fairfax became commander-in-chief and Major General Philip Skippon commander of the infantry.

Only after weeks of argument did the existing commanders consent to stand down and allow Fairfax to organize his new command. Extensive supplies and large bodies of men flowed in during the early spring, while Fairfax instituted tough discipline to reduce the number of desertions and to instil in the men a sense of purpose. Executions or beatings were introduced for looting or dereliction of duty, but at the same time more regular pay was instituted for the troops. Even then Parliament only gave Fairfax the right to command on his own behalf in June 1645, shortly before battle was joined; and only on 10 June was the MP Oliver Cromwell, who had managed to win exemption from the Self-Denying Ordinance, made Lieutenant Commander of Horse, in charge of the cavalry. Fairfax promoted men who had proven military worth, and Cromwell, as it turned out, was an inspired choice. With his troop of 900 'Ironsides', well-trained and mounted men, Cromwell was to play a major part in the battle that unfolded in the middle of June.

It was not clear where the first test of the New Model Army would take place. Both the king and Parliament continued to divide their forces to cope with local sieges or military crises, but in late May, confident that there was nothing about this New Model Army that could really threaten the royal forces, Charles and Rupert set out to seek battle. On 31 May, they captured and brutally sacked the Parliamentary city of Leicester and then moved south in force towards Northamptonshire. The royalist army failed to realize that Fairfax had now consolidated his scattered forces and was close by, near the small town of Naseby. The discovery was made on 13 June and the king and his commanders finally decided on a fight. The two armies closed towards each other and the following day drew up in battle order.

There is still much dispute about the exact size of the forces opposed at Naseby. The royal army was somewhere between 9,000 and 12,000, consisting of infantry and two large forces of cavalry; Fairfax had perhaps between 15,000 and 17,000, divided into infantry, two cavalry wings (the left under General Henry Ireton; the right under Cromwell) and a force of 1,000 mounted dragoons under Colonel John Okey. After early morning manoeuvring, the armies faced each other from two low ridges north of Naseby, the Parliamentary army largely concealing itself from view by forming up below the brow of their ridge to hide its size and composition. The foot on both sides carried either long pikes or halberds, 4.5 to 5.5 metres (15 to 18 feet) in length, or heavy matchlock muskets, which a skilled musketeer could fire at the rate of one shot per minute, with mixed effect. Enemy foot soldiers were difficult to break with musket fire, but a cavalry charge could be disrupted as horses and men were hit by random balls. The cavalry on both sides had light armour, pistols and heavy swords. Artillery was present but played, it seems, almost no part in the fight. The New Model Army differed hardly at all from its adversary, though part of it may well have been better trained. What did distinguish it was the shift over the course of 1645 to the idea of merit as the qualification for command.

The exact chronology of the battle differs in the many seventeenth-century accounts. Recent archaeological research suggests that Okey and his dragoons, concealed behind a hedge at right angles to the enemy, moved towards the royal army and opened fire on the right wing of the cavalry. Other accounts have the battle starting when Prince Rupert led his horse in a charge at Ireton on the Parliamentary left, throwing it into disorder until he was fired on by Okey's musketeers. Rupert's charge was pell-mell, taking him and his horsemen off the battlefield as far as Fairfax's baggage train, where skirmishers seem to have held them at bay. The royal infantry then charged the

Parliamentary centre, pushing it back towards the reserves, and the battle stood in the balance until Cromwell led his cavalry in a fierce charge against the horsemen on the royalist left, routing them comprehensively and then wheeling round to attack the royalist foot from the rear. Ireton's men had regrouped to join Cromwell and between them and the Parliamentary infantry, roused to greater efforts by a bare-headed Fairfax at the thick of the fight, the royal army was crushed. Charles wanted to rally his reserves and charge into the mêlée but was restrained from risking almost certain death or capture. The remnants of the royal army fled north, away from the destruction, leaving an estimated 1,000 dead and 4,000 prisoners.

The Parliamentary forces lost fewer than 700 dead, and gained all the king's baggage, artillery and private papers. They also found hundreds of women, chiefly army wives and camp followers; assuming them to be prostitutes of the royal army, a hundred of them were slaughtered and others mutilated in the most savage episode of the day. The impact of Naseby was profound, and the king surrendered within a year. In the 1650s, Cromwell, who had distinguished himself at the battle as a tough and disciplined commander, became Protector of England. The New Model Army continued after the restoration of the monarchy in 1660 in the guise of the Horse and Coldstream Guards.

40. BATTLE OF POLTAVA
28 June 1709

In late June 1709, a large Swedish army led by the ambitious young king Charles XII, which had swept into Russia to enjoy one victory after another, met its match at the hands of a Russian army under the command of the reforming tsar, Peter the Great. The victory went against the expectations of Europe, where the martial skills and courage of the Swedish forces enjoyed a formidable reputation. The Swedes had expected another victory against an enemy they always underrated. Peter, on the other hand, knew that he had to turn his unskilled peasant army into a real fighting force. The explanation for Russian victory lies in Peter's use of mass artillery. Its success marked the opening of an age in which large guns came to dominate the battlefield.

The battle came at the climax of the long conflict known as the Great Northern War. Tsarist Russia was the one remaining obstacle to Swedish domination of a large area of northeastern Europe. The Swedes began a major offensive in 1707, which took them on a long and bloody march across present-day Poland and Belarus, and on into Ukraine. The Russian army refused to stand and face a major engagement and used harassing, guerrilla tactics to exact a persistent toll of Swedish forces. Charles wanted a major engagement because he was confident that in a pitched battle his disciplined troops would overwhelm the Russian masses. In May 1709, his forces arrived at the small town of Poltava in southern Ukraine, 1,600 kilometres (1,000 miles) away from the Swedish homeland. Here they laid siege and waited to see if the Russians would seek battle.

Tsar Peter now moved his large army closer, crossing a river north of Poltava and, on 26 June, setting up a large fortified camp a few miles distant. His engineers began work on a system of fortified redoubts on the approach to the camp. Peter brought with him around 25,000 foot soldiers and 9,000 cavalry, with numerous Cossack irregulars in support. Above all, he had more than 100 pieces of artillery and large supplies of cannon balls, grenades and canisters – deadly projectiles of wood or iron containing scraps of metal, flint, lead shot or nails, capable of killing and maiming many soldiers at once. Russian artillery was reorganized to make it more flexible on the battlefield: cavalry units had their own mounted artillery to support them in action, while regimental commanders of infantry also had control over their own artillery, moving it around the battle to support their troops. Heavier artillery, capable of firing 10-kilogram (20-pound) or 20-kilogram (40-pound) projectiles, was less mobile but could be concentrated to provide devastating long-range fire.

Against this novel field of fire, the Swedes, whose king preferred his men to fight rapid, mobile contests, unburdened by artillery, were armed with just four three-pound guns and a few ammunition wagons.

Battle was not yet inevitable, but having come so far, with dangers all around them, the Swedish leaders could see that they had to inflict a decisive defeat or be worn down piecemeal on the wide Ukrainian plain. Charles and his leading field marshal, Carl Gustav Rehnsköld, decided to move from Poltava under cover of night in four large columns, with the cavalry following, and fall on the Russians before they awoke. The plan was to sweep through the redoubts, with their dangerous guns, and then for the cavalry to destroy the Russian horse on the flank, while the infantry stormed and destroyed the Russian camp. The reality was a tactical disaster. At night the infantry found it difficult to form up in their units; they arrived late in front of the Russian redoubts, and then had to wait for both wings of cavalry, which had lost their way in the dark. A Russian scout spotted them in the murky dawn and the element of surprise was completely lost. Fire began to pour onto the Swedish army. Two soldiers next to the king were killed by a cannon ball. Charles had no alternative now but to order the advance. At 4 a.m., the blue and yellow army began to move.

For the Swedes the situation went from bad to worse. The first two redoubts were stormed and their guns captured, though not spiked. The third redoubt was more sturdily built and had a deep ditch. Repeated efforts to storm it ended in failure and piles of Swedish corpses lay below the makeshift walls. Heavy gunfire cut gory swathes through the Swedish ranks. The Swedish left wing, under command of General Carl Gustav Roos, became stuck in the redoubts while the rest of the Swedish line skirted them and moved towards the Russian camp. As a result, one-third of the Swedish infantry lost contact with the rest. The Russians reoccupied the redoubts that had first been captured and turned the guns round to fire at the rear of Roos's force. The Swedish left was surrounded and worn down. No quarter was given on either side. Roos finally negotiated surrender for himself and the handful of men left, a mere 390 out of the 2,600 men he had set out with.

The rest of the Swedish right moved towards the Russian camp until they realized that the left wing was missing. Rehnsköld called a halt to wait for the remaining cavalry and infantry to reform, hoping that Roos would join them. After a long delay it was evident that one-third of the Swedish army had been lost. The Russians waiting in the camp were puzzled by Swedish inaction, but in the end Tsar Peter ordered them to form up and march out to engage with the enemy. They were sprinkled with holy water as they marched past their monarch, battalion after battalion, with artillery pieces in the gaps between them. Cavalry protected each flank and heavy guns stood behind them, ready to fire their lethal missiles over the Russian ranks. The Swedish infantry now numbered around 4,000 against 22,000 Russians. They were ordered forward into attack as the only method they knew. Russian grapeshot, canisters and balls opened up a terrible fusillade, smothering the battlefield with a smoky fog. The Swedish ranks thinned, but marched on. 'It was like a heavy hail from Heaven,' recalled one of the Swedish survivors; hundreds were mown down or mutilated by the hail. Somehow enough got through to begin to push the Russian tide back on the right of the line, but the Swedish cavalry, crushed behind the foot soldiers at the start of the advance, could not organize their units in time to support their front line. On the left, the weight of fire broke the Swedish line and soldiers began to panic. What had briefly looked like an unlikely Swedish victory now turned into a spectacular rout.

The Swedish commanders swiftly lost control of the battlefield entirely, covered as it was by dense smoke and islands of disorganized resistance. The Russian elite cavalry, under the command of Prince Alexander Menshikov, swept round the faltering Swedish line and attacked it from the rear. The line split apart, the left running in disordered flight, the right increasingly isolated by a press of Russian infantry and horse. Those who were caught in the trap were slaughtered almost to a man, the Russian infantry scenting victory, eager to kill any survivors and loot their weapons and clothes. The battlefield descended into a terrible chaos, but it was the Swedish soldiers who lay dead and dying in heaps, stripped naked, torn apart by the almost 1,500 rounds fired by the Russian guns. The remnants of the Swedish army, grouped around the wounded figure of the king, staggered back to their base camp and the baggage train. Peter did not order a large-scale pursuit, which would have resulted in complete annihilation, but instead ordered a halt in order to celebrate a triumphant victory. The ragged remains of the army were allowed to move away to the south. Charles hoped to reach Ottoman territory, but the Russians caught up with him at the village of Perovolochna. The king managed to cross the river there and make good his escape, but the only senior Swedish commander left, the infantry general Adam Lewenhaupt, after consulting with his men, surrendered to Menshikov on 1 July. Except for 1,300 men, many wounded and sick, who left with the king, all the other Swedes went into captivity. Sweden's army disappeared.

At Poltava the Swedes lost half the army, killed, wounded or captured. The rest went into captivity three days later. The thousands of captured Swedes were kept prisoner and only slowly returned to Sweden, the last thirty-six years after the battle. Swedish power was broken permanently. The Russians lost just 1,345 on the battlefield. Thanks to the devastating effects of the massed artillery, the 'primitive' army of Russia had become a force to be reckoned with. Poltava marked the beginning of the long and painful ascent of the Russian superpower.

41. BATTLE OF SOLFERINO–SAN MARTINO

24 June 1859

For the battle that took place around the northern Italian towns of Solferino and San Martino in June 1859 between the armies of the Austrian Empire and those of France and Sardinia-Piedmont, explanations often centre on innovations – such as the use of railways to bring in reserves, or the development by the French of the rifled artillery gun, which increased range and accuracy remarkably. But the real innovation that arose from this battle was supplied by Henri Dunant, a young Swiss businessman, who arrived in the aftermath of the battle and was shocked by the plight of the thousands of wounded soldiers lying untended on the field. Four years later, Dunant hosted the founding meeting of what became the Red Cross organization, committed to helping the sick and wounded on both sides. This commitment was enshrined in the first Geneva Convention, which was signed by the majority of the states of Europe on 22 August 1864.

The battle that Dunant witnessed was the final confrontation in a war that began on 29 April 1859 when Austrian forces crossed the border between Austrian Italy (the provinces of Lombardy and Venetia) and the independent Kingdom of Sardinia-Piedmont. The conflict was really over the creation of an Italian nation, an aspiration that had been crushed by the Austrians during the revolutions of 1848–49. A decade of military reforms made the army of Vittorio Emmanuele II of Piedmont a more modern and effective force, but it was still not strong enough to confront the vast Austrian army. The Piedmontese prime minister, Count Camillo di Cavour, persuaded the new French emperor, Napoleon III, nephew of the great Napoleon, to give military support to the effort to expel the Austrians. Some of the senior commanders in the French army had fought with Napoleon III's uncle and saw the conflict with Austria as unfinished business. Napoleon agreed with them. The Piedmontese strengthened the frontier with Lombardy, and when they refused an Austrian demand to disarm, war was declared.

The balance strongly favoured the Austrian 2nd Army, commanded by Field Marshal Ferenc Gyulai, which outnumbered the Piedmontese by two to one. But confusion over what strategy to adopt gave the French time to mobilize and to arrive in strength, thanks to the railway, by mid-May. The Austrians were defeated at Montebello, Palestro and a major battle at Magenta, and Gyulai was forced to pull back from the Lombard capital at Milan and concentrate Austrian forces on the 'Quadrilateral' of major fortresses at Peschiera, Verona, Legnago and Mantua. He resigned after his failure to halt the French advance and was replaced by Field Marshal Count Schlick, a veteran of the wars against the first Napoleon. The Austrian emperor, Franz-Joseph, now insisted on assuming overall command himself. The Austrian 1st Army, under Field Marshal Franz von Wimpffen, joined the 2nd, and 119,000 infantry, 9,500 cavalry and 429 guns moved onto a wide plain stretching from Lake Garda to Mantua. The forces were centred on the town of Solferino, protected by its high walls and the ridges and hills of the surrounding area.

After inflicting so many defeats, the French and Piedmontese had been uncertain about Austrian intentions. On 23 June, they could see Austrian activity in front of them as they crossed the River Chiese south of Brescia, and Napoleon III, like Franz-Joseph the overall commander-in-chief, ordered an advance during the night to avoid the scorching sun of the day. On the north wing, 38,600 Piedmontese, including Giuseppe Garibaldi's irregulars, advanced towards the village of San Martino; in the centre and south, 83,000 French infantry and 9,000 French cavalry, supported by 240 of the new rifled cannon, moved towards Solferino and, further south, towards Guidizzolo and the Plain of Medole. At 5 a.m., while many Austrian troops were still breakfasting, the two armies clashed. The battle divided into three. The Piedmontese tried all day to dislodge General Ludwig von Benedek's VIII Corps, who were ensconced on a hill around the village of San Martino. French armies in the centre, led by General Patrice MacMahon and Marshal Baraguay d'Hilliers, pushed into Solferino and its surroundings, while French armies in the south, heavily outnumbered, tried to force the Plain of Medole.

The battle was won in the centre, where determined French attacks, aided by more effective artillery and cavalry (though won in the end at the point of the bayonet), pushed the Austrians out of Solferino by the early afternoon. The Austrian commander ordered a retreat and by 3.30 p.m. the French had occupied the town of

Cavriana, which shortly before had been Franz-Joseph's headquarters. Once the breakthrough was achieved in the centre, the position of Austrian forces on both wings deteriorated. Despite their fierce defence of San Martino, Benedek was forced to withdraw by the early evening to avoid complete encirclement. In the south, the battle was sharper and the Austrian 1st Army fought desperately to hold onto a line across the Plain of Medole. French artillery fire and cavalry drove the Austrians slowly back, and the loss of Solferino released more support for the southern wing. By 4 p.m., the French were threatening Guidizzolo on the far side of the plain. Suddenly the fierce sunshine that had tortured the men of both sides with unendurable thirst gave way to a spectacular storm of rain, hail and thunder. Under the darkening skies, the Austrian 1st and 2nd Armies withdrew across the River Mincio, abandoning permanently, as it turned out, the whole of Lombardy.

The battle was fought at close quarters with bayonets as deadly as any more modern handheld weapon. Losses were high, 17,000 for the French and Piedmontese, 22,000 for the Austrians. It was the wounded from the battle that Dunant saw that evening. He had come to petition Napoleon III personally for help in a business venture in Algeria, but found himself an onlooker to the fighting. He was sickened by the stench of battle and the cries of the wounded, more than a third of whom required amputations. There were few medical facilities and the Austrians had withdrawn many miles away. Dunant immediately began to organize local villagers to supply water and clean linen for the wounded of both sides. On 27 June, he ordered from Brescia, the nearest large city, lemons, camomile, sugar, shirts and tobacco. Men from both sides were helped – 'all brothers', Dunant told his suppliers. The neglect of the wounded and the prisoners affected him so much that he gave up his business (Napoleon had refused to help him anyway) and devoted himself to recruiting Europe-wide support for the idea of formal medical assistance on the field of battle for sick and wounded soldiers. Of all the innovations associated with Solferino, this was the most important and most enduring.

42. BATTLE OF KÖNIGGRÄTZ (SADOWA)

3 July 1866

Few major battles have been affected so decisively by a single new weapon as the confrontation that took place near the small town of Königgrätz in Austrian Bohemia in early July 1866, at the climax of the contest for supremacy in Germany. The weapon in question was the Prussian needle-gun, a breech-loading rifle capable of delivering ten to twelve shots a minute, much faster than the muzzle-loaded guns still used by most of Europe. Its effect was devastating against the standard Austrian tactic of the storm attack. Within minutes, whole battalions were reduced to a fraction of their strength, the ground littered with corpses in gruesome heaps so dense that at the end of the battle Prussian horsemen had to dismount to cross the battlefield.

The needle-gun was the invention of the Prussian gunsmith Johann von Dreyse. Developed from 1836, it was finally adopted by the Prussian Army in 1848 and was standard issue by the 1860s. The paper cartridge was inserted by bolt action, and its paper construction meant that the cartridge case did not have to be unloaded before reloading, increasing the speed of fire. The failure of the Austrian Army to adopt the needle-gun was not based simply on a lack of imagination. It was a far from perfect weapon. Its 600-metre (2,000-feet) range was shorter than conventional muzzle-loaded rifles, and after a few shots the escaping gas from the explosion of the cartridge caused burns, forcing troops to fire the gun from the hip. The needle that pierced the paper cartridge when the trigger was pulled was also prone to break or wear out. The one advantage of the new weapon lay in the rate of fire, which exceeded that of anything else until the first machine guns. But even this advantage might not have been fully exploited had the Austrian army not chosen the massed frontal assault as its principal battlefield tactic.

The long struggle to determine the future of the German area, dominated for centuries by Austria, and organized since 1815 as a loose German Confederation, was always going to be a contest between northern Protestant Prussia and the multi-national, mainly Catholic, Habsburg Empire, with Austria at its heart. German patriots wanted a single German nation, but the Habsburgs were solidly opposed to it because their multi-national dynastic empire would collapse if nationalism succeeded. The Prussian monarchy was not particularly enthusiastic about a German nation either, but it became clear that promoting a unitary state separate from Austria would only be to Prussia's benefit as the most powerful kingdom in Germany. A clash was not inevitable, though likely. In 1866, the Austrian government decided to test the question of who dominated Germany. A Prussian–Italian treaty signed in April, designed to support Italian efforts to remove Austria from its remaining Italian territories, proved enough. The Austrian emperor, Franz-Joseph, ordered mobilization first in Italy and then, in late April, of the Austrian Northern Army under commanding general Ludwig von Benedek. The Austrians prepared to concentrate their forces in the Bohemian plain where they could use their storm tactics effectively.

The Prussian chief-of-staff, General Helmuth von Moltke, divided his army corps into three distinct forces, all of which converged on the Bohemian plain: the 2nd Army was based in Silesia, the 1st Army in Prussian Saxony, and the Army of the Elbe, which included forces from Prussia's German allies, based in Saxony once it was occupied. By the third week of June, the Prussians had invaded Saxony and deployed the last of their armies in a wide 400-kilometre (250-mile) arc around Bohemia. This was a risk, since the larger Austrian forces could defeat the Prussian enemy one army at a time if they moved quickly and boldly. However, when Moltke ordered the invasion on 22 June, a pessimistic Benedek dithered over his strategic options until he finally decided to move initially against the Prussian 1st and Elbe armies and, having defeated them, to turn east again to defeat the

2nd Army marching from Silesia. The first major engagements at Podol and Stralitz were a disaster, the needle-gun mowing down advancing Austrian infantry. Benedek changed his mind and decided to retreat in order to deal with the Silesian threat first. His armies converged on the banks of the River Elbe, in front of the town of Königgrätz, where he hoped they could rest and nurse their early wounds. The long marches in difficult weather with poor logistical support undermined the Austrian forces and Benedek recommended suing for peace. Franz-Joseph would not hear of it, and on 3 July the Austrians faced the prospect at last of a major battle against the encircling Prussians.

The Prussian forces had their own difficulties. Although the battle is often remembered as one decided by the more efficient Prussian railways, the two sides arrived at the same time in June, while the Prussians suffered from problems of supply once the troops had been transported. The 124,000 of the 1st and Elbe armies were outnumbered by the 265,000 Austrian soldiers and 650 cannon, and needed the 100,000-man Silesian Army to march to their help as quickly as they could. On 3 July, Moltke ordered the Prussian 1st Army to attack Benedek's larger force, but the troops were tired and hungry and the early engagements found the Prussian front held down by heavy and accurate Austrian artillery fire. The new Krupp 2.7- and 1.8-kilogram (6- and 4-pound) guns had shorter range and were poorly concentrated; artillery innovation was not, as is sometimes suggested, a key to Prussian victory. The answer was the needle-gun. On the left of the Prussian 1st Army, the commander of the 7th Division occupied the Swiepwald, a small area of forest. The Austrian right decided to clear the forest in order to attack the Prussian flank, but after four hours of attacks by much larger Austrian forces, twenty-eight out of forty-three Austrian battalions had been decimated by needle-gun fire. The forest was in Austrian hands but no flank attack was possible. Instead, Benedek found that a large hole had developed in his front at a critical moment.

The Prussian 2nd Army, commanded by Crown Prince Friedrich-

Wilhelm, had made its way slowly over muddy roads and awkward terrain. It debouched onto the battlefield by mid-day with the whole Austrian flank exposed before it. Helped by the geography of small ridges and tall crops, the Prussians filtered forward under heavy artillery fire. The needle-gun was a lethal advantage and soon the Prussians overwhelmed the defences around the town of Chlum, threatening the whole Austrian army with encirclement and anni-hilation. A fierce Austrian counter-attack to retake Chlum was stopped in its tracks by volleys of fire. The roadway to the small town was quickly nicknamed 'Dead Man's Way'. When the Prussian 1st Corps arrived, the Austrian assault died out. Benedek ordered his one remaining reserve corps to attack the oncoming Prussians, but within half an hour 10,000 of them were dead or wounded by needle-gun fire, half the strength of the corps. Before the Prussians could snap the jaws of their trap shut, Benedek ordered a general retreat across the still-intact Elbe bridges. Not a single infantry unit was any longer combat effective. The Austrians left 22,000 dead or wounded and 9,200 prisoners, against Prussian losses of 9,172, including 1,935 dead. Three weeks later the Austrians sued for an armistice. The future of a German nation was now to be determined by Prussia.

The outcome of the battle was not inevitable, since Prussian strategy had been at risk if any one element of its elongated line had been defeated quickly by the greater Austrian numbers. For most of the day, Moltke was uncertain about whether his side was winning, and there were moments when Prussian commanders thought retreat might be necessary. Prussian artillery performed poorly compared with Austrian. The needle-gun gave the outnumbered Prussian Army the edge it needed. Austrian forces took terrible casualties as they were propelled forward against the Prussian firing lines. The fact that they continued to attack even when experiencing such losses compounded the problem. An older form of battlefield practice, based on élan and aggression, was giving way to a battlefield dominated by fire.

43. BATTLE OF SHANGANI

25 October – 1 November 1893

In 1884, Hiram Stevens Maxim, an American inventor who made his home in London, developed the first recoil-operated machine gun. Unlike existing machine guns, which had to be cranked by hand, the water-cooled Maxim gun used the energy from the recoil to eject a bullet and insert the next. This prevented overheating of the barrel and allowed rates of fire of up to 600 rounds per minute. Orders were placed by the British army in 1888, and a prototype was ready a year later. The first true test of the new gun came in the First Matabele War in present-day Zimbabwe, when a British expeditionary force was sent to impose conditions on the powerful king of the Matabele (Ndebele), Lobengula Khumalo. The five Maxim guns carried by the British column were all that was necessary to destroy a Matabele army more than ten times larger.

There is still much argument about who started the First Matabele War. British settlers and traders had been moving inexorably out from their base in the South African Cape colony in pursuit of farmland, minerals and gold. By the early 1890s, they had established an unstable frontier with the Matabele kingdom, but the urge to exploit its economic potential made further encroachment hard to resist. The pioneer colonists Cecil Rhodes and Dr Leander Starr Jameson brokered an agreement with the Matabele king to allow some mineral exploration in his lands, but Lobengula rightly concluded that the long-term intention was to colonize his kingdom. Rhodes's British South Africa Company occupied Mashonaland to the south of the Matabele, enforcing control with a company police force and paid paramilitary troops. The Mashona were traditionally a source of women and cattle for Matabele raiding parties and it was an argument over just such a raid in July 1893 that finally provoked conflict. A Matabele *impi* (a Zulu term for an armed body of men), intending to punish a Mashona chief, entered the colonists' base at Fort Victoria, killed Mashona servants and ransacked a number of European houses. British insistence that Lobengula suspend raiding into the Company's area of Mashonaland was more than the king's honour would permit. More *impis* were raised and deployed on the roads leading from the king's capital at Bulawayo.

Jameson and Rhodes, without explicit approval from the British authorities in Cape Town, bought horses and recruited troopers for a Company expeditionary force into Matabeleland. The volunteers were each promised a 2,400-hectare (6,000-acre) farm, 20 gold claims and half the expected booty. In early October, two columns left Forts Victoria and Charter and crossed the River Umniati into Matabeleland; they met up at Iron Mine Hill on 14 October, a force of 700 white troopers, 155 auxiliaries from the Cape and 400 Mashona porters and labourers. Between them they had five Maxim guns, a number of other machine guns and two 7-pound (3.1-kilogram) artillery pieces. On 12 October, Lobengula called a council of his chiefs (*izinduna*) and ordered the *impis* to prepare to meet the invading force. He sent a letter to the British High Commissioner in Cape Town claiming that his people were blameless: 'your people must want something from me – when you have made up your mind to do a thing it is not right to blame it on my people.'

The letter was not delivered until 22 October, by which time conflict had become unavoidable. The Company columns had to pass through the Somabula forest that day and a force of Matabele waited in ambush for them, only to find that the enemy column had passed well to the left of where they were waiting. On 24 October, the Company force crossed the River Shangani onto a grassy plateau where they set up their fortified camp. At 3.55 a.m. on the following day, an estimated 5–6,000 Matabele warriors led by the *izinduna* Mjan attacked the camp. They followed a simple tactic of a crescent-shaped frontal assault, some with rifles, most with the short *assegai* stabbing spear. The Maxim guns barked out a hail of fire that stopped the warriors in their tracks. The elite Insukamini regiment charged repeatedly and bravely at the guns and was decimated. Its wounded commander, Manonda, hanged himself on a tree. The battle was over by 8.30 a.m. 'I doubt if any European troops,' wrote one observer, 'could have withstood for such a long time as they did the terrific and well-directed fire brought to bear on them.' And indeed, the Maxim machine gun was to go on to reap an even grimmer harvest of European soldiers only twenty years later.

As the Company column moved towards Bulawayo, on 1 November, a force of 7–8,000 Matabele, including two royal regiments, the Imbezu and Ingubu, attacked the camp set up at Imbembesi. The battle began at mid-day and was over two hours later, with the same result. In the first battle at Shangani only one trooper was killed; in the Imbembesi battle four were killed and seven wounded. The numbers of dead Matabele were evidently very large but have not been recorded. The survivors later admitted that they had not been worried by rifle fire, but could not withstand machine-gun fire that mowed them down like hay. On 4 November, the victorious column entered Bulawayo to find it a smoking ruin. Lobengula had left and so a small force was sent off to bring him back. The Shangani patrol, as it has become known, failed to find him, and on 4 December, the small detachment was ambushed and slaughtered by Matabele warriors still willing to resist the loss of their kingdom. Lobengula died the following January, possibly of smallpox, and one after the other local *izinduna* submitted to South Africa Company representatives. Five Maxim guns had been enough to destroy a powerful African kingdom that tried to block the imperialists' lust for riches.

44. BATTLE OF TSUSHIMA
14–15 May 1905

One of the most decisive naval victories in all history was inflicted by the Imperial Japanese Navy, then barely thirty years old, on the Navy of the Russian Empire, with two centuries of tradition behind it. A large squadron of Russian warships arrived in Japanese waters in May 1905 and was sunk, captured or scattered in a matter of hours, the first time since the start of European imperial expansion that a European navy had been defeated by a non-European power. The Japanese triumph has a number of explanations, but the real key was invention. Japanese shells had much greater destructive power, Japanese range-finders were the most modern available, and the Japanese navy had successfully adopted modern wireless telegraphy.

The battle came about as a result of a war between the Russian and Japanese empires, which began with a Japanese attack in late January 1904 on the Russian Pacific fleet stationed at Port Arthur, a new Russian base on the Chinese coast that threatened Japan's recent expansion into the Korean peninsula. The war went badly for the Russians, whose army and navy had to be deployed at the furthest distance from European Russia against a power whose military potential had been completely underestimated. The Russian fleet remained bottled up in Port Arthur, unable to break the Japanese naval blockade. On 15 October 1904, the Russian tsar finally dispatched a squadron of around 50 ships, including almost all Russia's battleships, old and new, to undertake a 29,000-kilometre (18,000-mile) voyage from the Baltic Sea to the Sea of Japan, where it intended to inflict a comprehensive defeat on the upstart state.

The journey was one of the most remarkable ever undertaken by a naval force. Sailing around the Cape of Good Hope (Britain refused the Russians access to the Suez Canal), the squadron picked up coal and supplies where it could. The journey took seven long months, during which the crews became bored and demoralized, cooped up with poor food and few amenities. In May 1905, the squadron arrived at Cam Ranh Bay on the coast of French Indo-China (now Vietnam), but by this time Port Arthur had fallen to a Japanese attack. The commander of the Russian fleet, Rear Admiral Zinovy Rozhestvensky, a tough, scrupulous disciplinarian, ordered his squadron to break through to Vladivostock, a new port on the Russian Pacific coast, and if possible to avoid an early showdown with the Japanese Navy. Of the possible routes to Vladivostock, the shortest and safest was through the narrow strait of Tsushima that separated Korea from the Japanese archipelago. The ships steamed north, many now in need of repairs, with their keels fouled by the long voyage.

Rozhestvensky commanded a fleet that on paper should have presented the Japanese with a real challenge. The first column consisted of five new battleships, including the commander's flagship, *Suvorov*, and three older battleships; a second column commanded by Rear Admiral Nikolai Nebogatov consisted of four older battleships and three large armoured cruisers. They were supported by another four cruisers, nine destroyers and a number of auxiliary vessels. Against this array, the Japanese naval commander, Admiral Togo Heihachiro, who had done his early training in England, could muster forty ships, including four modern battleships (among them his flagship *Mikasa*), two armoured cruisers and numerous torpedo boats and destroyers for night attacks. However, the numbers disguised important technical differences between the two fleets. The Russian vessels were slower by several knots, a gap made wider by the fouling of the keels; they carried guns of mixed calibres, while the Japanese favoured heavy guns; wireless communication was poor in the Russian fleet, but was modern and effective for the Japanese; the Japanese had also developed a new explosive, *shimosa*, which spread fire quickly, and a new thin-cased shell, *furoshiki*, which burst on impact rather than having to pierce armour plate. Above all, they had the 1903 Barr & Stroud range-finder, which gave accurate firing at 6,000 metres (20,000 feet), against the 4,000 metres (13,000 feet) of the Russian model. Small though these technical differences might seem, they were to prove vital in the coming battle.

On the night of 26–27 May, fortunately shrouded in deep mist, the Russian fleet entered the Korean Strait. To Rozhestvensky's relief, there was no sign of the Japanese. But a scouting cruiser, *Shinano Maru*, spotted a Russian hospital ship with its lights blazing (as was permitted under international law) and immediately telegraphed to Togo that the Russians were coming. Unable to see where the Japanese were, the Russian fleet continued on its way, aware that unseen dangers were all around. On the morning of 27 May, the crew put on clean underwear, a ritual preparation for possible death; while the officers were lunching and drinking champagne, four Japanese battleships and eight cruisers suddenly appeared out of the mist.

Rozhestvensky hesitated. He first thought to order his ships line abreast, but found that the manoeuvre would be too complicated in such a short time, and instead the Russian vessels remained in two columns, unable to bring their great firepower to bear on the Japanese fleet as it was invited to cross the 'T' of the approaching enemy. Togo exposed his force briefly to fire from the leading Russian ships, but once in position across the front of the Russian columns, his modern ships delivered accurate and deadly fire at the leading craft. The Russian warships in the rear could do nothing for fear that their fire might hit Russian vessels in front of them. They could only watch as superior Japanese gunnery and the new shells destroyed the cream of the Russian fleet.

The shells rained down on *Suvorov* with shattering effect. Soon the captain was mortally wounded; surrounded by six dead officers, Rozhestvensky watched as his flagship burned around him. Finally splinters hit him in the heel and head and he wandered around his ship until he was found, weak and losing blood, and transferred to a Russian torpedo boat. By this time the other three modern battleships were suffering the same massive fusillade: one after the other, *Alexander III*, *Oslyabya* and *Borodino* were blasted into wrecks and sank. The Japanese fleet was hardly damaged at all as the Russians continued to shell wildly amidst the fires and explosions on deck. The gap between the two sides in terms of technology and training was cruelly exposed. At the sight of the destruction of all Russia's modern battleships, the remaining Russian warships, now under Nebogatov's command after Rozhestvensky, semi-conscious and delirious, had abandoned his role, tried to break through to Vladivostock. Night fell and the Japanese torpedo boats and destroyers hovered round the Russian warships like jackals circling a dying prey. The battleship *Navarin* was sunk with just one survivor; the battleship *Sisoi Veleki* and the cruisers *Admiral*

Nakhimov and *Vladimir Monomakh* were scuttled by their crew after crippling damage. The following morning, 28 May, Nebogatov found his five surviving ships surrounded by twenty-seven Japanese vessels. He surrendered to Togo, though one Russian captain, unable to swallow the humiliation, took the *Izumrud* through a gap in the Japanese circle and escaped, only to be wrecked on the coast on the way to Vladivostock.

The battle destroyed Russia's navy and established Japan as a major Pacific power. The Japanese lost just 117 killed and 500 wounded, and three small torpedo boats. The Russian squadron lost 4,380 killed and 5,917 captured (including the two commanding admirals); all the battleships were sunk or captured, along with six out of the nine destroyers and four out of eight cruisers. Three cruisers escaped to Manila, where the Americans interned them; only one reached Vladivostock, together with two of the destroyers. One of the cruisers at Manila, *Aurora*, was to play a part twelve years later in the Russian Revolution when its crew joined Lenin's Bolsheviks in storming the Winter Palace in St Petersburg. One of the junior officers in the Japanese fleet was Isoroku Yamamoto (who lost two fingers of his left hand from a Russian shell). He later went on to command the Japanese Imperial Fleet in its devastating attack on the American fleet at Pearl Harbor, where training and technology again combined to bring the Japanese a stunning victory.

45. SIEGE OF EDIRNE

3 November 1912 – 26 March 1913

The siege of the Turkish city of Edirne – the former Ottoman capital – in the winter of 1912–13 was a remarkable victory for the small Bulgarian army against that of its much larger Turkish neighbour. But it is perhaps most memorable as the battle in which bombs were dropped from an aeroplane for the first time. Grenades had been thrown at Turkish soldiers by an Italian pilot in the Libyan War of 1911–12, but not bombs. A Bulgarian airman and engineer, Simeon Petrov, modified grenade shells by adding stabilizing fins and a fuse, creating what came to be known as the 'Chataldzha' bomb. There is some dispute about who first dropped them. The claim is usually given to the Bulgarian observer, Lieutenant Prodan Tarakchiev, flying in an Albatros F-2 aircraft piloted by Radul Milkov, who is said to have dropped bombs on Karaagac station on 16 October 1912 near the besieged city of Edirne. Another account has Major Vasil Zlatarov dropping the bombs from an aircraft piloted by an Italian volunteer, Giovanni Sabelli, on 17 November 1912. Whichever is correct, the Bulgarian air force, with its twenty-three aircraft, launched the long century of aerial bombing that followed.

The air attacks took place during the First Balkan War, in which an alliance of Bulgaria, Greece, Serbia and Montenegro took advantage of the fact that the Turkish Empire was engaged in war with Italy in North Africa. The aim was to expel Turkey from its remaining European territory, which stretched from Constantinople to the Adriatic coast of Albania. The war was launched by Montenegro on 9 October 1912, but the armies of the other three allies joined soon afterwards, rapidly driving the Turkish forces from the frontiers. In four weeks, Bulgaria moved its army of 400,000 a distance of 260 kilometres (160 miles) against collapsing Turkish resistance until it was only 65 kilometres (40 miles) from Constantinople on the fortified Çatalca Line. By 3 November, the city of Edirne (Adrianople) was surrounded by the 2nd Bulgarian Army under General Nikola Ivanov, supported by units of the 2nd Serbian Army led by Field Marshal Stepa Stepanović. There were 154,000 troops surrounding the town, together with 520 guns. Inside the city, one of the most heavily fortified of Turkish settlements, were an estimated 50,000 soldiers commanded by Mehmet Sükrü Pasha, but the flight of Turkish and Muslim refugees had doubled the civilian population to 150,000.

Edirne held a special place in Turkish culture as the former capital of the original Ottoman state and it quickly became the symbol of Turkish resistance to the Balkan League. The press highlighted the plight of the encircled population, short of food and, after the supply was cut off by the Bulgarians in November, short of water, too. The disaster shocked Turkish opinion. One senior officer later recalled that Turkey regarded Bulgaria as a nation 'that did not know about anything except raising pigs', but the Bulgarians proved adept and hardy soldiers and were soon being compared with the Japanese or the Gurkhas – famously tough and effective fighters. Conditions in the city quickly deteriorated as salt and sugar disappeared and rations were limited to bread and cheese. Soldiers had little to eat and became, according to one eyewitness, 'inhumanly emaciated'. On 15 November, the Bulgarian air force initiated another aspect of future air power by dropping leaflets over the city calling on the garrison to 'come and surrender'. It was two days after this that bombs were dropped for the first time on the town, an inauspicious start to the long history of civilian bombing from the air. The bombing was reported in Turkey as an outrage, but in reality it was only a gesture. On 2 December a delegation came from the Bulgarian lines asking Mehmed Sükrü to surrender. 'We have not yet given battle,' he retorted, but three days later a ceasefire was agreed along all fronts.

The pause gave the soldiers and citizens in Edirne no respite, since the Bulgarian and Serbian troops remained in place. The garrison expected food to be sent from Constantinople but nothing came, while 180 trains laden with food and supplies passed along the city rail route to supply the besieging forces. In January 1913, unable to accept the surrender of Edirne in a future peace settlement, a group of young officers staged a government coup and rejected the proposals then under consideration. On 4 February the siege began again, with Bulgarian artillery blasting the centre of the city incessantly. 'Being besieged within a fortress,' wrote Rakim Ertür in his journal during the battle, 'is an experience that resembles none other on earth – neither prison, nor exile.' The hungry population begged and stole food, increasingly anxious about what surrender might mean. By late March, the Bulgarians

A painting by the French artist Louis Philippe Crépin (1772–1851) depicts the action at the Battle of Trafalgar in 1805. The battle demonstrated the extent to which modern naval war could only be fought effectively by wealthy states with developed industries, able to supply and pay for large and well-equipped fleets.

The Battle of Gaugamela is illustrated in this tapestry, based on a painting by the 17th-century French artist, Charles Le Brun (1619–90). Le Brun undertook a series of paintings in the 1660s and 1670s depicting the triumphs of Alexander the Great, as homage to his wealthy patron, King Louis XIV.

One of fifty scenes from the Bayeux Tapestry, woven at Bayeux Cathedral in the late eleventh century on orders from William the Conqueror's brother, Bishop Odo, depicts the Norman soldiers with their cavalry mounts. Hundreds of horses were transported across the English Channel from Normandy, but Duke William had to be sure of victory since there was no way to resupply his knights with mounts if the war became drawn out.

A print showing the Mongol emperor Genghis Khan (c.1162–1227). After uniting all the Mongol tribes under his leadership, Genghis Khan conquered the whole of northern China, ruled by the Jin dynasty, including the siege and conquest of the vast capital city at Zhongdu.

In this nineteenth-century print by an unknown artist of the Battle of Austerlitz on 2 December 1805, Napoleon Bonaparte can be seen on his white horse in the centre of the picture, on top of the Pratzen Plateau, which had been captured from the Austrians during the day.

A nineteenth-century image of the Battle of Volturno in October 1860 shows Garibaldi's red-shirted Italian patriots driving the Neapolitan army to the far side of the aqueduct of Ponte della Valle. The victory brought Italian national unification a decisive step nearer.

Guerrilla leader Fidel Castro drives into the Cuban capital, Havana, following the victory of his irregular forces over the larger and better-armed Cuban army.

King Alfred sits in the shepherd's cottage in Somerset where he is scolded for allowing the cakes to burn while he contemplates his Danish enemy. This illustration by James William Edmund Doyle (1822–92) appeared in the *Chronicle of England* published in 1864.

An early fifteenth-century illuminated manuscript from the *Chroniques* of the French historian Enguerrand de Monstrelet (c.1400–53) shows two armies using the deadly longbow that proved such a decisive weapon at the Battle of Agincourt.

This painting of the defence of Rorke's Drift during the Anglo-Zulu War of 1879 was made a year later by the French artist Alphonse de Neuville (1835–85). The scene shows the blazing hospital building and the evacuation of the ill and wounded. In the background can be seen some of the food bags that were used to build an improvised defensive barrier. When the picture was exhibited in London, 50,000 people paid to see it.

Japanese soldiers guard British and Commonwealth prisoners following the fall of the city of Singapore on 15 February 1942. Around 130,000 surrendered to a Japanese force only half that size.

A nineteenth-century manuscript depicts the Parthians' use of metal plates to protect both rider and horse, and the technique of turning to shoot the arrow over the back of the horse, a tactic to which the Roman infantry found no answer.

This image of the Battle of Crécy fought between the army of the English king, Edward III, and the king of France, Philip VI, on 26 August 1346 appears in the chronicles of the French author Jean Froissart (c.1337–c.1405). The key to the English victory was the longbow, which could be shot faster and further than the French crossbow, visible on the lower left.

This painting of the Battle of Poltava in 1709 by Pierre-Denis Martin was commissioned by Tsar Peter the Great to mark his decisive victory over the Swedish Army of Charles XII. Russian success was brought about by the development of extensive and effective artillery fire.

At the Battle of Königgrätz (Sadowa) on 3 July 1866, the major difference between the Prussian forces, pictured here, and their Austrian opponents was the effective firepower of the new Prussian needle-gun, capable of firing ten to twelve rounds a minute.

This photograph of an early model of the Maxim Automatic Machine Gun was published in 1900. With its water-cooling system, the gun could fire up to 600 rounds a minute, transforming the nature of modern battle.

This Bulgarian reproduction of the F-2 Albatros aircraft was built in 2012 for the centenary of the 1912 fight by Bulgarian aviators over the Turkish lines at Edirne, which dropped the first primitive aerial bombs. The Bulgarian bomb was later adopted by the German army during the First World War.

The Supermarine Spitfire was the iconic aircraft of the Battle of Britain. Armed with eight machine guns, it had great speed and manoeuvrability and became the mainstay of RAF Fighter Command throughout the war.

A mushroom cloud rises from the second atomic bomb dropped on Japan on 9 August 1945. The attack on the Japanese port of Nagasaki was made at the last moment when the main target became obscured by cloud. Around 74,000 died as a result of the attack.

This section of a carved frieze from the Ramesseum Temple at Luxor shows Pharaoh Ramses II deciding how to punish two spies caught from the Hittite army at the Battle of Kadesh. The captives were supposed to supply the Egyptians with false information about their enemy.

This steel engraving of the Trojan horse dates from 1876. Once the wooden horse had been dragged inside the walls of the city, Greek soldiers hiding inside were supposed to have descended at night to open the city gates to the waiting Greek army.

An illustration c.1460 from *Les Grandes Chroniques de France* shows the emperor Charlemagne discovering the dead body of his favourite, Roland, after an ambush by Basque soldiers near the Roncesvalles Pass in August 788. In medieval France the story came to symbolize the virtues of a Christian knight.

A painting by an artist of the sixteenth-century Spanish School shows the soldiers led by Hernán Cortés walled up in the royal palace of Tenochtitlán where they have kidnapped the Aztec king, Moctezuma II (1466–1520). The king was killed by a missile from one of his own warriors as he tried to address them, and Cortés escaped.

A painting of the battlefield of Blenheim by the British artist John Wooton (1682–c.1765), now hanging in the National Army Museum, London, shows the point towards the end of the afternoon when the French cavalry broke in the face of heavy fire from Marlborough's platoons of infantry.

This eighteenth-century engraving is based on a drawing made by a soldier in Major General James Wolfe's army. It shows the British victory in September 1759 over the French on the Plains of Abraham in front of the city of Québec. The successful transfer of troops up the steep cliff face, seen in the foreground, gave Wolfe the advantage of surprise over his French adversary, General Louis-Joseph de Montcalm.

An 1889 lithograph depicts Custer's last stand at the Battle of the Little Big Horn in June 1876. Though a romanticized view of the conflict, the narrow defiles from which the concealed warriors moved to attack the US cavalrymen can be clearly seen in the background.

An eighteenth-century engraving shows the aftermath of the Battle of Lechfeld in 955 when the emperor Otto I defeated a large Magyar army. As the Hungarians retreated they were harried by garrison troops in the nearby cities who butchered the cavalry and caught and hanged the Magyar leaders.

An illustration by William Overend (1851–98) for Cassell's *Illustrated History of England*, published in 1874, shows the British ship *Asia* engaging two Turkish ships during the Battle of Navarino Bay on 20 October 1827. The vessels were only a few metres apart during the bombardment.

A painting entitled *Hancock at Gettysburg*, by the Swedish-American artist Thure de Thulstrup (1848–1930), depicts the charge of Major General George Pickett's Confederate troops on the last day of the Battle of Gettysburg. Major General Winfield Hancock (1824–86) was a corps commander on Cemetery Hill when the Confederate troops charged. They were decimated by Union artillery and rifle fire.

A grim roll-call of the 1st Battalion, Lancashire Fusiliers, taken on the afternoon of 1 July 1916, the first day of the Battle of the Somme, after the unit had attacked Beaumont Hamel during the morning. The battalion had suffered 163 deaths, including 7 officers, plus 323 wounded or missing.

Red Army soldiers fight in the ruins of the Red October Factory in the heart of Stalingrad in January 1943, shortly before the final defeat of the German 6th Army. Both sides displayed an exceptional endurance in harsh conditions and under continuous fire. More than 600,000 soldiers died during the gruelling five-month battle for the city.

A fifteenth-century Turkish miniature shows the Ottoman sultan, Mehmet II, at the siege of Constantinople in 1453. After weeks of fruitless bombardment, the city was taken when a small door in the city walls, the Wooden Circus Gate, was left open by mistake by the defenders.

German troops prepare to fire from the shelter of a long wall in East Prussia during the Battle of Tannenberg, which lasted from 24 to 30 August 1914. Victory over a numerically superior Russian force was only achieved by rapid deployment of German forces at the critical moment.

A painting of the Battle of Midway by the American artist Robert Grant Smith (1914–2001), who became famous for his depictions of naval aviation. Here two Douglas-SBD-3s fly over the Japanese aircraft carrier *Akagi*. Only three bombs on target were required to turn the Japanese flagship into a blazing inferno.

A Royal Navy Sea Harrier jet flies into action during the campaign to recapture the Falkland Islands from Argentine occupation. In the background can be seen the aircraft carrier HMS *Invincible*. The small number of aircraft available represented a narrow margin between victory and defeat.

judged that the garrison was too weak to resist any longer. On 24 March, the troops covered the metal of their uniforms and weapons with tissue to deaden noise and to conceal their gleam, and that night stormed the city. They captured the fortified enclave and the following night captured the fortress in the city centre. Mehmed Sükrü surrendered the following morning. The Bulgarian army allowed three days of looting and violence against the population, no doubt a deliberate echo of the Islamic law that specified this exact length of time for seizing booty. For centuries the victims of Turkish atrocities, Bulgarians could see no reason not to repay their enemy in the same coin.

Edirne was to pass to Bulgarian rule following agreements reached in a peace conference in London, but the Balkan states fell out over their territorial gains and while Bulgaria was under attack from her recent allies, Turkish forces crossed the newly agreed frontier and reoccupied Edirne on 22 July 1913. It has remained in Turkish hands, except for a brief Greek occupation in 1920–22, ever since. One of those who reoccupied the city was a young colonel, Mustafa Kemal, destined to go on to become modern Turkey's first ruler. The 'Chataldzha' bomb also enjoyed a later reputation. The design was passed on by the Bulgarians to the German army and became the prototype for German bombs in the First World War. What began as a modest and militarily insignificant engineering experiment grew, within a generation, into the most destructive weapons yet devised.

46. BATTLE OF CAMBRAI
20–21 November 1917

The tank is one of the most significant inventions in modern war, but it took some time before the primitive and slow contraptions built during the First World War developed into the fast, heavily armoured, battle-winning vehicles of the wars that followed. Combined with battlefield aviation, the tank brought a renewed flexibility and striking power to modern armed forces. The first time the tank-air combination was used was at the Battle of Cambrai on the Western Front in November 1917, when the British attempted to unhinge the apparently impregnable German defences of the Hindenburg Line. It was not an entirely auspicious start, but nonetheless it marked the advent of a new age of war.

The tank was developed through the efforts of a number of ingenious naval and army officers who saw that the stalemate of trench warfare would only be broken by technical or tactical innovation. The British War Office was sceptical when first shown the clumsy tracked vehicle, but with the support of the Minister of Munitions, David Lloyd George, the first forty Mark I tanks were ordered, and by May 1917 they were organized into the Tank Corps under the command of Lieutenant Colonel Hugh Elles. Doctrine for the tanks' use emerged piecemeal, but all those involved in their development recognized that their impact would only be achieved *en masse*.

That was not how the first few tanks were used. The new British commander-in-chief, General Douglas Haig, wanted them to support his massive assault on the Somme, which began in July 1916. A total of forty-nine Mark I tanks were used for the first time on 15 September in small packets, but despite the initial shock caused to the German defenders, the tanks were knocked out by shellfire or disabled by mechanical failure. Haig was sufficiently impressed to order 1,000 more, but it was not until the late summer of 1917, after the failure of the Passchendaele offensive, that they were used in larger numbers. On muddy, cratered ground the tanks had made little progress. They moved at only around 3–5 km/h (2–3 mph) and once immobilized were an easy target for enemy gunners or for German riflemen armed with new armour-piercing bullets. Elles tried to persuade Haig that tanks needed to be used *en masse* and on ground suitable for tracked vehicles. The new Mark IV tank was faster, with better armour, and had a more advanced track design.

At Cambrai, near the River Scheldt in northern France, the ground was sufficiently firm and flat and the sector was held by seven weak German divisions. Elles suggested using the British 3rd Army to mount a major raid towards Cambrai with a large body of tanks supported by aircraft. Haig, desperate for positive news, finally agreed.

A force of 474 Mark IV tanks was assembled in great secrecy on the Cambrai front. They were brought in by rail and concealed in woods and sheds. To be sure of crossing the wide trenches of the Hindenburg Line, each tank carried in front a huge bundle of wood, or fascine, to be dropped into the trench so as to allow the tank across. Elaborate tactics were worked out. Infantry would follow the tanks, and between them they would carve out a gap in the line for British cavalry to move through and capture the German forces from the rear. This bizarre mix of old and new had a symbolic feel to it. Tanks were slow and potentially deadly, but horses were fast and flexible; yet the tank had a military future to it, while the days of the cavalry were numbered. The operation was ready by 19 November 1917, after weeks in which every effort was made to prevent alerting the Germans.

The enemy was thus caught almost completely by surprise when, on the early morning of 20 November, columns of tanks lumbered out of the morning mist, led by Elles himself. All along the line the Germans sent up SOS rockets, adding their bright lights to the flashes of shells bursting from the tanks, and from the British field artillery firing over them at the retreating Germans. One tank would patrol a trench, firing at the soldiers inside, while a second one dropped its fascine into the trench. After it had crossed, this tank patrolled the far side of the trench while the first tank got across. The infantry followed, mopping up the few dazed German defenders. The dense walls of barbed wire were crushed by the tanks, some of which were tasked with rolling the wire into giant balls to clear the ground for the expected cavalry attack. Inside the tanks, the crews of ten struggled with the noise, the fumes, hot shards of metal from shell impacts, and the unbearable heat. A direct hit from a German shell could turn the tank into an inferno in which the men were roasted alive. Overhead the Royal Flying Corps, with 275 fighters, bombers and scouts, harried the small force of 75 German aircraft, many of which were lost in the poor weather as they tried to find the front line. Within hours the tanks had forged a salient 8 kilometres (5 miles) deep and 10 kilometres (6 miles) wide towards the town of Cambrai and had breached the Hindenburg Line, capturing 8,000 men and 123 guns. The scene was set for the first tank victory.

In the end it was not to be. The Germans fought boldly back and were soon reinforced by reserves. Key geographical points proved difficult to capture, particularly the Flesquières Ridge overlooking Cambrai, where a legendary German artillery officer had single-handedly knocked out five tanks before being killed. Tanks broke down or were destroyed by accurate fire. By the end of the day, there were only 195 tanks left, many of these needing mechanical overhaul. Above all, the key lessons of tank warfare had been ignored. The infantry were not quick enough to exploit the breakthrough achieved by the tanks, while the cavalry were held too far back and failed to rush through the gap created by the tanks until it was too late.

In London, news of the day's fighting was greeted with jubilation. But the following day the advance slowed, losses mounted and German reinforcements began to appear. Over the week that followed, German forces reversed the British gains. A few of the remaining tanks, just 38 from the original force, prevented the British salient from being eliminated by a flanking attack – showing what potential the tank still had – but by early December most of the ground gained had been lost. Each side suffered losses of around 45,000 men, and the brave tank crews suffered casualties of 29 per cent of their original number. The battle, despite its eventual failure, marked the arrival of the tank as a battlefield weapon. On the same ground a quarter-century later, the German army demonstrated what it had learned from the lessons of Cambrai.

47. BATTLE OF FRANCE

10 May – 17 June 1940

German victory over British, French, Belgian and Dutch forces in the Battle of France in May and June 1940 has often been seen as the inevitable result of heavy German rearmament in the 1930s compared to the late and insufficient preparation of the Allies. Yet on paper the balance between the two sides was much more even, while a large part of French territory was defended by a solid wall of fortifications, the Maginot Line. It is a commonplace that the attacker has to outnumber the defender by two or three to one to overcome the advantages of prepared defences. In the Battle of France this prescript was overturned. German forces demonstrated that it was battlefield innovation that mattered, not the balance of numbers.

The battle is best remembered for the triumphant display of what was widely called *Blitzkrieg*, or lightning war, although the German armed forces did not use the term themselves at the time. They focused on the first effective use of a combined arms offensive, making the most of modern tracked and armoured vehicles, principally tanks, mobile motorized infantry and battlefield air power – fighters, dive-bombers and medium bombers.

The roots of this lethal combination of striking power lay in the period immediately after the First World War when Germany was disarmed by the Treaty of Versailles. The German Defence Ministry set up a large number of study groups to learn the lessons of the previous conflict. Although they now had no tanks or military aircraft, the German armed forces worked out the effectiveness of enhanced mobility and aerial striking power as a battering ram to pierce the enemy front line and allow the mass of infantry to follow, encircling and annihilating the enemy. This was what they had wanted to do in 1914, but they had lacked the mobility and firepower. After six frantic years of rearmament, by the eve of the attack on 10 May 1940, German forces had mustered 2,439 tanks and 3,369 aircraft.

On paper, the Western Allies still outnumbered the Germans. With the addition of Dutch and Belgian forces, which were attacked at the start of the campaign to clear one of the avenues for the German approach, the Allies could count 4,204 tanks and 4,981 aircraft; they deployed 152 army divisions against the German 135. The difference between the two sides was the way those forces were exploited. Most of the British air forces were defending Britain or posted overseas; French aircraft were spread across metropolitan France protecting industrial zones or defending the French empire in North Africa. The British sent only 250 aircraft to northeastern France opposite the German line of attack, the French only 500. They faced 2,741 German aircraft concentrated in two air fleets to support the armies on the ground. French tanks were spread throughout their army units rather than concentrated in mobile armoured divisions, while some were posted to defend the Maginot Line of fixed fortifications.

Concentration of force was not the only strength of the German campaign. The ten armoured and motorized divisions carried with them mobile anti-aircraft batteries to defend them against enemy air attack. Battlefield anti-aircraft artillery was significant in destroying the slow-flying light bombers of the RAF expeditionary air force. The Germans also had an effective means of radio communication, which meant that army units on the ground could contact the supporting air fleet for immediate assistance from bombers and dive-bombers, whereas the British army had to send requests for help via London, which could take hours. The rate at which German aircraft operated was also critical. German fighters averaged four sorties a day, the French fighters less than one. German tanks were mainly light and underarmed, but the secret of combined arms operations was to bring the mobile infantry, artillery batteries and engineers together in one integrated body, capable of exploiting a breakthrough, where the British, who did have armoured units, concentrated too much on a preponderance of tanks at the expense of infantry and artillery.

The Battle of France was not a conventional battle lasting a day or two with a clear conclusion, but a series of operations that lasted six weeks, with regular large-scale fighting all along the line of German attack. Within five days the Dutch army surrendered; the Belgian army was pushed back rapidly until it met up with units of the British Expeditionary Force as it moved into Belgian territory, but Belgium surrendered on 28 May. German forces moved forward quickly through the Low Countries, but this was not the main axis of attack. Large German mobile forces were concentrated in the region of the Ardennes Forest, north of the Maginot Line. Long considered impassable for modern armies, the Allies neglected the sector. The German plan was to use this area as the launch pad for a heavy armoured thrust at the French line to create panic and allow for the encirclement of much of the Allied front. On 13 May, the tanks of General von Kleist's five armoured divisions rolled out of the forest; there had been long queues of vehicles and the rugged terrain and narrow roads made it difficult to manoeuvre. If the Allies had understood the threat and sent aircraft to bomb the vehicles, the outcome might have been different, but the air forces were too busy opposing the bulk of the German air force further north.

Once out in the open, the armoured divisions poured across the River Meuse, opening up a wide gap in the French front. Within six days German armour, continuously supported by bombers and dive-bombers, had reached the Channel coast at Abbeville, surrounding the British forces, the French 1st Army and the remnants of the Belgian divisions. The British could see that the battle was lost and ordered an evacuation. A total of 338,000 men were shipped to safety from Dunkirk. The German army turned south again and destroyed what remained of French resistance in two weeks, using the same irresistible combination of ground mobility and air power. By 19 June, the forward units had reached the Atlantic coast. Two days earlier, the French had sued for an armistice.

It is worth reflecting that this battle was effectively won in six weeks for the loss of 29,640 German servicemen and 1,200 aircraft. Hitler was one of the many who had served for four years in the First World War, when the German army lost almost two million men and could make no progress in France for most of those four years. His air force adjutant, writing on 29 May, celebrated the 'unheard-of pace' of the campaign and the triumphant combination of tank and bomber; when the armistice was requested, he observed a Hitler 'overwhelmed with emotion' and it is not difficult to see why this common soldier turned generalissimo could scarcely believe his luck. The innovation in operational performance had been there for every power to emulate, but in 1940 only the Germans had learned the lessons of the First World War. Over the next three years, the British, Soviet and American armies and air forces each had to learn the hard way, but by 1945 they were all fighting as the Germans had done in 1940. Innovation could win a battle but it could not win the war.

48. BATTLE OF BRITAIN
July – October 1940

In the late summer of 1940, one of the most important battles of the Second World War was fought out between the British Royal Air Force and the German Luftwaffe in the skies over southeastern England. Since the start of the war in September 1939, the German armed forces had defeated and occupied seven European states – Poland, Norway, Denmark, The Netherlands, Belgium, Luxembourg and France. Britain had sent an army to France to help defend against a German attack, but it was defeated and expelled from continental Europe in late May and early June 1940. German forces occupied northern France and the Low Countries and prepared for the next war of conquest against Britain. The German leader Adolf Hitler, who was also the supreme commander of the German armed forces, planned to invade southern England with Operation Sea Lion, but first he needed his large air forces, stationed in northern France and the Low Countries, to defeat the RAF so that the Channel crossing and the capture of beachheads in Kent and Sussex could be achieved with a reduced threat from the air or from the Royal Navy. Upon the outcome of the air battle depended the future of democratic Europe. A British defeat would mean a German hegemony in Europe; a British success would not defeat Hitler, but it would keep resistance alive. The battle hinged on whether the new technology available to the RAF would work effectively.

The Battle of Britain did not resemble a land battle with a clear shape and a definitive day on which victory was secured. It was a battle of attrition that went on throughout the summer and autumn months. The German aim was to destroy RAF Fighter Command in a few days and then to deploy the large German bomber force to knock out military and economic targets in southern Britain before attempting a landing. The day chosen by the Luftwaffe commander-in-chief, Hermann Göring, for the start of the campaign, codenamed 'Eagle Day', had to be postponed because of poor weather, and the date eventually chosen, 13 August, was less than ideal for flying. Half the force was called back, and in the end the full weight of the German air attack was brought to bear only on 18 August against Fighter Command targets, and particularly the fighter stations of Air Vice Marshal Keith Park's 11 Group in southeast England. For the next two weeks repeated attacks were made on fighter stations but despite persistent bombing only three were closed, and then only for a short time. Every day RAF aircraft took a heavy toll on attacking fighters and bombers. Although German air intelligence regularly reported that the RAF was close to collapse, the Spitfire and Hurricane fighters appeared every day ready to meet the incoming German aircraft.

The Germans never guessed that the secret of the RAF's success that summer lay in a complex network of communication based around the use of radio direction finding (RDF or 'radar'), which had been developed in Britain from 1935. Other countries developed it too, but none applied it so systematically to aerial defence. By 1940, a chain of twenty-one radar stations had been set up around Britain's southern and eastern coastlines for detecting high-flying aircraft, and thirty-six so-called Chain Home Low stations to detect aircraft flying lower than 300 metres (1,000 feet). The information from the stations was fed to a central Fighter Command operations room at Bentley Priory just north of London, where the commander-in-chief of Fighter Command, Air Chief Marshal Sir Hugh Dowding, had his head-quarters. It was sent on to the Fighter Group headquarters and from there to individual sector stations. Information had to be transferred in a matter of minutes to give fighters time to scramble into the air to intercept, and it relied on a strategic set of telephone cables, laid by the General Post Office, that held the whole communications struc-ture together. The system did not always work perfectly, but it ensured that the RAF could use its fighters sparingly. They would be in the right place rather than flying long patrols with no knowledge of enemy movements. The Luftwaffe assumed that RAF fighters were tied inflex-ibly to the area around their bases, and never realized that the presence of British aircraft was achieved through a vital scientific breakthrough. Without the system of central control and early warning, Germany's air fleets might well have inflicted irreparable damage.

The German side consistently exaggerated the damage being done to the RAF. By September, Fighter Command, with over 700 aircraft, had more fighters operationally available than it had had when the battle started, and there were never fewer than 1,400 pilots on hand. The Luftwaffe suffered from poor supply from German factories of aircraft and bombs and a slow, if thorough, training system. In the last weeks of combat the German fighter force was down to 700–800 operational pilots and 600 aircraft. The combination of radar, an effective communication system and a regular resupply of RAF planes and pilots ensured that the German side could not win air superiority over southeast England, even though the RAF had its own weaknesses in the quality of fighter armament and the rigid flying pattern initially adopted by fighter units.

On 7 September, the Luftwaffe switched the weight of attack to London in preparation for Operation Sea Lion, but lost so many aircraft over the week that followed that daylight bombing had to be abandoned. On 15 September, now celebrated as Battle of Britain Day, one-quarter of the Luftwaffe's forces were shot down or damaged. This was a level of loss no force could sustain and 15 September, the day Hitler had originally planned to invade, marked the end of the major daylight air battles, and the end of the invasion threat to Britain. On 17 September, Hitler postponed Sea Lion indefinitely. During October, the German fighter force undertook regular hit-and-run raids to lure the RAF into combat, but they petered out by the end of the month. Over the course of the battle from July until the end of October, the Luftwaffe lost 1,733 planes, RAF Fighter Command 915. Radar became one of the most important technical developments of the Second World War, a classic example of how a technical lead, even a temporary one, can transform the face of battle. Radar was also used in the anti-submarine campaign and in all the air battles of the war, and laid the foundation for today's electronic battlefield.

49. PEARL HARBOR
7 December 1941

In 1921, Brigadier General Billy Mitchell of the United States Air Service conducted tests to demonstrate his contention that modern warships were highly vulnerable to air attack. The captured German battleship *Ostfriesland* suffered severe damage during the exercise and Mitchell claimed that his point was proved. The navy took offence and Mitchell was court-martialled in 1925 for going too far in his criticism of service short-sightedness. A little over twenty years later, the pride of the United States Pacific Fleet was struck in harbour by Japanese torpedo and fighter bombers attacking in waves. The raid on Pearl Harbor was not the first to knock out warships from the air, but it was by far the most damaging and it confirmed Mitchell's argument that sea power was no longer viable if unsupported by air.

The Japanese navy was among the first to develop aircraft carriers and high-performance naval dive-bombers and torpedo-bombers. Geography dictated the necessity of protecting the ocean surrounding Japan's empire, while power could only be projected further south and east by using ships and aircraft together. The prospect of a Pacific theatre of war came closer in the early 1940s as America tightened embargoes on scrap metal and oil in an attempt to pressure Japan into ending its drive into China and threatening French Indo-China. The Japanese navy needed oil and the rich pickings of Southeast Asia beckoned. The government in Tokyo hoped to negotiate an end to the embargo; the United States was determined to make no concessions unless Japan agreed to end its aggression. In October 1941, the new prime minister, General Hideki Tojo, finally set a deadline for talks. If America would not negotiate, then war would follow.

Under its supreme commander Admiral Isoroku Yamamoto, the Japanese navy planned a daring operation to cripple the US Pacific Fleet anchored at Pearl Harbor, the main base on the Hawaiian island of Oahu. A pre-emptive strike, it was hoped, would make the Americans accept negotiation more readily. By 22 November, a carrier fleet comprising six carriers, two battleships and a number of smaller vessels had gathered in readiness for possible war in the Japanese Kurile Islands, under the command of Vice Admiral Nagumo Chuichi. The naval pilots were the elite of the service, subject to long hours of training in cross-ocean flight, dive-bombing and torpedo attacks. The force carried around 600 pilots and 460 aircraft, enough to do serious damage. On 1 December, the government accepted that further talks were fruitless. Nagumo was instructed to strike on the morning of 8 December (7 December Honolulu time).

Yamamoto knew that this was a risky operation and the Japanese navy prepared for opposition or accident. Yet everything went according to plan. The weather in the northern Pacific concealed their approach. The American military did not anticipate an attack and aircraft were sent south to other American islands, or to reinforce the Philippines where an attack was expected. Hawaii was on high alert for possible sabotage, but as a result, the anti-aircraft batteries were not fully manned and the level of alert for air attack was low. The American intelligence agencies could read Japanese diplomatic traffic but failed to alert Hawaii to what was happening, even when intercepts revealed instructions to the Japanese consul to provide a grid map covering the port and its shipping. The message indicating that a state of war would exist from 7 December (Washington time) was not decrypted in time to give any reasonable warning. When one of the few radar stations detected the incoming Japanese carrier planes, no action was taken because a group of B-17 bombers was expected that morning.

When the first wave of Japanese aircraft arrived over the island at 7.49 a.m., the forces of Rear Admiral Husband E. Kimmel and Lieutenant General Walter Short were taken completely by surprise. Pilots saw the clouds part obligingly and the whole island was laid out clearly before them. The 173 attacking aircraft destroyed or damaged all but 47 of the 394 American planes on the island and inflicted heavy damage on the port area. The second wave at 8.50 was made up entirely of bombers and dive-bombers aiming for the main warships. By 9.45, the battle was over for the loss of only twenty-nine Japanese aircraft. Nagumo abandoned the third wave of attack against repair and oil installations for reasons which have never been clear. Six American battleships were sunk and two damaged, including *Arizona*, *Oklahoma* and *West Virginia*; a further ten smaller vessels were disabled. A total of 2,403 civilians and servicemen were killed and 1,178 injured. Mitchell's ghost had returned with a vengeance.

In Japan the news was greeted with delight. The radio played 'The Battleship March' in between special announcements. 'The whole nation bubbled over,' one Japanese sailor remembered, 'excited and inspired.' The parting of the clouds over Oahu was taken as a divine omen. In Washington, the Japanese attack united American opinion. President Roosevelt announced the declaration of war on 8 December with the famous words, 'a date which will live in infamy'. The US navy had learned its lesson. The Japanese battle fleet was reduced slowly over four years to a mere shell, hammered into the sea by attacking waves of naval dive-bombers and torpedoes. Combined air-sea co-operation became standard practice in all the world's navies, a commitment whose roots reach back to the two destructive hours at Pearl Harbor in December 1941 rather than the wreck of the *Ostfriesland*.

50. BATTLE OF THE ATLANTIC

March – May 1943

What Winston Churchill called the 'Battle of the Atlantic' was a major struggle waged by the Royal Navy, abetted by the Canadian and US navies, against the submarine arm of the German *Reichsmarine* for control of the trans-oceanic shipping lanes. The German plan was to sink enough merchant shipping to blockade Britain and undermine any attempt to invade mainland Europe; the Allied strategy was to break the stranglehold of the U-boats and so maintain the flow of supplies, resources and troops to Britain. The course of the battle was determined not only by the naval vessels assigned to the convoy operations, but by the introduction of very long-range aircraft, advanced radar equipment and a scientific system for cracking German naval codes. The breakthrough for the Allies came at the last moment in spring 1943, in time to avoid a growing crisis.

In the course of 1942 German submarines sank 7.8 million tons of shipping – 1,662 ships in all. They hunted the convoys and single vessels in 'wolfpacks' of anything up to thirty or forty vessels. A lucky convoy might avoid contact altogether, and many did so, but the real danger to the Allies was an attrition rate so high that shipping lost could not be replaced in time. This meant finding an active way to inflict losses on the submarines. By 1942, many innovations had been introduced: large, armed escorts protected the merchantmen and hunted for submarines; improved air-to-surface radar helped Allied aircraft to locate submarines more accurately; a large spotlight (the Leigh Light) was introduced so that submarines that surfaced at night could be illuminated for attack. Better anti-submarine projectiles were developed, including the Hedgehog, which fired twenty-five small bombs fitted with contact fuses, so that an explosion would indicate clearly a submarine hit. The German submarine arm, commanded by Admiral Karl Dönitz, reacted to these changes, but the main effect was to push the wolfpacks to the so-called Atlantic Gap in the central part of the ocean, between Greenland and the Azores, where long-range aircraft could not yet reach. By late 1941, the German *B-Dienst* serving naval intelligence had cracked Anglo-American codes and could track convoys, while in February 1942, after a long period in which the German encrypted Enigma messages could be decoded and read (known in Britain as Ultra intelligence), the German navy changed its Triton cypher and kept the Allies in the dark until December 1942, when German naval traffic could be read again (with a brief pause in March 1943), and the submarine packs tracked.

The battle was poised by the end of 1942. Submarine losses were at last starting to mount. Only three had been sunk in the Atlantic between January and June, but between July and December the total was thirty-two. Allied shipping losses were high in 1942 and the morale of merchant seamen, thousands of whom lost their lives in the cold and remote seas of the mid-ocean, was low. The cost of building new ships challenged even the wealthy economy of the United States. But over the first months of 1943, the balance began to tilt towards the Allies, thanks not only to the painstaking work of directing convoys onto safer routes, and the growing expertise of the aircraft and escort vessels hunting the enemy, but also to a number of vital technical changes in the Allied force that came together all at once, and at the moment of greatest crisis.

The first innovation was a new radar set, ASV-III, using the newly discovered cavity magnetron that permitted much more accurate sets based on narrow centimetric wavelengths. The Germans had been able to block the ASV-I and ASV-II sets that used long radar waves, but they had nothing to stop the new sets. The new radar could even detect a periscope in calm seas, transforming the capacity of aircraft to detect submarines.

The second change was the advent of very long-range aircraft, principally the B-24 Liberator bomber, designed to close the Atlantic Gap and give air cover for the whole convoy voyage. This was something the Royal Navy had wanted for a long time but they had been frustrated not by the enemy but by the resistance of the US navy chief-of-staff, Admiral Ernest King, and the commander-in-chief of RAF Bomber Command, Air Chief Marshal Arthur Harris, neither of whom had been willing to divert long-range aircraft from other operations. But this change came only after a fierce battle between submarines, ships and aircraft in the middle of March 1943 that signalled the peak of the Battle of the Atlantic.

The battle was fought against thirty-eight submarines, organized in three wolfpacks, *Raubgraf*, *Stürmer* and *Dränger*, in the heart of the Atlantic Gap. Intercepted signals warned the Germans that two large convoys, SC122 and HX229, were on their way, a total of ninety-one vessels. The weather was appalling, with squalls of snow and hail, fog, and heavy grey seas. Contact was made with the convoys when U-653 sighted the ships of HX229 and alerted the rest of the packs. Radar was less useful with the high swell of the waves and the submarines pressed home their attacks, sinking a total of twenty-one ships of 141,000 tons. Only one submarine was lost, sunk by a B-17 'Flying Fortress' on duty from the Hebrides Islands. But during the battle, two B-24s were used for the first time over the Gap; neither scored a kill, but their presence caused the submarines to be more cautious. The British commander of the Western Approaches in the eastern Atlantic, Admiral Sir Max Horton, sensed that, despite the high losses, the balance of technology was swinging the Allies' way. Rather than urging greater caution, Horton insisted that the next convoys sail into the waiting jaws of the wolfpacks, where long-range aircraft and escorts armed with centimetric radar would seek out and fight the submarines.

This was risky and convoy sinkings continued, but at only half the losses experienced in March. More significant, the losses of submarines escalated. Between March and May 1943, fifty-six submarines were sunk, with thirty-three in May alone, one submarine for every merchantman sunk. In mid-May, convoy SC130 with thirty-seven merchant vessels set out across the gap. Supported by a large naval escort and very long-range Liberators, the waiting submarines were decimated, losing six of their number but sinking not a single ship. Dönitz, whose son died on one of the submarines in this battle, bowed to reality. On 24 May, he withdrew his submarines from the Atlantic so that they could be refitted and he could assess the new Allied tactics and technology, but their battle was all but over. It took time for the Allies to realize what had happened, but by June, when only four ships were sunk for the loss of twelve submarines in all waters, it was clear that the battle had been won. The submarines never posed a serious threat again.

51. HIROSHIMA AND NAGASAKI
6 and 9 August 1945

The dropping of the atomic bombs on the Japanese cities of Hiroshima and Nagasaki did not, strictly speaking, constitute a battle. Nevertheless, the two air operations have been seen ever since as the decisive blow in ending the total war that began with the Japanese attack on the American Pacific Fleet at Pearl Harbor four years earlier. The two bombs represent the culmination of thousands of years in which military forces have vied for the weapon that would give them a permanent advantage. Here was an innovation that both simplified and complicated the history of war: simplified because it reduced operations of huge destructive power to one bomb and one aeroplane; complicated because it put into the hands of modern soldiers and politicians a weapon that could quite literally destroy the globe.

The story of the atomic attacks comes together from two different directions. The first came from Britain in 1940, where scientists began researching the possibility of creating a weapon using what was then known about atomic physics. Much of the key research had been done by German émigré scientists who contributed to the development of the world's first atomic weapons, initially in Britain, then from 1942 onwards in the United States. The programme – codenamed the Manhattan Project – cost more than $2 billion and took three years of work, which chiefly involved finding industrial ways of producing the fissile material. The Germans and Japanese worked on nuclear projects, too, but lacked the resources to make them a top priority. The Anglo-American allies worried all the time that they might be beaten to the nuclear draw, and so gave it high priority. On 16 July 1945, the new weapon was ready for testing at Alamogordo in the New Mexico Desert. In the early morning the test was carried out with complete success. It was, wrote one eyewitness, 'as if somebody had turned the sun on with a switch'.

The second direction came from the war with Japan. The bomb came too late for it to be used on targets in Germany (whose leaders had surrendered on 7 May), but it seemed the ideal weapon to end Japanese resistance, save American lives and bring the conflict to a swift conclusion. The American Air Force had secured bases in the Marianas, to the southeast of the Japanese home islands, which now lay within range of the new American super-bomber, the Boeing B-29. The bomber had destroyed miles of Japan's urban areas using incendiary bombing. Neither this nor the stranglehold on Japanese trade had provoked surrender, though Japanese politicians and soldiers were trying to find a way to persuade the hard-liners to give up. President Truman, who had succeeded Roosevelt in April 1945, gave equivocal approval for an atomic operation, and the US 21st Bomber Command was told to go ahead.

The operation hinged on where to bomb. A small handwritten note has survived in papers belonging to the American air force commander-in-chief, Henry 'Hap' Arnold, with 'Atomic Bomb Cities' underlined at the top. There were five cities on the list – Hiroshima, Nagasaki, Niigata, Kokura and Kyoto. These had not been bombed for a number of reasons, but one was to save a target in case atomic weapons became available. Kyoto was ruled out because it was the historic home of the imperial family. Arnold ticked Hiroshima, Kokura and Nagasaki, an almost casual selection that doomed whole cities to a form of destruction no-one could yet imagine. On the morning of 6 August 1945, the B-29 *Enola Gay* set out for Hiroshima carrying a 4,000-kilogram (9,000-pound) uranium bomb, nicknamed 'Little Boy'. The bomb worked as planned, wrecking 13 square kilometres (5 square miles) of the city and killing 80,000 people in an instant. Another estimated 40,000 died from radiation effects, making this the worst bombing raid of the war. Three days later, a 4,600-kilogram (10,000-pound) plutonium bomb known as 'Fat Man' was flown to Kokura only to find it covered by cloud; Nagasaki was the secondary target. Around 74,000 of the population died. Eyewitnesses watched as a terrified stream of injured refugees fled from the bombings, their skin hanging in folds, lymph leaking from their flesh, their bodies caked in sores. The operations were one-sided: the triumph of military science against a defenceless civilian population rather than the armed forces of the enemy.

The effect of the second bomb was to spur Emperor Hirohito into finding a way to surrender without losing his throne and without dishonouring Japan entirely. Historians are divided over whether the atomic attacks really did cause the surrender. The Soviet armed forces began their invasion of Japanese-occupied Manchuria on 8–9 August and overwhelmed the Japanese Kwantung Army in a matter of days, killing 80,000 soldiers. The last thing the Japanese leaders wanted was to be occupied by the Soviet Union and this may well have been the key factor in deciding on surrender. Army fanatics tried to stage a coup by storming the imperial enclosure, but they were overcome and on 15 August 1945, Hirohito broadcast to the Japanese nation that the war would have to end. A formal surrender came on 2 September in Tokyo Bay on board the American battleship USS *Missouri*.

The two bombs opened the nuclear age. By the 1960s, the twin superpowers, the United States and the Soviet Union, had the means to obliterate each other's cities. An American strike was designed to kill 80 million Russians. Mutual Assured Destruction – MAD, which it surely was – kept a precarious peace, and nuclear weaponry has not been deployed in war since 1945. Since these weapons have never been used, it is difficult to describe what kind of military revolution they ushered in. Conventional warfare, using more and more sophisticated weapons but of lower lethality than nuclear arms, has continued unabated. What the bombs did do was to spark an immediate debate about the morality and legality of using them. The American secretary of war, Henry Stimson, described the choice as 'the least abhorrent', compared with the costs of invading Japan or starving her population. In moral terms, however, the atomic attacks returned the world to the military values of much earlier battles in world history, when cities were sacked and burnt to the ground and their inhabitants slaughtered without distinction. Modern though the technology might be, the atomic attacks fit seamlessly into millennia of savage battles lost or won on the back of invention.

52. OPERATION DESERT STORM
17 January – 28 February 1991

The brief campaign in which the American-led Coalition compelled the Iraqi army of Saddam Hussein to abandon its occupation of Kuwait was the first test of a whole generation of modern weaponry. The outcome of the final 100-hour battle was made possible by the significant technical margin between the two sides. Nevertheless, as with all innovations, victory also depended on the way in which the forces using them were deployed operationally on the battlefield. Here there also existed a decisive contrast between the two sides.

The technical gap between the Iraqi and Coalition forces was not the result of simple asymmetric warfare. Iraq had fought a long war against Iran in the 1980s; its army had plenty of battle experience and the Iraqi forces possessed an impressive array of modern weaponry. The army had an estimated 4,200 tanks and 3,100 artillery pieces; the air force had around 700 aircraft and helicopters, while Iraq was shielded by a modern air-defence system, including radar and SAM missiles and anti-aircraft artillery. It was perhaps because of the scale of his forces and the relative modernity of his weaponry that Saddam risked an assault on his tiny oil-rich neighbour, launched by 2,000 tanks and 100,000 troops on 2 August 1990. Invasion of Kuwait was followed by a build-up of forces along the Saudi Arabian border. In the West, fears began to spread at the prospect that Iraq might control one-half of the world's known oil reserves.

The Saudi appeal to the United States for protection against a possible Iraqi attack coincided with a United Nations resolution calling on Saddam to withdraw unconditionally from Kuwait. The American commander, General Norman Schwarzkopf, established a vast military camp on Saudi soil to set up a defensive line. Desert Shield, as it was called, was composed of units from thirty-four countries in the United Nations, though the largest contribution next to the American was British. Saddam rejected the call for withdrawal, hopeful that the Coalition might fall apart, or lack the public approval to wage actual war. On 29 November 1990, the United Nations issued Resolution 678 setting a final deadline for withdrawal of 15 January 1991. Schwarzkopf moved from defensive to offensive posture and 700,000 Coalition forces arrived in Saudi Arabia and the Persian Gulf.

Schwarzkopf had at his disposal a cluster of new weapons, much of which had not yet seen combat. In almost all cases, they represented an important step beyond the modern weaponry available to Saddam. They included the M1A1 Abrams tank, the M2 and M3 Bradley fighting vehicles, the Apache and Black Hawk helicopters, the Patriot air defence missile system, the F-117 Nighthawk flying wing (capable of avoiding radar), satellite mapping, AWACS, and – among the most important innovations – night goggles and thermal imaging. Thermal imaging and weapons locator systems meant that in many cases the Americans could strike at tanks and artillery before the enemy even knew that they were under attack. The Iraqi air-defence system could be destroyed using the F-4 Wild Weasel with its high-speed anti-radiation missiles that locked on to enemy radar. The new range of weaponry rendered Iraq's sizeable arsenal all but obsolete and showed the extent to which Iraqi intelligence had failed to appreciate that fighting the Coalition would not be the same as fighting Iran.

The Coalition victory was certainly not a formality, but the new weaponry was tied to an operational plan that also out-thought the Iraqis. Imitating the German Afrika Korps commander, Erwin Rommel, Schwarzkopf planned a frontal assault on Kuwait City to pin down Iraqi forces, while two army corps positioned further west along the Saudi–Iraqi frontier would swing round behind them and cut off their retreat. While the final preparations were in progress, the Coalition air forces began a four-week campaign on 17 January to knock out key military and war-economic targets. A total of 110,000 sorties were flown and 46 aircraft lost, though not one from air-to-air combat. Most Iraqi aircraft flew to Iran while 146 were destroyed on the ground or in the air. The air campaign, Operation Instant Thunder, claimed 1,300 enemy tanks, 1,100 guns and 850 armoured personnel carriers, but the difficulty of identifying targets in urban areas, with a technology still in its teething stage, resulted in the death of more than 3,000 civilians. As the air campaign drew to a close the air forces prepared to support the ground war. The movement of 200,000 troops to the western zone had been kept secret, itself a remarkable achievement, and despite the torture of the few Coalition personnel that had fallen into Iraqi hands. On 24 February, the ground war began, as 575,000 troops, 3,700 tanks and 1,500 guns moved forward against a much-depleted Iraqi force.

The technical edge supplied by the Coalition's weaponry devastated the Iraqi defenders, but the speed and scale of success also depended on the operational plan. The two army corps designed to swing round and outflank the Iraqi line moved forward remorselessly, demolishing any resistance in their path. Within hours, 13th Corps had reached the Euphrates Valley and could cut off the Iraqi forces stationed in and around Kuwait. The 7th US Army Corps was slower, hampered by smoke and dust, but it, too, moved irresistibly, opening up space for the British First Armoured Division to swing into place to the north of Kuwait City. The assault on the city was so rapid that the chief problem was coping with the thousands of Iraqi soldiers who surrendered. Iraqi resistance all but evaporated save for a few units of the elite Republican Guard. They fled down the road to the southern Iraqi city of Basra, but they were sitting targets. Two thousand vehicles were destroyed from the air in what came to be called the 'Highway of Death'. At Medina Ridge north of Kuwait, one of the toughest tank engagements of the battle took place, but only one Coalition soldier was killed. The gap in fighting power between the two sides proved unbridgeable.

On 28 February, with Kuwait clear of Iraqi forces and the Iraqi defensive line destroyed, the Coalition announced a ceasefire. On 3 March, in a tent at the Safwan airfield, just inside the Iraqi border, Schwarzkopf dictated the terms of the armistice to Iraqi representatives. The battle was a disaster for the large Iraqi army. Only 7 of its 43 army divisions remained operational, while 3,800 tanks, 1,450 armoured personnel carriers and 2,900 artillery pieces had been destroyed. The best estimate is that 25,000 Iraqi soldiers were killed while 85,000 became prisoners of war. Coalition forces lost 240 dead in combat, 235 killed in accidents and 785 wounded. The battle had provided the opportunity to test weaponry that was state-of-the-art but still in development. When Iraq was invaded twelve years later in the Second Gulf War, the new battlefield bristled with electronic, laser and information technology equipment to which Saddam still had no answer.

CHAPTER 4
DECEPTION

Deception is as old as battle itself. Perhaps the most important force magnifier is the ability to deceive the enemy of your intentions, the size of the force, even your whereabouts. In the first recorded battle, at Kadesh in 1285 BCE, the Hittite king managed to conceal his entire army before unleashing it on the unsuspecting Egyptians. The story of the mythical battle for Troy is centred on a clever ruse. Indeed, so universal are the many different forms of deception and surprise that it seems remarkable there should be any battles fought at all on transparent terms, with both armies in full view of each other, ready for combat.

Deception takes a wide variety of forms, though its intention – to throw the enemy off-guard and secure a battlefield advantage – has remained reasonably constant. There are large-scale strategic deceptions in which the true destination of an army (less commonly a navy) is masked in order to present the enemy with a sudden and unexpected menace. Marlborough's rapid march to the Danube before the Battle of Blenheim is a well-known example; so too Washington's success in masking his destination before Yorktown. Arguably the most significant was the deception practised for the Normandy invasion in June 1944, when it was imperative that the German army should have no clear forewarning of the invasion area. The deception operation, codenamed 'Fortitude', was on an enormous scale and involved the most sophisticated of deception measures; it made possible a successful lodgement in France in unpredictable military circumstances.

These examples constitute what might be called 'grand deception'. In most other cases, deception operated at a more mundane level, though with effects just as significant. Spreading rumours and misinformation to confuse the enemy or to stimulate overconfidence or fear is a stratagem that goes back millennia. The outcome of the Battle of Carrhae depended on a double agent working for the Parthians who lured the Roman army into a trap. Before the Battle of Hohenfriedberg, Frederick II had sent infiltrators into the enemy area to spread the rumour that he and a scattered army were retreating, while in fact he was concentrating his army for another deception, an arduous night march to catch the enemy army at dawn before it could organize a defence. The use of 'deserters' who arrive in an enemy camp with misleading news from the other side was commonplace, and perhaps explains Stalin's reluctance on the eve of the Barbarossa invasion to believe the news of an imminent attack brought to Soviet lines by German deserters who claimed to be communists.

Deception can also take the form of simple concealment or surprise, dictated by geography as much as by strategic planning. The use of ambush, or the exploitation of a topographical feature regarded by the enemy as a secure barrier, has been commonplace. Spartacus and his band of runaway slaves climbed down the sheer side of Mount Vesuvius against all expectations, just as General Wolfe's men climbed up the cliff face to the Plains of Abraham to surprise the French. Shrewd use of cover by Wellington at Waterloo gave Napoleon a misleading view of British strengths and disposition, while a ravine or narrow valley was an ideal site to conceal an ambush against an unwary or overconfident enemy, of which there are many examples.

The only way to prevent the effect of deception in battle was to have excellent intelligence on the enemy and his intentions. This is a feature that has varied widely over time. In a great many battles, such intelligence was impossible to procure, or was carelessly neglected. Right at the start of the historical record of battles, at Kadesh, Pharaoh

Ramses II captured two enemy scouts and tortured them into revealing information, though too late to prevent a surprise attack by the Hittite king. Scouting parties were commonly sent out to find enemy soldiers who could then be compelled to reveal the whereabouts or plans of the enemy, if they knew them. But these could also be planted to supply misinformation. For a commander it was difficult to judge the extent to which intelligence was to be trusted. Deception depended on creating this sense of uncertainty so that battle could be joined with a psychological advantage to the attacker. It could not guarantee victory, but time and again it has balanced out uneven odds or tipped the scales or, as at Troy, quite literally opened the gates to victory.

53. THE FALL OF TROY
c.1200 BCE

The most famous deception operation in all history is the wooden horse of Troy. After laying siege to the city for ten years, so the story goes, the Myceneans (Greeks in the modern account) finally packed up and rowed away, leaving a giant wooden horse as a tantalizing gift for the Trojan people. After much argument about its purpose, the Trojans hauled the horse into the city and spent the night carousing in victory. A handful of enemy soldiers hidden inside the horse climbed out, overwhelmed the guards at the gate and let in their comrades who had rowed back unseen to the shore a few miles away. Troy was burnt to the ground, its people butchered and its treasures stolen.

How much of this story could be true? It has come down to us as myth, allegedly written by the blind Greek poet Homer in the eighth century BCE, hundreds of years after the events occurred, if they occurred at all. There is no historical record of the famous names

– King Priam of Troy, the Greek heroes Achilles and Ajax, and the beautiful Helen, wife of the Greek king of Sparta, Menelaus, whose kidnapping by the Trojan Prince Paris was the reason for the siege in the first place. The very site of Troy itself was unknown until it was excavated for the first time in 1871 by the German archaeologist Heinrich Schliemann. It has been excavated many times since, and a much better understanding has been gained about the city, its hinterland and the civilization in which it flourished.

Troy certainly existed as a place. It was known by the Hittites, who inhabited Anatolia (now modern Turkey) as Wilusa, called Wilion by the Greeks, and then Ilion (after which Homer's *Iliad* is named). It lies on the western shore of modern Turkey, overlooking the Dardanelles Straits. It was rebuilt many times after sackings, earthquakes or fires. It lived on trade and was, by the end of the second millennium BCE, a wealthy city with solid walls and defences and a population of perhaps 7,500 people. The rulers of Troy dominated a region known as the Troad, which supplied food and horses. The peoples of the region probably acted as Troy's allies when the city was threatened. Most archaeologists argue on the basis of the evidence that the siege of Troy took place at some point around 1200 BCE. A layer of fire damage has been unearthed to show that the city was gutted around that time, together with an arrowhead that is identifiably Greek.

If the Trojan War did take place, it is a plausible supposition. The Mycenean Greeks were a seafaring, violent and piratical people. They lived from raiding and stealing and trade, and their sturdy vessels, illustrated on archaeological finds, would have brought them easily to the shores of the Troad, while Troy's reputation as a centre of wealth was a likely magnet. Most research suggests that the ten-year siege with its tumultuous battles outside the city probably never took place. The story of the war derived from Homer and the so-called 'Epic Cycle' of six other Greek poems written around the same time, used literary devices to convey the epic story – 10 years or 100,000 men were figures of poetic speech, not reality.

It is almost certain, however, that something happened at Troy.

The written version 500 years later clearly derived from traditions of epic poetry passed on by word of mouth from generation to generation, like many other narratives in the civilizations of the Middle East before they were consigned to the written word. It is not unlikely that Greek raiders, perhaps on some excuse such as the pursuit of Helen, arrived at Troy to seek its treasures. Modern estimates guess at perhaps 300 ships and anything up to 15,000 men, if the Greek kingdoms had united their forces. Trojan forces and their allies numbered perhaps another 15,000. It is likely that the siege was short, and that the Greeks pillaged and raided the hinterland around the city before finding a way through its defences.

The idea of using deception to undo a city under siege was not unusual in the classical Middle East, when a city could be betrayed by a fifth columnist. The choice of a horse is also consistent with what is known from late Bronze Age archaeology of the special place horses had as offerings. A clay model of a horse from exactly this period was excavated from the ruins of Troy itself. The Greeks were skilled boat-builders and would have had no difficulty putting together a horse made of wooden planking. They would have left the horse, returned to their ships and sailed out of sight, perhaps behind one of the small islands a few miles from the coast, to await a signal that the horse had been taken into the city and that the gates would be opened by the soldiers hidden inside it. It has been calculated that the Greek ships would have taken perhaps two hours to row back to shore during the late evening and another two hours to march the 8 kilometres (5 miles) to the city. Once inside the gates, in the dead of night, with a Trojan population quite unprepared for assault, the Greek victory was assured.

This is all supposition, but it is consistent with what is now known about the Greek and Turkish world 4,000 years ago. The rest is myth, but it could clearly rest on a truth embellished over centuries of oral tradition. Much of the story rests on established patterns of behaviour in ancient warfare. The use of champions as surrogates for whole armies was not uncommon, from the Biblical Goliath to the fatal clash between Hector, son of the King of Troy, and the Greek champion Achilles. The sacrifice of prisoners to satisfy the gods – ordered by Achilles in front of the bier of his favourite, Patroklos, according to Homer – was a common practice, later recorded by Herodotus in his account of the Persian invasion of Greece. Finally there is Helen, who started it all. Modern research has not found a real Helen, but accounts of wars in nearby areas in surviving texts show that a supposedly personal motive for a war that was actually for treasure or land or power was common enough. We are left to imagine a beautiful queen seduced by the smooth-talking Paris, abducted only half against her will, pursued to Troy by her angry husband Menelaus and the Greek commander Agamemnon, where after mighty battles the city was finally taken by a famous ruse and Helen reunited with her vengeful husband, who only stopped his sword, so the story goes, when Helen showed him her breasts. The story of the Trojan Horse is the most famous story of deception, the ancestor of centuries in which tricks have been used to overturn a powerful enemy or to turn an uncertain outcome into victory.

54. BATTLES OF MOUNT VESUVIUS
Summer – autumn 73 BCE

The slave revolt in southern Italy that began in 73 BCE resulted in humiliating defeats for the legions of the Roman army sent to suppress it. The principal slave leader (there were a number) was a tall, fit Thracian gladiator from what is today Bulgaria, known as Spartacus – a Latin version of his Thracian name Sparadakos, meaning 'famous for his spear'. When he escaped from captivity with a band of seventy-three gladiators, a mix of Thracian, German and Celtic fighters, he had little chance of defeating a Roman force in open battle. Spartacus and his improvised army relied on stealth, surviving, as gladiators had to do in the arena, on strength and guile.

The historical record on the Spartacus revolt and its key battles is sparse, but enough is known to reconstruct something of the remarkable year in which the runaway slaves inflicted a series of defeats on the armies sent to crush them. Spartacus had once been trained to fight as a Roman soldier. Why he was subsequently made a captive and forced to fight in the arena as a heavily armed gladiator (named after the short Roman sword, or *gladius*, that they used) is not known. At some point in 73 BCE, he and around 200 fellow captives decided to escape from the gladiators' enclosure in the southern city of Capua. Fighting their way out, only seventy-four escaped, together with an unknown Thracian woman – the mistress of Spartacus and a devotee of the Greek god Dionysus, deity of wine and the dance, who is alleged to have given the gladiators the god's blessing.

The band moved south, destroying a small detachment of men sent from Capua to recapture them. Thirty kilometres (20 miles) away they arrived at Mount Vesuvius, then thought to be extinct, and climbed it to camp in its broad dormant crater. How many slaves joined the march south is not known. Roman writers speculated that there were 10,000, later 20,000, but at this point it seems unlikely that there were more than one or two thousand, using their new-found freedom to rampage through the countryside. A slave revolt was regarded in Rome as a police matter – a *tumultus* or 'commotion' that had to be quickly snuffed out using what men were available. Since Rome's best armies were on distant battlefields in Spain, the Balkans and Turkey fighting wars of pacification, one of the eight Roman *praetors* (an elected office-holder, one rank down from the two consuls who conducted Rome's affairs) named Gaius Claudius Glaber was chosen to finish Spartacus off. He marched south with an estimated 3,000 foot soldiers, bearing in front the famous *fasces* – the bundle of rods tied round an axe, which signified life or death, later adopted by Mussolini's fascist party. Glaber arrived at Vesuvius, camped at or near its foot and blockaded the slaves. The only narrow path down the side of the volcano was guarded. Glaber probably assumed that it was only a matter of time before hunger drove them down.

The slave band was led not only by Spartacus but by two Celts, Crixus and Oenomaus, who commanded the unknown number of Celts among the band. Like Thracians, Celts from all over Europe had a reputation as tough and brutal fighters: tall, tattoo-covered, bearded, they must have seemed both exotic and terrifying to the local population. The classical sources agree on what happened next, though the details are scrappy. The slaves wove the wild vines growing on Vesuvius into ropes. They used the ropes to climb down the steepest and most difficult route on the far side, which the Romans regarded as impassable and had left unguarded. This subterfuge allowed them to arrive, probably at night (which Thracians preferred for ambushes), on the outskirts of the Roman camp. The sources vary on how the slaves approached the camp, but with the advantage of surprise and inherited woodcraft, it is likely that they silently killed off the sentries placed outside the stockades, before rushing forward to attack the soldiers sleeping in their rows of leather tents.

For the Roman militia collected by Glaber, the attack was unexpected. On the Roman frontier, surrounded by barbarian tribes, a sudden assault was routine. Here the frontier had been brought into the heart of the Roman countryside: an uncommon silence, followed by the ritual roars and shouts of the slave warriors as they burst into the enclosure. The camp was captured, an unknown number of Roman soldiers killed and the stocks and weapons plundered. Glaber, it seems, escaped, but his praetorian headquarters was in slave hands. The sources agree that now thousands more slaves, commonly used to farm the rich soil around Vesuvius, flocked to join Spartacus. News of Glaber's humiliation reached Rome and two more *praetors*, Publius Varinius and Lucius Cossinius, were chosen to lead two entire legions (around 12,000 men) to avenge the defeat. The army made its way south in large cohorts, but separated from each other. The slaves ambushed the advance guard of Lucius Furius with 2,000 troops, killing Furius and annihilating his force. They then tracked Cossinius's slow march south and chose their moment to ambush the second cohort. Cossinius was taking the waters in a villa at Salina, near

Pompeii, when he and his guards were surprised by a slave attack. He fled back to his camp but was slaughtered along with many of his soldiers. Varinius, with a force now much reduced, met the same fate. He gathered together the remnants of the other armies and tried to bring the slaves to battle. The details of the final defeat are not known, but an army of perhaps 40,000 slaves seized his camp, slaughtered his forces and captured his standards and *fasces*, though he himself seems to have escaped.

In six months of fighting around Vesuvius and the rich countryside of Campania, four Roman armies had been annihilated by European slaves who had fewer arms and little training but a great deal of brutal cunning. In the end the revolt failed. In 71 BCE, after long marches up and then down the Italian peninsula, Spartacus and some 40,000 slave warriors were defeated not far from the sites of his original victories. He died fighting with a raw courage under a hail of blows and javelins. The few survivors were crucified and left to rot alongside the Appian Way to Rome. The revolt lived on to become a symbol for Marxist revolutionaries, centuries later, of an ancient class struggle, slave against master, the ancestor of their struggle for proletarian emancipation.

55. BATTLE OF RONCESVALLES
15 August 788

The events that took place in a high gorge in the western Pyrenees one August day in 788 were turned three centuries later into one of the most famous European epic poems, the *Chanson de Roland*, the 'Song of Roland'. The author of the poem is not known, and indeed the historical circumstances to which the poem alludes are sketchy in the extreme. The poem has Roland as a brave Christian hero, betrayed by his jealous step-father Ganelon during a campaign in Spain by the

Frankish king Charlemagne. As the Frankish army returns through the mountains to France, Roland and the rearguard are ambushed by thousands of pagans (Muslims) and the nobles are slaughtered. Roland dies, sword in hand, and his soul is taken to heaven by angels. Ganelon is later caught by Charlemagne, tortured, and finally, still alive, torn to pieces by four horses.

There is enough truth in the epic to indicate that over 300 years an oral tradition passed down an embellished Christian version of the death of Roland, prefect of the Breton March, during the withdrawal of Charlemagne's army from an unsuccessful campaign against the Muslim state of al-Andalus that dominated most of Spain. The poem itself is a fantasy, for little is known of the circumstances of the defeat of Charlemagne's rearguard at or near the town of Roncesvalles in the present-day Basque country, though it was certainly not a show-down between Islam and Christianity, as the *Chanson* suggests. The first medieval accounts of Charlemagne's reign passed over the defeat. Only the ninth-century biography of Charlemagne, the *Vita Karoli*, written by the monk Einhard, has a few hundred words about the ambush. There remains considerable uncertainty about the site of the battle, who organized the ambush, and even if the 'Hruodlandus' mentioned in the text really is 'Roland'. For the details of the ambush itself, this is the only real record. The one thing that seems reasonably certain is that the Franks caught by the men concealed on the forested mountainsides were massacred.

The background to the Roncesvalles ambush gives at least some clues as to what might have happened. In 777, the rulers of small Muslim states in eastern Spain, led by Suleiman al-Arabi, governor of Barcelona and Girona, sent an embassy to Charlemagne in Paderborn asking him to help them in their struggle against the Muslim ruler of al-Andalus, Abd al-Rahman. There were hints that Charlemagne might gain territory or vassals if he helped them. Since the Frankish kings had spent decades slowly pushing back the Muslim control of southwestern France, Charlemagne was probably attracted to the idea of establishing a Spanish March in the areas of the Pyrenees. He mustered a major army from across his dominions and marched in two columns, one west, and one east of the mountain chain. They met up and moved on Zaragoza, whose ruler, Al-Husein, went back on his promise to co-operate with the Franks. Charlemagne spent a fruitless few weeks trying to besiege the city but abandoned the attempt when he was warned that the troublesome Saxons were again threatening the eastern part of his kingdom. He took Suleiman al-Arabi as a hostage and set off with his army through the passes that linked the Basque territories of northeastern Spain with Gascony, in southwest France.

According to the surviving annals, Charlemagne had a difficult retreat. Some sources suggest that a Muslim attack was made to free Suleiman and other hostages. When Charlemagne reached Pamplona, he found the Basque and Muslim inhabitants no longer willing to submit to him, so he captured and sacked the city. By the time his army began to wind its way through the pass across the Pyrenees, the local Basques and probably some Arab allies had plenty of reason to want revenge on the Franks. The rearguard was their target as it contained the baggage train and treasure taken from Charlemagne's temporary Spanish allies. Einhard's account describes a country where ambushes were everyday affairs, easy to mount 'by reason of the thick forests'. As the rearguard entered the pass (the exact one is not certain), they were suddenly assailed by a more mobile and lightly armoured enemy. They were hurled down 'to the very bottom of the valley', where they were slaughtered as they struggled in heavy armour and unhelpful terrain against an enemy evidently familiar with the advantages of deception. Before any help could come from the rest of the army, the ambushers melted away in the dusk, bearing all the booty with them. Einhard confirms that pursuit was useless: 'not the least clue could be had to their whereabouts'.

The story consists of little more than a classic opportunistic ambush that reversed the odds against what was certainly a large and powerful army. Charlemagne did not return to Spain for another twenty years, but the Carolingian Empire did eventually construct a Hispanic March to end any further encroachment from Muslim Spain. The death of Roland, if indeed it was he, is supposed to have weighed heavily upon Charlemagne. A chronicle in 829, the first time the defeat at Roncesvalles was admitted, claimed that 'this wound that the King received in Spain almost totally erased from his heart the memory of his success there'. The ambush has since become the famous climax in the *Chanson de Roland*, the founding work of French literature, enjoying an unexpected afterlife long after any of its details could be recalled. In the poem, Charlemagne takes his revenge on the pagans, but in reality the ambush remained unavenged, a brief moment of triumph for the unruly Basques against the main power of Christian Europe.

56. BATTLE OF KLEIDION-STRUMITSA

July – August 1014

Two battles fought in the space of a few days in the summer of 1014 between the Byzantine emperor Basil II and the Tsar of the First Bulgarian Empire, Samuel, were won by the use of deception. The first, near the village of Kleidion (Klyuch in modern Bulgaria), resulted in a Byzantine victory; the second a few days later gave the Bulgarians revenge in the Battle of Strumitsa, thought to have been fought in the Kosturino gorge south of the town. In both cases surprise was the key that unlocked a military situation which otherwise seemed difficult to overcome, and in both cases concealment resulted in an annihilating victory.

War between the two empires had been persistent ever since the establishment of a Bulgarian Empire in the Balkan Peninsula in the seventh century. But under Byzantine emperor Basil II, who came to the throne in Constantinople in 976, the destruction of the Bulgarian state became a central ambition, even an obsession. By 1004, the eastern half of the Bulgarian Empire was lost to Byzantium. For the next decade, Basil campaigned in the Balkans each year, pillaging and burning the countryside and destroying one Bulgarian outpost after another. The Bulgarians' strategy against their powerful neighbour was to rely on ambushes and raids, avoiding pitched battles, but in 1014 Samuel, whose empire was now confined to the mountains of Macedonia and Albania, decided to confront the next Byzantine invasion. Basil usually followed a route through the Kleidion Pass, which runs between the Belasitsa and Ograzhden mountains to the upper valley of the River Struma. Here Samuel set up palisades and earthworks to block Basil's path.

The details of the battle that followed are only known in outline. The Bulgarians fielded perhaps 15–20,000; the size and composition of the Byzantine force is unknown, though it would have included armoured cavalry. Samuel sent south one of his commanders, Nestoritsa, to threaten the Byzantine city of Thessaloniki and compel Basil to turn back, but the Bulgarian raid was defeated by the governor of the city, Theophylactus Botaniates, a close companion of the emperor, who then brought his army to join Basil at Kleidion. Fruitless assaults on the wooden fortifications strung across the Struma Valley persuaded Basil to find an alternative. One of his generals, Nicephorus Xiphias, suggested a deception: while the army hammered away at the palisade, he would lead a force across the forested mountainside of Belasitsa to circle the Bulgarian army and attack it from the rear. The ruse worked. On 29 July, Basil attacked the Bulgarian defences while Xiphias, safely and secretly through the forest, attacked the enemy from the rear. The result was a devastating defeat for Samuel, who narrowly escaped with his life, fleeing on horseback to the castle at Strumitsa. Early Byzantine chronicles claimed that 14–15,000 were taken prisoner, but a late-medieval Bulgarian account suggests little more than half this figure.

The defeat was heavy but not, despite the later Byzantine

accounts, comprehensive. Basil moved on to invest Strumitsa. Further south, he found that the road to Thessaloniki was also blocked by ramparts set up by his enemy. While he surrounded the town, Basil sent Botaniates to open the road, but this time the Bulgarians, by no means completely routed, deceived Basil. On his return from clearing the road, Botaniates and his army were ambushed in a gorge, probably at Kosturino, and slaughtered to a man by a hail of boulders and arrows. Botaniates himself is said to have been speared by Samuel's son, Gavril Radomir. When Basil heard the news of the death of his favourite, he raised the siege on Strumitsa and returned towards Constantinople. At some time after the battle, Basil ordered the Bulgarian prisoners to be blinded and sent back to their tsar, a punishment, it was said, for the death of his beloved Botaniates. Out of every hundred men, one was blinded in only one eye, so that he could lead the others back to Bulgaria. The number mutilated was almost certainly smaller than the 15,000 claimed by Byzantine accounts, but the sorrowful trail of blinded men was too much for Samuel. When they arrived in early October, the shock is said to have killed the Bulgarian emperor, already lying ill in the city of Prespa. Samuel had an apoplectic fit, revived briefly and then died on 6 October 1014.

The two battles in and around the Struma Valley each showed the merit of concealment and stratagem in different ways. Ambushes were common devices used by irregular forces to offset the numerical or tactical advantages enjoyed by a stronger and well-organized enemy. The use of mountainous terrain to conceal an outflanking movement was as old as Thermopylae and probably older. The outcome of the two battles was nevertheless not a draw. The death of Samuel provoked confusion and conflict among the surviving Bulgarian commanders and within four years the whole Bulgarian Empire was defeated and occupied by Byzantium. The Byzantine Empire now extended its authority throughout the Balkan Peninsula, reaching the highpoint of its medieval revival. Basil II earned the nickname by which history has remembered him, *Boulgaroktonos* – the 'Bulgar-slayer'.

57. BATTLE OF MANZIKERT

26 August 1071

The Battle of Manzikert (Malazgirt in modern Turkey) was a battle full of surprises. When it was over the emperor of Byzantium, Romanos IV Diogenes, was brought before the victorious Saljuq (Seljuk) Turk leader, Muhammad Ibn Da'ud Alp Arslan, covered in dirt and dried blood, and it was some time before the Turkish sultan would believe that this could possibly be the ruler of the Eastern Roman Empire. Romanos was not deliberately in disguise and the ragged emperor was soon identified. His hapless state was the product of a long and exhausting battle in which the Turks used their traditional skill at deception to confuse and frustrate the larger imperial force they were confronting.

Romanos assumed the imperial title as regent in 1067 after a century in which the Byzantine lands in the Balkans, Anatolia and Armenia – the heart of the empire – had been subject to raids and losses to different Turkic peoples from the central Asian steppes. The most successful were the Saljuq Turks, who established their rule across an area from the Sea of Azov to modern Iran and Iraq, and raided Armenia and what is now present-day Turkey. Under Alp Arslan ('Heroic Lion'), sultan from 1063, the Saljuqs began to encroach ever further into Syria and Armenia. Romanos saw his appointment as regent as an opportunity to stabilize the eastern frontier of the empire and if possible to inflict a damaging longer-term defeat on the Saljuqs. In March 1071, he mustered a large army of foot soldiers and cavalry from all over the empire, an ethnic melting pot that included the famed Varangian Guard composed of Normans and Germans, as well as some Turkish mercenaries. Estimates from medieval texts vary widely, but it is thought that he led at least 30–40,000 men, supported, according to one account, by a huge train of baggage and siege equipment mounted on 3,000 carts.

Neither side knew what the other was intending. Alp Arslan collected an army to capture cities in Syria and then to threaten the

Fatimid Caliphate in Egypt, but he failed to capture the besieged city of Aleppo. Romanos's army tramped across Anatolia in the direction of Lake Van and the cluster of fortified towns around it, including Manzikert, recently seized by the Saljuqs. When news arrived that the Sultan was stuck in Syria, Romanos assumed he would have an easier time securing his goal. When Alp Arslan abandoned the siege and moved east, Romanos thought he had been defeated and was no longer a threat. This was to be the first of many surprises. The sultan was much better informed about the Byzantine progress and abandoned Aleppo in order to gather a fresh army in northern Iran (then Azerbaijan) to meet the Roman threat. Taking with him only 4,000 of his best *ghulam* (professional cavalry), he called to arms the Kurdish and Turkic tribes to the north and arrived in eastern Anatolia, quite unknown to Romanos, with an estimated 20–30,000 (the exact figures will never be known) and a hard core of 15,000 skilled horsemen.

Both armies arrived north of Lake Van at almost the same time. On a flat plain, broken by ridges and shallow gorges, dominated by the snow-covered peak of Süphan Dag, more than 4,000 metres (13,000 feet) high, the two armies set up camp. Alp Arslan was careful to make sure his camp was concealed to increase the degree of surprise when he faced an enemy he knew to be much stronger. Still ignorant of the threat, Romanos sent part of his army south, under the command of Joseph Tarchaniotes, to capture the city of Ahlat. The news reached Alp Arslan, who despatched 10,000 of his cavalry to intercept the force. They drove it back westwards, away from contact with the main Byzantine army. Manzikert fell to Romanos's impressive show of force the same day, 23 August. No news came of the disaster at Ahlat, and Romanos was so confident that there was no immediate threat that no reconnaissance was undertaken. Only when foragers sent out from his camp were attacked in force by Turkish soldiers did it suddenly become clear that he might have miscalculated. On 25 August, Saljuq emissaries arrived to see whether an agreement could be reached, perhaps because the sultan could see just how imposing the Byzantine force looked in its large fortified camp. They were humiliated by the emperor and sent back to the sultan. Romanos was confident that in a pitched battle, even one so unexpected, his army was a match for an army of Turks.

After a parade of icons and crosses, the Byzantine army marched out in three broad sections with a fourth reserve section behind it. Romanos commanded the best troops and the heavy cavalry in the centre, armed with lances. After commending his soldiers to the will of Allah, Alp Arslan drew up his army in a crescent shape, a centre and two wings, dominated by horsemen with bows and spears. Appearances were deceptive, however, because many of the Saljuq army were in hiding waiting to ambush the approaching Byzantines. Romanos was lured on as the Turkish crescent bent and the centre retreated. A cloud of choking dust arose from the marching feet and hooves, driven across the Turkish lines by a strong wind. As the Turks moved back under the cloud, the formation of the Byzantine army began to lose coherence while Turkish horsemen suddenly appeared from nowhere to harass the enemy units, disappearing again behind ridges and rocks, only to spring another ambush further ahead. The elusive enemy tactics wore down the patience and morale of Romanos's forces, and he decided to withdraw from a fruitless pursuit. His signal was mistakenly read as an indication that the centre had been defeated and a panic set in as the structure of the Roman force broke up. The rearguard failed to come to the assistance of the front line as it gave way. Sensing the crisis, Alp Arslan ordered his whole force forwards with cries of 'Alluhu Akbar' ('God is Most Powerful'). The Byzantine centre, the Varangian guard and Romanos himself were surrounded and cut down, the emperor falling from his horse. It was here, dusty and wounded, that an unknown *ghulam* is supposed to have found and captured him, leading him the following day to the humiliating meeting with the incredulous sultan.

The battle was not the massacre it was once thought to be, since it is now evident that many soldiers escaped as fast as they could back to Constantinople and safety. Romanos was generously freed, perhaps because Alp Arslan guessed what was in store for a defeated emperor. His enemies conspired to take his throne and after a brief civil war, he was captured, hideously blinded and died of his wound in July 1072. Alp Arslan was killed in November the same year, stabbed by a rebel prisoner he had just condemned to execution. The battle nevertheless opened the way to Turkish encroachment and conquest of Anatolia and the slow extinction of the Eastern Roman Empire.

58. BATTLE OF LAKE PEIPUS
5 April 1242

At the climax of the Russian director Sergei Eisenstein's epic film *Alexander Nevsky*, made in 1938, is a scene in which the Teutonic Knights, German thirteenth-century crusaders against the Russians of Novgorod, are lured into a battle on the ice of Lake Peipus (Chud) and plunge into the icy waters as the weakening spring ice gives way beneath the heavily armoured men and horses. Deceived by the presence of the enemy on the far bank of the lake, the Germans fail to realize that they have been tricked onto the ice. This was a prescient allegory. Only two years later, German armies roared across the Soviet frontier in Operation Barbarossa, a name also plucked from Germany's medieval past, only to be frustrated and destroyed by a modern-day Russian army.

Almost everything about the battle on the ice was in reality the product of centuries of literary embellishment of an event about which almost nothing is known. The only certain facts available come from a handful of medieval texts, the earliest written fifty years after the battle. According to these accounts, the battle took place on 5 April 1242 near the lakes west of Novgorod. After a tough struggle, victory went to Alexander Nevsky and a number of German crusaders were killed or captured. The very first account has the battle taking place 'on the grass'. Not until a century after the battle is there an account mentioning that the knights were fought 'on the ice', and not until 1500 is there a source that claims the Germans were chased 'across the ice'. There is no agreement about who started the battle, although it suited Russian chroniclers to assume that the German knights were the aggressors. The very first account has Alexander as the aggressor, coming to the lands of the Teutonic Order to 'rob and burn'. Later histories suggest that Alexander was summoned by the people of Novgorod to protect them against an approaching army of German knights and local, probably Estonian, foot soldiers.

Alexander Yaroslavich himself was not a fiction. He was commander of the army of the Republic of Novgorod in what is present-day northern Russia. In 1240, he defeated a Swedish invasion at the Battle of the Neva, from which he got his title 'Nevskii'. That year the Livonian Order, a branch of the crusading Teutonic Knights, under their commander Dietrich von Grüningen, had invaded and captured a number of towns up to the edge of Novgorod itself. Alexander drove them back the following year, and in 1242 seems to have taken the offensive against Livonian territory in present-day Estonia. The early chronicles make it clear that Alexander arrived somewhere between Lake Peipus and Lake Pskov, linked by the narrow Teploe Ozero, or Warm Lake, and that he drew up his army near Raven's Rock Island, a landmark close to a promontory jutting into Teploe. This is an area of water that modern research has shown to contain warm currents that make the ice shallower and more brittle. Most early accounts have the Livonian Order and their Estonian troops attacking Alexander's army. The Teutonic Knights usually employed a wedge-shaped formation, attacking and breaking the enemy line by sheer physical power. This was probably how the battle began. The very first chronicle describes a fierce battle in which the Novgorod army used archers to attack the knights, while 'swords were heard cutting helmets apart'. This account reports 20 dead Livonian knights and 6 captured; later medieval accounts talk of 400 or 500 dead from the Order and 50 captured.

That is the full extent of what is known. Modern-day estimates of the numbers involved are mere guesses, though a few thousand on each side seems a not unreasonable speculation. The idea that the knights drowned as they struggled on the breaking ice is a modern invention for which there is no historical evidence. Indeed, the first indication of such an outcome can be found in Eisenstein's film. The film was shot in the summer so all the vegetation on the outdoor set had to be painted white, while the famous lumps of ice on the lake had to be held in place by gas-filled balloons. Eisenstein himself claimed to have been inspired not by the legend of Alexander's victory but by the scene of the battle in heaven from John Milton's *Paradise Lost*, in which the Host of Satan is driven back and plunges into 'the wasteful Deep' down to the 'bottomless pit' of Hell.

The story of the battle on the ice has existed as myth, used to symbolize the centuries-long struggle between the Russians and enemy invaders. The film proved awkward after the German–Soviet Pact of August 1939 had been signed, and it was not shown. When Operation Barbarossa began, *Alexander Nevsky* was brought out again and widely screened now that the heroic defence of Russia against the savage German foe had become the main focus of Soviet propaganda. The battle is a curious phenomenon, projected backwards onto a past otherwise silent about its details. Between 1958 and 1961, the Soviet authorities, interested to find out more about a battle they had appropriated for their own purposes, despatched an archaeological expedition to the supposed site of the Battle at Teploe Ozero. Exploration underground and underwater could not find a single trace of any battle, though heavy silt deposits now covered the lake floor. This was perhaps the greatest deception; the battle on the ice remains permanently elusive.

59. FALL OF TENOCHTITLÁN
28 May – 13 August 1521

In the sixteenth century, the capital of the Aztec Empire, Tenochtitlán, site of present-day Mexico City, was one of the largest and most populous cities in the world. It was the heart of a remarkable warrior civilization that dominated central America for 200 years, and was ruled by a 'chief speaker' (*tlatoani*) chosen by the Aztec nobility. It survived by exacting heavy tribute from the subject peoples of the area, including regular human sacrifices to appease the Aztec gods. It was into this world that the Spanish adventurer Hernán Cortés arrived from the Spanish colony of Cuba in the spring of 1519 with 600 men and a number of horses. He came seeking new sources of wealth for Spain and fresh converts for Christianity, but his arrival heralded doom for the Aztecs. Their capital was destroyed two years later, thanks in part to Cortés's decision to build a fleet of small warships on dry land in order to take the Aztec city in the middle of Lake Texcoco by surprise.

The destruction of the Aztec Empire was not inevitable. There were many opportunities for the Aztecs and their vassals to destroy the invaders, despite the disparity between the stone clubs of the Aztec warriors and the Spanish weapons forged from Toledo steel. Accompanied by only 450 men, Cortés entered the city in November 1519 to meet the chief speaker Moctezuma II (also known as Montezuma). The thousands of Aztec warriors held back from killing him because of a suspicion that the Spaniards might be gods. But following the Spanish slaughter of hundreds of Aztec nobles who had gathered for a celebration in the Great Temple, Cortés and his men were besieged by a crowd of angry warriors dressed in traditional jaguar and eagle costumes and armed with slings, spears and the deadly *macuahuitl* – a wooden club embedded with obsidian blades. The Spaniards, together with a number of allies recruited from the Tlaxcalan people, who were hostile to the Aztecs, managed to fight their way out on 30 June 1520 and across the lake causeways, but they lost 800 of the Spanish garrison of 1,300 in the process. Cortés himself almost drowned in the lake. The events of 29–30 June 1520 – the 'night of sorrows' as it came to be known – almost brought the Spanish expedition to an end. Cortés retreated to the mountains north of the capital together with his Tlaxcalan allies. The Aztecs pursued them but were defeated in a battle on the open plain, where Cortés's few surviving cavalry could operate effectively.

It was in the mountains that the Spanish leader decided to build a fleet of boats, concealed from the distant Aztecs, to be hauled down to the lake and used to launch a surprise attack on the city. Only one carpenter had survived the massacre. With the help of local labour, trees were cut, planks were hewn, and thirteen small boats, 13 metres (42 feet) long and 3 metres (9 feet) wide, known as 'brigantines', were constructed over the winter of 1520–21. They were built with flat bottoms to make it easier to navigate the lake. In the spring of 1521, the boats were hauled with considerable difficulty down to Lake Texcoco. By this time, Cortés had received military supplies and a small number of infantry and cavalry sent from Cuba. His total of 90 horsemen, 820 soldiers and 18 small cannon, supported by perhaps as many as 100,000 unreliable local allies, planned to defeat an Aztec army estimated at perhaps as many as 300,000.

The Aztec leaders were now certain that the Spaniards were not gods. During the fight in the city, Moctezuma had been killed by Aztec slingshots as he tried to calm his people. A new 'chief speaker', the eighteen-year-old Cuauhtémoc, was determined to eradicate the Spanish threat once and for all. Tenochtitlán had been ravaged by a smallpox epidemic during the winter, but the surviving warriors still constituted a formidable force. In late May, the main aqueduct into the city was cut by a Spanish posse. Cortés divided his small force into three and posted them at the entrance to each of the causeways into the city. Then at the beginning of June the brigantines, manned by 300 Spanish soldiers and a handful of cannon, were secretly launched onto the lake. The ships were something the Aztecs had never seen before and in the ensuing battle hundreds of Aztec canoes were destroyed or sunk. The ships remained throughout the ensuing siege, firing at the city in support of the forces trying to cross the causeways.

The siege of Tenochtitlán lasted ninety-three days and was in truth an almost continuous and exhausting battle. Nearly every day the Spanish and their allies fought thousands of Aztec warriors who pressed forwards on each of the three causeways regardless of losses. Cortés himself was almost captured several times, and those Spaniards who fell into Aztec hands met a grisly end. They were stripped naked and taken to the sacrificial table of the Great Temple where the priests ripped open the victim's chest with a stone dagger and plucked out the still pulsating heart. The soldiers besieging the city could see the sacrifice in the distance and hear their comrades' screams. Hands and feet were severed and parts of the body eaten. The flayed skin of the dead Spaniards' faces and chunks of their roasted flesh were thrown at the besieging forces to terrorize them. Many of the local allies who had joined Cortés melted away from the battle but enough stayed to impose on the Aztecs a level of attrition that in the end was unsustainable. Conditions on both sides deteriorated over the summer weeks as food shortages left both armies tired and emaciated. Slowly the causeways were cleared and building by building the Spanish destroyed the city to prevent the enemy from sustaining any form of urban guerrilla warfare.

Cortés appealed to Cuauhtémoc a number of times to abandon the struggle and avoid further death and destruction but the Aztec rulers now sought only death or victory. An estimated 40,000 died in the final defence of the city, though Cuauhtémoc finally chose to flee in a canoe across the lake. On 13 August, the Aztecs fought to a standstill, with women and children joining the struggle for the city, but most were too debilitated by starvation and disease to resist. The Spaniards and their allies fought across piles of bodies in the streets until the final massacre ended resistance. The din of Aztec kettledrums and trumpets and the yelling of Aztec commanders suddenly ceased after weeks of deafening battle. Cuauhtémoc was captured and begged to be killed, but Cortés spared him, impressed by his valiant defence of the city. The slaughter and destruction of the capital by Cortés's *conquistadores* ended the 200 years of Aztec civilization and ushered in the age of the Spanish American Empire.

60. BATTLE OF BLENHEIM
13 August 1704

Widely regarded as the most significant victory in English military history, the battle in and around the small Bavarian village of Blindheim (usually spelt Blenheim in English) had an English commander and a core of English soldiers and horsemen, but was a multi-national battle, as most early eighteenth-century battles were, in which more Germans, Dutch and Danes served than English. There is no doubt, however, that the English commander, John Churchill, Duke of Marlborough, was the inspiration behind the victory over a larger French and Bavarian army in what was one of the critical battles of the War of the Spanish Succession. It was a battle that might never have happened if Marlborough had not deceived his allies, his government and above all his enemies about his plans for an unexpected offensive campaign deep in the heart of Europe.

Marlborough was the commander of a confederate army of European states that objected to the decision by Louis XIV of France to support his grandson's claim to the vacant throne of Spain following the death of the feeble-minded King Carlos II in 1700. The crisis in Europe developed slowly but in May 1702 an alliance of England, Holland (the United Provinces) and the Austrian Habsburg Empire declared war on France. The armies of Louis XIV had not been defeated in forty years and posed a formidable challenge to Marlborough. By the spring of 1704, it seemed likely that Vienna would be captured by the advancing armies of France and her ally, Maximilien Wittelsbach, the elector of Bavaria, a move that would bring about the collapse of the coalition. Marlborough was stuck in Holland because his Dutch allies were unwilling to send their home troops on so distant and dangerous a campaign, and a major crisis loomed.

The deception at the heart of the eventual triumph at Blindheim was simple but risky. Without telling anyone except his monarch, Queen Anne, Marlborough pretended that he was taking part of his coalition army of 70,000 men to campaign in the Moselle Valley, close enough to Holland if the Dutch needed protection. Two French armies were positioned opposite the frontiers and could threaten his line of march, so he needed to persuade them, too, that he was staying in the north rather than moving to the aid of distant Vienna. He left Holland on 19 May with his secret still safe, though he had already made careful preparations to keep his men supplied and provisioned as he began the 400-kilometre (250-mile) trek down the Rhine and into Bavaria as far as the River Danube. By the time the Dutch found out that he had marched beyond the Moselle it was too late. At Koblenz, he ordered his surprised army across to the eastern bank of the Rhine and after five weeks of slow progress, as fast as the vast baggage train would allow, he reached Bavaria. Halfway along he had tricked the French again by pretending to throw bridges across the river as if to attack through Alsace and threaten Strasbourg. Only when he had finally arrived on the Danube, now with a coalition army of 80,000, was his intention evident.

Marlborough captured Donauwörth on the Danube on 2 July 1704, despite taking heavy casualties. Placing his armies between the approaching French and Bavarians and Vienna, the imperial capital, Marlborough joined up with the 20,000 imperial troops under Eugene, Prince of Savoy, and another force led by the tetchy Louis-William, Margrave of Baden. Facing them were the 56,000 French and Bavarians. The French armies were commanded by the veteran Marshals Count Ferdinand de Marsin and Camille d'Huston, Duke de Tallard, who had brought his army through the Black Forest with great difficulty, and with the loss of one-third of the horses from an epidemic of glanders. The French chose to make camp on the north bank of the Danube on the plain of Höchstädt, between the villages of Blindheim and Lutzingen, which was ideal ground for a major cavalry encounter, but also an ideal defensive position, protected in front by a small marshy river, the Nebel, and a slope difficult to assault against stiff resistance. Tallard was confident that his enemy would not risk battle.

Marlborough and Eugene camped further east along the river near Donauwörth. To get their awkward ally out of the way they dispatched the Margrave of Baden to capture Ingolstadt. Then they worked out how to deploy their 60 guns and 52,000 soldiers and cavalry to achieve victory. On the face of it, their prospects were not good. French forces occupied the Danube village of Blindheim on one flank and the village of Oberglau on the other. Any chance of encircling the enemy was nullified by the large Bavarian force stationed on the French left in Lutzingen and the surrounding woodland. Once again deception was to play a part. As Marlborough moved his army forwards towards the enemy on 12 August, he sent ahead men who would allow themselves to be taken by the French. The prisoners pretended that the coalition armies were moving north to protect their lines of communication. Since this was exactly what Tallard had expected – position, rather than actual battle, was everything in eighteenth-century warfare – the French and Bavarians slept soundly that night. Marlborough's men did not sleep well. They were already moving into position ready to ford the Nebel and seek battle. Tallard's camp was still asleep when the nine enemy columns converged on the plain.

Marlborough's plan for an offensive depended on the willingness of his men to accept a high level of sacrifice. The British left was to storm Blindheim, while the Germans and Danes on the right were to neutralize Oberglau, thus removing the threat from infantry on the flanks, while allowing Marlborough's larger cavalry force, intermingled with infantry, to confront the concentration of French horsemen on the Höchstädt plain. Meanwhile Eugene was to move through the woods and streams on the far right to pin down Marsin and the elector around Lutzingen, leaving Tallard without reserves. The plan was even riskier than it seemed in the light of what actually happened. The attack was delayed because of Eugene's difficulty in getting his men and guns in place over difficult ground, and the French and Bavarians, despite the initial surprise, were able to organize a coherent defensive line. Only at mid-day was it possible to start the battle with a fierce infantry assault against the fortified village of Blindheim. Deception had its limitations.

Marlborough was fortunate that the plan unfolded much as he had hoped. The attacks on Blindheim were repelled with heavy losses, but when the French army's elite *Gens d'Armes* cavalry was sent in to finish off the attackers, they were hit by the sudden appearance of Hessian infantry, hidden in the marshy bank of the Nebel. The cavalry panicked and fled in disorder, creating a disturbing uncertainty throughout Tallard's army. The French commander at Blindheim was so disconcerted that he gathered most of the French infantry into the village, leaving 12,000 soldiers to be bottled up by only 5,000 of Marlborough's men. After savage hand-to-hand action against Irish soldiers fighting for France, Oberglau was overrun after Marlborough's prudent deployment of his cavalry reserves. Eugene's imperial forces suffered heavy casualties on the right wing, but held Marsin and the Elector in place for the entire day.

By 5 p.m., with the French visibly tiring, Marlborough finally brought up his fresher lines of cavalry, supported by infantry four rows deep, firing by platoon rather than by line (a tactical innovation to ensure greater accuracy of fire), and launched them against the massed French cavalry. After a fierce engagement all along the line, the French cavalry broke, with many trying to cross the Danube where up to 3,000 are thought to have drowned. Tallard himself was captured by a Hessian trooper and invited to sit in Marlborough's command coach. Marsin and the elector made their escape in good order, but the collapse left Blindheim isolated, and an hour later it surrendered, bringing 10,000 prisoners of war. The initial bluff had paid off handsomely. Some 100 guns and 14,000 prisoners were captured, as well as 129 infantry colours and 110 cavalry standards, a shameful loss for any eighteenth-century regiment. The cost, however, was high – 14,000 of the coalition side were killed or wounded, against French and Bavarian casualties estimated at 20,000. Tallard eked out his years as a prisoner in England, where he introduced celery to the English diet. Marlborough was fêted on his triumphal return to London in December 1704, but it was to be a further nine years before the long war had run its course.

61. BATTLE OF HOHENFRIEDBERG
4 June 1745

Frederick II of Prussia – Frederick the Great after this battle – needed a victory in 1745 to stamp his authority on the Prussian army after the disastrous winter campaign of the Second Silesian War. The thirty-three-year-old king was unlike almost any of his European adversaries. Cultured, philosophically inclined and a noted flute player, the diminutive monarch was also fascinated by battle and an avid student of the wars of the past. The victory he sought against the vast military resources of the Habsburg Empire was made possible by the simplest of deceits: a forced march during the night to take the enemy camp by surprise at sunrise. For all the attention later lavished on Frederick's operational genius, the simplicity of this stratagem was its most significant characteristic.

The war was fought between an upstart Prussia, a state carved out of northeastern Germany over the previous half-century, and the empire of Maria Theresa, whose claim to the Habsburg throne in 1740 had precipitated a general European conflagration against her. Frederick had used the opportunity to seize the Habsburg province of Silesia in southeastern Germany (now Poland) to mark his own accession to the throne. Maria Theresa bowed to reality in 1742 and acknowledged Frederick's acquisition, but she was never reconciled to it and in 1744 war was resumed. Frederick raised a large army of 140,000 men, some conscripted from the Prussian cantons, others German mercenaries from the smaller German states, all led by a military aristocracy whose status owed more to battle competence than to land ownership or birth. Frederick marched them into Bohemia and occupied Prague, but no army came to engage him. Since winter was approaching and supplies from distant Prussia were difficult to maintain, he had no alternative but to retreat to his kingdom. His forces were demoralized, desertion was rife, and illness and cold depleted the remainder. This was why a victory was so important to him in 1745.

The army he raised for the next campaigning season was much smaller. It included some 42,000 foot soldiers and 17,000 cavalry. He was ready by late May, but he had to entice the enemy to fight rather than simply manoeuvre around him. 'A battle,' he concluded, 'is my only option.' A large Austrian and Saxon army was camped out in the Bohemian mountains, the Riesengebirge. It comprised around 60,000 men led by Prince Charles of Lorraine. Frederick's use of deceit began early in June, when rumours and disinformation were spread, intended to reach the enemy camp. He wanted the enemy to believe that his forces were dispersed or even retreating so that they would come down from their secure positions in the heights onto the plain below, where Frederick's army had more advantage. The Habsburg commanders took the bait and moved towards him. On 3 June 1745, they camped near the village of Hohenfriedberg in the Sudetenland, spread out along a small river. So confident were they that the Prussians were on the run that no temporary fortifications were thought necessary.

Frederick had achieved the surprise he needed. He drew his forces quickly together and ordered a night march towards Hohenfriedberg. Camp fires were left burning in case any Austrian spies crept near to reconnoitre. The men were ordered to keep absolute silence and not to smoke. Discipline was harsh in the Prussian army so the men obeyed. The infantry crossed fields while the guns struggled along dirt roads, with the sound of their movements muffled as much as possible. They arrived in front of the enemy camp at sunrise. Surprise was almost complete, but the camp was much wider than Frederick had realized and his first units ran unexpectedly into enemy infantry. He ushered his cavalry forward, leading by example – the first time he had fought on the battlefield himself. A large force of Austrian and Saxon horsemen quickly found their mounts and met the Prussian charge. A fierce engagement followed in which Frederick had insisted that no quarter be given. The balance gradually turned in his favour. While the horsemen battled each other, the Saxon infantry, encamped on the Habsburg left, formed up and prepared to defend their position. Nine Prussian infantry battalions were ordered to shoulder their muskets and march straight at the fusillade of musket and cannon fire coming from the Saxon ranks. They did so keeping an extraordinary discipline, then at the last moment, only yards from the enemy, they fired their muskets. A confused battle ensued until the Saxons, hoping every minute for reinforcements from their Austrian allies that never came, finally broke at around 7 a.m.

By this time, the whole Austrian camp was attempting to come to terms with what had happened and organize a satisfactory defence. Frederick, realizing that his original plan was already compromised, instead ordered the bulk of his foot soldiers, supported by the remaining cavalry, to attack the Austrian lines head-on. They had to cross the small river and as they did so the one bridge collapsed. As the Austrian cavalry advanced, the remaining Prussian cavalry found a ford further downstream and charged to help their stranded comrades. Shocked by the force of the Prussian charge, the Austrian horse broke and scattered. The infantry struggle was intense, with disciplined lines exchanging point-blank musket fire, but at 8.15 some 1,500 horsemen of Frederick's 5th Bayreuth Dragoons, who had not taken part in the earlier cavalry charge, saw through the smoke of battle an inviting gap opening up in the Austrian lines. They charged at full gallop, crashing into a battalion of Austrian grenadiers who were put to the sword. With no cavalry left, the Austrian line collapsed in minutes and by 9 a.m. the battle was over. The dragoons captured some 67 regimental colours and 2,500 prisoners. Fighting had been brief but savage and 4,700 from the Prussian army were dead or wounded. Austrian and Saxon losses were three times as great. Frederick had the captured colours set up in his head-quarters tent, as if he could not quite believe his good fortune.

The war ended a few months later with the Peace of Dresden, and Silesia remained for the moment in Prussian hands. Frederick composed a march in honour of his victory. News of Hohenfriedberg made Frederick overnight into a European military celebrity but the victory, which owed much to the element of surprise, was brought about partly through luck and partly through the disciplined fighting power of Prussian units when faced with taking initiatives in their own part of the battle. Deception, however effective it might be, still required a thorough exploitation in combat to make it worthwhile, as Frederick, the philosopher-king, found out in his first battlefield action.

62. BATTLE OF THE PLAINS OF ABRAHAM

12–13 September 1759

Almost as famous as the image of Admiral Lord Nelson dying at the Battle of Trafalgar is the 1770 painting by Benjamin West of Major General James Wolfe as he breathed his last in the closing moments of a battle against the French outside Québec, then the capital of Canada. The battle is best remembered for Wolfe's inspirational idea to scale the sheer cliffs of the St Lawrence River and surprise the French army at their summit. In reality, the deception happened by chance, through the hazard of the unpredictable tides of the river. The effect of surprise on the subsequent battle was decisive. As news arrived that the French were fleeing in disorder after a battle that lasted no more than a few minutes, Wolfe is said to have uttered the words 'I die contented.'

The struggle between the French and the British for control of North America, supported by the local emigrant population and American Indian allies, reached its peak during the Seven Years War (1756–63) in which French claims in America and India were defeated by British arms. In 1759, the British government decided that the moment had come to besiege and capture the capital of New France at Québec. Wolfe was sent 7,400 officers and men, supported by 300 gunners, to capture the city. At the end of June 1759, his flotilla arrived in the St Lawrence and the force disembarked at Île d'Orléans, a few miles downriver from Québec, which stood on a high promontory protected by cliffs, woods and water. The most favourable approach to the city was across a wide and shallow river beach known as the Beauport Shore, and it was there that the French commander, General Louis-Joseph de Montcalm-Gozon, Marquis de Saint Veran, positioned most of his forces and artillery in anticipation of a British assault.

The natural protection afforded to Québec made a direct approach dangerous. When Wolfe finally attempted a limited raid on Beauport on 31 July, the attackers took heavy losses from entrenched French fire, leaving 210 dead and 230 wounded. He continued to undertake probing reconnaissance for weeks, but could find no suitable spot from which to attack. Ill and despondent, he asked his subordinate commanders for their opinions. They unanimously favoured moving further upriver to find an undefended section of shore. Wolfe was reluctant, but his options were narrowing. With every passing week came the looming threat of ice at the mouth of the St Lawrence. British ships sailed upriver. In response, the French moved troops and cavalry under Colonel Louis-Antoine de Bougainville to defend an area over 20 kilometres (12 miles) from Québec. As Wolfe sailed up and down the river between the fleet and his camp at Île d'Orléans, he observed an entry point that had been overlooked, a narrow road leading up from the river, sided by cliffs, at Anse au Foulon. Dismissing the earlier plan, he ordered his forces to land at Foulon on 13 September so that they could reach the plain in front of the city at dawn before the French could react.

The famous scaling of the cliffs below the Plains of Abraham came by accident. The units assigned to disembark and capture the narrow road from the small French picket posted there were swept further down the beach by the tide and found themselves at the base of a cliff about 50 metres (160 feet) high. While some troops went to capture the road, William Howe led the light infantry up the cliff face, clinging to ledges and scrub, until they reached the top. A highlander, Captain Donald MacDonald, spoke enough French to persuade the French picket in the dark that his soldiers were their replacement, allaying suspicion. While Howe led his men up the cliff, Wolfe and the rest of his force cleared the defensive fortifications on the narrow road and toiled up to the plain, carrying at least two of their artillery pieces. He formed his 3,111 men in a horseshoe formation, with 1,750 of them facing the French army camped outside the city, and the rest on each side facing the French Canadian sharpshooters and militia. The British were drawn up in two lines, prepared for alternate shooting, one line after the other, but the central battalions had been instructed in a new tactic by Wolfe. As a French column approached, Wolfe had told his men to hold their fire until the last moment, then to open their ranks to let the column pass through, firing all the time at the column's now-exposed flanks.

Montcalm was caught entirely by surprise. He had expected an imminent assault on the Beauport Shore. He ordered his army, estimated at 1,960 regulars and 1,500 militiamen, to engage the enemy but it emerged disorganized and unprepared. His columns moved forward firing at will and were hit by fierce flank fire from the left and right of Wolfe's line at a distance of only 40 metres (130 feet). The centre held their fire until the French were only 20 metres (65 feet) away, when they released a deadly fusillade that killed most of the approaching officers. Subjected to further heavy flanking fire, the French broke up, turned and fled back towards the city, leaving 150 dead and 370 wounded on the field. The whole battle lasted only a few minutes, but long enough for Wolfe, as he stood on a small rise to observe the course of the battle, to be hit three times by Canadian marksmen hiding in the nearby bushes. He died a few minutes later as his own officers rushed up with news of the French collapse.

Québec surrendered five days later, and although the British garrison was defeated in a second engagement on the plains on 20 April 1760, the city was not recaptured. Three years later, the French conceded defeat and New France was granted to the British. Much had depended on the success of surprise and it had taken Wolfe months to work out how to effect it, even if the final scramble up the cliffs had been a purely serendipitous event. In war, wrote Wolfe in 1757, 'something must be allowed to chance and fortune'.

63. SIEGE OF YORKTOWN
29 September – 19 October 1781

The surrender of a British garrison at the small Virginia port of Yorktown on 19 October 1781 proved to be the key moment of the American War of Independence. When the British prime minister, Lord North, was told of the disaster he famously exclaimed, 'Oh God! It's all over.' Yet it was a battle that might never have taken place but for a key deception perpetrated by the American Continental Army's French ally. George Washington, the American commander-in-chief, wanted to besiege and, if possible, capture the British-held area of New York. The French commander, Lieutenant General Comte de Rochambeau, thought New York too well defended and instructed an approaching French fleet to sail for Chesapeake Bay, off the Virginia coast, not to New York. Washington's hand was forced. He ordered a move south, with the British headquarters at Yorktown as his destination.

The campaigns prior to 1781 left the balance poised between the British with their royalist American allies on the one hand, and the American Continental Army with its French allies and local irregular militia on the other. The British army in the south, commanded by Lieutenant General the Earl Cornwallis, having failed to take control of North Carolina, set out for Virginia in April 1781. Here Cornwallis was reinforced by troops sent from New York and the local British garrison. Instructed to find a port on the Virginia coast that he could fortify, he chose Yorktown near the mouth of the Chesapeake. On a high promontory, he calculated that it would be difficult to take as long as the Royal Navy could supply him. Control of the sea was essential to British strategy in the American war. On 29 July, he moved 7,000 British and Hessian mercenary troops into the town. Across the estuary was the small town of Gloucester, which Cornwallis saw as a possible site to which his forces could retreat if Yorktown were threatened.

That summer the initiative lay with Washington. He asked Rochambeau to bring his 5,500 soldiers to join him at White Plains, New York, with a view to investing the city. The French accepted Washington as their commander, too, but when news came that the French Rear Admiral François de Grasse had escaped the British blockade of France and was heading to the West Indies, Rochambeau used the opportunity to undermine his ally's strategy. He wrote in secret to de Grasse that his substantial fleet of twenty-six ships should sail for Chesapeake Bay, not for New York. This would make a move south, under the protection of French guns, more sensible. When Washington discovered that de Grasse was intent on sailing to Virginia he accepted that New York would now indeed be difficult to capture. A move south, however, required a second deception. The British commander-in-chief in America, General Sir Henry Clinton, was based at New York, uncertain of Washington's plans but anxious to strengthen his position. He assumed New York would be the principal battlefield in 1781, and even ordered Cornwallis to send 3,000 men north to assist him. Very few were in fact sent, but Washington fuelled Clinton's anxiety by keeping up the pretence that New York was his goal. Dummy camps were set up and filled with regular activity for the British to see, boats were built for possible river crossings and spies and rumour-mongers were sent into the British-held zone to confirm that a great siege of New York was in preparation.

On 19 August, Washington and Rochambeau set out for the 700-kilometre (450-mile) march to Yorktown. Extensive preparations had been made in advance to ensure supplies of cereal and animals along the way, while large siege guns were found for shipment by sea and river. A sizeable army of 4,000 was left in front of New York to sustain the deception. The remaining 4,000 French and 3,000 American troops began the march as if going to New York, then swung south. By the time Clinton realized he had been duped, it was too late to organize a large rescue mission for Cornwallis, and reinforcements did not finally sail until the very day that Yorktown was surrendered, 19 October. On 14 September, after three arduous weeks of marching and sailing, the American and French force arrived in Virginia, where it rendezvoused with troops serving under Major General Marquis de Lafayette, the young French officer who had devoted his career to the cause of American independence.

Altogether Washington now commanded an army of 19,000 men, 12,000 of them regular soldiers. As Washington moved south, a battle being fought at sea was to give him a decisive advantage. The French fleet arrived at Chesapeake at the end of August and was challenged a few days later by the British squadron lying off New York, commanded by Rear Admiral Thomas Graves. Neither side won a clear victory, but on 13 September, Graves retreated north, allowing a small French squadron under Admiral Comte de Barras to come south with supplies and reinforcements under the protection of the larger French fleet. Yorktown was now cut off from help from the sea.

Cornwallis had used his two months in the port to build up its defences. Some sixty-five cannon were dispersed around the perimeter and at Gloucester. Eight redoubts were built outside the main fortifications as strongpoints to hold up the enemy. The town had reasonable supplies of food but ammunition was limited. On 29 September, the enemy arrived and surrounded the town, with three divisions commanded by Rochambeau on the left, and three divisions under Washington on the right. The French commander had experienced many sieges in Europe so his expertise was used to build the first parallel line opposite the British fortifications. The engineers and labourers worked only at night to avoid British cannon fire and by the end of the first week of October they had a system of trenches, bunkers and batteries in place. The siege guns were drawn along poor roads by teams of horses and oxen and were not all in place when Washington ordered the opening salvo at 3 p.m. on 9 October after more than a week of bombardment from British guns.

The unexpected arrival of the enemy army had alarmed Cornwallis, who ordered all but three of the redoubts to be abandoned without a fight. He posted some 1,500 men across the river in Gloucester to forage for supplies and food, but they were beaten back by a covering French force. The blockade was complete. The town was shelled mercilessly while Washington ordered red-hot cannon balls to be aimed at ships in the harbour. Two vessels burned out completely. After two days of firing Washington was confident enough to order a second parallel line to be constructed. Under heavy cannon fire, the engineers dug a line of trenches and artillery sites only a few hundred yards from the British line. Cornwallis sent a troop of 350 men to infiltrate the line and spike the cannon, and although under cover of darkness they succeeded in slaughtering the gunners and knocking out six guns, the cannon were back in action the following day. On the night of 14 October, Washington and Rochambeau ordered men forward to seize two redoubts that blocked the American line. They were captured after a fierce fight, bayonet to bayonet. Cornwallis could see that the remorseless cannonade would sooner or later breach the defences while it wreaked havoc in the town and port. On 16 October, he ordered his troops to board the small boats still left in the harbour to cross to Gloucester with the hope of breaking out through weaker

French lines. As the evacuation began, the weather turned stormy and the plan had to be abandoned.

On 17 October, after conferring with his officers, Cornwallis decided to surrender. It took two days of negotiation, but on the morning of 19 October Cornwallis signed. It was a humiliating moment for British arms. The 8,087 British and Hessian soldiers and sailors were made to walk a mile through the lines of French and American troops to a field where they deposited all their weapons. All except the senior officers became prisoners-of-war. Losses for both sides had been low, given the importance of the victory. The French and Americans lost 75 dead, the British 156. For fewer than a hundred men, Washington sparked off the process that led to negotiations in Paris the following spring and, after protracted discussion, to the Treaty of Paris that secured the independence of the United States of America.

64. BATTLE OF THE LITTLE BIG HORN

25 June 1876

Among the modern legends generated by war, few are more compelling than the story of Custer's 'Last Stand' in the Indian wars of the 1870s. Today, visitors to the battlefield are shown Last Stand Hill. There are heroic paintings of George Armstrong Custer, surrounded by American Indians, battling vainly to the last bullet. The reality, however, bore little resemblance to the legend. The battle's outcome was the product of Custer's hubris – he thought of himself as the greatest Indian-fighter of his day – and of his sheer tactical incompetence. Above all it was testament to the cunning and courage of the Lakota and Cheyenne warriors, among the last American Indians to bend the knee, and of their remarkable commander, Chief Sitting Bull.

The battle came at a point when the government of President Ulysses Grant had decided no longer to tolerate the alleged threat posed by Indian tribes to white settlers and prospectors in the distant Black Hills of Dakota. These tribes, which so far had eluded the policy of placing them on permanent reservations, included the many branches of the Lakota people (the Teton Sioux) and of the Cheyenne. They were loosely grouped under the leadership of the Hunkpapa Lakota leader, Sitting Bull. The government considered any group refusing to enter the reservations to be in a state of war with the United States. Sitting Bull responded by declaring that he, too, was at war. When the 7th US Cavalry, led by Lieutenant Colonel Custer (though formally commanded by Brigadier General Alfred Terry), entered the Black Hills territory in June 1876, conflict was almost certainly unavoidable.

Thousands of his fellow warriors and their families rallied to Sitting Bull. A few weeks before Custer's arrival, Sitting Bull had undertaken the ritual mutilation of his arms with an awl to appease the Great Spirit (Wakan Tanka). He had then performed the Sun Dance for two days and was visited by a vision of white soldiers 'falling like grasshoppers'. The augury seemed good, and although Sitting Bull preferred to avoid open conflict by regularly moving his growing tepee camp, his people interpreted the vision as evidence that the American soldiers could be beaten. By the time the Lakota and Cheyenne had set up a camp of hundreds of tents on the banks of the Little Big Horn tributary, crowded with more than 8,000 of their people and 20,000 horses, the young warriors were eager for battle. Some had already attacked another army column under General George Crook near the Rosebud River, but had been driven off. Had Custer known of this encounter, it might have warned him of the size of Sitting Bull's forces, and of their willingness to engage in open battle rather than withdraw, as was often the case. His regiment arrived in the valley of the Little Big Horn on the morning of 25 June hoping to find Sitting Bull's camp.

The topography, of bluffs and hills shielded by forest, made it difficult to see anything ahead, so Custer took the unusual step of dividing his small regiment of around 550 troopers. Major Marcus Reno was sent to scout the south bank of the river, while Custer proceeded along the north face of the valley. Captain Frederick Benteen was detailed to go north to search out the Indian camp and was soon lost to view. The division of his force sealed Custer's fate. Reno led his men to a grassy slope from which some of Sitting Bull's camp (though not its vast extent) was visible. He ordered his troop to charge, only to find, as his tired cavalrymen stirred up a heavy dust, that there were hundreds of warriors forming in front of him. The troop halted, dismounted and tried to establish a firing line, but the Lakota, angered by the unprovoked attack, swept on, with perhaps as many as 800–900 warriors against Reno's 160 troopers and scouts. The US cavalry were armed with the powerful Springfield carbine, but this was a single-shot firearm. Many of Sitting Bull's men (and women) carried the Winchester repeater, which was fired with little accuracy, but which could overwhelm an enemy unit. Reno ordered a ramshackle retreat to a small wood. While the frenzy of the Lakota was temporarily appeased as they killed the wounded, then stripped and mutilated the bodies, Reno's survivors attempted an escape from the wood. More were caught and killed on the way but the few survivors met up with Benteen's troops returning with Custer's pack train.

Custer made his way with the remaining troopers, some 215 men, along a ridge beside the Little Big Horn. He decided to divide his force once again, leaving one group on a small hill to await Benteen's expected arrival, and leading the rest of his troop towards the river to find a ford across it. If Custer had a plan at all, it is most likely that he hoped to seize women and children in the camp and use them as hostages. He still had little idea of the size of the enemy he was facing. This was largely because the ground he had chosen was split with small, bush-covered gullies and ravines. The Lakota and Cheyenne were adept at concealment in their familiar landscape, and filed silently and almost invisibly into the network of gullies. As many as 2,000 remained hidden from the cavalry as they slowly snaked their way towards the group Custer had stationed on top of a hill. The deception was devastating for the morale of the frightened men waiting on the hillside. Suddenly the thousands of concealed warriors, led by Yellow Nose and Lame White Man, leapt out, firing rifles and shooting arrows in a deadly, smoke-screened hail. What followed was short, sharp and bloody. 'The firing was quick, quick,' one Cheyenne witness later recalled; 'Pop – pop – pop, very fast.' The Lakota warrior, Crazy Horse, found a way through a narrow defile behind the troopers and attacked them from the rear. Around twenty soldiers managed to escape to join Custer further along the small escarpment, now known as Battle Ridge. Those still alive were then rushed by the oncoming warriors and killed to a man.

How Custer reacted to the massacre can never be known. His remaining men gathered on what is now Last Stand Hill. More Lakota and Cheyenne crept forward under the cover of the ravines until, as before, they rose like an army of dragon's teeth from the ground. Some forty troopers tried to make a break for freedom down towards the river but they were overwhelmed and annihilated. Others tried to hide in a large ravine, where they were battered to death or shot. Custer stayed at the hill and took a bullet just below the heart. The evidence of a second wound through his temple suggests that his brother Tom may have given him the *coup de grâce*. Then Tom, too, joined the dead. Not one soldier survived. Custer's naked body had awls jammed into his ears, to make him hear better, according to the Lakota account; an arrow was used to pierce his penis. How many of Sitting Bull's men died is not known with any precision. The following night and day his warriors tried to annihilate the 400 troopers still commanded by Benteen and Reno, but most survived behind a makeshift barricade on top of a ridge above the river. On 26 July, Sitting Bull struck his camp and moved on.

The defeat of Custer shocked American opinion, not only because of the loss of a legendary 'Indian-fighter', but because it was the centenary year of American independence, when defeat by indigenous peoples was no longer thought possible. The army pursued the Lakota and Cheyenne to force them into reservations. Sitting Bull escaped to Canada but returned and surrendered in 1881. He was killed while resisting arrest in November 1890. The victory at Little Big Horn had a symbolic significance for both sides. Custer's Last Stand was treated as an iconic act of American heroism. Sitting Bull's victory came to be seen as a final monument to the struggle of American Indians protecting their vanishing birthright.

65. BATTLE OF ALAM HALFA
30 August – 4 September 1942

The five-day battle for the desert ridge at Alam Halfa has always been overshadowed by the greater victory secured at El Alamein two months later, yet it was, as one German field marshal later recalled, 'the turning point in the desert war'. British Commonwealth and Axis forces had battered each other back and forth across North Africa since 1940, but in 1942 the tide turned suddenly in favour of the combined German–Italian force commanded by Erwin Rommel, whose armies were now poised on the Egyptian frontier. One more defeat for the Allies and Egypt, the Suez Canal, even the seizure of the oil of the Middle East might be within Rommel's grasp. Hurried efforts were made by the British to use deception to exaggerate their strength in Egypt, but the real deceit was the defensive strength of the British Commonwealth position holding the ridge. Rommel expected another walkover but fell into a well-prepared trap.

By August 1942, the British were making every effort to prevent the Axis enemy from capitalizing on the defeat of British Commonwealth forces in June, when Rommel had seized Tobruk in Libya and had raced to the Egyptian frontier. A deception operation codenamed 'Sentinel' was set up to introduce dummy gun positions into the Allied front line but time was against it. Another operation involved moving vehicles and dummy installations to simulate two whole divisions, one in defence of Cairo and another in front of the port of Alexandria. False information was leaked to the enemy to support the idea that there were 30,000 additional troops in reserve. What Rommel did not know was that the British could read his encrypted Enigma messages – Ultra intelligence – and this deception proved crucial because it allowed the new commander of the British 8th Army, General Bernard Montgomery, to eavesdrop regularly on Axis plans.

Montgomery knew that he had to prevent any further disaster and was cautious in his approach. While preparing a major counter-offensive, he had to be able to absorb any stroke by the enemy. When Ultra revealed Rommel's intention to strike by the end of August, before American assistance to the British became too strong, it also revealed that Rommel was going to undertake his attack desperately short of fuel. An intensified and successful effort was made to sink or bomb all the Axis vessels trying to bring oil to North Africa, and the fuel shortage limited what Rommel could do in his renewed offensive. For his part, Rommel prepared a predictable operation, launching spoiling attacks against the main Allied line while he concentrated most of his armour on a southern axis for a surprise attack that would allow his forces to get behind the British lines and destroy them from the rear. Speed was of the essence, as it had always been in *Blitzkrieg* warfare. Though he did not know it, the tank balance slightly favoured him. There were 234 German and 281 Italian tanks to 478 British, which were mostly older and less well-armed models. Only in the air was he outnumbered, a situation made worse by the poor supply of aviation fuel and problems of maintaining aircraft for combat in the desert.

Knowing his enemy's plans in advance certainly made Montgomery's task easier. He strengthened the deep belt of mines on his southern front and dug in his tanks and anti-tank guns along the Alam Halfa Ridge, a shallow hill that dominated the whole line. Rather than be lured onto the desert where German tanks and the feared 88-millimetre anti-tank gun would destroy Montgomery's weaker vehicles, he opted for a plan to lure Rommel onto his guns, a case, as he famously said, of 'dog eat rabbit'. This was not what Rommel expected and the deception, made necessary by experience of the desert war, proved decisive. On the night of 30–31 August, Axis armour rolled forward towards Montgomery's southern flank. Rommel realized at once that the minefields were a much more complex barrier than had been thought. Suddenly flares burst in the air above his immobilized tanks and vehicles and tons of bombs were dropped accurately by the aircraft of the Desert Air Force. Co-operation between the Allied army and air force was critical to Montgomery's success. A relentless barrage from the air was kept up throughout the following three days while the German air force, suffering from fuel shortages and with its bases subjected to regular bombing, lost control of the skies on the first day.

When Rommel's army finally emerged from among the mines, the Germans were forced to wait for the Italian armour, still stuck in the minefield, to catch up. Further air attacks killed a number of senior German commanders, leaving the force decapitated at a critical moment. Rommel hesitated, but the lack of surprise and the loss of fuel, eaten up in the delays during the night, meant that his tanks could not press on east to surround the British Commonwealth line, since many would have been forced to come to a halt – sitting ducks for Allied artillery. At lunchtime Rommel changed tactic. He directed his panzer divisions to attack the Alam Halfa Ridge, hoping to lure out British armour so it could be destroyed. Instead his armour and vehicles came under withering tank, artillery and anti-tank fire and a ceaseless pounding from the air. When a German breakthrough seemed possible, Montgomery moved in the Royal Scots Greys from the reserve, and with the 1st Rifle Brigade they halted and turned back the German assault.

Rommel was nonplussed by British tactics but aware that he had little room left for manoeuvre. On 1 September, the 15th Panzer Division moved forward to assault the ridge again, but with the same result. Trapped between Montgomery's strengthening forces to the north and east, and with the impassable Qatarra Depression to his south, he was compelled to order a withdrawal. The sensible decision by Montgomery to hold a firm defensive line rather than run risks was confirmed when he released the New Zealand Division to try to drive the Germans further back on 3 September, only for the offensive to result in a high proportion of the casualties suffered during the battle – 1,140 out of a total of 1,750. Axis losses were not as great as might have been expected from the aerial pounding – 2,910 casualties and tank losses estimated at between 52 and 67 tanks – but hundreds of other vehicles were lost and the Axis forces were subjected to a demoralizing level of bombardment that left many dazed and disoriented and Rommel himself close to physical collapse. It was the turning point of the desert war, and no-one was more surprised than Rommel. An enemy he had constantly underrated, led by a commander whose caution the Germans misinterpreted, was not only not surprised by his attack, but had surprises in store for him. When it came to the more famous Battle of El Alamein two months later, Montgomery's use of deception to mask his intentions sprang one more, decisive, surprise.

66. THE NORMANDY INVASION
6 June 1944

Up to the very hour of the invasion of the Normandy coast on the morning of 6 June 1944, the Western Allies had succeeded in concealing from the Germans the exact destination of the vast amphibious operation – known as 'Overlord' – that had been preparing in southern Britain for months beforehand. Normandy was certainly on the Germans' list of guesses, but their failure to anticipate exactly where Allied forces would land meant that the German armies were divided between all the probable options and this fatally weakened their ability to react quickly enough to drive the invaders back into the sea. One of the greatest deception operations in history, code-named 'Bodyguard', allowed the Allies to achieve almost complete surprise and the first firm foothold in Adolf Hitler's 'Fortress Europe'.

Planning for the invasion had begun in April 1943, when the United States and Britain (supported by the British Commonwealth and Empire) finally reached a very provisional agreement for an operation to be mounted sometime in the spring of 1944 against the northern French coast. The British lacked confidence in the invasion; the Americans were determined to carry it through, but understood its many serious dangers. A way of reducing the risks was to mislead the enemy and weaken his initial response. However, to keep secret the destination of 4,000 ships, 2 million men and 12,000 aircraft was an unprecedented challenge. It seemed at the time almost impossible that the plan to invade Normandy (the date was not yet fixed) could be kept secret for six months. Practical measures could be taken: no-go zones were established around the southern coasts of Britain; travel restrictions were imposed, preventing anyone not on official business from leaving Britain in the last weeks before the invasion; mail was severely censored, and, in the weeks just before the invasion, mail to destinations abroad was suspended altogether. These precautions were designed to reduce the risk of information leaking out – an issue of secrecy rather than deception.

The Allies soon realized that a daring plan of misinformation was needed to convince the German leaders that they had correctly guessed the main destination of the invasion. In December 1943, 'Bodyguard' was launched, codenamed after Churchill's wry dictum that in war truth had to be concealed 'by a bodyguard of lies'. The plan was divided into two separate operations. 'Fortitude North' was designed to persuade the German High Command that a diversionary attack on Norway was planned using forces stationed in Scotland. This was to compel the German army to keep or even enlarge its forces there. 'Fortitude South' had to make it appear that the major invasion force was stationed in southeast England, ready to cross to the Pas de Calais and threaten western Germany. 'Fortitude North' had limited success, not only because Hitler had always worried about a Norwegian invasion and kept a larger garrison there than commitments on other fronts justified, but also because the German radio intercept system in Norway was tuned in to the approaching Soviet enemy and paid little attention to the false radio traffic signalled from Scotland. Much more rested on the success of 'Fortitude South'.

The operation in the south involved a complex web of deceit. In the first place, a vast phantom force was set up in the southern and eastern counties of England under the bogus title of First United States Army Group (FUSAG). Command was given to the most famous and flamboyant of American commanders, the pistol-toting General George S. Patton. This was given as public knowledge, to persuade the Germans that FUSAG must really exist. The falsehood was sustained by huge parks of dummy tanks made from rubber (built by prop-makers at the Shepperton film studios), landing craft of wood and fabric, and numerous air bases with dummy buildings and fake aircraft, and all illuminated sufficiently for the benefit of German night reconnaissance, but not so much as to make the deception evident. On a line west of the south-coast town of Portsmouth, where the real invasion forces were stationed, everything was dark and darkened – tents were covered, towels changed from white to khaki, smokeless stoves installed. By day, the Germans' aerial reconnaissance was hazardous, but their aircraft were allowed to photograph the FUSAG area in order to provide evidence of this as the main invasion force. Double agents in Britain – German spies who had been caught and turned, some for years – fed small drops of information to confirm the existence of FUSAG. One agent in particular, an elderly Dutchman known as 'Albert van Loop', originally recruited by the German secret service, then turned by the FBI, fed the Germans a diet of false military unit numbers. This was plausible because the American army numbered regular units from one to twenty-five and reserve units from seventy-six onwards, leaving plenty of numbers free in between. By January 1944, German military intelligence had identified fifty-five divisions in Britain when there were only thirty-seven, and by May had identified seventy-nine when there were only forty-seven.

The deception worked better than the Allies could have hoped. Hitler became convinced that Calais was the principal target. The Germans had evidence to show that Allied forces were clustered in southwest England, too, but it was assumed that this was for a diversionary assault in Normandy, not the real thing. This forced the German army to divide its forces in the West: fourteen divisions of the 7th Army were stationed in Normandy and Brittany; twenty divisions of the 15th Army were in the Calais region. More divisions were held in southern France in case of an invasion there. The idea that Normandy might be a ruse to divert the Germans west and allow FUSAG to attack an undefended Calais lodged so firmly in Hitler's mind that not until 7 August, long after the Allies had almost defeated the German army in France, did he order 15th Army to move. The timing was less important than the disposition of forces. The German army was weaker in Normandy than it would have been; even knowledge of the date of Operation Overlord would not have persuaded Hitler to risk putting all his eggs in the Normandy basket.

The story of D-Day itself is well known. The weather in early June seemed too poor to launch an invasion and the Germans relaxed. The commander of the coastal defence, Field Marshal Erwin Rommel, was away in Germany celebrating his wife's birthday; most of the junior commanders had been sent away on an exercise to Rennes. On the night of 5–6 June, paratroopers slowly descended into the Normandy countryside to secure bridges and roads. In the early morning of 6 June, German sentries on the coast were greeted by the staggering sight of an armada of 4,000 vessels emerging out of the mist. Soon, over 2,500 heavy bombers were pounding the German guns and concrete bunkers, followed by waves of rocket-firing fighter-bombers and a ferocious fusillade from the Royal Navy. On the three beaches assigned to British and Canadian forces – codenamed 'Gold', 'Juno' and 'Sword' – a lodgement was made by mid-day with modest casualties; on Utah Beach, assigned to the American army, a bridgehead 10 kilometres (6 miles) deep had been achieved by evening. Only on Omaha Beach, where neither the heavy bombing nor the naval barrage had done sufficient damage to the defenders, was the struggle bitter and costly, but here, too, a small beachhead was secured by evening. Over the next few days a more secure front was established and the invasion battle was over. Hitler and the High Command regarded Normandy as a sideshow and anticipated an assault on the Dieppe area further east some time in mid-June. 'Fortitude South' had done everything expected of it, confirming once again that in situations where the danger is great, surprise can be the most precious strategic asset of all.

67. OPERATION BAGRATION
22 June – 3 July 1944

The Russians in the Second World War were masters in the art of strategic deception. So important was this tactic that it was known in planning by a special term, *maskirovka*, meaning 'camouflaging of intentions'. From the successful defeat of Axis forces in November 1942, when deception had been critical in the strategy to surround Stalingrad, misleading the enemy as to strength and intentions was central to the revival of Soviet military fortunes. In late spring 1944, the head of German Army Intelligence in the east, General Reinhard Gehlen, told Army Group Centre, the major element in Germany's front line, to expect a 'calm summer'. Three weeks later the Soviets launched their biggest assault to date, destroying the resistance of Army Group Centre in Belorussia in one of biggest battles of the war. They gained almost complete surprise against an enemy on its guard against surprises.

The most important element in a deception is to work out what the enemy expects and to play on those assumptions, as the Western Allies did for the invasion of France. On the Eastern Front, the main effort of the Red Army in the winter and early spring of 1943–44 had been in Ukraine and southern Russia, where the geography favoured the rapid movement of mobile armies. The Germans assumed that this momentum would be maintained in the same area during the summer of 1944, and concentrated their armoured forces against the threat. Army Group Centre in Belorussia was the largest army group, dug in behind solid defences and protected, so it was thought, by the swampy, wooded Pripet Marshes to the south, where mobile warfare would be difficult. Any threat in the centre was expected to be a feint, to mask the real campaign from the direction of Ukraine.

In Moscow, these assumptions were exploited in the Red Army's planning. Every effort was made to make it appear as if the southern front were the main axis, while in complete secrecy massive forces were deployed into the area facing the centre. The result would confuse German planning and make a Russian success possible in both sectors – in Belorussia and Ukraine. Security began right at the top. Only five people knew of the plan – Stalin, his deputy Marshal Georgy Zhukov, the chief-of-staff Marshal Alexander Vasilevski, his deputy, General Alexei Antonov, and the chief of operations, General Sergei Shtemenko. They imposed on themselves a ban against mentioning the operation by telephone, telegraph or letter. They deliberately set no date. Officers from the central front had to report only two or three at a time, and in person. No-one was told more than he needed to know for his small part of the preparations. Only in a state as habitually paranoid as Stalin's Soviet Union could such a shroud of secrecy be woven with any hope of success.

In Belorussia the Red Army was ordered to make a show of digging in for the summer, creating a defensive line along the central front. Complete radio silence was imposed and all the main Soviet radio stations on the front closed down. Further south towards Ukraine, however, an entire dummy force was set up, with fake tanks and gun parks protected by real anti-aircraft fire to enhance the subterfuge. A second dummy force was constructed further north, on the Baltic front. German air reconnaissance was difficult in 1944, given the Red Air Force's overwhelming superiority, but the Soviet side allowed German aircraft to fly over and photograph the fake forces. The Germans had previously relied on information from Russian informers or spies, but these sources dried up as the Red Army advanced, victorious and vindictive. Gehlen and his intelligence department swallowed the bait. Additional armour was sent south to strengthen the front opposite Ukraine. Army Group Centre had only 553 tanks and self-propelled guns against a Soviet force of over 5,000, and only 775 aircraft against 5,300.

With the odds so heavily in its favour, the Red Army might not have needed deception at all. But the purpose of the campaign was to annihilate Army Group Centre swiftly, without mistakes or delays. Deception made the task on the battlefield much more straightforward. So it was that 1 million tons of supplies and 300,000 tons of oil were moved surreptitiously into place behind the four army groups designated for the operation. Train drivers were not told their destination, only the number of the train they were to drive. On the way to the front, soldiers and workers had to remain on the train at stations under guard, so they would not know where they were. The most elaborate preparations took place in the 'impassable' Pripet Marshes, where Soviet engineers, as noiselessly as possible, set up long wooden causeways strong enough to hold Soviet tanks as they passed across the swampy ground. Like the German penetration of the Ardennes Forest in May 1940, which unhinged French resistance, the sudden emergence of large units of Soviet tanks from out of the marshes would break German morale at a critical moment.

The Soviet battle line was drawn up in June. The operation was given the codename 'Bagration' after the Georgian prince Pyotr Bagration, who was killed defending Moscow from Napoleon. The date was finally fixed for 22 June 1944, two weeks after the Allied landing in Normandy. On the German side, Field Marshal Ernst Busch, with headquarters at Minsk, had only 792,000 men in 51 divisions. Facing him were four army groups, two commanded by Zhukov, two by Vasilevski, with a total of 2.6 million troops. On the eve of the assault, the German side received the first clues: partisans systematically targeted German rail links in the region, while Soviet bombers pounded German bases and supplies. Surprise was nevertheless almost complete. On 22 June, by chance the anniversary of the start of the Barbarossa campaign of 1941, armed forays were made into the German defensive line, and the following day the tidal wave of Soviet armoured forces struck the hapless defenders. While struggling to cope with this onrush, the Germans were then suddenly presented with the armour of Marshal Rokossovsky's First Belorussian Front rushing at them out of the marshy land to the south.

The battle was over quickly. Four major towns, designated special 'fortified zones' by Hitler's headquarters, were encircled and captured by 29 June. The leaders in Moscow lost no time in contrasting the speed and completeness of Soviet success with the slow progress of the Allies in Normandy, which were kept bottled up by a German force far smaller than Army Group Centre. On 3 July, Minsk was captured along with the whole of the German Fourth Army, and the battle was all but won. Some 300,000 German soldiers were killed or captured. The Red Army pursued the fleeing Germans to the River Vistula in Poland, campaigning across almost 500 kilometres (300 miles) in just six weeks. German reinforcement was impossible, not only because of the battle in France, but because on 13 July the Soviet southern front unleashed its campaign towards Lvov, the gateway to central Europe. On 17 July, the Red Army marched 57,000 German prisoners through the streets of Moscow, including 19 generals. After they had left, cleaning lorries passed along the same streets symbolically spraying disinfectant. Bagration was one of the greatest battles of the Second World War and an annihilating victory for the Red Army. Deception was key to making sure that the victory was sure and swift, as it had been for the Germans three years before. It could hardly have tasted sweeter.

68. THE SIX DAY WAR
5–10 June 1967

The Six Day War is in some sense a misnomer. What happened in the second week of June in the territories bordering the young state of Israel was a single colossal battle of manoeuvre between a greatly outnumbered Israeli Defence Force and the armies and air forces of almost all Israel's Arab neighbours. After six days, the battle was over, with Israel the bloodied victor. Deception mattered in the battle for two very distinct reasons. First, the Israeli armed forces successfully masked their intentions right up to the decisive moment when enemy aircraft were caught by surprise and destroyed, followed shortly by the invasion of the Sinai Peninsula. But second, the Arab states deceived themselves repeatedly during the battle by pretending all the time that they were winning when the truth was exactly the reverse.

Self-deception is a corrosive and dangerous influence in war. The Arab states – principally Egypt, Jordan, Syria and Iraq – had waited many years to stamp out an Israel that they had failed to emasculate in 1948 and again in the brief Suez war in 1956. Their anti-Semitic hostility was expressed in visceral terms, while for years in the 1960s they brought ever larger military resources in preparation for the moment when they could begin again to reclaim land they saw as properly Arab. By 1967, they were convinced that the military balance was at last decisively in their favour; the Soviet Union was supportive and encouraging, because it condemned Israel as an outpost of American capitalist imperialism, while the United States, it was thought, was bogged down with the war in Vietnam. When the Soviet Union mischievously (and wrongly) informed the Egyptian president, Gamal Abdel Nasser, that Israel was massing troops on the northern frontier opposite Syria, the Arab states moved closer to a showdown they were overconfident of winning.

The path to conflict was a complex mix of diplomacy, threats and military planning, but the decisive step was taken by Nasser when he reoccupied the demilitarized zone on Sinai and closed the Straits of Tiran to Israeli shipping in the third week of May 1967. Nasser's commander-in-chief, Abd al-Hakim Amer, drew up a battle plan for a major advance into Israel that would link up with the army of King Hussein of Jordan. The plan was poorly prepared and communicated, but Amer was confident that Egypt's 420 aircraft, 1,500 tanks and 200,000 men would sweep the Israelis away. Jordan was less convinced, but Hussein cemented an alliance with Nasser that compelled him to take part. Syria was more circumspect, but with the arrival of Iraqi reinforcements, the planned Operation Victory seemed more certain of success.

The Israeli government was caught between conflicting pressures – from Arab neighbours who were clearly, at least from the evidence, gearing up for a major war, from the Soviet Union, which was constantly warning Israel of its support for the Arab cause, and from the United States, which was desperate to persuade the Israelis not to provoke or be provoked into war. This locked the Israeli leadership into a vicious circle: either accept the changed balance in the Arabs' favour, or risk starting a conflict from which they were likely to be the losers. Chief-of-staff Yitzhak Rabin and Prime Minister Levi Eshkol opted for military preparations. Israel's 200 aircraft, 1,100 tanks and 275,000 reservists were primed for battle in case it came. To deceive the Egyptians, dummy movements and camps were simulated to make it look as if the chief threat was along the north coast of Sinai, when the bulk of Israeli armour was further south. A daring plan was worked out to neutralize enemy air power by a stealthy and unexpected first strike. Given the material imbalance, surprise and deception were valuable allies.

War came a step closer when, due to popular demand, the flamboyant ex-soldier, Moshe Dayan, with his distinctive eyepatch, was finally appointed Minister of Defence with the right to make key military decisions. He was all for pre-emption. 'We're not England here,' he told his cabinet colleagues, 'with its tradition of losing big battles first.' On 4 June, the Israelis decided to strike first while Nasser made sabre-rattling speeches in Cairo and all the Egyptian high command was away from Sinai. The operation began at 7 a.m. on 5 June when almost all Israel's 200 aircraft were airborne. Flying low under the radar, some made a wide loop to attack Egypt's bases from the west while others flew towards bases on Sinai, keeping complete radio silence. The surprise was an overwhelming, almost unbelievable success. No anti-aircraft guns fired because no-one expected an attack. The runways were pitted with bombs, radar installations blown up and 286 out of Egypt's 420 aircraft destroyed. One-third of Egypt's pilots died on the ground rather than in the air. Over the following two days the same destruction was meted out to the Jordanian, Syrian and Iraqi air forces.

The Arab forces and public were instead told that the Israeli air force had been destroyed and that the Egyptian army was advancing into southern Israel. Amer did not learn the full truth until later, and then became almost insensible with the crisis, locking himself in his office and communicating with no-one. The air strike, however, was only the start of the Israeli programme of deception. At 7.50 a.m. the invasion of Sinai began, first along the coast, which was heavily defended, because the Egyptians had been fooled into thinking the main thrust would come here. Then, gradually, major Israeli offensives with tanks and heavy artillery opened up further south. The tactics were a model of what *Blitzkrieg* strategy was thought to be. Moving as fast as possible, outflanking or surprising the enemy, using heavy air support, the Israeli attack was, as Ariel Sharon, commander of one of the southern divisions, described it, 'a continuous unfolding of surprises'. The enemy defended stoutly, but in the absence of clear commands or adequate intelligence and with only negligible air support, the front crumbled. The Egyptians made a disorganized retreat and Israeli tanks reached the east bank of Suez by 9 June. Arab soldiers were utterly confused and demoralized by the contradiction between Cairo radio, constantly broadcasting news of phantom victories, and the evidence all around of dead and dying soldiers, burned-out tanks and vehicles and the order to retreat at all costs back to Egypt.

Self-deception also encouraged the Jordanians to take advantage of the battle in Sinai. Listening to constant communiqués on the smashing of the Israeli air force and the advance into southern Israel, Hussein's commanders launched their own artillery attack with heavy guns from the West Bank, while Jordanian tanks tried to surround Jerusalem. Though Israel had wanted to avoid simultaneous conflicts to east and north, the threat could not be ignored and over the following three days fierce engagements, which resulted in some of the heaviest Israeli casualties, destroyed Jordan's smaller armed forces and captured not only the whole of Jerusalem but the entire West Bank. Syria had been hedging its bets, but joined in the propaganda chorus of Arab victories. Syrian guns devastated northern Israel until finally, despite fears of Soviet intervention, Israeli forces battled onto the Golan Heights in southern Syria and were poised, if they wanted, to march to Damascus. At 6 p.m. on 10 June, Israel agreed to enforce a ceasefire. Its territory was now more than three times greater than it had been before the battle.

The cost for the Arab cause was catastrophic. The Egyptians lost most of their air force and an estimated 10,000 military dead, as well as 85 per cent of their military equipment, while Jordan and Syria lost over 1,100 soldiers. Israel lost 679 dead and 36 planes, but the surprise attacks destroyed 469 enemy aircraft in the most comprehensive air strike of the century. Cairo radio's broadcasts switched from strident fabrications of victory to sombre reflection on defeat. Nasser broadcast his resignation (later rescinded) after he described the shock of the Israeli deception: 'We expected the enemy to come from the east and the north, but instead he came from the west.'

69. TET OFFENSIVE
30 January – 8 April 1968

In September 1967, General Vo Nguyen Giap, commander-in-chief of the communist North Vietnamese Army (NVA), announced a strategy to 'directly hit the enemy in his deepest lair'. The enemy was the Military Assistance Command Vietnam, a force of almost half a million American men and women supporting the South Vietnamese government and the Army of the Republic of Vietnam (ARVN). Rather than engage in a single pitched battle on unequal terms, the North Vietnamese plan was to infiltrate the whole of South Vietnam and attack hundreds of government buildings and military bases simultaneously. For the strategy to work, absolute secrecy was required. The preparation for what became known as the Tet Offensive involved one of the largest and most complex deception plans ever mounted in warfare.

Secrecy was necessary because the North Vietnamese Army and the southern communists, or Viet Cong, were not only greatly outnumbered by American and ARVN forces, but possessed only a fraction of the sophisticated military equipment available to the enemy. The deception involved two approaches: first, it was necessary to persuade the Americans that the real threat came in the North, from NVA incursions across the demilitarized zone between North and South Vietnam; second, it was necessary to infiltrate thousands of soldiers and guerrilla fighters into the towns and cities of the South in order to build up reserves of equipment and ammunition and to dig numerous bunkers and tunnels concealed from the enemy. This was done without divulging the overall plan to those involved, or the date of the operations. Over the winter months an estimated 65–80,000 communist regular and irregular troops moved into position around South Vietnam. To make surprise more certain, the North Vietnamese decided to launch the offensive during the Tet New Year celebrations at the end of January when a period of truce traditionally existed between the two sides. A seven-day truce was agreed from 27 January to 3 February, during which it was assumed that the South Vietnamese armed forces would be on low alert. The assault on the towns would also make it more difficult for the Americans to deploy the tanks, aircraft and helicopter gunships that they used in open country.

On 20 January, the NVA began the active part of its deception by launching a surprise assault on the American Marine base at Khe Sanh, near the northern border of South Vietnam. The redoubts around the base were attacked using rockets, mortars and machine-gun fire. The base itself came under heavy fire and a 1,500-ton ammunition dump exploded. The runway was hit, leaving only a 600-metre (2,000-foot) strip still viable. Using trenches and bunkers dug almost up to the base perimeter, the NVA kept up a remorseless fire. Khe Sanh threatened to become another Dien Bien Phu.

Both deceptions worked up to a point. The Americans' gaze was directed at Khe Sanh and their efforts went into reinforcing the threatened base. Although intelligence sources suggested that something was going to happen in the rest of South Vietnam, there was no clue as to when or how extensive the offensive might be. The Tet holiday was celebrated in North Vietnam a day early, a decision explained to the population by an apparently favourable configuration of the Earth and the Sun that day. In the South, soldiers began leaving for the annual celebrations, though a state of alert was finally ordered. The surprise was not total, but the scale of the offensive was quite unanticipated. In and around Saigon, the southern capital, two Viet Cong divisions and thirty-five NVA battalions had infiltrated, quite undetected.

In the end the deception was undone by the need for secrecy. The local units in the South did not understand the importance of co-ordination. The date for the attack was changed at the last moment from the night of 30 January to the night following, but some units failed to receive the instruction, and in the early hours of the morning of 30 January attacks began in twelve towns in the north of the country. The American commander, General William Westmoreland, still thought that this was a diversion to mask a greater assault planned across the demilitarized zone. Only when the following night showed communist attacks right across the country did the nature of the offensive become clear. The insurgents hit 5 out of 6 cities, 36 out of 44 provincial capitals and 64 out of 245 district capitals. Using automatic weapons, rockets and mortar fire, government buildings and military bases were either bombarded or, once communist sappers had done the work of cutting the wire and removing mines, infiltrated by NVA and Viet Cong forces. Fierce firefights broke out across the country, though in many cases the attacks were halted and the insurgents killed or captured. The strong assault on Quang Tri was defeated in a day of fighting. Only in three towns did a major battle develop, with heavy casualties on both sides.

The longest battles took place in Da Nang, Hue and Saigon. Da Nang, headquarters of the US 1st Corps, was subjected to two weeks of intermittent attack, including the destruction of aircraft on the Da Nang airfield. The American forces suffered 681 casualties in the struggle, the communist forces 1,300. In Hue, the NVA succeeded in taking over and occupying the town citadel. Fighting in difficult conditions around the city, the US Marines assigned to the battle found conditions not unlike Stalingrad. When buildings were cleared of the enemy in the day, they were stealthily reoccupied again at night. Not until 2 March was the city again in South Vietnamese hands. In Saigon, the communists concentrated on the Chinese suburb of Cholon, though attacks were also made on the US Embassy and the presidential palace. The street fighting in Cholon lasted a month, though the rest of Saigon was secured in a few days. Across the South and the Mekong Delta, hundreds of incidents brought a countrywide series of skirmishes and ambushes, but nothing on the scale of the continued battle at Khe Sanh, which more closely resembled a conventional battlefield. Here major redoubts at Lang Vei Camp and Alpha 1 were overrun, with heavy American casualties. At Lang Vei, 300 of the 487 defenders were killed, wounded or missing. Reinforcements battled their way in, but the key effort was made to re-open Route 9, the main road to the base. 'Operation Pegasus' involved 30,000 troops, the largest single deployment of the war. On 8 April, the siege was lifted and the NVA retreated back to the North.

The Tet Offensive failed on a military level, leaving an estimated 32,000 communist dead. The communist purpose had been to use the offensive to spark a revolutionary uprising among the South Vietnamese population and this it failed to do. There was, however, one major political achievement: the deception shocked American military commanders and the American public and accelerated the winding-down of the American commitment in Vietnam. By 1972, the Americans had withdrawn altogether. World opinion understood that the American assurances given in late 1967 that the war was almost over were entirely misplaced. In this sense, Tet was a turning point in the communist struggle to create a single Vietnamese nation by attacking the 'deepest lair'.

CHAPTER 5
COURAGE IN THE FACE OF FIRE

In a very real sense soldiers and sailors through all the ages of battle have been called on to display remarkable courage in the face of enemy fire. It is what they were expected to do even if forced to fight rather than volunteering. For professional soldiers it is the test they are trained for. A French paratrooper trapped at Dien Bien Phu in the Viet Minh siege asked his commander what to expect as the enemy closed in. 'You're a para,' was the reply. 'You're there to get yourself killed.' Courage in this case, as in so many others, is about accepting the strong possibility of death but remaining steadfast under the most threatening of battlefield conditions.

The psychology of courage is a complex question because it involves not only the explanation for why men keep their ground as they come under fire or attack but also the explanation for why that courage cracks at certain moments and terror-stricken flight takes over. For sailors the choices are, of course, narrower. Throwing yourself into the sea is not much of an option. For airmen, in the twentieth century, options were also very narrow, though in an emergency the parachute gave in most cases the opportunity of safety. For submariners the courage demanded was considerable, since from a stricken submarine there was often no escape. For armies the possibility of flight is usually an option, though throughout history it has often been as dangerous a choice as holding ground, since enemy horsemen and infantry give chase and cut down anyone they catch.

The test of courage is evidently something that all soldiers think about. In some cases military service was required of all men, even of all ages, as in Mongol society or in Menelik's Ethiopia, so that fighting was considered a social obligation and cowardice a sign of failed masculinity, to be punished usually by death. But even fighting as a sign of gender status will leave men pondering on the eve of battle what combat will be like and what are the chances of survival. Clearly group solidarity is a critical factor in explaining how men face fire. The universe of moral commitment becomes very small in battle, confined to you and your companions, for whom the pressure to give mutual aid and to fight as effectively as possible is, in battle, perhaps a stronger bond than the requirement to obey what chiefs or commanders order you to do. Prowess has little to do with it (though trained men will evidently fight more competently than an untrained mob), because courage can be displayed by men with little military experience or competence. The American Civil War exacted exceptional levels of casualty from men drawn from a civilian milieu and thrust within weeks into battle, where they learned to stand and fight through a brutal apprenticeship.

Courage on the battlefield is also sustained by the superstitious hope, often cemented by religious faith in the hereafter, that you will not be the one killed that day. The ranks of French soldiers and cavalry at Borodino that stood in line waiting for the move forward while Russian ball and canister shot repeatedly smashed one or more of them to pulp, displayed an apparently inexplicable courage not to wheel around and run back out of range. The arbitrariness made battle a gamble and in most of the battles described here the overwhelming majority survives, even in the face of defeat. Complete or near complete annihilation, such as Custer faced at Little Big Horn or Harold at the Battle of Hastings, is unusual. The hope for survival acts as a counterweight to the inescapable anxiety felt by the average soldier about the prospect of death. One Confederate officer writing after Gettysburg confessed that 'enthusiasm of ardent breasts in many cases ain't there...the thought is most frequently, Oh, if I could just come out of this charge safely how thankful would I be!' He charged nonetheless and half his division became a casualty.

The courage required in the face of fire is near universal since no part of a battlefield is particularly safer than another; even the baggage train will be captured, ransacked and put to the sword in the event of defeat. The spectrum of courage displayed is nevertheless a wide one, and in battle the example set by commanders, who even as late as the eighteenth century could be monarchs as well, plays a critical part, spurring on more timid troops or trying to stop a pell-mell flight if it occurs. The Ethiopians understood this at Adwa and told marksmen to pick out the Italian officers, in their splendid white uniforms and coloured sashes, knowing that the troops they commanded would flee once their leaders were dead. Fear was as infectious as courage, for once troops become leaderless, uncertain and conscious of probable defeat, the psychological power that kept them fighting bravely can evaporate in moments. Courage in the face of fire needs to be nurtured and sustained in the heat of battle. Natural courage is rarer, though it certainly exists.

70. BATTLE OF MARATHON
Summer 490 BCE

The Battle of Marathon is best remembered today for the 42-kilo-metre (26-mile) race named after it. Following the battle, the Athenian messenger Thersippos (or Phidippides – there remains some uncertainty) ran from the plain of Marathon all the way to Athens where he shouted out the news of the Athenian victory and fell down dead. This story, like many accounts of Marathon, is probably a fiction. But running did feature in the battle itself, and may well be the explanation for the Greek victory that Thersippos died for.

There might never have been a battle at Marathon had it not been for the persuasive skills of the Athenian general, Miltiades. In the summer of 490 BCE the Greek city was faced with a difficult choice. After taking part in a raid in Anatolia against the vast Persian Empire, ruled by the emperor Darius I, the Athenians knew that they faced the threat of retaliation from an army that held the whole of the Middle East in thrall. Darius is generally thought to have been a benign autocrat towards those peoples who accepted Persian suzerainty; to those who crossed him, however, he was capable of a studied cruelty. In 490, he ordered Datis, a Mede in his service, to lead an expedition to capture the islands of the Aegean and enslave the Athenians. He set off in an estimated 300 boats. The number of men and horses with him grew much larger in the telling. Modern estimates suggest around 12,000 soldiers and perhaps 1,000 horses, more than enough, it was assumed, to complete the task. The Athenians had no cavalry and lacked the large body of trained and toughened archers and horsemen Datis brought with him.

Datis took a winding route from Rhodes, past the island of Naxos (which he sacked) and on to the city of Eretria, which was also slated for destruction and enslavement. After a six-day siege, traitors let in the Persians, who burned and looted the town and put 780 in chains on a temporary prison island. Athens faced a victorious and potentially unstoppable force. The Athenian assembly debated their prospects. Miltiades, who had already clashed with the Persians elsewhere, was in favour of fighting, and his arguments won the day. Athens was the largest Greek city and could raise perhaps 10,000 hoplites (the heavily armed infantry) and 8,000 lightly armed men, but no horsemen. The

Greek commander was Kallimachos, but Miltiades seems to have been the inspiration behind the Greeks' subsequent strategy.

Datis arrived with his boats off the coast of the plain of Marathon. He probably chose the site because it afforded ample ground for his cavalry to deploy. He camped and waited. The Athenians, joined by perhaps 1,000 allies from Plataea, marched to the southern side of the plain. Here the ten Athenian generals (one for each of Athens's tribes) argued again about whether to fight or not. Miltiades prevailed with the casting vote of Kallimachos (not for nothing was Athens the home of democracy). The fighting began when it was the turn of Miltiades to be the general in charge.

Recent accounts suggest that it was Miltiades who worked out how Athens might defeat the larger, more experienced and well-armed enemy in front of it. He probably observed that the cavalry was camped some distance from the infantry, possibly divided from them by a small lake, and that it would take time for all the horses to deploy onto the plain. Some historians have suggested that the cavalry had already gone back on board ship, with a view to sailing round to Athens by sea, but that would seem a strange decision, given the importance of the battle, and horses are evident on a sarcophagus in the northern Italian city of Brescia, on which the Greek painting of the battle, made just thirty years after the event, was reproduced in marble. The Athenians' plan was to urge the Greek army to run across the plain (approximately a mile) and engage the Persian archers and infantry before the cavalry could intervene. This was a risky plan, and it forced the Greeks to shed some of their protective armour to run as lightly burdened as possible. It also meant that the whole Athenian army would be exposed during its ten-minute run across the plain to the withering fire of the Persian archers. This required a special courage.

Sacrifices to the gods carried out beforehand suggested good omens, which may have shored up any doubts among the Greek soldiers: Miltiades led them onto the plain, his line thicker on the two wings, deliberately thinner in the centre, until they were about a mile (eight *stadia* in the ancient Greek units of length) from the Persian lines. A trumpet sounded, and Miltiades gave the order, 'Rush at them!'

Those ten minutes of running, not too fast to exhaust them but fast enough to disconcert the enemy, were a formidable trial for the Greek army. The Persian archers shot cascades of arrows, but they were less effective at a running target, and the Greek line held. Before the Persian horses could join the action, the Athenians crashed into the Persian line, warmed up, like modern sportsmen, from the run. There is no record of how long the battle with sword and spear lasted, but when the Persians broke through the weaker centre, the two wings, where the Greeks had succeeded, wheeled round to envelop the advancing enemy from the side and rear. The Persians probably panicked, and tried to fight their way back to their boats. At this point the Athenians exploited their advantage ruthlessly, killing the Persians with their better thrusting spears or drowning them at the edge of the sea. Only seven ships were captured as Datis made his getaway, but the Persian dead numbered 6,400. It is said that the Athenians lost 192, including Kallimachos, who, legend has it, died holding onto a Persian ship with his teeth after losing both his arms. The enemy corpses were stripped of gold and left to rot.

Marathon has been hailed many times as the battle that saved Western civilization from oriental despotism. More than a single battle was needed to achieve that, but it confirmed the special status of Athens and paved the way for the later victories that really did end Persian ambitions in Attica. It has also left a permanent imprint on the modern view of ancient Greece. The brave and disciplined run across the plain at the enemy was the key to victory; it is echoed in the awful run through no-man's land forced on the infantry of the First World War, which brought a bitter stalemate rather than a rich and legendary victory.

71. BATTLE OF THE CATALAUNIAN FIELDS (CHÂLONS)

20 June 451

One of the most famous battles of antiquity occurred at an unknown site in northeastern France in June 451 between a mixed Roman–Gothic force and the raiding army of Attila, commander and king of the fearsome Huns, a nomadic people from Central Asia. Their reputation for ferocity has echoed down the ages, and 'Hun' was the pejorative term chosen by the Allies to describe the Germans in the First World War as an indication of how savage and barbarous their war-making was considered to be. In the late Roman period, the approach of the Huns struck terror into peoples who had become accustomed to the regular incursions of other nomadic invaders. The Huns were seen as an unstoppable force and their menace almost apocalyptic. The victory over Attila – it was in truth closer to a draw – showed that, in the right circumstances, no force is unstoppable. However, the army that gathered at the Catalaunian Fields to oppose him did not know that. They needed a double courage to confront the Huns and the terrible reputation that preceded them.

In 451, Attila, after campaigns in the Eastern Roman Empire, decided to launch a large raid into Roman Gaul from his base in modern Hungary, there to seek further booty. His advance caused consternation, and later Christian chroniclers saw him as the scourge of God, sent to punish Christian communities for their lack of faith. Attila sacked Metz and Rheims (their murdered bishops became instant martyrs, and later saints) and laid siege to Orléans. His army, according to the Byzantine historian Jordanes, writing a century later, numbered half a million. It was almost certainly a fraction of this figure, but nevertheless a formidable host composed not only of Hun tribes but also eastern Goths under three brothers, Valamar, Thiudimer and Vidimer.

However, besieging a large, well-defended city was not a Hun speciality, and when news arrived that a large Roman army was approaching from the south, Attila broke off the siege, apparently anxious to avoid a major confrontation. The Huns began to withdraw, but were caught by their enemy at some point on the plain of Champagne between Rheims, Châlons (from which the battle has generally taken its name) and Troyes.

The presence of a Roman army was not accidental. The westward march of the Huns clearly made the loss of Gaul, a major territory in the Western Roman Empire, a possibility. This danger alerted the Roman general Flavius Aetius, who had at one time allied with Hun tribes for his own purposes, to the defence of Gaul. The common threat also brought the local king of the Visigoths, Theodoric, together with his eldest son Thorismund, into alliance, along with the Burgundians and Bagandae from eastern Gaul, who had already suffered at the hands of the Huns, and the Alans from the west. The allied armies numbered perhaps 30–50,000, though the exact numbers are not known. Attila's host has been estimated at around the same size, but both figures are largely guesses. The Huns fought with their traditional cavalry armed with bows and swords and lassos, but also fought on foot with swords and axes. The Roman–Visigothic army had heavy cavalry, light cavalry, traditional Roman infantry with sword and javelin, and more lightly armed troops from the non-Roman allies. Aetius, who as a hostage with the Huns many years before had developed a shrewd understanding of their battle tactics, opted for a formation that put his weaker forces in the centre and his stronger forces on the wings. Attila adopted the contrary pattern, with his stronger veterans in the centre, but more vulnerable forces on either side.

It is thought that the battle began in the early afternoon and went on to a bloody crescendo at dusk. The combat hinged around a low ridge overlooking a sloping plain. The Roman army attacked it from the right, the Huns from the left, but the fight for the crest of the ridge fell to the Roman side, aided by a flanking attack from the Visigothic cavalry. The Huns were pushed back on their flanks and finally broke back down the slope. Attila is supposed to have admonished them to stand and fight: 'For what is war to you but a way of life?' They charged back up the slope but were always at a disadvantage. Bitter hand-to-hand fighting followed. The gore-soaked ground was supposed to have turned a small river running across the fields red with blood. Theodoric was killed in the mêlée. At the end of the battle Aetius was unable to find his camp, so he stayed with his Gothic allies overnight. But the clear result was the retreat of the Huns, worn down by the long battle, who returned to their camp of encircled wagons and waited to see what the following day would bring.

This was indeed a historic moment and it was achieved by a mixed army of men whose individual motives and fears explained their courageous stand against the waves of Hun cavalry and foot soldiers. They showed that the Huns were not invincible, though it had been an unfamiliar contest for Attila, who preferred weaker opponents or a battle on the run rather than one against a large, disciplined army. The memory of that victory lingered on in European folklore as the moment when Europe was saved again from the domination of Asia. In truth, Attila was followed over the centuries by waves of other nomadic invaders from the east, but nothing has stayed in the collective consciousness of the West so firmly as the turning of the tide against the Huns.

Over the days that followed the battle, the Visigoths and Romans broke camp and left, allowing Attila the opportunity to take his battered army swiftly back to Hungary. According to the best-known account, he died two years later from a nosebleed that choked him to death after a night of heavy drinking. As so often in the ancient world, Aetius was not thanked for his pains. Three years later he was suspected of attempting to usurp the imperial throne, and was slain at court in Ravenna by the emperor Valentinian himself, wielding a meat-cleaver. Savagery was not a Hun monopoly.

72. BATTLE OF POITIERS-TOURS
25 October 732

Few battles in European history are more famous than the defeat of an Islamic army somewhere between the northern French cities of Poitiers and Tours in October 732. For centuries this has been seen as the battle that finally turned the tide of an inexorable Arab expansion and saved Europe from an Islamic future – a battle, therefore, of world-historical significance. As in so many medieval conflicts, however, the battle is shrouded in mystery. Almost everything about it, including the exact site, the number of soldiers present, the pattern of the battle and the number of casualties, has to be surmised from the scantiest of surviving manuscripts and from the topographical evidence. What is certain is that the battle came to symbolize the turning of a tide of conquest that had seemed remorseless. The Arab incursion into Spain in 711 had proved unstoppable; the capture of southwest France was completed by 725; heavy raids into the rest of southern and central France had followed. If no-one had stopped the raid of 732 it is difficult not to assume that sooner or later much of France would have become an Arab province.

The stumbling block to further Arab expansion was the Frankish Merovingian kingdom, ruled for decades not by the king but by the 'mayor of the palace' whose position came by inheritance. The mayor in 732 was Charles, nicknamed Martel after the word for 'hammer'. He had twenty years of campaigning behind him defending his empire from the barbarian east and from the rival claims of ambitious French nobles and bishops. He had not fought the Arab armies, though he knew of the raids they had carried out deep into French territory, while the Arab rulers of Spain (known then as al-Andalus) knew little about the Merovingians or their military prowess. In 731, the new governor of al-Andalus, Abd al-Rahman al-Ghafiqui, planned a major raid (perhaps even an invasion) into the western French territory of Aquitaine. Booty and slaves may well have been the principal motive, but it cannot be ruled out that this was indeed an exploratory excursion preliminary to more permanent settlement. The call went out for volunteers, many of whom came from the Berber territories of Arab-ruled North Africa. Starting out from Pamplona in northern Spain, Abd al-Rahman led an army of perhaps 15–20,000 (various estimates suggest a lower or much higher number) towards Bordeaux and the rich pickings of western France.

Aquitaine was ruled by Duke Eudes (generally known as Odo the Great). Caught between Arab expansion from al-Andalus and the ambitions of Charles's Merovingian kingdom, Eudes tried to maintain his independence. In spring 732, Abd al-Rahman marched unexpectedly through the difficult passes of the western Pyrenees and arrived in southern Aquitaine. Within weeks he had captured and sacked Bordeaux. He then destroyed Eudes's army at the Battle of the River Garonne, where Christian refugees were slaughtered. Eudes threw himself on the mercy of Charles Martel by agreeing to become a Merovingian vassal. Charles seems to have been keen to prevent the Arab army reaching his own territory in northwest France and sent out a call to muster his scattered forces. He led them to the city of Tours, where the wealthy monastery of St Martin was probably the Arab goal. After three months ravaging western France and amassing wagon trains of booty and slaves, Abd al-Rahman moved north towards Poitiers and Tours. How far he went is not known with certainty. It is clear that the advance took place in the middle of October as far as, or perhaps across, the River Vienne. From here on, the evidence is almost non-existent.

So little did the Arab army think of the threat from the Franks that scant effort seems to have been made to scout far ahead. It is likely that the usual Arab advance guard and skirmishers ran into Charles's army camped south of Tours and pulled back. By 18 October, the Arab army was behind the Vienne where it set up camp. Charles, it is assumed, followed at a distance, crossed the river, and then drew up in a defensive position of his own choosing. The two sides were organized and armed differently. Abd al-Rahman's army consisted of a core of Arab warriors and a large number of Berber levies; both

forces were on horseback, probably using stirrups (a point of continuing controversy), and were armed with swords and spears. There
was a smaller body of infantry using bows, slings and javelins. The
Frankish army was mainly infantry, using long spears, swords and
axes in a phalanx formation. How many cavalry were present is simply
not known. Both were experienced armies rather than raw recruits.
How many men Charles had with him is again mere speculation,
though a similar number of 15–20,000 is possible.

The course of the battle is again open to conjecture. By chance
the date, Saturday 25 October, is known with certainty from both
Arab and Christian sources. Brief accounts, written later in the
century by 'Anonymous of Córdoba' and in *Continuator of Fredegar's
Chronicle*, suggest that Charles drew up his army in a strong defensive
line, supported by cavalry commanded by Eudes, and perhaps sheltered on both flanks by thick woodland. Here the Arab cavalry
probably attacked head-on and were beaten back (the Franks managed
to 'grind them small in slaughter' according to the *Chronicle*). Eudes
may have outflanked the Arab army and attacked its large camp, full
of loot and Berber families and followers. It seems likely that Abd
al-Rahman retreated back to his camp to save it from being pillaged
and that it was here that he was killed, possibly by a javelin. The
camp was not captured but the defeat was clearly heavy enough to
compel the Arab army to withdraw during the night, leaving the
tents and most of the wealth behind them. They made their way
back to Narbonne in the Arab southwest and thence back to al-
Andalus, an intact, if defeated, force.

Historians argue over the significance of the victory at Tours or
Poitiers, and about the unrecoverable details of the battle. The Arab
name for the battle is 'The Road of Martyrs', which suggests heavy
losses. The figures given later range from 1,000 to an implausible
300,000, but losses there would certainly have been. The victory did
not stop further Arab depredations in France over the next four years,
but they were confined to major raids. By 759, most of southwest
France, including Narbonne, had fallen under Merovingian rule. The

battle was perhaps not the grand clash of religions as it has so often been presented. Charles Martel did not see the Arab threat as much different from the threat from his unruly vassals or his pagan neighbours; the Umayyad Empire was also crumbling from within, so Poitiers could be seen as more effect than cause. Nevertheless it was a battle worth winning against an enemy that the battered Christian populations of Europe had thought might scourge them for ever.

73. BATTLE OF LECHFELD
10 August 955

The battle that took place over a number of days in and around the Bavarian city of Augsburg in 955 signalled a dramatic change in European history. The defeat of an invading Hungarian (Magyar) army, organized on principles that had dominated warfare in Eurasia for centuries, brought to an end the long age of violent migrations from the Asian heartland. The only object that stood in the way of Hungarian conquest was an army of Germans hastily brought together by the Saxon king Otto I early in August. The Saxons knew their enemy, for German armies had suffered a catastrophic defeat at the hands of Hungarian horse-archers forty-five years earlier on the plain of Lechfeld. Otto understood that the hail of arrows likely to greet his men had destroyed most armies that had suffered such an attack, from the Parthian defeat of the Romans at Carrhae onwards. He led his army towards the invaders hoping that courage and luck would be enough.

The battle was sought by the Hungarian leaders, among whom the best-known was the general Horka Bulksú. Their aim was to impose Hungarian military domination on central and southern Germany and even beyond, but above all they wanted booty and tribute. Otto had troubles of his own with local insurrections and Slav wars to the east, but in the summer of 955, these dangers were dwarfed by the threat of Hungarian military might undermining the whole region of central Europe. When emissaries from the Hungarians arrived in late June at Otto's base in Magdeburg, it was evident that they were there to assess his readiness for war. What they saw reassured them, and a large Hungarian army of infantry, siege weapons and, above all, an estimated 9–15,000 horsemen, lightly armoured but carrying the lethal short bow of the steppe archer, set out for southern Bavaria. They crossed the River Lech and ravaged the countryside over a wide area, taking plunder but also creating a barren waste for any approaching army. They then laid siege to Augsburg, ruled by a very martial bishop, Ulrich, in the hope of tempting Otto south for a decisive battle.

Otto was told of the invasion by messengers from Bavaria. He took only a few of his Saxons with him, since the Saxon army was still battling with its Slavic neighbours, and called on levies from Bavaria, Swabia and Bohemia to join him. His son-in-law, Conrad the Red, brought 1,000 Franconian horse. By early August, they had gathered near Ulm to cross the Danube and confront the enemy. Augsburg was not yet captured, thanks in part to a brief sally by Ulrich's professional soldiers to drive away a Hungarian assault on a weakly held city gate, but when the Hungarians got news of the advance of Otto's army, they withdrew to their camp on the east side of the River Lech. There they prepared a strategy to lure Otto onto the plain, the Lechfeld, where their mobile archers would surround and annihilate the Germans once again. The infantry were to be put in front, to entice the enemy horsemen, while part of the cavalry would sweep northwest to outflank Otto's army and attack the rear as the main Hungarian force waited on the edge of the plain to smash the Germans fleeing from the flanking attack. The horsemen each had spare mounts and a large supply of arrows.

The details of the battle are little known, since the two main accounts, both written some years later by contemporaries, gloss over the actual combat. There are no reliable estimates of the size of either force, though Otto's eventual victory was hailed as a remarkable triumph against overwhelming odds. What is known is that Otto, afraid of exposing his men to encirclement and probable annihilation by the enemy archers, organized his army into six columns, protected at the back by units of Bohemians guarding the baggage train, and marched them through the forest northwest of Augsburg, in rough, wooded terrain where horsemen and arrows were equally disadvantaged. This was too late to prevent the Hungarian horsemen sent to outflank him from attacking the Bohemians and either destroying them or driving them off. Greed or overconfidence led them to loot the baggage rather than finish off the Germans. This was a tactical error, since suddenly out of the forest stormed Conrad's column of Franconians, who, it seems likely, killed the pillaging Hungarians. No quarter was usually given.

The battle that followed was not fought, despite the name, on the Lechfeld, but further north on the edges of the Rauherforst. Otto chose battle with the shelter of the trees behind him and his left flank protected by high cliffs to prevent any outflanking movement. What happened next is not known, but the best estimates suggest that Otto probably did what Epaminondas did at Leuchtra when he routed the Spartans – he concentrated his main force on one wing, and used it to drive the enemy back and encircle them. The strategy, if such it was, seems to have half-worked this time. The Hungarian infantry was pushed back, surrounded and annihilated to a man, but the archers tried to lure Otto onto the plain by feigning retreat. Otto understood the dangers and refused to be drawn. As it was, his army was subjected to volley after volley of light and deadly arrows, which could penetrate armour when shot in a long arc. Conrad the Red fell to an arrow as he loosened his armour to cool off. The critical factor seems to have been the discipline of the Germans, who neither gave way in the face of heavy casualties nor risked pursuit and the danger of encirclement.

Puzzled, exhausted or both, the Hungarian cavalry retreated past Augsburg, allowing Otto to capture their camp. The decisive nature of the defeat, however, was due to what happened next. Over the following two days, the Hungarian cavalry were separated into small groups and ambushed by soldiers from the smaller fortified cities behind them. Most seem to have been killed or captured; their leaders, including Horka Bulksú, were taken to Regensburg to be hanged in public. Why this happened has eluded clear historical explanation, but the best guess is rain, or, as contemporary Christians called it, the 'tears of Saint Lawrence', a Christian martyr whose feast day fell on 10 August. Heavy summer storms are now thought to have followed the engagement by the Rauherforst, swelling the rivers that were usually passable by cavalry and, crucially, rendering the highly crafted composite bows, on which Hungarian military success depended, all but useless. Damp and rain led the bows to unravel or limited their operational effectiveness. Left to wield rather brittle sabres, it is thought that the Hungarians had nothing to match the heavy lances and swords of German and Bohemian cavalry. This remains the most plausible explanation for the catastrophic Hungarian defeat, which ended their depredations for good, allowed Otto to claim the title of Holy Roman Emperor a few years later, and earned the fiery Ulrich his sainthood.

74. BATTLE OF ARSUF
7 September 1191

Among the great battles of the Christian crusades in Palestine, the Holy Land, one of the most remarkable was the sharp defeat inflicted on the Muslim Kurdish leader, Salah ad-Din (better known as Saladin), by the combined might of a European army led by the king of England, Richard I, the 'Lionheart'. The Arab chroniclers respected Richard (never, one wrote, was there 'a subtler or a bolder opponent'). The conflict at Arsuf, near the Mediterranean coast of present-day Israel, was a model of medieval crusading warfare. It involved extraordinary courage and patience under constant harassing attack from Saladin's mounted archers, who had triumphed at Hattin, four years earlier. The outcome at Arsuf resolved little, but Richard showed that Saladin and his army were not invincible if heavy European cavalry was used in the right way, combined with supporting infantry.

The Third Crusade was going nowhere when Richard arrived in 1191. The crusaders were laying siege to the port of Acre and were themselves besieged by Saladin's army at their rear. The crusaders had solid defences, but Acre had equally solid walls and did not easily give way. It had taken almost two years to starve the city into submission when Richard arrived in time to march in and plant his standard. Saladin reached an armistice with the crusader leaders, biding his time to raise more fighters from across the Middle East, but he failed to honour his pledge to pay ransom for the prisoners taken at Acre, and on 20 August 1191, Richard ordered 3,000 of them slaughtered in cold blood in sight of Saladin's men. Richard was a cautious strategist, however, and determined to march on Jerusalem, the key prize for any crusader, only after first securing the ports of Jaffa and Ascalon as supply bases for his march on the Holy City.

The soldiers allegedly left Acre with some reluctance, detained by prostitutes, according to the Arab account, 'tinted and painted...with nasal voices and fleshy thighs'. But Richard was adamant. The women were ordered to remain behind while he deployed the army in a way that made strategic sense, but which required him to impose a tough discipline on all those under his command. For the march south, he divided his forces into three divisions of heavy cavalry with a strong rearguard composed of the Knights Hospitaller and the Templars. He had the sea on one side as a natural protection and as a source of regular supply by merchant vessels plying down the coast. His numerous infantry and archers were divided into two – one force marching on the seaward side, one on the other flank protecting the horsemen, as was usual in Frankish warfare. They crossed over and exchanged roles as the landward troops became tired from the constant skirmishing with Saladin's archers, a system of rotation that worked well as the long column wound its way through the hilly and wooded country running down to Jaffa.

The strategy was designed to conserve the force and prevent a second Hattin. Richard knew, just as the Arab strategists knew, that his knights were vulnerable as soon as they were isolated from their main body. Once their horses were killed, they were easy prey. Richard ordered the heavy cavalry to stay in column and on no account to rise to provocation from the enemy or charge them without his order. This meant keeping tight formation for days while Saladin's shadowing force rode up close, showering the crusaders with missiles. At a distance, their arrows had limited penetration and infantry could be seen still fighting with arrows stuck in their thick leather tunics, like so many walking pin-cushions. The danger of not keeping formation was shown when the rearguard fell back too far and enemy horsemen rode in to attack the baggage train, but Richard hurried back from the front of the column to restore order.

The marching army had to show extraordinary perseverance under constant attack, and exceptional patience. For horsemen in armour, in conditions of exhausting heat and dust, the forbearance must have seemed a laborious penance. Heat exhaustion claimed victims as did the spears and arrows of the circling enemy. Somehow Richard stamped his authority on the men toiling through the heat. Saladin decided they could only be halted by a pitched battle and he chose the plain north of Arsuf to mass his army. Richard kept going, commanding an even tighter formation and insisting that no charge should be made by his knights until the right moment, signalled by six trumpet blasts, two each at the rear, in the centre and in the van. The object, if it came to it, was to hit the enemy with a massed charge of concentrated power to destroy his capacity to revive and retaliate. By mid-morning Saladin had seen enough and he ordered his cavalry to attack. Enveloped in a cloud of dust a menacing wave of horsemen bore down on Richard's column, accompanied by the sound of braying trumpets and pounding drums. This was the critical point for the heavily armoured crusaders, who had to stay in formation, taking casualties but unable to fight back, while their infantry fought off the cavalry as best they could.

The final charge by Richard's cavalry began by chance. Provoked beyond endurance, the Hospitallers at the rear, without waiting for the agreed signal, suddenly charged at the encroaching enemy, riding unexpectedly through the ranks of their own infantry. Richard saw at once what had happened and ordered the rest of his knights to charge as well, making a powerful battering ram of horsemen aimed at Saladin's tiring forces. The impact was exactly what Richard had hoped for. Saladin's forces retreated, then tried to rally for a counter-blow. Richard and William des Barres then led the Norman and English knights, who had been held back in reserve, for a final hammer blow against the enemy. Richard did not earn his sobriquet 'Lionheart' for nothing. The Arab chroniclers described a man with a 'burning passion for war'. Christian writers praised the 'force of his arm', reaping enemy soldiers like corn. But if Richard's leadership was necessary, victory rested above all on the willingness of the whole crusader army to take remorseless punishment, day after day, and still hold together. Yet for all its bravery, the army never occupied Jerusalem. Richard abandoned the attempt in appalling weather just 19 kilometres (12 miles) from his goal, his reputation tarnished in the eyes of Christian pilgrims for failing to capitalize on his victory.

75. BATTLE OF BORODINO
7 September 1812

Around the Russian village of Borodino, lying astride the road that led from Smolensk to Moscow, there took place one of the bloodiest battles fought by any European army before the age of mass slaughter in the trenches of the First World War. It was here that the

Grande Armée of the French Emperor Napoleon was confronted for the first time by the bulk of the Russian army under the veteran commander Field Marshal Mikhail Kutuzov. As the two armies fought back and forth, the soldiers were met by withering musket fire and a deadly cannonade from more than 1,000 guns. Both sides stood their ground with an exceptional courage. At the end of the day, 75,000 were dead or wounded, one-third of all those who took part.

Napoleon had not wanted to fight in Russia, but the vast, ramshackle empire that he had constructed across Europe faced numerous threats. The Russian tsar, Alexander I, refused to accept the trade blockade of Britain (the so-called 'Continental System') and was consolidating Russia's strategic position in the Baltic and Black Sea regions. Napoleon gathered a huge army of almost half a million men (only 200,000 of them were French) to march through Poland and pressure Alexander to accept a humiliating treaty that acknowledged Napoleon's domination of Europe. He anticipated, at most, a battle or two in Lithuania or Belarus, not a major campaign deep inside Russian territory. Alexander was not to be intimidated, and appointed Kutuzov to meet the threat from France. On 24 June 1812, Napoleon crossed the River Niemen and captured the Lithuanian capital of Vilna (Vilnius). He expected a major battle but the Russian marshals pulled their forces back. On 9 July, he left Vilna and marched into the interior seeking the elusive grand battle that would decide the future.

As Napoleon marched from Vilna towards Vitebsk, the problems that his army was to experience for months became evident. Freak blizzards, burning sun, an absence of fresh water and food, and the slow plod of the baggage wagons far in the rear, resulted in a line of dead and dying men and horses along the road. Napoleon was moved by the loss. 'I have marched too far,' he confessed to himself, but he was too committed to battle to give up. Russian armies gathered in defence of Smolensk, but after two days of indecisive fighting, which cost Napoleon 20,000 men, the Russians once again made off in good order, sucking Napoleon inexorably deeper into the savagely hostile terrain. Advised by all around him to halt and recover, Napoleon was driven on by his inner demons. He had left Vitebsk with 185,000 troops; he marched down the Smolensk–Moscow highway with his army reduced to perhaps 130,000 tired, malnourished and anxious soldiers. Napoleon fell ill with a heavy cold; he had swollen legs and a painful bladder.

By chance the Russians chose an opportune moment to stand and fight. Kutuzov stopped at Borodino in early September and set out a prepared battlefield with earthworks and redoubts. He was popular with his men but his marshals saw him as lazy and unimaginative. Dressed only in a green frock coat and white cap, he sat a great deal, wrote little and paid scant attention to the battlefield. Both men, Kutuzov and Napoleon, could have won the battle at Borodino decisively if they had been fit and active enough. As it turned out, the battle was commanded by two men who fought like lumbering punch-drunk boxers, unable to inflict the knock-out blow. Kutuzov deployed approximately 150,000 regular soldiers, Cossack horsemen and Moscow militia in a broad semi-circle with a powerful redoubt in the centre (the Raevsky). The right wing under Marshal Barclay de Tolly was shielded by a small river; here the bulk of the infantry and cavalry were placed. The left wing under Prince Piotr Bagration was much weaker; Kutuzov sent a fresh corps to hide in the woods behind the left wing in order to attack any French effort to outflank Bagration, but the local commander ordered the corps out into the open.

The Russian position was weak because it gave little chance for manoeuvre and risked encirclement, but Napoleon failed to exploit the possibilities open to him. After inspecting the Russian dispositions in detail on 5 and 6 September, Napoleon chose a frontal assault, placing his key commanders – Michel Ney, Joachim Murat and Louis Davout – in a strong centre, with the Polish commander Prince Josef Poniatowski on the right and Prince Eugène Beauharnais on the left. His generals found him uncharacteristically indecisive and lethargic. Though his troops were hungry, racked with dysentery and, in some cases, shoeless, Napoleon chose the most dangerous and costliest form of attack. At 6 a.m. on 7 September, the guns of both sides broke out a deafening roar. The troops had to stand waiting while the cannon balls and canister-shot crashed remorselessly into their ranks, removing a head here, an arm there, or tearing a horse literally in half.

Both sides were exposed, and they remained so for much of the day. Yet they kept formation even while their ranks were decimated by cannon and musket fire, a rare courage displayed by both sides. The Russians in particular stood to the last man, giving ground as little as possible before they collapsed in heaps of dead. Napoleon was puzzled that they did not give up: 'These Russians let themselves be killed like automatons.' The result was an ebb and flow on the battlefield in which both sides took horrifying losses as they hacked and stabbed their way forward only to be driven back once again. Reserves waiting to be thrown into the cruel mêlée were too close to the front to avoid being killed by the guns where they stood. One French cavalry unit lost one-third of its men and horses without seeing action. The exceptional bravery in the face of fire owed something to a tough discipline instilled in both armies, but it was also a mark of desperation, since neither side wanted to risk the grisly consequences of defeat. Prisoners were few.

Each time the French forces stormed a redoubt or an earthwork, a second line of Russian soldiers stood in front of them a few hundred metres further back, making a second charge necessary. The struggle for the Raevsky redoubt came late in the afternoon and it soon turned into a swarm of soldiers from both sides fighting hand-to-hand to the death. But when the French stormed it, there was a second line of Russian infantry forming a new wall 800 metres (2,500 feet) away. Napoleon could find no way through and failed to outflank his enemy. His 25,000-strong Imperial Guard was held back throughout the battle when it might have won it in the last hours. At around 6 p.m., the battle petered out and the Russians withdrew a few kilometres to the east. Their withdrawal allowed Napoleon to claim Borodino as a victory, but it was a hollow success. He inspected the battlefield with its piles of corpses and wounded. In the Raevsky redoubt, they lay bleeding or senseless six to eight deep. The French forces lost forty-nine generals killed or wounded; the Russians lost twenty-nine, including Prince Bagration. French losses were estimated at 28,000, but thousands more died of wounds that could not be treated for lack of medical supplies and doctors. Russian casualties were put at 45,000.

The Russian army reformed to the south but abandoned Moscow, which Napoleon entered on 15 September. Borodino made no difference in the end to either side. Alexander still refused to make peace. Short of food and water, harassed constantly by angry peasants and booty-seeking Cossacks, uncertain as to the future, the French armies became quickly demoralized. Napoleon was forced to retreat, and the long road back from Moscow left him in the end with only 20,000 tattered, emaciated and frozen troops when the army arrived outside Vilna. Napoleon hastened back to Paris, leaving perhaps 400,000 dead littering the wide Russian steppe. 'Fortune,' Napoleon is supposed to have said on the eve of Borodino, 'is a fickle courtesan.' For all the courage of his army, fortune abandoned them as it abandoned him.

76. BATTLE OF LEIPZIG
16–19 October 1813

The Battle of Leipzig was almost certainly the largest land battle fought in Europe before the First World War. It has been called the 'Battle of the Nations', but it was in truth a battle of monarchies – the Sixth Coalition of Austria, Prussia, Russia and Great Britain against the upstart emperor of France, Napoleon Bonaparte. Smaller monarchies joined in or changed sides, but the deciding struggle was between the big players, and the stakes were very great. This time the old monarchies of Europe wanted to be rid of Napoleon for good, even though they could not agree among themselves under what terms the defeated emperor would be tolerated once he was contained in France. The final showdown around the Saxon city of Leipzig in eastern Germany turned into a fierce face-to-face battle as the troops from both sides took and inflicted high casualties. The raking fire was nothing new to a Napoleonic battlefield, but this time all the armies involved understood that it had to be endured for what was evidently a climactic confrontation.

The army of 177,000 men that Napoleon mustered for the final battle was not the army of his earlier campaigns. After the disastrous adventure in Russia in 1812, Napoleon was forced to scrape the bottom of the recruitment barrel. Young, raw recruits, older men, disabled veterans, 20,000 naval marines and gunners and units of the National Guard militia were drawn together, seasoned with the few remaining veterans and professionals. There was a severe shortage of cavalry horses, and the new horsemen recruited compounded the problem by not understanding how to care properly for their mounts, which died in thousands on the campaign. There was also a shortage of heavy horses to pull the guns and not enough time to train new animals to cope with the stresses of the work. The whole campaign in 1813 was dogged by a shortage of trained cavalrymen and difficulties in keeping open long lines of communication into central Europe.

The campaign in 1813 was complicated for both sides because fighting was taking place in three separate theatres: in Italy, in the Low Countries and northern Germany, and across the central German area of Saxony. Two major battles were fought at Lützen on 2 May and at Bautzen on 21 May; in each case Napoleon, whose army was divided, was able to bring up strong reinforcements in time to compel the Russians and Prussians to withdraw, though not to defeat them. Both sides took heavy casualties, and for a number of months a ceasefire existed. In the interval, Napoleon tried to win over the Austrians, but he could not agree to their demands and the Austrian chancellor, Prince Metternich, brought Austria into the Coalition camp in August. Napoleon now had almost the whole of Europe ranged against him. The Coalition comprised an Army of the North numbering 120,000 under Napoleon's former marshal, Jean Baptiste Bernadotte, who was now king of Sweden and had taken the name Carl Johan; the Army of Silesia under the Prussian general Blücher, with 95,000 men; and the Army of Bohemia with 240,000 men. The overall commander was the Austrian field marshal, Prince Karl zu Schwarzenberg. Napoleon had armies stretched out across Europe, a total of 473,000 men. For the next two months they fought indecisive engagements against part of the enemy force as the two sides manoeuvred for advantage, but in the process Napoleon lost tens of thousands of his carefully garnered troops.

The climax finally came in October. Leaving a force of 45,000 at Dresden under Marshal Joachim Murat, Napoleon took 150,000 men to try to pin the Prussians down to a decisive battle. Blücher avoided combat, but suddenly Napoleon had news that the Austrians and Russians, under Schwarzenberg, had returned from their sojourn in Bohemia and were pushing Murat back towards the city of Leipzig. What followed was a three-day battle on a truly awe-inspiring scale as half a million men were pitted against each other for the future of Europe. Napoleon had left 177,000 men, though few cavalry, to confront his approaching enemies. He attacked the Army of Bohemia, expecting to have support from other French armies further north. But they now faced stiff combat from the Prussians moving rapidly south. Napoleon's offensive came to a halt, and on 17 October both sides regrouped for a final showdown. Though 14,000 more men reached Napoleon, the pause gave time for the Army of the North and additional Russian units to arrive at Leipzig, bringing the Coalition total to 256,000 infantry, 60,000 cavalry and 1,382 guns. The two gigantic armies then crashed together again on 18 October, but this time Napoleon was surrounded by a great semi-circular arc of enemy troops, who attacked in six columns, pushing the French back towards Leipzig.

The fighting was fierce and confused for much of the day, but the direction was clear. When the traditional three cannon shots signalled the end of the day's fighting, Napoleon had no alternative but to order a general retreat, and at 2 a.m. on 19 October, his armies began to withdraw westwards as best they could. The rearguard held the enemy at bay but was finally swamped by sheer numbers in fierce hand-to-hand fighting. Throughout, both sides had fought in the face of withering fire and heavy cannonades, with battlefield casualty rates among the worst of the war. For the French there was still one more tragedy. The single bridge over the River Elster at Leipzig had been mined for detonation by French engineers. A French sergeant blew up the bridge prematurely while it was still crowded with French troops, leaving 30,000 men to be captured or killed on the wrong side of the river. The 38,000 French dead and wounded from the three-day battle, added to the loss of the rearguard, took the heart out of what was left of the *Grande Armée*. The ferocity of the final days of fighting could be judged by the 54,000 casualties on the Coalition side. When the British ambassador to Vienna, Sir George Jackson, crossed the battlefield two days later he was shocked by the scene. He later wrote that 'a more revolting and sickening spectacle I never beheld.' He witnessed bloated horses, headless corpses, heads without bodies and thousands of 'upturned faces of the dead, agony on some, a placid smile on others.'

The 'Battle of the Nations' satisfied dynastic ambition at last and demonstrated that the armies of Prussia, Russia and Austria had learned something from the long campaigns against an ailing military genius. Napoleon turned back again to France, where he faced months of fruitless argument over seeking peace and a bitter and hopeless defence against a vast invading army. On 2 April, the French Senate deposed him as Coalition forces finally entered Paris. On 28 April, he was exiled to the island of Elba, off the Italian coast. Most of the battles in the revolutionary and Napoleonic era were not decisive in any meaningful sense, but Leipzig was.

77. BATTLE OF NAVARINO BAY
20 October 1827

The modern states of Greece and Egypt both owe their path to independence to a battle fought at an inlet in the western Peloponnese between a small squadron of British, French and Russian ships and the fleet of the Ottoman sultan. The battle had not been planned by either side, nor was it clearly directed at the independence or otherwise of either of its eventual beneficiaries, but it helped to end centuries of Turkish domination in the Balkans and did so in the most dangerous of circumstances. The battle in Navarino Bay was fought at close quarters after a mixed squadron, commanded by Vice Admiral Sir Edward Codrington, had sailed into the midst of the enemy fleet to frighten the Ottoman leaders into abandoning a savage campaign against the local Greek population. Crews on both sides bravely kept their place when they suddenly found themselves subjected to point-blank fire. Although at an immediate tactical disadvantage, the European ships stuck to their task with a grim and courageous determination and won an unexpected conflict.

The Greek struggle against Ottoman rule had begun in 1821. By 1827, a ferocious campaign of repression waged by the Turks and their Egyptian vassals had left only a few areas of Greece in nationalist hands. Despite public sympathy in Christian Europe for the Greek cause, concern that the balance of power would be upset by an Ottoman defeat prevented any formal commitment to the Greeks. The atrocities in Greece nevertheless called for a response and in July 1827, Britain, France and Russia signed the Treaty of London, in which they agreed to pressure both sides in the war to accept mediation and end the violence. A small fleet set off from Russia commanded by Admiral Count Lodewijk van Heiden, while the British and French Mediterranean squadrons were instructed to engage in a 'friendly demonstration of force' to make sure an armistice was observed. Codrington found the expression puzzling, since force could seldom be friendly, while the Sultan in Constantinople and the Egyptian commander in Greece, the shrewd and ruthless Ibrahim Pasha, rejected out of hand any idea that the European powers had the right to intervene in their efforts to crush Greek insurrection. Instead, they assembled a large fleet in Alexandria and sent it to the Peloponnese to help finish the task of suppression. The fleet entered the small bay at Navarino on the western coast of Greece.

The orders sent to the three European naval squadrons were never very precise and Codrington arrived off the coast at Navarino uncertain how to proceed. He was joined by the French ships under command of Admiral Henri de Rigny, while Heiden's force was still on its way through the Mediterranean. The British and French commanders met Ibrahim Pasha on 25 September in an attempt to persuade him to accept the armistice, which the Greek nationalists had already done. Ibrahim refused, and a few days later he slipped out of Navarino Bay with part of his fleet to sail for Patras and drive out the nationalist garrison there. Codrington, though outnumbered, forced him to return. Ibrahim defiantly set off by land and began a campaign of renewed savagery against the local Greek population. This proved too much for Codrington and his allies, who were all pro-Greek, and on 18 October they decided to sail into the bay at Navarino, under the shadow of Turkish guns, to intimidate the Ottoman forces into abandoning the repression and dispersing their hostile fleet. Codrington later insisted that this move was not meant as a precursor to battle, but it is difficult not to see the entry of the European ships as a direct and humiliating challenge to which the Turkish–Egyptian fleet was honour-bound to respond.

On paper, the balance of forces favoured the Turkish–Egyptian fleet commanded by Tahir Pasha and the Egyptian admiral, Moharrem Bey. Their combined fleet had 65 ships with 2,000 guns, with a small number of fire ships. The European fleet comprised 12 British, 8 Russian and 7 French ships, mounting between them 1,298 guns. The Turkish vessels were drawn up in a horseshoe formation around the bay as if already expecting battle, with the major fighting ships at the front, and the fire ships and smaller sloops behind. At 1.30 p.m. on 20 October,

Codrington led his Royal Navy squadron into the bay, followed at a distance by the French under de Rigny, and finally by the Russians. Arguments have raged ever since about who started the fight, but Codrington had been keen to avoid it if possible. Both sides had itchy trigger-fingers; the guns were primed and the fire ships ready to go. When a red flag was raised as an apparent signal to the Turkish vessels, activity could be seen on the first of the fire ships. A small British boat was sent to order the crew of the fire ship to cease their preparations, but the sailors were fired on and the officer killed. A few minutes later a Turkish ship fired on de Rigny's flagship *Sirène* and a general battle started almost at once, with the ships from both sides firing from only a few metres' distance apart – point-blank cannonades backed by rifle fire from the marines.

What followed was an extraordinary mêlée as the ships, mostly at anchor, tried to shift away from the worst of the broadsides while inflicting as much damage as possible on the enemy. European guns and gunnery were generally superior, but the Turkish sailors stuck to their task with exceptional bravery, as British accounts later confirmed, even while their ships caught fire, or, in some cases, exploded with a deafening roar. Codrington's flagship *Asia* destroyed the Turkish flagship of Tahir Pasha before turning to wreck the *Warrior*, flagship of the Egyptian commander, who had been reluctant to enter the fray at all. The water was soon filled with wreckage, struggling sailors and mutilated corpses; many Turkish sailors were chained to their posts and unable to escape into the sea. The only tactic, one British sailor later wrote, was 'burn, sink and destroy'. When Heiden's squadron finally sailed into position, firing with great effect, the battle had already been decided. Heiden's flagship *Azov* sank three frigates, one corvette and a sixty-gun ship of the line, which blew up after half an hour of bombardment.

After more than three hours of fighting, the Turkish fleet abandoned the contest with most of its ships destroyed or incapable. Not a single European ship was lost, while only 174 Europeans were killed; the Turkish fleet lost 60 ships and an estimated 6,000 dead. A number of the ships still afloat were deliberately blown up by the defeated Turks during the night. The battle made extraordinary demands on the crews, who found themselves in a situation from which they could not escape and which exposed them to direct and crippling fire. When Codrington visited the dying commander of *Genoa*, Captain Walter Bathurst, he told him, with some justice, 'you die gloriously'. Yet little of this sacrifice was appreciated once it had been made. Codrington was summoned back to England and made to explain to a hostile parliament why he had allowed the battle to happen at all, while Ibrahim Pasha continued his depredations until compelled, under the terms of the Treaty of Adrianople two years later, to withdraw. The battle was, nevertheless, a turning point. Egypt finally rejected Turkish rule; Ottoman Turkey began its long decline as the 'sick man of Europe', and Greece recovered its independence after centuries of servitude.

78. FIRST BATTLE OF MANASSAS (BULL RUN)

18–21 July 1861

The first major land engagement of the four-year American Civil War was fought around a small rail junction at Manassas, Virginia, close enough to the Union capital at Washington to make this a battle that Union generals wanted to win. Instead it was a major victory for the Confederacy, the group of breakaway states that hoped to retain slavery and defy the northern and western states of the Union. The forces were evenly matched in the numbers that actually fought, but neither side had anything like a disciplined body of men used to fighting on a battlefield. Both armies nevertheless displayed a robust courage under unfamiliar fire, though it was the

Confederate units who stood firmest when the test came for their exhausted, thirsty and fearful men. Confederate stamina was exemplified by the famous stand of Brigadier General Thomas Jonathan Jackson, whose nickname 'Stonewall' was earned at Manassas as his unit stood firm against the tide of Union attacks and suffered more casualties that day than any other.

The military leaders of both armies had been reluctant to fight this battle so soon, but the pressure from popular and political opinion on both sides to get to grips with the enemy as quickly as possible proved irresistible. The Union commander, General Irvin McDowell, had gathered around 35,000 troops in the Washington area, most of them green and untrained, many of them the newly recruited 'ninety-day men', who had been conscripted to serve for just ninety days before returning home. President Abraham Lincoln favoured action and ordered McDowell to attack the Confederate forces gathering around Manassas Junction in the hope that a major victory would open the way to the occupation of Richmond, the new capital of the Confederacy in Virginia, which was within easy reach from Washington. On the other side, the preferred strategy was to hold a line defending Virginia from Union encroachment, but public outcry demanded action against an enemy rated poorly compared with southern soldiers. The local commander at Manassas, General Pierre Beauregard, and the commander of the Army of the Shenandoah, General Joseph Johnston (who, under the nose of Union forces, slipped out of the valley with 11,000 men to join forces with Beauregard), could between them call on around 30,000 men for the battle, a little less than Union strength. Artillery was more even: fifty-five Confederate guns against fifty-seven of the Union.

McDowell took the initiative when, on 16 July 1861, he marched his army away from Washington in the direction of Manassas. Forewarned by spies in Washington, Beauregard drew up a defensive line behind the Bull Run River, stronger on the right than on the left, because he expected McDowell to try to capture the rail junction. Union troops made slow progress, but information from his scouts about the strength of the Confederate line forced McDowell to change his original plan to turn the enemy's right flank and to undertake instead a large sweeping movement against the exposed and weaker left flank. At mid-morning on 21 July, the leading Union units, after marching for hours in a scorching summer heat, were finally ordered to assault the smaller Confederate force in front of them. Both armies fought with great courage and a raw military skill that belied their improvised training, but at times they also displayed a tactical ineptitude that only experience would overcome. For most, this was a terrible baptism of fire. Men watched companions blown to pieces or bayoneted to death. Some soldiers had only a makeshift uniform, so that many on each side wore the same colour, resulting in a great deal of confusion on the battlefield as friend and foe merged into one. An unknown number of men on both sides fell to the shells and musket balls of their comrades. The most exposed of all were the northern *zouave* regiments, dressed in imitation of French soldiers with baggy red trousers, an easy target for Confederate marksmen.

McDowell's strategy might well have worked had he been able to concentrate his forces and co-ordinate their movements, but his regiments were fed in piecemeal on a narrow front, made harder by the hills, woods and rivers across which the battle was fought. The smaller Confederate force on the left was pushed back in disarray from Matthew's Hill, and a new line was formed on Henry Hill (named after the Henry House, whose senior occupant, the widow Judith Henry, refused to move and was killed by a shell). At this point the Union column of around 15,000 men could have swept forward against a demoralized Confederate force of little more than 3,000, but McDowell, riding among his men with shouts of 'Victory is ours!', delayed the pursuit. Beauregard moved more men to the left and Johnston's forces, arriving pell-mell from the railhead, supplied fresh reinforcements. On Henry Hill both sides threw in regiments one after the other, charging and falling back in a confused mêlée, with no clear evidence of victory for either side.

It was at this point that Jackson set up his defensive line with his Virginia regiments. General Barnard Bee, riding behind the lines, shouted out, 'Look at Jackson there standing like a damn stone wall.' Bee was killed shortly afterwards, and the meaning of his words has been much debated. But whether Bee was censuring Jackson for not being more active or applauding the stoicism of his troops, Jackson inspired the Confederate army to stand and fight and prevented a Union victory. By late afternoon, the Union regiments, still being sent in one after the other, were nearing exhaustion. Jackson ordered his Virginians to fix bayonets and charge, shouting at the tops of their voices. The cry (later described as 'Woh-who–ey!') was a terrifying hurrah that stoked up Confederate morale and struck fear into Union units that were already starting to dissolve under the barrage of constant fire.

Henry Hill was retaken and slowly the Confederates pushed their enemy back. By 4 p.m., with Confederate reinforcements evening up the balance between the two sides, Beauregard sensed that the Union was a fading force. He ordered a general advance against the whole enemy front, which rapidly collapsed. Despite exhortations from the officers, the Union soldiers had had enough of the carnage, heat, hunger and thirst and fled in disarray towards Washington. The Confederate officers ordered a pursuit, but soon halted when they realized that their own men were in the same state. Victory was not complete, but it was enough to ensure that the Civil War would not be over in ninety days. It would be fought to the death over four grimy years in which the soldiers of both sides learned how to fight and die. Jackson died of pneumonia two years later after the Battle of Chancellorsville where he was shot in error by his own side. The courage shown by his Virginians at Manassas Junction made 'Stonewall' Jackson a symbol for the undeviating resistance of the south against the fading odds of war.

79. BATTLE OF GETTYSBURG
1–3 July 1863

The battle that raged for three July days in 1863 around the junction town of Gettysburg, Pennsylvania, provoked extraordinary stories of courage and endurance on both sides in America's Civil War. On the third day a young Union cavalryman, George Armstrong Custer, at twenty-three the youngest brigadier in the Army of the Potomac, led his 7th Michigan troopers in a charge against the approaching Confederate cavalry. 'Come on you Wolverines!' he called, and was at once caught up in the mêlée, thrusting with his sabre at the whirling Confederate horses. He lost two horses under him but found a third, riderless mount, and carried on battling from the front. His brigade accounted for 86 per cent of the Union losses in the brief engagement that drove away the Confederate troopers. His men followed him willingly into the teeth of a ferocious battle, as did thousands of others at Gettysburg.

The battle at Gettysburg, famous though it has become, was an unexpected confrontation. After the Confederate victory at Chancellorsville, Virginia, in May 1863, General Robert E. Lee, the commander-in-chief, decided to risk an advance north into Union territory in Pennsylvania. His aim was to capture the state capital, cut Union communications and even, it was hoped, force the Union to seek peace. His army of Northern Virginia was reorganized into three infantry corps and six cavalry brigades of 75,000 men. Living off the land, the army moved northwest, sending south into slavery any free blacks it captured. Lee was uncertain where Joseph Hooker's Union Army of the Potomac was; after Chancellorsville, the Union still had 90,000 men in the field. Hooker trailed behind Lee, pressed by an anxious President Lincoln to act. His hesitation brought his dismissal and the Union army that crossed the Potomac into Pennsylvania was led from 28 June by General George Meade. Only now did Lee's army learn that the enemy was moving north towards it.

The two armies nevertheless met by chance. On 1 July Lee sent

Lieutenant General Ambrose Hill to secure a large supply of shoes said to be found in the small town of Gettysburg. When the Confederate force arrived it found two Union cavalry brigades already in occupation of high ground to the northwest of Gettysburg. The outnumbered Union troopers bravely held off the enemy for two hours; the tough 'Iron Brigade' of Midwestern recruits in their distinctive black hats lost two-thirds of their number. As reinforcements arrived for both sides, the 24,000 Confederate forces drove back the 19,000 Union soldiers through Gettysburg to a defensive line of high ground south of the town, running from Little Round Top, across Cemetery Ridge to Culp's Hill further north. Lee could see that this was an ideal position for the Union to occupy and urged Lieutenant General Richard Ewell's 2nd Corps to seize it before dusk fell and so secure yet another Confederate victory. Ewell hesitated, and by the evening the Union had a firm line running across the high ground, reinforced during the night by three more corps hurriedly led there by Meade himself.

Lee was confident that his men, fresh from a string of victories, were capable of a frontal assault, and he ignored the advice of General James Longstreet that he should make a strong flanking attack instead, bringing the southern army between Meade and Washington and rolling up the Union line. Longstreet was instead given the task of attacking the Union left wing at Little Round Top while Ewell would pin down the Union right until it was weakened enough to assault. Longstreet delayed until 4 p.m. on 2 July, giving the Union plenty of time to prepare the line of defence. When he attacked he found that the Union left, commanded by Major General Dan Sickles, had moved to high ground away from the main line, creating an exposed salient and leaving Little Round Top undefended. Here both sides engaged in fierce firefights, with neither willing to give way. The 15,000 Confederate soldiers, with their fearsome war cry, drove back Sickles' two divisions step-by-step through ground that was littered with the dead and dying. Meade hastily sent reinforcements to try to plug the opening gaps. When it seemed that the Confederates were about to capture Little Round Top, a regiment was sent to stop them. The 20th Maine, commanded by a former professor of rhetoric, Colonel Joshua Chamberlain, held off the uphill attacks for two hot, smoke-filled, gruelling hours. Finally, out of ammunition, Chamberlain ordered a bayonet charge. The approaching Alabama soldiers were taken by surprise and hundreds surrendered. More Alabamians were held up in the centre of the Union line by another brave charge, this time by the remaining 262 men of the 1st Minnesota regiment. Only forty-seven came back, but the front was saved. As dusk fell the exhausted Confederate forces once again fell back; the line from Little Round Top to Culp's Hill was still intact.

The following day proved decisive. Lee was determined to have his crushing victory and felt that the gains of the first two days justified him. He planned for Ewell to pressure the Union right at Culp's Hill and perhaps turn a position that had been subjected to fierce attack in the evening and night of 2 July; the Confederate cavalry under Major General James 'Jeb' Stuart to outflank the Union left; and Longstreet to attack the Union centre, commanded by Major General Winfield Hancock, with three fresh divisions. The final battle plan went wrong from the opening hours of 3 July. Ewell's offensive, led by Major General Jubal Early, became bogged down at Culp's Hill where a Union counter-attack regained ground lost the previous evening. Nevertheless Lee ordered Longstreet to bombard the centre and then launch a charge across 1,100 metres (3,600 feet) of open ground. At 1.07 p.m. 150 guns opened up the heaviest Confederate bombardment of the war, made more confusing and deafening by the Union reply from more than 100 artillery pieces on Cemetery Ridge. Dug into position, the Union troops suffered much less than expected from the cannonade. When the 14,000 men led by the division of Major General George Pickett finally charged, the Union defenders were able to smash the advance with artillery and musket fire from front and flanks. A few hundred of the doomed Confederate soldiers reached the Union line but the rest were mown down as they advanced across the open with a display of remarkable courage.

They broke and turned, leaving half the men behind on the ground. Pickett's charge cost him two-thirds of his division, including all his senior officers.

Meade still had 20,000 men to throw into the conflict but he hesitated, aware of how skilful his enemy had been on earlier occasions. A decisive victory might have been gained, but Meade did not counter-attack, and the Confederate army, moving south in disarray, was allowed to cross the Potomac at Williamsport back to comparative safety without engaging in another major battle. The turning point promised by Gettysburg failed to materialize and the war dragged on for two more years. The exceptional courage displayed in the three-day battle was evident from the total of more than 45,000 casualties suffered by the two sides in three days of bitter fighting. The Army of the Potomac had 22,813 casualties, including 3,149 dead; the Army of Northern Virginia suffered 22,625 casualties of whom 4,536 were killed. This was close to a quarter of the forces involved. On 19 November President Lincoln arrived at Gettysburg to inaugurate a national cemetery on the aptly named Cemetery Hill, where he announced that the dead had not died in vain but had ushered in a 'new birth of freedom' with their sacrifice.

80. BATTLE OF TACNA
26 May 1880

After liberation from colonial rule, South America experienced few prolonged wars. The longest and bloodiest was the War of the Pacific, fought between Chile on one side and Peru and Bolivia on the other. The conflict began over claims to the rich nitrate sources in the province of Antofagasta in southern Bolivia but it soon developed into a power struggle between the three states over control of the Pacific littoral. The decisive battle near the small city of Tacna in southern Peru was a crude clash of arms between three armies that relied on the courage and discipline of men who had little experience of combat as they charged and countercharged under a hail of fire.

The Bolivian government's threat to confiscate the Chilean Nitrate Company in Antofagasta prompted a swift response. Nitrate production was essential to Chile's economic survival because it could be traded against European goods. Chile's small army, no more than 2,500 strong, occupied the port of Antofagasta. The invasion activated a secret alliance made in 1873 between Bolivia and Peru. This prompted Chile to declare war on both states on 5 April 1879. A prolonged naval battle opened the conflict as Peru and Chile used their tiny navies in a bid to win control of coastal sea lanes. Chilean naval success opened the way to a land invasion, and in November 1879 the Chilean commander, Erasmo Escala, landed in the Tarapacá province of southern Peru. The efforts of the Peruvian and Bolivian armies under General Juan Buendía to co-ordinate their operations broke down when the Bolivian commander Hilarión Daza deserted. Following victory over the Peruvians at Dolores, Chile occupied Tarapacá. The presidents of Peru and Bolivia were replaced, and the new Bolivian president, General Narcisco Campero, assumed command of the army in the field.

By this stage the tiny armies had grown through conscription, with many of the recruits drawn from the local Indian population. In February 1880, 13,000 Chilean soldiers were disembarked at the port of Ilo, further up the coast of Peru, in an attempt to seize the nitrate-rich province of Tacna. Escala had by now been replaced by General Manuel Baquedano Gonzalez, a more aggressive and effective commander. He moved inland, over difficult terrain that took a steady toll of his force, intent on reaching and capturing the main port of Arica. After a difficult month's march his army arrived at the Campo de la Alianza, an arid plain in front of the town of Tacna, with a gentle slope on one side, and sandy dunes along its edge. It was here that Campero, now the overall commander of the Bolivian and

Peruvian troops, decided to establish a defensive line to await the arrival of Baquedano.

Campero commanded somewhere between 9,000 and 12,000 men, supported by 16 cannon and 7 Gatling machine guns. The Chileans numbered around 14,000, according to the official history (11,000 according to other accounts), supported by 37 field guns and 4 machine guns. Baquedano was advised by the Chilean war minister, José Vergara, to try an outflanking attack in order to preserve manpower, but his artillery commander recommended a frontal assault along the whole line to prevent the enemy from moving men from one part of the defence to another. Baquedano agreed and divided his force into five divisions, to attack the enemy defences head-on in a human wave.

The battle began with an artillery duel that had little effect as shells buried themselves in the soft sand. At 10 a.m. the first line of Chilean infantry attacked up the slope but was driven back under heavy fire. Thinking they were retreating, the commander of the left wing of the Peruvian–Bolivian army, Colonel Eliodoro Camacho, sent his men forward, only to be destroyed by accurate fire from Chilean artillery and machine guns. After a brave hour's fighting, Camacho had lost around four-fifths of his force. Along the rest of the line the Chileans were pushed back by intense fire as they tried to storm across the open ground. The effort to reinforce Camacho with reserves weakened the right wing and it was here that the line cracked as waves of Chilean soldiers attacked with bayonet charges in the face of continuous fire. When Baquedano sent in the Chilean reserve division to force a path round the right flank of the enemy, resistance crumbled. The remnants of the Peruvian and Bolivian divisions staggered back to Tacna where they surrendered after a brief Chilean bombardment at 6.30 p.m.

The harsh nature of the contest between soldiers who were ordered back and forth against determined fire was evident in the exceptional level of casualties. The Chilean Army suffered 500 dead and 1,600 wounded – around 20 per cent of the force engaged on the battlefield. The Atacama and Santiago regiments lost one-half of their men. The defenders suffered even more, losing between 3,500 and 5,000 men. Only 400 Peruvians escaped from the battle and the surrender of Tacna. The high cost of Baquedano's tactics prompted one Chilean journalist to suggest that the triumph should be celebrated by a 'dance of death' rather than a victory ball. But Baquedano was unrepentant and in two further battles in 1881 to capture the Peruvian capital, Lima, 1,300 Chilean soldiers died in tough frontal assaults.

The victory at Tacna did little to end the war, though it confirmed Chilean occupation of the three coastal provinces of Tacna, Tarapacá and Antofagasta and cut Bolivia off from the sea. After two years of frustrating occupation in Lima, fighting a growing Peruvian insurgency, a peace was finally signed at Ancón on 20 October 1883, ceding Tarapacá to Chile. Bolivia signed an indefinite truce with Chile in April 1884, on the assurance that Chilean occupation of Antofagasta would be only temporary. The slaughter experienced in the War of the Pacific prompted the Peruvian writer Manuel Prada to reflect a few years later on the primitive nature of combat: 'When man leaves behind his atavistic ferociousness, war will be remembered as a prehistoric barbarity...'

81. BATTLE OF VERDUN
21 February – 15 December 1916

It is difficult to imagine a more horrific battle than that waged for control of a small fortified region to the east of the French town of Verdun during the height of the First World War. Unlike all the battles of earlier ages, this one lasted for almost a year and involved millions of soldiers from both the French and German sides. Yet it was clearly a 'battle', with the Germans pushing forward for months against stiff French resistance, then French troops pushing the other way for months until the Germans abandoned the field. To fight in conditions where the death rate was staggeringly high, the ground a mess of rotting bodies, shell fragments and eviscerated countryside, where the supply of food and water was irregular, was to fight with a raw, primal courage dredged from the depths of the human spirit. 'Hell,' wrote one French soldier, 'cannot be this dreadful.'

The French did not expect this battle. Verdun was surrounded by a network of eighteen defensive forts, but the French high command did not regard it as a critical part of the Western Front and the forts were undermanned and short of heavy artillery. The German army chief-of-staff, General Erich von Falkenhayn, decided to use the Verdun area for a major assault. His aim was to impose such a crippling attrition of French troops that it might push France out of the war. It was the only major German offensive between 1915 and 1918 and its strategic objectives were risky, since the French army had to respond to the challenge while German armies had no particular territorial goal to aim for.

'Operation Gericht' was planned to open in February 1916 and a rapid victory was expected. Concealing its movement as far as possible, the 140,000 men and 1,400 artillery pieces of the German 5th Army were brought into place. The artillery included giant 420-milimetre (16-inch) siege guns. Storm troopers carrying flamethrowers and clusters of grenades were to follow the bombardment, which was designed to punch holes in the French line and create panic among the defenders.

The German assault was opposed by the French 2nd Army, which had just two divisions in this sector of the front compared with nine German. Warnings from local French commanders were ignored and only at the last minute did the French commander-in-chief, General Joseph Joffre, allow a limited number of additional troops and guns to strengthen the front. 'Gericht' was supposed to open on 12 February but a fierce blizzard forced postponement until the early morning of 21 February, when the huge siege guns began to fire shells over distances of 30 kilometres (20 miles), dropping so far behind the French front that soldiers in the forward forts and trenches did not realize the offensive had started. At 7 a.m. began the fiercest artillery barrage of the war so far. It churned the countryside into mud and waste, buried hundreds of French soldiers alive and left the survivors dazed and disorientated. German infantry stormed forward when the barrage ceased but to their surprise found French soldiers still able to man the surviving artillery and machine guns. In the first two days the German front moved forward up to 3 kilometres (2 miles) but soon met stiffening resistance as French reinforcements were rushed to the scene. Although Fort Douaumont, the most easterly of the major defences, was taken on 25 February without a shot fired, the French line did not collapse, though the army suffered 26,000 casualties in the first few days.

The weakness of Falkenhayn's plan was evident not just in the fanatical defence of the line in front of Verdun by the still disorganized and battered French army but in the fact that attrition was a two-way affair. By the end of February the German 5th Army had suffered 25,000 casualties and the further it moved forward, the harder it was to move up supplies by lorry or horse-drawn cart across a landscape of mud and craters.

On 28 February General Philippe Pétain was made commander of the French army at Verdun. He immediately set out to establish a complex line of defensive fire using machine guns and the famous French 75-milimetre (4-inch) artillery. He saw that supply was critical, as indeed it was, and organized a remarkable single-track supply line between Bar-Le-Duc and Verdun that came to be known as the 'Voie Sacrée', the sacred way. This track, together with a single rail track, moved thousands of tons of supplies daily into the maelstrom of battle. The German offensive slowed down and the two sides battled in the mud, driven on by a mixture of desperation and fear as the constant thudding of shells and the staccato rattle of machine-gun fire signalled the death and mutilation of tens of thousands every week.

How the two armies continued to fight under such conditions is hard to explain, but neither side would give way. They were men, as

Henri Barbusse, the writer and front-line soldier put it, 'carrying their own graves'. Battling in the mud it was difficult to tell friend from foe as uniform colours and insignia were swallowed up in the wet earth. Both sides fought surrounded by the decaying corpses of comrades and the enemy, while rats gorged themselves on the dead. In some encounters, soldiers ran forward over piles of swollen, decomposing bodies, their feet bursting the bloated flesh as they stumbled on. The battles were not entirely suicidal, but survival was simply a matter of luck. Troops were pulled back out of the line after a few weeks to rest, but more were sent in to feed the terrible machinery of death. By the end of the battle three-quarters of all French soldiers had served some time at Verdun.

In early May, the German army renewed the offensive with no very clear purpose except to impose continuing losses on the army in front of it. In early June, the 600 defenders of Fort Vaux, many of them wounded, were subjected to a horrific bombardment but held firm. Under the command of Major Sylvain Raynal, the garrison retreated to the cellars where it was attacked by flamethrower and toxic smoke. Efforts to relieve the defenders were beaten back and in the early morning of 8 June, crippled by thirst and unable to escape, the defenders surrendered. They had suffered around 100 casualties, the German attackers 2,740. This imbalance of losses says much about the futility of Falkenhayn's enterprise. Though the German 5th Army pushed forward against fierce counter-attacks through June, the opening of a major offensive on the Eastern Front on 4 June (the Russians' Brusilov offensive) and the launch of the Battle of the Somme on 1 July by a combined Anglo–French force compelled the German high command to move reserves to stem these new threats. The Verdun offensive came to a halt and in August Falkenhayn was forced to resign. On 19 October it was the turn of the German side to experience devastating artillery fire as the French, determined to avenge the early months of battle, smashed German resistance in turn, using the new tactic of the creeping artillery barrage, with infantry following just behind. When the infantry assault began on 24 October the French recaptured in a day much of the ground it had taken the Germans months to occupy. Fort Douaumont was retaken that day, Fort Vaux on 2 November. By 15 December the battle came to a bitter conclusion, with almost all the territory captured by the Germans once again in French hands.

The cost of the battle was colossal. The French lost 156,000 dead and 195,000 wounded. The German side suffered attrition almost as severe, with 142,000 dead or missing and 187,000 other casualties. Like the later Battle of Stalingrad, Verdun has gone down in history as a monument to the courage, endurance and determination of men who were placed in circumstances of almost indescribable horror. 'All these deaths at once crush the soul,' wrote Barbusse in his novel *Under Fire*. 'But we have a vague idea of the grandeur of these dead. They outdistanced life, and there is something superhuman and perfect in what they did.'

82. FIRST DAY OF THE SOMME
1 July 1916

There are few better symbols of desperate courage in the face of war's futility than the experience of the British troops on the first day of the Battle of the Somme. That day, 1 July 1916, there were 57,470 casualties, 19,240 of them dead. This was the worst day of losses in the history of the British army. Most of the men had been mown down by accurate machine-gun and rifle fire as they slowly made their way, weighed down by 30 kilograms (70 pounds) of equipment, across open ground towards the enemy lines. How soldiers could heave themselves out of their trenches and dugouts, already under a hail of bullets, and march off to their deaths still challenges the modern imagination, not least because a better-executed and more tactically adept assault might have left many of those men still alive at the end of the day.

The battle that took place north and south of the River Somme, between Gommecourt in the north and Dompierre in the south, was originally part of a general plan by the Allied powers – Britain, France, Russia and Italy – to undertake concerted offensives in 1916 against all enemy fronts. The German attack on Verdun, which began in February 1916, changed the options in the West. Instead of a general Franco–British offensive, the French commander-in-chief, General Joseph Joffre, asked the British army, now commanded by General Douglas Haig, to make an early offensive to relieve the pressure on the French. The plan was agreed in a meeting at Amiens on 31 May. The British 4th and 3rd Armies under Generals Henry Rawlinson and Edmund Allenby, with fourteen divisions and four in reserve, would attack the seven divisions of the German 2nd Army, commanded by General Fritz von Below. They would be supported by a more limited French offensive on the right of the British line using five divisions with six in reserve. The German defence was composed of three trench lines, well embedded in the wooded and hilly countryside. The chief advantage enjoyed by the Allies in this sector was a superiority in air power (386 aircraft compared with the German 129) and in artillery (2,981 guns against 844). Even this would make little difference to the infantry, however. Their task was to capture the bombarded German lines and create the conditions for a possible breakthrough.

In recent years historians have been keen to show that the overall plan for the battle and the tactical instructions given to the front-line troops were considerably sounder than they seemed after the awful bloodletting of the first day. The problem was the gap between plan and reality. The battle began with a seven-day bombardment of the German lines, launching 12,000 tons of explosive. This already invited problems. A high proportion of the British shells were shrapnel, which had little effect on troops dug deep into bunkers, and at least a quarter of the shells proved to be duds. French artillery fire further south proved to be more accurate and effective. Though the front trenches were pulverized in places, the dense barbed wire barricade was not completely cut, nor were the German troops' firing platforms eliminated. Worse still, a message sent *en clair* from Rawlinson to his men on the night of the attack wishing them good luck was intercepted by the Germans so that any element of surprise was eliminated.

The soldiers who were ordered to clamber out of their trenches on the morning of 1 July were not supposed to be mown down in no-man's land. The expectation was that the artillery barrage, the heaviest British barrage of the war so far, would have so disorientated the enemy that the infantry advance would seize the German trenches without difficulty. The idea was to use artillery to creep ahead of the troops, who would then move on to the next objective before the enemy soldiers had had time to recover. None of this worked except in the south, where the Germans had fewer divisions and guns. Here the British divisions fighting alongside the French 6th Army made greater progress and the 'creeping barrage' worked more effectively. The iconic images of British soldiers tramping across the killing-fields come from the main part of the British line, where infantry progress was so slow that the artillery barrage hit areas too far ahead, leaving the German troops plenty of opportunity to emerge from their trenches and foxholes, covered in mud and dirt, to man the machine guns. At 7.30 a.m. on 1 July, shortly after the explosion of massive mines laid below German positions by British engineers, officers blew their whistles to signal the advance. Men clambered over the parapets and into the field of fire.

The whole northern line of the battle was a disaster. A diversionary attack on Gommecourt in the far north with two divisions suffered appalling casualties and was back in the British lines again two hours later. The attack by the 'Pals Division', composed of brigades drawn from a particular city or area, soon became suicidal. The men were instructed to march in line and only to break and run at the enemy 18 metres (60 feet) from the trench. According to all accounts, they kept a remarkable discipline even as the enemy artillery and machine guns swept the fields to leave a litter of shattered bodies and dying men. The attack uphill against the village of Serre proved impossible and the 31st Pals Division lost 3,600 men in the space of a few minutes. As each divisional attack failed, so the next division in line found its expected flank support evaporating, opening it up to a merciless fire. Somehow a handful of men made it through even to the German second trench line, but they were captured or killed in the attempt. In the famous assault on Beaumont Hamel, the 1st Newfoundland Regiment, the only Empire force committed that day, was a reserve force ordered forward from behind the British front line. So cluttered were the trenches that they were forced into the open and were shot down even before they had left British lines. Somehow the survivors struggled forward across a no-man's land already piled high with corpses and a handful reached the German trenches. The regiment was obliterated, suffering 91 per cent casualties.

The disastrous results of the first day on the Somme must have reminded Haig of the day, eighteen years before, when, as a young captain, he had watched the Mahdist forces at Omdurman surge relentlessly towards the British Maxim guns. Half the forces sent in on that first day on the Somme were casualties, and three out of every four officers. The German troops were also given a terrible taste of modern war. The week-long artillery barrage was an experience likely to traumatize the hardiest soldier, and despite the ease with which infantry assaults were blunted, the cumulative effect was to impose more than 40,000 casualties on the German side in the first days of the offensive. The campaign went on for a further 150 days, leaving 620,000 Allied and 465,000 German casualties, a terrible bloodletting for a few kilometres of ground, though the campaign did ease the pressure on Verdun.

Attrition warfare made terrible demands of the men on both sides. The capacity to absorb that damage and not to crack was testament to a remarkable degree of social discipline and self-sacrifice among men, many of whom, only months before, had been civilians. Despite the claim of some historians that the battle eventually achieved its purpose, the first day of the Somme was, as one eyewitness called it, 'monotonous, mutual mass murder'. Another eyewitness, the soldier-poet Siegfried Sassoon, caught the spirit of brave resignation that animated many soldiers that day in a poem written on 3 July, shortly before he was wounded: 'Crouched among thistle tufts I've watched the glow/ Of a blurred orange sunset flare and fade;/ And I'm content. To-morrow we must go/To take some cursèd Wood...'

83. GUADALCANAL
7 August 1942 – 8 February 1943

One of the longest and toughest battles the American army and navy had to fight in the Second World War was the struggle against the Japanese for control of the isolated, jungle-covered island of Guadalcanal in the British Solomon Islands. For months a small American beachhead had to be defended against wave after wave of Japanese attacks by air, sea and land. It was a harsh baptism of fire for the Americans. This was their first experience of combat against a Japanese army that had been fighting in China for years and had conquered Southeast Asia in a matter of weeks.

The island represented one of the furthest points reached in the violent burst of Japanese expansion that followed the strike on Pearl Harbor on 7 December 1941. The outer perimeter in the southwest Pacific ran through New Guinea and the Solomons. On Guadalcanal the Japanese decided to build an air base and a small port that would allow them to interrupt Allied supplies to Australia and act as a possible launch point for further aggression. The American high command decided to make the island the first point at which to pierce the Japanese perimeter and neutralize the threat to American shipping. A task force was assembled and 19,000 US marines, commanded by Major General Alexander Vandegrift, were disembarked on 7 August

1942 under cover of darkness. After a tough two-day fight they had control of the Japanese airfield at Lunga (renamed Henderson Field) and the small port at Tulagi. This was to prove only the start of a fierce battle that raged on the island for six long months.

The Japanese commanders in the South Pacific, based further north at Rabaul in New Britain, reacted immediately. A large Japanese naval force arrived and the American naval commander, Vice Admiral Frank Fletcher, was compelled to withdraw after losing four cruisers. The Japanese ships ferried the 17th Army under General Haruyoshi Hyakutake to the island and Japanese units swarmed towards the airfield to drive the Americans into the sea. Short of supplies and air support, the marines dug in. They found Japanese tactics almost suicidally primitive. Unarmed Japanese, reported one marine officer, would continue to attack armed marines until they were mown down. Some swam across from small nearby islands without weapons and little uniform to join in the fight. From 670 Japanese defending the islands around Tulagi, 655 chose to fight to the death rather than surrender. When the newly arrived Japanese army units began to attack, almost all the 900 Japanese were killed in the first wave, for the loss of 40 marines.

Over the weeks that followed the marines faced an extraordinary ordeal. Hit from the air and subject to regular naval bombardment, they held on to a small segment of the island while wave after wave of Japanese soldiers tried to dislodge them. On 12 September around 6,200 Japanese soldiers were in position to storm the airfield. They chose as their main advance line a small ridge to the south, which was defended by Colonel Merritt Edson's Marine Raiders – around 840 marines who had earlier raided the nearby Japanese base, seizing supplies and documents. They had been sent to the ridge for a brief rest. Instead they found themselves facing the main axis of the Japanese assault. For two nights around 3,000 Japanese fought to gain possession of the ridge. The marines were exhausted, deprived of sleep and short of ammunition, but, inspired by their commander, they fought endless lines of Japanese infantry charging towards the one remaining defensive position, Hill 123, with fixed bayonets. When American morale began to suffer, Edson rallied the men tirelessly, standing all the time rather than taking cover. Fighting with bayonets hand-to-hand stifled all attempts at infiltration, but Japanese soldiers were expected to fight to the death. Their constant assaults, recalled another marine, were 'like a rain that subsides for a moment and then pours the harder...'

The Japanese commanders finally abandoned the attempt; their men were also exhausted and hungry, with some units down to no more than one-fifth of their strength. It was the first major defeat for the Japanese army since the start of the Pacific campaign. At least 830 Japanese were killed for the loss of 80 marines. The Battle of Edson's Ridge – or Bloody Ridge – was the turning point of the whole battle and it depended on the remarkable courage of a few hundred marines fighting their first major engagement against an enemy that was expected to triumph or die in the attempt. The victory on Bloody Ridge not only secured the survival of the first American invasion of Japanese-held territory but exposed the myth of Japanese invincibility that had taken root after the first months of Japanese military successes.

In October the Japanese commanders on the island again tried frontal assaults against the airfield perimeter but were once again repulsed with heavy losses. In November the decision was made to expand Japanese forces sufficiently to overwhelm the small American enclave. Japanese naval vessels navigated the narrow strait running the length of Guadalcanal to deliver men and supplies – the so-called 'Tokyo Express'. By 12 November, the Japanese army reached its largest extent on the island but a series of naval engagements on the nights of 12–13 and 14–15 November cut off Japanese attempts to land more men and supplies, and new American army units arrived to strengthen the garrison. The Japanese high command reluctantly accepted that the island could not be held and planned an eventual withdrawal. More than 20,000 Japanese died on Guadalcanal against the loss of 1,752 American servicemen.

On 8 February 1943 the last Japanese left the island in a well-concealed evacuation. Vandegrift went on to command the Marine

Corps; General Hyakutake lived out the last years of the war hiding in the jungle on the island of Bougainville, in the northern Solomons. Colonel Edson fought in most of the major Pacific island campaigns, rose to the rank of major general, and committed suicide in 1955.

84. STALINGRAD
19 August 1942 – 2 February 1943

Stalingrad was one of the longest battles of the Second World War and the bloodiest. It has rightly come to symbolize the epic struggle between the German armed forces and the Red Army. It was regarded at the time as a turning point in the war against the Axis states, and has remained a firm favourite for anyone reflecting on the key moments when the tide turned in the conflict. The battle was also an exceptional test of men under fire, first for the Soviet 62nd and 64th Armies as the Germans advanced into the city, then for the German 6th Army as it faced encirclement and annihilation. Men on both sides were pushed to the limits of endurance and beyond. More than 400,000 lost their lives in the effort.

Neither side had predicted the battle. Hitler decided to open his summer campaign in the south of Russia in 1942, and detailed his forces to capture the Caucasus oilfields and cut the Volga river link with northern Russia around the city of Stalingrad. He expected a quick victory, and thought the Red Army would crumble. Stalin and his generals expected a renewed assault on Moscow and put the bulk of their forces in the centre and north of the Soviet–German front line. When the German Operation Blue opened on 19 June, the German army found the south to be even weaker than expected. Progress was rapid and by 19 August the German 6th Army, commanded by General Friedrich Paulus, and units of the 4th Panzer Army had arrived at the outskirts of Stalingrad. Paulus expected to capture the city in days and to cut the vital Volga trade route.

The city was defended by the Soviet 62nd and 64th Armies, which had retreated in growing disorder across the steppe and into the city. Here they dug in and waited for the Germans. They were supported by no more than 300 aircraft, and the artillery and rocket launchers on the far side of the river. Otherwise the Soviet defenders were outnumbered and outgunned by the 250,000 Axis forces (including Italian and Romanian divisions) that had begun the campaign. On 19 August Paulus began his assault and four days later he had reached the Volga north of the city. On 23 August 600 German bombers pounded the city, reducing great areas to ash and rubble. Slowly the defenders were pushed back towards the river until they controlled only a factory area in the north, the area around the Central Station and the small hill, Mamayev Kurgan, which dominated the central area. Under constant bombardment, they fought in many cases to the death. A few weeks before, Stalin had issued Order number 277 'Not a Step Back', by which any retreat or withdrawal was to be treated as cowardice.

On 7 September the Soviet commander in the city, General Alexander Lopatin, did order a withdrawal and was promptly sacked. He was replaced by General Vasily Chuikov, a tough, brave, no-nonsense commander, who shared the hardships of his men and risked his life over and over again. The Stalingrad front was placed under General Andrei Yeremenko, who, like Chuikov, was a tough commander who was wounded seven times during the battle, but continued to command from his hospital bed. A week after Chuikov arrived, Paulus launched what the Germans thought would be the decisive push to drive the Red Army out of its last redoubts and capture the western bank of the Volga. The German advance was remorseless; the 62nd and the 64th were divided when the Germans reached the Volga to the south of the city. The Central Station changed hands fifteen times. Mamayev Kurgan was charged by one side, then by the other. A trickle of reinforcements and supplies made its way to Chuikov; ferries full of the wounded crossed the other way.

The courage of the Soviet defenders was exceptional. Some failed to cope and it is claimed that over 13,000 were shot for desertion or dereliction of duty. For the rest Stalingrad became a symbol for which they were prepared to give their lives. Chuikov bullied his men but he also inspired them. They became adept at the art of street fighting, a form of urban guerrilla warfare that has become familiar since 1945, but which had not yet been seen in the war. By day German forces, supported by tanks and aircraft, blasted their way forward street by street, block by block; by night Soviet soldiers would work their way back through the ruins, using knives and bayonets to kill their opponents silently, or sometimes rushing an isolated German unit with terrifying yells and machine-gun fire. German soldiers learned never to show themselves for fear of Soviet snipers – skilled hunters who killed anything that moved. The ruins proved a useful asset for the Red Army, slowing down the movement of tanks and providing hundreds of foxholes and hidden alleyways from which to launch a sudden ambush.

Unknown to either side in Stalingrad, the Soviet high command had devised a way to end the battle. In September General Zhukov, Stalin's deputy, and the chief-of-staff, Alexander Vasilevski, drew up a plan to cut across the long, exposed Axis flank, strike at the weaker Italian and Romanian divisions, and encircle the 6th Army, cutting it off from effective rescue. It was a bold plan but Stalin accepted it and agreed to use all the reserves to build up, in complete secrecy, a force of over 1 million men, 14,000 guns and 979 tanks on either side of the long Axis flanks. German intelligence failed to detect it. The whole plan depended on the ability of Chuikov to keep his small and battered force fighting for the month it took to organize the counter-strike. This was the supreme test. On 9 November Paulus prepared one more assault to clear the remnants of Chuikov's forces. Bitter hand-to-hand fighting left both sides exhausted. On 12 November the fighting slowed down and the Germans dug in.

Chuikov's small force had done enough. On 19 November the counter-strike, Operation Uranus, began. The weaker Axis divisions crumbled and within five days the two prongs of the Soviet attack met at Kalach on the Don Steppe. Paulus was encircled with 330,000 of his men. Hitler refused to allow him to break out and an attempt by Field Marshal Erich von Manstein to drive through the Soviet lines to rescue the 6th Army was too weak in deteriorating winter weather. The fighting resumed in Stalingrad, but this time it was the German army doing the desperate defending. Operation Kol'tso ('Ring') began on 10 January and the 47 Soviet divisions and 300 tanks quickly cleared the approaches to the city. With nowhere to go and with constant orders from Hitler's headquarters to stand firm, Paulus and his men displayed a remarkable courage, fighting against heavy odds an unwinnable and pointless battle. On 31 January Paulus finally surrendered. German forces to the north of the city surrendered three days later. Famished, poorly clad and ill, the defenders trudged into captivity where most died on the route. The extraordinary courage of the Soviet defenders had made it possible to inflict the largest defeat the German army had ever experienced: 147,000 dead and 91,000 prisoners. For the final siege the Red Army paid with 485,000 dead, injured or missing. Chuikov went on to become a marshal and to capture Berlin; Paulus was recruited by the Soviet side as leader of a 'Free Germany' movement among German prisoners of war and ended up in retirement in East Germany.

85. FOURTH BATTLE OF MONTE CASSINO

11–18 May 1944

The Battle of Monte Cassino is usually remembered for the destruction by bombing on 15 February 1944 of the fourteenth-century Benedictine monastery on the mountaintop overlooking the small

Italian town of the same name, Cassino. Yet the battle for the mountain top really began after the monastery had already been destroyed. Here German paratroopers from the First Fallschirmjäger Division, part of the Gustav Line set up by the German army in central Italy in late 1943 to block the advance of Allied armies, dug into defensive positions high above the Allied forces and withstood every effort to dislodge them until the assault that began on 11 May by two divisions of Polish soldiers. The Poles succeeded, under withering fire and in the toughest terrain, in capturing the heights, an achievement of remarkable audacity.

The scale of the Polish success can be measured against the repeated failure to dislodge the Germans from the heights in three battles for Monte Cassino that took place between January and March 1944. The aim of the Allied armies, under the command of the British general Harold Alexander, was to push up the Italian peninsula towards Rome, with US General Mark Clark's 5th US Army on the left and General Oliver Leese's 8th British Army on the right. Progress was slow as a result of poor weather and a landscape of hills, mountain crags and small rivers that made mobile warfare difficult. Snow, mud and rain made tracks impassable except by mule or horse. German artillery and machine-gun emplacements could easily be concealed in this topography and a lethal field of fire established over the narrow valleys and defiles. On 22 January 1944 an attempt was made to outflank the Gustav Line by landing on the coast at Anzio, south of Rome, and attacking the German forces commanded by General Fridolin von Senger und Etterlin from the rear. The Anzio assault failed to break out of the beachhead. In the end the only way out of the impasse was to assault the Gustav Line directly, which meant attacking the Monte Cassino massif. The first battle began on 17 January but American troops made little progress against two ridges, Snakeshead and Phantom, which dominated the mountaintop and the monastery, and the operation was called off on 11 February. A second assault by the 4th Indian Division began on 15 February but petered out three days later with no gains. An assault on Cassino itself by the

New Zealand Corps between 15 and 23 March took massive casualties but failed to dislodge the enemy.

The assault was halted until large new resources could be brought forward. Alexander's staff drew up a new plan, Operation Diadem, designed to outflank the German defenders and drive down the valley of the River Liri towards Rome. A French corps was to take the Aurunci Mountains to the south; British, Indians and Canadians were deployed for the attack on the valley, but the critical task of finally clearing Monte Cassino and the ridges around it was given to the Polish 2nd Corps under General Władysław Anders, who was given ten minutes by the British commander to decide whether or not to accept the assignment. Anders saw the risks but wanted a Polish success, so that the cause of Poland would be brought 'to the fore of world opinion', and he agreed. The Polish Corps had been formed from Polish prisoners of war in the Soviet Union, who had been allowed to leave Russia and join British forces in North Africa. The Polish units had a good number of mountain troops, accustomed to the forbidding terrain, and a great deal of unrestrained enthusiasm for killing Germans. In early May huge supplies of equipment and ammunition were secretly moved into position (but much smaller quantities of food and water). The Poles were forced into a silent and patient wait for the start of the operation, a situation for which they were temperamentally ill-suited. Finally at 11 p.m. on 11 May a massive artillery barrage opened up on German positions. Anders told his men to remember the sacred slogan 'God, Honour, Country' and two hours later the Polish divisions were released up the slopes of the mountain, one towards the strongpoint known as Point 593 on Snakeshead Ridge and the other towards Colle Sant'Angelo on Phantom Ridge.

Conditions for both sides were appalling. Dry, dusty weather made water supplies imperative, but military equipment took priority. Artillery and mortar fire shattered the rocks and cliff face, sending shards of rock as lethal as shrapnel in all directions. Dead bodies were left where they fell and quickly decomposed. German paratroopers were issued with gasmasks to keep out the putrefying odour. The

Poles had to cope with mines on every track, including the S-Mine, nicknamed the 'de-bollocker' by the British because it was triggered to leap in the air, spraying ball-bearings at groin height. There was little cover for the attackers. The Poles were forced to fill sandbags with stones to provide some rudimentary protection. On the first day of action the 1st Carpathian Brigade, assaulting Point 593, had only one officer and seven men left alive and unwounded. There were 4,000 Polish casualties in the first assault, for little gain. Since the wounded were difficult to evacuate, they were treated where they lay and in many cases carried on fighting. Hand-to-hand combat between small groups of soldiers characterized much of the fighting and neither side readily took prisoners. The Germans took high losses, but fought in many cases to the death because of the persistent rumour that the Poles killed out of hand any German they caught.

The Poles had much to prove and Anders was keen that his force achieve the impossible and 'cover Polish arms with glory'. After a rest of a few days, spent precariously dug into the mountainside, a fresh assault on the mountains began on 17 May, coinciding with a heavy attack by the 8th Army in the Liri Valley that aimed to prevent the Germans from switching their shrinking reserves and artillery fire between the two fronts. Major General Sulik's 5th Kresowa Division stormed the slopes of Phantom Ridge but failed to dislodge all German resistance while continuing to take high casualties. One unit ran out of ammunition and hurled rocks at the Germans, all the while singing the Polish national anthem. The 3rd Carpathian Division fought for Point 593 and Snakeshead Ridge above the monastery. Under heavy fire, the Poles struggled bitterly for every metre, taking, losing and retaking the Point several times. On the night of 17 May the Poles were forced to rest and consolidate their costly gains, but during the night German movements could be detected. The Polish assault had proved too much for their embattled enemy. The monastery was abandoned by the morning and an incredulous unit of Polish lancers cautiously approached it. Only the German wounded were left. An improvised Polish flag was hoisted to the cheers of the onlookers. At

10.15 a.m. a Polish bugler stood on the monastery walls to play the Kraków Hejnal, the historic Polish trumpet call, while Polish soldiers wept with emotion. Savage fighting continued on the other ridge where the trapped paratroopers fought to the last out of fear of Polish vengeance, but finally Colle Sant'Angelo was in Allied hands as well.

The battle cost the Polish Corps 3,682 casualties, 860 of them killed. German losses are harder to calculate because the units moved during the battle to other fronts. After the battle German and Polish bodies could be found in a deathly embrace, having fought with knives and bayonets to the last, a brutal physical conflict with little quarter given. The hardships endured by the Polish attackers were exceptional but their courage under fire was unquestioned. Anders recommended one-third of the attackers for the Polish Cross for Valour. The dead were later buried in a cemetery between the monastery and Point 593. General Anders asked that he be buried beside them and when he died in 1970, his wish was fulfilled.

CHAPTER 6
IN THE NICK OF TIME

A t the height of the Battle of Adwa, in which a huge Ethiopian army destroyed an invading Italian–African force, General Matteo Albertone sent a laconic note back to the Italian commander: 'Large enemy force before me. Reinforcements would be welcome.' The help never came and Albertone's force was destroyed, but his plight reflected the hope that any armed force caught in a closing trap was bound to have, that at the last moment it would be saved by the appearance of powerful friends. Just occasionally the absence of reinforcement in a critical situation could be survived. Troops coming to help at Rorke's Drift, another African conflict in which a small European imperial force was surrounded by thousands of enemy tribesmen, saw the burning settlement in the distance and decided their assistance would come too late. The tiny garrison survived nevertheless, saved in the nick of time not by their compatriots but by the decision of the Zulu army to leave, just as their ammunition was running out.

The nick of time is not entirely the same as luck (since a commander may well know that reinforcements are on the way) yet in many cases a piece of good fortune at the last moment has played a part in deciding a battle one way or another. The fall of Constantinople in 1453 depended on the discovery of a small gate left open inadvertently through which Ottoman troops could pour; the victory in the Pacific War at Midway depended on just ten bombs that found their target in the final attack, and disabled four aircraft carriers. The destruction of the Magyar army after the battle at Lechfeld was due to a lucky downpour of rain which no-one could have predicted. Luck operates in battle in a hundred different ways, large and small, though the advantage granted by luck often depends on the skill of commanders who can react to an opportunity with decisive improvisation.

The most common examples of victory achieved or defeat avoided in the nick of time are the result of the appearance of reinforcements at a decisive moment. This is not the same as a force kept in reserve, though the timely exploitation of reserves has been a battlefield practice since the very first wars. Distant reinforcements may not arrive in time if they are held up or diverted, but when they do the effect can be deeply demoralizing for the side left without assistance. The victory at Stalingrad depended on the Soviet 64th and 62nd armies holding on to a shrinking finger of riverside territory, bombarded from all sides, until when all seemed lost, a massive Soviet counter-offensive smashed into the enemy flank, encircled Stalingrad and saved the embattled urban fighters. The Battle of Waterloo may have been won by Wellington or it may not, but the approach of a large Prussian army forced Napoleon to divert troops at a critical time to hold off the prospect of a crushing attack on his right flank.

The failure to co-ordinate forces so that they can all be brought to bear at once on the battlefield demonstrates how in just hours an expected victory turns into defeat. At Tannenberg in 1914, the Russian armies of General Samsonov desperately needed the Russian armies of General Rennenkampf to swing southwest and support his offensive, but help never came. At First Manassas in the American Civil War, a good proportion of Union troops never saw action, but their timely deployment in the heart of the fighting might have swung the battle the way it had been expected to go. Many battle post-mortems have consisted of speculation as to what might have happened if only help had arrived, whether in the form of ammunition, fuel or men. The margin can often be frustratingly small between triumph and failure, as Rommel found at Alam Halfa and Second Alamein, when a tanker or two of oil and a hundred more aircraft might have secured German conquest of Egypt.

Battle after battle in the 100 selected here has hung on a knife-edge for many hours of evenly matched combat. Many victories have come in the nick of time for reasons not always easy to discern. The element of chance in war is one that historians are often loath to accept when a rational calculation of odds, whether of materiel, leadership or morale, suggests a historically plausible outcome. The element of chance is not everything in battle, but it is an element that an astute leader must be aware of even when things look at their worst: 'If you engage in ten great undertakings,' wrote Prussian king Frederick the Great at the height of the Seven Years War, 'and are lucky in no more than two you make your name immortal.' Shortly after, in the last of thirteen fruitless hours battling the Austrians at Torgau, when the Austrian commander had already left to report his triumph, the Prussians made one final desperate push and at the last moment it proved just enough for victory.

86. BATTLE OF KADESH
1285 BCE

Kadesh (or Qadesh) is the earliest recorded battle for which there is definite information about both the forces involved and the operational sequence of events. It was long assumed to have been a major Egyptian victory because that is how the young pharaoh, Ramses II, portrayed it on his return from Syria to his Nile capital. He left both a 'poem' and a 'bulletin' (to accompany the relief carving of the battle), which were for years the only sources. Archaeological evidence has now come to light at Boghazköy in Turkey, which sheds light on the campaign from the point of view of Ramses's Hittite enemy, Muwatalli II, and suggests that there was no clear winner at Kadesh. What seems certain is that Ramses might well have lost the battle entirely had it not been for the timely arrival of a division of mercenary allies. About this the sources seem as reliable as can be expected.

The battle came as part of an Egyptian campaign in the thirteenth century BCE to recapture territory and influence in Syria, which was dominated by an amalgam of small communities owing allegiance to the Hittite kings. In the fourth year of his reign, Ramses set out from Egypt with an army reckoned at 20,000, divided into four divisions named after Egyptian deities – Amun, Re, Set and Ptah – and perhaps 2,000 chariots. Egyptian chariots were light two-man vehicles, allowing one man to fire his bow or use his spear while the other controlled the reins. Critical for the battle, as it turned out, was the addition of a body of mercenaries, probably from Canaan, described as the Ne'arin or *nrrn*.

Ramses led his force north through present-day Israel and Syria to recapture the cities of Amurru and Kadesh. His first division, Amun, reached the town of Shabtuna on the approach to the fortified city of Kadesh. It was here that Muwatalli positioned two nomad spies, intending that they should be caught. The spies told Ramses that the Hittite army was 200 kilometres (120 miles) away near the city of Aleppo. Relieved, Ramses established a camp for his lead division, Amun. The other divisions were still some distance behind, dangerously spaced apart. When Egyptian scouts brought in two Hittite prisoners, they were tortured in order to confirm the previous intelligence, but instead revealed the dismaying truth: Muwatalli was only a few kilometres away, hiding behind the town of Kadesh with a large force.

The Hittite army was composed of infantry and chariots. According to modern estimates, there were perhaps 20,000 foot soldiers and 3,000 chariots; Hittite chariots each carried three men, making them slower and less manoeuvrable than those of the Egyptians, but nevertheless they were the ancient version of a heavy tank attack when massed together. The Hittite king exploited the element of surprise perfectly. As the second division, Re, approached the Egyptian camp on the exposed banks of the River Orontes, the first wave of Hittite chariots forded the water and overwhelmed the exposed division in front of them. The survivors fled to the Amun camp, pursued by the enemy chariots. Amid the panic of retreating soldiers and looting Hittites, Ramses gathered his personal bodyguard and any soldiers still fighting and charged at the chariot force, driving them back, probably to the shelter of Kadesh. Muwatalli then released another 1,000 chariots to attack the Pharaoh, and it was during this second confrontation that the Ne'arin arrived after a march from the coast and fell on the Hittite flank.

According to the existing accounts, it was now the Hittites' turn to panic and flee. They abandoned their chariots and tried to cross the Orontes 'as fast as crocodiles swimming', according to the Egyptian version of the battle. The nimbler Egyptian chariots, though less stable than the heavier Hittite vehicles, were ideal for the pursuit. What happened next is not known with certainty, but it seems clear from both the Egyptian and the Hittite texts that Ramses failed to capture Kadesh and subsequently withdrew his army back to Egypt. The Hittite king had used only the chariots, which had been repulsed, but the rest of his army was still intact. Most modern accounts describe the battle as a draw, since Ramses was denied his goal, but nevertheless inflicted a local defeat on Muwatalli. Without the timely arrival of the Ne'arin, the outcome might have been very different since the other Egyptian divisions were still on the road moving north towards Kadesh, too far away to offer any assistance.

No-one in Egypt would challenge Ramses's version and the relief carving shows the victory for all time. But in truth, the Egyptian campaigns in the eastern Mediterranean were futile attempts to stem the encroachments of the Hittites and their allies. In 1258 BCE, the first surviving peace treaty was drawn up between the two empires demarcating their territorial spheres. The tablets are now in a museum in Istanbul, but there is a copy in the United Nations building as the first example of an agreement for peace in a region now plagued again by conflict. Kadesh was a first in every sense – the first recorded battle; the first evidence of the use of mass chariots; and, following Ramses's fortunate escape, the clash that paved the way for the first brief recorded armistice in centuries of war.

87. BATTLE OF ZAMA
202 BCE

The Battle that decided the long struggle between the Romans and the African empire of Carthage, in the Second Punic War, was fought by two armies led by veterans of the disastrous Roman defeat at Cannae. Hannibal Barca had been the victor at Cannae, while his opponent, Publius Scipio ('Africanus' as he became known), had been on the losing side, surviving the massacre by luck. This time, the Battle of Zama, in present-day Tunisia, was finely poised, but Scipio had learned important lessons. At the last moment, the Roman cavalry did to Hannibal what he had done to the Romans fourteen years earlier. It was a narrow margin, but enough to seal a historic triumph for Rome and the start of centuries of Roman domination.

The Second Punic War was fourteen years old when Scipio, who had taken most of Spain from the Carthaginians, set out from Sicily in 204 BCE with 40 warships and 400 transports to attack the enemy on their home territory in North Africa. The aim was to finish the war once and for all and to force Carthage to acknowledge Roman supremacy. For Scipio, given temporary supreme command of Roman forces, the campaign was designed to secure his political position in Rome against his jealous rivals. He faced two opponents in Africa, not only Carthage but also the Numidian kingdom ruled by King Syphax, who had long supported his neighbour against Rome. Political rivalry among the Numidians, however, brought Scipio an important bonus. Prince Masinissa took 2,000 of the fine Numidian cavalry over to the Roman side and fought against his former master. In the first engagement between the two sides in the early summer of 203 BCE, Scipio and Masinissa destroyed the Carthaginian and Numidian camps in the Battle of the Great Plains. After marching towards Carthage, Scipio exacted tough armistice terms from the alarmed Carthaginian senate. Masinissa pursued Syphax to Numidia, where he defeated him and declared himself king.

In secret, the Carthaginian assembly summoned Hannibal and his army back from southern Italy, where they had stayed on after Cannae, in the hope that the legendary general could turn the tide in Africa. By spring 202 BCE, the Carthaginian leaders were more confident that the armistice could be overturned and Scipio defeated. Hannibal gathered a new large army, estimated at 36,000 infantry and 4,000 cavalry drawn from all over North Africa and the Iberian Peninsula. The host fielded a variety of weapons, including the long Greek *sarissa* pike and the fearsome curved *falcata* steel sabre, which could cut through a Roman shield. Scipio had a mix of mercenary soldiers and veteran legionaries, some 29,000 in number, supported by 6,000 Roman and Numidian cavalry. They carried the conventional Roman spear, short sword and dagger. The two forces settled in camps a few miles apart at a site known as Zama, though its exact location remains uncertain. Modern estimates suggest a small plain near the present-day town of Sidi Youssef. It was here, halfway between the two armed camps, that Hannibal asked Scipio to meet him for a parley, to see if he could extract terms and avoid an unpredictable battle. Scipio is said to have asked for unconditional surrender. Hannibal turned on his heel and the two commanders prepared for combat on the following day.

Hannibal planned his battle predictably, which helped Scipio a great deal. He placed his infantry in three ranks, one behind the other, first mercenaries, then the Carthaginian levies, and finally his veterans from the Italian campaign. On either flank were placed 2,000 cavalry, while 80 elephants, the tanks of the ancient world, were placed at the front. Hannibal's plan was to break up the opposing infantry with an elephant charge and deploy his cavalry, as at Cannae, to drive back the enemy flanks and envelop the entire enemy force. Scipio understood all this. His infantry were drawn up in three similar ranks, mercenaries at the front, hardened veterans at the rear. The novelty in Scipio's plan was to create corridors concealed by lightly armed infantry, the *velites*, through which the elephants would be ushered to the rear and killed or incapacitated, while the ranks of Roman soldiery closed up behind them. Once the charge was over, Scipio planned to release his two superior cavalry forces, including Masinissa's Numidians, to destroy Hannibal's horsemen. What would happen next was in the lap of the gods, to whom both sides commended themselves before the battle.

It was later recorded that Scipio had addressed his soldiers on the eve of battle with the stark demand that they 'conquer or die'. Certainly both commanders realized that a great deal depended on the battle. The contest began when Hannibal released his elephants, backed by the first lines of infantry, against the Roman army. No battle had ever used so many animals, and neither side was quite sure what would happen. Scipio's plan did not go perfectly, but it worked well enough. Some of the elephants ran through the corridors to be finished off at the rear; others were so terrified by the deliberate blare of Roman trumpets that they stampeded from the field or turned back, trampling the Carthaginian cavalry. Seeing the disorder, the two cavalry commanders – Masinissa on the right, Gaius Laelius on the left – charged Hannibal's two cavalry wings and routed them with such enthusiasm that they were chased well beyond the battlefield, leaving the contest for the moment as a simple clash of infantry.

The two blocks of soldiers pushed one way and the other, neither side quite strong enough to gain the advantage, until Scipio's more experienced second-line soldiers finally broke the Carthaginian mercenaries and levies, leaving just Hannibal's Italian veterans in front of them. Hannibal stretched his line out, putting the survivors of his first two lines on the wings in the hope that a long line might envelop the shorter Roman line in front. But Scipio quickly reorganized his own forces so that the tough veteran legionaries stretched in a long line to match that of the enemy. While these two lines swayed and fought amid the piles of corpses and wounded, the battle hung on a knife-edge, both sides now deploying their toughest and most experienced troops. Suddenly back onto the plain galloped the Roman and Numidian cavalry, arriving behind the Carthaginian lines. They slaughtered Hannibal's veterans just as his horsemen had slaughtered the Roman legions at Cannae. Estimates in Roman histories suggest 20–25,000 Carthaginian dead and almost all the rest prisoners, for the loss of only 1,500 Romans. These figures are certainly exaggerated, but it seems that few escaped. Hannibal himself fled to his headquarters near Carthage, leaving his men to their fate.

Hannibal travelled to the capital at once to announce his defeat and recommend surrender. By spring 201 BCE, terms had been agreed and ratified in Rome, and Rome's political power now extended to Africa. Both commanders ended their lives in exile. Hannibal killed himself with poison in Anatolia in 183 BCE to prevent the Romans from taking him prisoner; Scipio was victimized by rivals in Rome, accused of corruption and embezzlement, and died in exile at a villa in Campania in southern Italy a year before his famous rival, embittered by the ingratitude of a people whose empire he had helped to secure.

88. THE BATTLE OF ADRIANOPLE
9 August 378 CE

The fall of the Roman Empire in the late classical age was a slow but irresistible process. Few battles signalled its eventual fate more completely than the battle outside the town of Adrianople (modern-day Edirne in western Turkey), where an army of Gothic tribes all but annihilated a large Roman army led by the emperor himself, Flavius Valens Augustus. The defeat had not been a foregone conclusion, as the Goths had been nervous of a pitched battle with seasoned Roman troops. The tide was turned by the late arrival of reinforcements for the Goths. From a position of numerical inferiority, they suddenly found themselves on equal terms with the enemy. Valens's prevarication and incompetence then turned what might have been a military stalemate into a comprehensive rout.

Leading up to the battle, the Roman Empire had been trying to find ways to live in peace with the settlers and warriors who were moving in large numbers from mainland Asia into the heart of Europe. In the mid-fourth century, beyond the frontier of the empire in the Balkans, the Huns emerged as a powerful and predatory new kingdom in central Asia, causing major movements of population. The Huns pushed back the Alans, whose pressure in turn pushed the Gothic Greuthungi and Tervingi kingdoms further west and southwest. In 376, large numbers, perhaps hundreds of thousands, of refugee Tervingi arrived on the Danube frontier with Rome and petitioned for permission to cross into Roman territory to escape the apparently unstoppable Huns. Negotiations took time as the emperor was in Antioch, on the southern coast of modern Turkey, not in Constantinople. Valens decided to agree to a treaty that would allow the Goths to cross the river, in the hope that he could use their manpower for his wars in the east against Persia. The Goths crossed over the river and were immediately subjected to harsh treatment by the local Roman generals, who stole the food allocated to the refugees and traded dog meat instead, at the rate of one dog in exchange for a Gothic child to be sold into slavery.

While the Tervingi were being dispersed south, the leaders of the Greuthungi Goths, Alatheus and Saphrax, who had been refused entry to the empire, slipped across the Danube unnoticed and set up a large camp unsupervised by the Romans. Meanwhile, the local Roman commander Lupicinus invited the leaders of the Tervingi, Fritigern and Alavivus, to a feast in his headquarters in Marcianople; it is not clear if he intended to kill them, but he killed their bodyguard. The Goths outside the city threatened to break in and Lupicinus thought better of his plot. Fritigern escaped but Alavivus was not seen again. As a result, the Goths rebelled against Roman abuse and laid waste to much of Thrace. The Roman armies in the west, led by Valens's young nephew Gratian, sent reinforcements, but the main army would not arrive until the late summer. Valens decided to snuff out the threat himself. He appointed Sebastianus as commanding general of his cosmopolitan army, drawn from all over the Eastern Empire, and on 11 June 378 set out from Constantinople to destroy the army of Fritigern. He set up camp in Adrianople and on the morning of 9 August, after rejecting overtures for an armistice from the Goths and receiving intelligence that the enemy numbered only 10,000, took his army out to the plain where the Goths had drawn up their forces. Valens was confident that a Roman victory was assured.

The record of the battle has not survived in great detail in the one classical account that we have. Gratian was approaching but would not arrive for some days or weeks. Valens thought his help was not needed, but he was outmanoeuvred by Fritigern. While the Roman army stood in the baking sun in its usual battle order, the Goths lit grass fires whose smoke, like a twentieth-century gas attack, was designed to leave the enemy troops temporarily incapacitated. At the same time, Fritigern sent further envoys to Valens, ostensibly to seek peace but in fact to stall for time while he waited for his adopted allies, the Greuthungi of Alatheus and Saphrax, to arrive. In the confusion, the right wing of the Roman army began engaging with the Goths in front of them. What followed was, by Roman standards, a chaotic battle. The Roman line was distorted and then, at the critical moment, perhaps 10,000 new warriors appeared – the army of the Greuthungi – to cave in the Roman left flank. The newcomers turned the tide as they overwhelmed the now numerically inferior attackers. The Roman cavalry on the left found they had ridden too far and were cut off and slaughtered. As a result, the unprotected infantry line bent back on itself, leaving the soldiers with insufficient room to fight. The Goths swarmed over the Roman line, killing thousands where they stood. Roman reserves melted away from the battlefield in fear. Two-thirds of the cream of Rome's eastern army were slaughtered, along with the emperor Valens, whose body was never recovered. It was later variously recorded that Valens had been shot by an arrow, or that he had been burnt to death in a nearby farmhouse. His senior commanders, Traianus and Sebastianus, also perished in the massacre.

For the Roman Empire, Adrianople was a disastrous and humiliating rout. It signalled around the known world that the Roman frontier could no longer act as an effective barrier, and hundreds of thousands of migrants pushed into the empire over the following decades. But it was a battle that, with better judgement, intelligence and operational understanding, the Romans might have won. Fritigern was fortunate that Alatheus and Saphrax arrived when they did. We do not know why they came to his aid, but their arrival helped write a new chapter in the history of the fall of Rome. Only forty years later, the Goths sacked the very capital of the empire.

89. FALL OF CONSTANTINOPLE
April – May 1453

Sultan Mehmet (Turkish for Muhammad) was an impatient ruler. He came to the Ottoman throne in 1451 and almost his first act was to order the murder of his baby brother to make sure there would be no fratricidal conflicts later in his reign. Though only nineteen at his accession, Mehmet was in a hurry to complete an ambition that had frustrated the Muslim east for centuries: the eradication of the last vestige of the centuries-old Byzantine Empire, the Orthodox Christian capital at Constantinople. The city boasted formidable fortifications, man-made and natural, which had frustrated earlier Turkish sieges. They almost defeated Mehmet after seven weeks of fruitless assaults on the city until two moments of good fortune opened the way to its conquest.

The young sultan wanted to mark the start of his reign in spectacular fashion. The Ottoman Turks now controlled a large empire in Anatolia (present-day Turkey) and the European Balkan peninsula. Christian Constantinople lay between the two, a thorn in the Ottoman side. Mehmet wanted the city for his capital rather than the Greek city of Edirne, and even at a young age was capricious and forceful enough to compel his advisers and commanders, including the more cautious grand vizier, Çandarli Halil Pasha, to accept his ambition. In 1452, he made a start by ordering a fortress to be built on the European side of the Bosphorus Strait above Constantinople to act as a 'throat cutter' for Byzantine trade. The fortress, Rumeli Hisari, was built in record time and heavy cannon backed by a rapidly constructed Ottoman fleet cut off trade routes to the city. Mehmet called on the Byzantine emperor, Constantine XI, to surrender. The emperor refused and sealed up the gates.

Constantine had little with which to challenge the huge Ottoman army that Mehmet summoned from all over his empire. There were probably no more than 6,000 regular soldiers and militia in the city, reinforced in January 1453 by 700 heavily armed Genoese under their commander Giovanni Giustiniani Longo. He quickly organized the defence of the city, repairing crumbling walls, stockpiling weapons, and instructing the anxious defenders in the best tactics to frustrate siege warfare. Their best protection, however, remained the 'Wall of Theodosius', a 20-kilometre (12-mile) fortification on the landward side of the city 60 metres (200 feet) in depth and 30 metres (100 feet) in height, with 192 towers, a fosse wall and a deep moat. The other walls of the triangular site on which Constantinople perched were protected by the Sea of Marmora to one side and the Golden Horn inlet on the other. These fortifications were all that stood between a frightened population, increasingly persuaded that God was punishing them for their sins by sending the infidel to scourge them, and the 200,000 Ottomans, 60,000 of them soldiers, who approached the city early in April 1453.

Mehmet knew that siege warfare did not sit well with Ottoman traditions of war-making. He therefore ordered the construction of giant cannon, supervised by a Hungarian gunsmith, Orban, and transported with great difficulty more than 150 kilometres (100 miles) from Edirne to the gates of Constantinople. He set up the siege a mere 250 metres (800 feet) from the Theodosian Wall, his men protected behind a ditch and rampart. The cannon, including one 8.5 metres (27 feet) long, with stone cannon balls weighing half a ton, were set up to bombard what looked like the weakest parts of the fortification. His forces captured small forts and outposts outside the city and displayed the unfortunate survivors – impaled naked on sharp stakes driven with a heavy mallet through the rectum and along the spine - in full view of the Greeks on the battlements of the city. Terror was also one of the weapons at Mehmet's disposal, but it was no more than Constantine and his soldiers expected. Ottoman tradition was to slaughter all those who resisted.

On 12 April, the siege began with a six-day bombardment, the largest artillery barrage yet mounted. The 'supergun' devastated the defending walls until metal fatigue caused it to explode, killing, so it was said, the helpful Orban. To the Ottoman besiegers, the damage must have looked impressive as each massive stone ball knocked down sections of towers and battlements, but when Mehmet ordered the first storming of the damaged walls on 18 April, the stout defenders blocked the narrow entryways and slaughtered any who tried to break through. The attacks were usually made in the dark, accompanied by yells, constant drumming and cries to Allah, but each was repelled with savage hand-to-hand fighting, while civilians poured down stones and burning pitch from the tops of the fortifications onto the mass of Ottoman soldiery. Mehmet had wanted a quick knock-out blow but was now faced with a prolonged investment. Arguments began in the Ottoman camp over fears that crusading Christians would arrive from Europe to save the capital of eastern Christendom or that frustration, disease and pointless casualties would evaporate the previously high morale of the Ottoman army. Further assaults, on 6 and 7 May, and a brief penetration of the city on 12 May by a group of Ottoman soldiers came to nothing.

Mehmet tried everything, including further offers of peace, even a new kingdom for the inhabitants in Greece, if Constantine would surrender, but the Byzantine leaders remained obdurate. The Ottomans recruited Saxon miners to tunnel under the walls, but a Scottish soldier resident in the city, John Grant, knew how to detect mining and managed to frustrate every attempt, burning or burying the miners underground. A huge wooden siege tower, even higher than the walls, was trundled into place but the Byzantine defenders threw barrels of gunpowder with lighted tapers and blew the contraption into the air. On 26 May, the Ottoman commanders debated with the sultan about what they should do. Halil Pasha thought it wise to abandon the siege, but the restless army needed the loot it had been promised (Ottoman soldiers were not paid) and Mehmet had already faced several near rebellions by his personal janissary guards. The assembled leaders accepted Mehmet's plea for one last attempt. On 27 May, an endless bombardment was set up against the damaged walls, where Giustiniani had improvised stockades and earthworks to fill the breaches. On 29 May at 1.30 a.m., accompanied by a cacophony of screams, drums and trumpets, the whole Turkish army ran at the walls.

They were beaten back relentlessly by the small and exhausted Byzantine army, until two pieces of luck suddenly undid the weeks of stout defence. A small gate, the Wooden Circus Gate, had been left open by neglect after a small group of Italian soldiers had returned from a sally. Some Ottoman soldiers saw it and rushed in. Within minutes they were on the battlements and Ottoman banners fluttered from the towers. At almost the same time, Giustiniani, in the thick of the battle, was severely wounded. His men carried him away to a Genoese ship still anchored in the Horn, and the rest of the Genoese followed, no longer willing to defend an apparently hopeless cause.

Their loss suddenly exposed the weakened defence. Mehmet now threw in his last trump card, the 5,000 imperial troops of his own bodyguard. They hacked and pushed their way through a narrow breach in the wall and slaughtered the enemy soldiers. Though no eyewitness was certain what happened to Constantine, whose severed head had been promised to the sultan, he died somewhere in the mêlée along with his garrison. In Islamic law, three days of pillaging and violence were permitted, though this time Mehmet allowed only one. An estimated 4,000 of the population were killed, the rest taken into slavery. What was left of the wealth of the city, which was much less than expected, was taken by the soldiers during an orgy of violence, looting and rape.

Mehmet's siege was rescued at the last moment and his ambition fulfilled, more by luck than by the panoply of siege equipment brought to bear on the city. Two days later, Halil Pasha was executed to punish him for his restraint. Constantinople developed as an Islamic centre and the Topkapi Palace was constructed in the city as Mehmet's refuge. The Christian West deplored the loss but had made almost no effort to come to Constantine's aid. Hundreds of Byzantine nobles, and the fortunate Giustiniani, made it through the Ottoman sea blockade to fight another day.

90. BATTLE OF SEKIGAHARA
21 October 1600

There are few battles in Japanese history more famous than the clash between the so-called Western and Eastern armies in a brief civil war to decide who would become the new military hegemon of Japan. The country's imperial system was dominated by the military leaders, who jockeyed for influence over the imperial court. At

Sekigahara on the island of Honshu, the great regional lords, or *daimyo*, clashed over the rival claims of the Tokugawa and Toyotomi clans to dominate Japan. The battlefield was as much a political as a military site. A number of *daimyo* fighting for the Toyotomi Western Army hedged their bets about the outcome, uncertain whether to switch loyalty to the enemy commander, Tokugawa Ieyasu. At the last moment, with the outcome in the balance, Kobayakawa Hideaki, son of one of the guardians of the young Toyotomi heir, switched sides and victory went to the Eastern Army, opening the way to the long and relatively peaceful Tokugawa era.

Japanese politics in the late sixteenth century was dominated by the Toyotomi clan and its leader, Hideyoshi, who by the 1590s had imposed a fragile political unity on the whole of Japan. Failure in war in Korea weakened the Toyotomi hold over the rival *daimyo*. That hold was further weakened when Hideyoshi died in 1599, leaving a five-year-old son, Toyotomi Hideyori, as his successor. Before his death, Hideyoshi established a board of five regents (*tairo*) to rule on his son's behalf and five administrators (*bugyo*) to oversee the running of the state. Within two years the two groups split into rival factions. While Hideyori and his mother sheltered in the powerful castle at Osaka, Tokugawa Ieyasu, the most senior military commander and a powerful landowner, built an alliance to support his efforts to supplant the Toyotomi. The *daimyo* still loyal to the Toyotomi succession, their land based chiefly in the west of the Japanese islands, gathered around the figure of Ishida Mitsunari, one of the leading *bugyo*. They also made their base at Osaka Castle, where the infant Hideyori was protected by the *daimyo* Mori Hidemoto, one of those who was to play a double game at Sekigahara.

The clash between the two sides gathered pace in the summer and autumn of 1600 as each side sought to win over the allegiance of *daimyo* who hesitated to commit themselves. The Western Army captured the Tokugawa fortress of Fushimi while Tokugawa Ieyasu gathered a force of 30,000 of his own followers and 40,000 from his allies and marched towards Osaka. Ishida's army numbered an estimated 80,000, but the reliability of many of his allies, already secretly in contact with Ieyasu, was doubtful. After a difficult march through heavy rain, the Western Army arrived at Sekigahara, where Ishida deployed his troops on hilly ground, protected on either flank by a stream, to await the oncoming Eastern Army. On 20 October 1600 (the Japanese fourteenth day of the ninth month), Ieyasu learned that the enemy was waiting for him at Sekigahara and the following morning, in heavy fog, the two armies stumbled into each other. As the fog lifted, the two armies stood face-to-face, an array of heavily armoured samurai armed with their traditional swords and bows, some on horseback. They were backed by a militia of light infantry carrying the traditional spear (*naginata*). Both sides had cannon, though Ishida's artillery was hamstrung by the rain, which had soaked the gunpowder. Ieyasu had brought a supply of arquebuses to add to the traditional weaponry of the Japanese soldiers. He placed his allies in the front line, his own retainers in the reserve. At mid-morning, his ally Fukushima Masanori began the battle by launching his advance guard along the River Fuji against the right wing of the Western Army.

The details of the battle are sparse. Ieyasu followed Fukushima's assault across the rain-soaked ground against the Western left. The samurai, like European knights, were the fighting elite, trained from a young age for mortal combat. 'The way of the samurai,' wrote one sixteenth-century soldier, 'is desperateness. Ten men or more cannot kill such a man.' As both assaults pushed forward, Fukushima's flank lay open to attack. Otani Yoshitsugu, a former 'chief-of-staff' of the Toyotomi army in Korea, crossed Mount Fuji to attack Fukushima's forces, who were already engaged in a fierce contest. At this point, Otani should have been supported by the 16,000 men of Kobayakawa Hideaki, stationed behind him on Mount Matsuo. Ieyasu ordered the arquebuses to open fire on the hill and as he did so, the young Hideaki, smarting from Ishida's accusation of incompetence and encouraged to defect by a Christian *daimyo*, Dom Daimia Kuroda, decided that his allegiance to the Western Army was no longer useful. He charged into the fray against Otani and turned the tide of the battle. Seeing

Hideaki's disloyalty, and fearing its consequences, four other commanders switched sides. Behind the Western Army stood the reserve of Mori Hidemoto, with 15,000 soldiers. He, too, doomed Ishida by remaining largely inactive. The political calculations on the battlefield made the difference between defeat and victory, for the Western Army was not only larger, but had more battle experience from the war in Korea. This army now disintegrated and fled. Ishida and two of his leading commanders, Konishi Yukinaga and Ankokuji Ekei, were captured and later publicly executed. The casualties suffered by both sides in a long and bitter battle are unknown.

The victory at Sekigahara confirmed Tokugawa Ieyasu as the military hegemon in Japan, though the defeated Western clans acknowledged his claim with reluctance. In 1603, the emperor Go-Yozei installed Ieyasu as *sei-i tai-shogun*, chief of the Japanese warrior estate and in effect the dominant political authority in Japan. Ieyasu took land away from the defeated *daimyo* of the Western Army and re-distributed it to his allies and those who had switched sides so auspiciously during the battle. The Christian *daimyo*, Kuroda, who played a key role in persuading Hideaki to change sides, was presented with a large fiefdom. In 1605, Ieyasu made his son Hidetada shogun in his place, initiating what was to be a 250-year dynasty of the Tokugawa.

91. BATTLE OF MARENGO
14 June 1800

One of the most famous portraits of Napoleon Bonaparte has him mounted on a rearing white horse crossing high in the Alps on his way to a stunning victory over the Austrians at the north Italian town of Marengo in the Po Valley. In reality, he made the journey partly on foot, partly on a more reliable mule, and the triumph at

Marengo was so close to turning into a battlefield disaster that the later legend which surrounded it required judicious amendment of many of the facts. The real hero that humid day in Italy was Lieutenant General Louis Desaix, who managed to get his tired men to march back 15 kilometres (10 miles) from where Napoleon had sent them, and to lead them into battle at the last moment against an Austrian enemy so confident that victory had been won that their guard was down. As he charged, Desaix was accidentally shot in the back and killed, leaving the legend of Marengo to the fortunate Napoleon.

The battle brought to an end the war of the Second Coalition, an alliance of Austria, Russia and Britain formed to overturn the conquests of revolutionary France in Italy, Germany and Switzerland. The war hinged on the ability of the Austrian army, commanded by General Michael von Melas and his chief-of-staff, General Anton von Zach, to drive the French out of northern Italy. Melas took 85,000 men on the campaign with the object of besieging the French garrison at Genoa and driving the army of Italy, commanded by General Louis Suchet, back over the frontier into France, to be followed by an Austrian invasion. The plan worked well enough at first. Suchet was pushed into Provence by mid-May while the 5,900 troops in Genoa finally surrendered on 1 June. The problem for Melas was the new French First Consul, Napoleon Bonaparte, who had been appointed in a coup in November 1799 in Paris. His responsibility was to overcome the crisis faced by the military effort to export the revolution to Europe. Napoleon understood how serious the Austrian threat was. The only way to get quickly to northern Italy with the new army he had raised, the so-called Reserve Army, was to cross over the Alps behind the Austrians, cut off their supply route, and leave them trapped between two French forces, one in their rear, one in Genoa.

Crossing the Alps was a severe challenge. It had to be done over the St Bernard pass, bringing 60,000 men, supplies and heavy guns along the snowy mountain tracks. Napoleon insisted on the risk, since success would place him right behind the Austrian army. Mules struggled along the treacherous paths laden with stores, while 100 soldiers pulled each cannon up the slopes. Yet the whole crossing, which had cost Hannibal heavy losses many centuries before, was undertaken in just three days. Most of the men and equipment made it safely across, and Napoleon moved towards Milan, which a smaller Austrian force then abandoned. Further south, he cut the main road used to move Austrian supplies along the Po Valley. What he did not know was that Genoa had already surrendered and Suchet's army driven back towards France.

Alerted to his enemy's movements, Melas turned to face Napoleon, concentrating most of his army of around 30,000 men at Alessandria. His chief-of-staff suggested a ruse to get Napoleon to disperse his forces, allowing the main Austrian army to batter its way along the main supply road and reach safety further east. A spy was sent by the Austrians to inform Napoleon that Melas was hoping to escape northwards towards Milan, in the hope that the French would then move north as well, exposing their flank to an attack from the main Austrian force. Napoleon was unsure how to treat the deception, though the spy reported to Melas and Zach that the ruse had worked. In the end, Napoleon did not move north, but he sent one division northeast to cut off any Austrian attempt at a breakout, and a division commanded by Desaix southwest, towards the Austrian forces that Napoleon assumed were still at Genoa. Napoleon set up camp, uncertain of his options.

On the evening of 13 June, the central French line clashed with a force of Austrians in and around the village of Marengo, close to the main bridge over the River Bormida and a few miles from the Austrian camp. Thanks to the spy, both sides misinterpreted the clash. Napoleon assumed this was Melas's rearguard, left in place as the Austrians tried to withdraw, while Melas and Zach assumed that it was a small French blocking force, sent to disguise the move of the French army further north. The following morning Melas sent the bulk of his army across the plain from Alessandria, over the Bormida Bridge, and on to Marengo. The rest were sent northeast with Field Marshal Karl Ott von Bártokéz to block what was expected to be the real advance guard of Napoleon's army. Both sides soon discovered their mistake. A crushing assault on the French line, now weakened by the dispersion of divisions north and south and the reserve held further back by Napoleon, was repulsed with difficulty. Twice more the Austrian force charged forward, both sides taking heavy casualties in bitter fighting. Napoleon at first believed the assault was a mere feint to mask the Austrian retreat and refused his front-line commanders' request for aid. He finally realized his mistake by mid-morning and sent a despairing note to Desaix, 15 kilometres (10 miles) down the road towards Genoa: 'For God's sake, come up if you still can.'

Slowly the French army, outgunned by the larger Austrian force, was pushed back from Marengo. At places there were only ten paces between the lines as men fired at point-blank range. Melas ordered a flanking attack on the French left, while Ott's force, finding that the French army was not advancing from the north, turned back to threaten the French right flank. By 2.30 p.m., after hours of stubborn, blood-soaked fighting, the French abandoned Marengo for a line of vineyards further back; the right wing faced collapse and at 3 p.m. Napoleon ordered the elite Consular Guard to attack Ott and hold back the threat of encirclement. The Guard found themselves isolated and were annihilated, and by late afternoon Napoleon faced a catastrophic defeat. Melas thought he had won and ordered a pause while the army organized for a pursuit. Bruised by two falls earlier in the day, he returned to the Austrian camp, confident of victory.

A short while elapsed while the French waited for the final humiliation when suddenly Desaix arrived to greet Napoleon. Among the many versions of what passed between the two men was one that suited the later Bonaparte legend. 'I think this is a battle lost,' Desaix is supposed to have said, to which Napoleon retorted, 'I think it is a battle won.' The 6,000 new troops were sent against the tired Austrian line after a brief and unexpected bombardment. Desaix was killed in the first attacks, but the momentum continued. When an Austrian rally threatened, General François Kellermann attacked with 400 cavalry and scattered the threat. Two more hours of bloody combat followed as the disheartened Austrians were pushed back through Marengo and the narrow river crossing. Here hundreds were crushed at the water's edge or drowned in the river. Unexpectedly, the Austrians now stared defeat in the face. When dusk came, they fell back in a battered line to the Austrian camp. Around 6,500 casualties were suffered by both sides; the French lost 5,000 as prisoners, the Austrians almost 3,000. An armistice was signed and Melas was allowed to retreat eastwards with his surviving army intact. On 2 July, Napoleon returned in triumph to Paris, where his reports on Marengo had already turned a battle he had almost lost into an undeserved monument to his masterful leadership and shrewd battlefield skills..

92. BATTLE OF WATERLOO
18 June 1815

The great Allied victory near the Belgian village of Waterloo against the final offensive of Napoleon Bonaparte has at its core the legend of the arrival of the Prussian army in the nick of time to save the day for the beleaguered forces under General Arthur Wellesley, Duke of Wellington. The claim has always encouraged arguments about the decisive moment in the battle. It is not untrue that the Prussians arrived as the struggle was near its end, and thus ensured a comprehensive rout and pursuit of the French army, but it is not necessarily the case that Wellington needed Prussian help. His management of a classic defensive strategy on ground of his choosing sealed the outcome of a battle that Napoleon had been overconfident of winning.

Waterloo was neither the longest nor the largest battle of the Napoleonic Wars, but it was decisive in ending the spectacular career of the Corsican-born emperor who had taken France and then Europe by storm. After defeat and exile to the island of Elba in 1814, Napoleon harboured ambitions for a return to glory. Escaping from his unwary British guardians, he returned to France in March 1815, overthrew the recently installed king, Louis XVIII, raised an army of veterans and admirers and prepared to fight Europe for his right to rule. Meeting at Vienna to argue out the terms of a peace settlement, the other Great Powers responded to the arrival of a fresh Napoleonic threat by immediately forming a Seventh Coalition. This included Great Britain, Prussia, Austria and Russia, which each pledged 150,000 troops to finish off Napoleon once and for all.

By early summer Napoleon had organized an army loyal to him, led by marshals and generals who had served him through conquests and defeats. His strategy in the past had relied on dividing his enemies and defeating them piecemeal. The armies of the Coalition were gathered slowly together, but the British army in Belgium under Wellington, with a mixed force of 90,000 soldiers from Britain, the Low Countries, Brunswick and Hanover, was the nearest and the most vulnerable. The Prussians, under Field Marshal Gebhard von Blücher and Lieutenant General August von Gneisenau, were forming an army of 130,000, but the two coalition forces were still stationed some distance apart – Wellington around Brussels, the Prussians further east around Namur. Napoleon chose to attack them separately before they had consolidated their forces. The Battle of Waterloo was in truth a battle of three days of position and manoeuvre as Napoleon sought to eliminate two of his powerful opponents. On 15 June, he launched his field army of around 100,000 men across the Belgian border. Part of it was to attack and drive back the Prussians, and part was to march on Wellington before he was ready and drive the British into the sea.

On 16 June, the French army attacked the Prussians at Ligny and Wellington's army at the village of Quatre Bras. The larger Prussian force resisted stoutly but took heavy casualties to prolonged French assault; they eventually fell back in good order having suffered 19,000 losses to 13,900 French. Marshal Michel Ney commanded the force against the British and initially he had 28,000 men to Wellington's 8,000. But more of the Coalition force arrived and they soon numbered around 30,000, allowing early French gains to be retaken. Wellington then disengaged with great discipline, moving his forces back to a position he had already reconnoitred on the road to Brussels, along a ridge at Mont-Saint-Jean near the village of Waterloo. In torrential rain the two sides moved into position to continue the contest. Napoleon was confident that the Prussians were fleeing eastward and sent Marshal Emmanuel de Grouchy to pursue them, but on 17 June Blücher informed Wellington that he was actually moving north in order to join him at some point on the following day, the very outcome that Napoleon had wanted to avoid. The bulk of the French army, around 72,000 men, moved up the Brussels road towards Wellington. On the morning of 18 June, through paths and fields turned to churning mud by heavy rains, Napoleon drew up his army for what he hoped would be a textbook victory against a British opponent he had consistently underrated.

Wellington had chosen his ground well. On either flank he was protected by a hilltop farm, Hougoumont on the right, La Haie Sainte on the left, both of which were heavily garrisoned. He placed his artillery along the forward slope to slow up the French advance, and held the bulk of his infantry and a reserve of cavalry on the rear slope, concealed from view and sheltered from the worst of the French artillery barrage. The foot soldiers were in ranks four-deep on the centre and right, though weaker on the left in expectation that the Prussians would soon arrive from that direction. Napoleon had once claimed that war was waged only with 'vigour, decision and unbroken will' but at Mont-Saint-Jean he was a tired commander, made sluggish by painful haemorrhoids and cystitis and a greater remoteness from the battlefield, whose management he left to Ney. Rather than try a battle of manoeuvre, he believed his force strong enough to sweep Wellington's army away with a firm frontal assault. The two redoubts at Hougoumont and La Haie Sainte were invested first; Hougoumont was never captured, La Haie Sainte only at 6.15 p.m., both attempts absorbing large numbers of French troops. At 1.30 p.m. the first wave of French infantry – four divisions under Count Jean Baptiste d'Erlon – attacked Wellington's centre. As they crossed in columns over the ridge, they confronted a line of defence that they could not break. The cavalry under Lord Uxbridge then charged, driving the French infantry back. The attempt by the French to dislodge the enemy on foot had failed.

As Wellington reformed his line, withdrawing some units, Ney thought his opponent was retreating. The French cavalry were now called on to charge the fleeing enemy. They were instead subjected to heavy fire from the forward British cannon even before they reached the crest; once across it they found that Ney had been wrong. Wellington's infantry were arrayed in thirteen solid squares that proved impenetrable after two hours of exhausting charges, each one made across an ever-growing pile of corpses and horse carcasses. Wellington spurred on his men in person as he moved from square to square, exposing himself to continuous danger. By 6 p.m. the French horsemen had had enough and more infantry were sent in, once more subject to heavy fire from front and flank. News was at last arriving among the French soldiers that the Prussian army was advancing from the left. Napoleon had already sent his Sixth Corps to block the German advance, removing a large part of the French reserve. At 7.30 p.m., with the British line still firm, Napoleon flung in the last of his Imperial Guard but the famed force cracked and Wellington at last ordered a general advance, with the cavalry and his disciplined line of foot overwhelming a broken and exhausted enemy. The Prussians began to arrive at 8 p.m.

Did the Prussians save the day? The threat certainly worked to force Napoleon to squander his reserves while the news of the Prussian advance demoralized a French army already suffering debilitating casualties. The French had 31,000 killed or wounded, almost half their force. Wellington's army had 16,200 casualties, 3,500 of them dead. Neither side had given much quarter. But the real damage had been done by the disciplined British line much earlier in the day. Colonel

Stanhope of the First Foot Guards welcomed the sight of the Prussian troops but remarked with some justice the next day, 'The French were beat before but this was a very pretty sight.' The defeat was comprehensive. Napoleon fled to Paris but his army was broken. Light resistance was swept aside as Wellington and Blücher advanced on the French capital, which they occupied on 7 July. Napoleon ended his days on the Atlantic island of St Helena, wondering where he had gone wrong; Wellington became and has remained Britain's most celebrated soldier.

93. BATTLE OF TANNENBERG
24–30 August 1914

The battle between advancing Russian armies and the depleted German forces in East Prussia just weeks after the outbreak of the First World War was one of the few really decisive battles of the whole conflict. It raises an important historical 'what if?' Had Russian armies swept the Germans aside and occupied Berlin, the war might well have been over by Christmas, as so many had hoped. As it was, German victory in an area of heath and forest around the small towns of Frankenau and Orlau (the village of Tannenberg was some distance from the fighting) meant that the German war effort could at least continue, and with it the long and bitter war of attrition that followed. But it was a close-run thing. New commanders were appointed in time to prevent a German disaster and the decisive operation was carried out with no room for mistakes, fully in the knowledge that with one error the path to Berlin would lie open.

The Russians mobilized and deployed their armies much more rapidly than the Germans had expected. The idea had been to leave a covering force in eastern Germany while France was defeated swiftly in the West, and then to turn the bulk of the German army against Russia. Instead the battle in France became bogged down while two large Russian armies attacked the 14 second-echelon divisions and 774 guns available to General Max von Prittwitz. The Russian 1st Army commanded by General Paul von Rennenkampf had 12 divisions, half of them cavalry, and 492 guns; the 2nd Army under General Alexander Samsonov amounted to 18 divisions and 1,160 guns. Together the 30 divisions and 1,652 guns on the Russian side outnumbered the German enemy by more than two to one.

The Russian general staff, however, weakened the impact of their larger force by dividing it in two. Rennenkampf was to advance north of the network of the Masurian Lakes into Prussian territory while Samsonov moved south of the lakes with the object of encircling and destroying the German forces as they struggled to contain the threat from Rennenkampf. Once that had happened, the Russian head-quarters (Stavka) gambled on being able to sweep into the heart of Germany with little oppostition. The German supreme command told Prittwitz to make limited offensives to try to hold up the Russians, but when he let the headstrong General Hermann von François attack Rennenkampf's advancing Russians at Gumbinnen on 20 August 1914, the German forces took heavy casualties. Uncertain of the outcome and conscious that Samsonov's much larger force was moving forward in the south and might cut off and encircle the German 8th Army entirely, Prittwitz ordered a retreat back to the River Vistula. But by this stage Samsonov's vanguard was already nearing the German rear, creating just the operational conditions the Stavka wanted.

Two things saved the Germans in the east. On 24 August, Prittwitz was dismissed and replaced by the aged General Paul von Hindenburg (called out of retirement) and the quirky, nervous General Erich Ludendorff, victorious conqueror of the Belgian fortress of Liège a few weeks before. When they arrived, they adopted a plan proposed some days before by Prittwitz's experienced chief-of-staff, General Max Hoffmann. He suggested sending some of the 8th Army by rail to hit Samsonov's approaching left wing, while the rest disengaged from the battle with Rennenkampf and marched south to hit Samsonov's right wing in the flank. The risk was immense, for if Rennenkampf realized that the Germans were moving away, he would pursue them and crush the force between the two Russian armies. But Rennenkampf and Samsonov had a sour professional relationship; communication between the two was poor, while radio messages were transmitted *en clair*, helping the Germans to calculate exactly how much time they had.

On 23 and 24 August, the movement began, taking all the forces facing Rennenkampf away and turning them south to confront Samsonov. The Russian 2nd Army was tired after an exhausting seven-day march, while supplies were a constant problem, particularly for the large contingent of horses. But Samsonov was also under the illusion that Rennenkampf was still marching westwards (and could thus bring to bear his forces as well) and that the Germans were in retreat back to the Vistula. Russian optimism encouraged him to push forward to try to encircle the fleeing Germans. On 24 August, his advancing army met the German 20th Corps between Orlau and Frankenau and what followed was a confused and unscripted four days of manoeuvre and counter-manoeuvre as each side tried to find a way to envelop the other. Both sides at times thought that the distant sound of battle indicated that Rennenkampf was nearing, but the effect played into German hands. Desperate to finish their envelopment rapidly, German commanders pushed on as fast as they could – in the case of François, in defiance of his orders. Samsonov, on the other hand, thought he could sense German collapse and hoped Rennenkampf would arrive to finish them off.

Both were wrong. Rennenkampf slowed to a halt, rested and turned north towards the fortified region around Königsberg, leaving Samsonov to battle on his own. His corps became separated from each other and easy prey for German flanking attacks, but the key was the drive into the two wings of the Russian 2nd Army. Both collapsed and the Russians found themselves encircled. On 28 August, Samsonov knew that he faced a catastrophic defeat. He and his staff retreated to the forest where, like thousands of Russian soldiers, they blundered about in the darkness not knowing where they were. Finally Samsonov slipped away and shot himself rather than face disgrace. His body was found by the Germans two days later. By this time, only 2,000 Russians had escaped in a confused final struggle in which neither side was certain of what had happened. Some 92,000 prisoners and 400 guns were captured and an estimated 50,000 Russians killed.

The battle was going to be called the Battle of Frögenau, after a nearby settlement. Hoffmann suggested instead taking the name of the village of Tannenberg, once the site of a famous battle between Slavs and Teutonic Knights in 1410 that had halted Prussian advance, a defeat that had now been avenged by modern Germany. Hindenburg became the greatest hero of the war, his gnarled, military portrait displayed everywhere. Victory had not been assured at Tannenberg, but the arrival of Hindenburg and Ludendorff proved just enough to turn the tide. The slender margin of success showed, as so often in battle, that improvisation at the last moment can turn imminent disaster into unexpected triumph.

94. THE FIRST BATTLE OF THE MARNE

5–12 September 1914

The First Battle of the Marne became immortalized by the story of the plucky Parisian taxi drivers who ferried half the French 7th Division out of the capital to fight the advancing Germans and at the last moment turned the tide of the battle. The story has become greater in the telling, though it is not untrue. If the strange cavalcade of taxis did not quite amount to the cavalry arriving in the nick of time, the men had to be moved somehow. The 7th Division was one part of the offensive by the French 6th Army against the encroaching German forces, an attack that distorted the German front line and opened the way for the hasty German retreat back across the River Marne. The taxi drivers did their bit to ensure that Paris did not fall to the oncoming enemy.

The crisis in early September 1914 had been looming since early August, when the bulk of the German army took the offensive through Belgium and further to the south through Luxembourg in order to carry out a version of the famous 'Schlieffen Plan', originally drawn up a decade before by the then German chief-of-staff, General Alfred von Schlieffen. The plan was to wheel through Belgium and northern France, encircle Paris and the left wing of the French defences, and then attack the remaining French armies from the rear. It was a gran-diose operation and it depended on speed and co-ordination before the French, supported in 1914 by a small British Expeditionary Force (BEF), could rally. An annihilating victory would then open the way to a similar destruction of the Russian forces in the east.

A modified version of the plan, directed by General Helmuth von Moltke (the Younger), came close to success. The French, Belgian and British forces in the north were driven back in a month of frantic and draining campaigns. By early September they had not yet broken but the soldiers were demoralized by weeks of retreats and some of the highest losses recorded throughout the four-year war. By early September, there were further signs of panic. The French government left Paris for Bordeaux on 3 September, and the roads nearing the capital were clogged with refugees streaming away from the conflict. The German advance was nevertheless achieved at great cost. High losses, the difficulty of supply over long distances and sheer exhaustion after a month of battling movement all took a toll. The French commander-in-chief, General Joseph Joffre, recognized that opportu-nities still existed. He shifted the focus of the French army away from Alsace-Lorraine, where the French 1st and 2nd Armies were trying to hold back a sustained German offensive, in order to meet the German sweeping manoeuvre towards Paris with a reformed and strengthened front. This was difficult to do with a rail system already under heavy strain, but by early September a new French 9th Army under General Ferdinand Foch and a 6th Army under General Michel-Joseph Manoury were forming against the onrush of General Alexander von Kluck's German 1st Army and the 2nd Army under General Karl von Bülow.

The critical point came by 3 September. The German armies decided to move south rather than encircle Paris from the west, which was beyond their capabilities. As they did so, von Kluck's forces ran ahead of von Bülow's, creating a growing gap between them and exposing Kluck's right flank. This news was understood by the commander of Paris, General Joseph Galliéni, who pestered Joffre for permission to use his garrison and the 6th Army to assault the German flank. It was at this point that the 600 famous taxis were ordered to drive out to Nanteuil-le-Haudoin with their military fares. They moved five infantry battalions, a total of around 4,000 men, along the 50 kilometres (30 miles) to the front line. The advance from Paris worked. The German 1st Army flank was fully exposed and von Kluck was forced to turn and defend himself. In doing so, a large gap opened between the two German armies and the French 5th Army and the BEF (which needed all Joffre's imploring to move again) poured into the gap, exposing von Kluck to attacks from the rear and von Bülow to an equally damaging flank attack. To make matters worse, von Moltke had now lost effective contact with his front commanders and did not know what decisions they had taken.

The answer was clear: the German army had tried to do something too large and operationally sophisticated for the tired forces at its disposal. Moltke sent a liaison officer, Lieutenant Colonel Richard Hentsch, from his headquarters in Luxembourg to find out what was happening. When he arrived on 8 September, Hentsch could see at once that the German plan was close to collapse. Despite von Kluck's assertion that the British and French he had fought were not up to scratch, it was evident that without a withdrawal, the German 1st and 2nd Armies risked being cut off and destroyed. Hentsch ordered both commanders to pull back behind the River Marne to rest and regroup. With reluctance they complied and within weeks the long, trench-covered Western Front solidified along the line where the Germans stopped their retreat. The French and British success was not decisive, since the war dragged on for four more years, but it ended the prospect of Germany defeating the Allies quickly and opened the way for the bloody war of attrition that followed.

The taxi drivers were rewarded for their pains. They had been allowed to keep their meters running throughout the two-day operation to move the troops and were paid on their return by the garage clerks, an average of 27 per cent of what was actually on the clock. The taxi drivers were even mentioned in dispatches for their 'keenness and devotion to duty'. Moltke, on the other hand, was close to a nervous breakdown and was replaced by General Erich von Falkenhayn on 14 September. Some thirty-three German commanders were sacked, but for the Allies General Galliéni and his taxis became the unlikely heroes of the hour.

95. DEFENCE OF TSARITSYN
22 September – 25 October 1918

The battle that took place to defend the town of Tsaritsyn on the River Volga in the autumn of 1918 against anti-Bolshevik forces was foster parent, in a number of ways, to the great battle of Stalingrad, fought twenty-four years later. During the key stages of the battle, the special plenipotentiary of Lenin's new Bolshevik government was a young Georgian revolutionary, Joseph Stalin. He gave the impression, both then and later, that it was only thanks to his courage, ruthlessness and energy that the enemy had been driven back. A number of myths began to emerge once the threat was over, one of which was the success of Dmitrii Zhloba's 'Steel Division', summoned by Stalin at the last moment from the Caucasus to save the embattled revolutionaries. Victory in the nick of time, Soviet propaganda later proclaimed, was thanks to the military genius of Stalin. Tsaritsyn was renamed Stalingrad in 1925 in memory of Stalin's heroic defence of the town. Stalin seems to have believed the myths himself. During the first years of the Soviet–German war in 1941–42, the long legacy of Tsaritsyn was enough to persuade the dictator that he could once again save the day.

The defence of Tsaritsyn was not, of course, all myth, even if Stalin's role in it was used in the 1930s to puff up his reputation once he had become dictator. The Bolshevik revolution of October 1917 provoked an almost immediate counter-revolution. By the spring of 1918, the new regime was being assailed from all sides by 'White' armies made up of a wide range of enemies, including the southern Cossacks commanded by Lieutenant General Pyotr Krasnov, the Ataman of the Don Cossack Host. Krasnov was armed by the Germans, who in 1918, following the Treaty of Brest-Litovsk made with Lenin's government in March, occupied the Ukraine. Krasnov built up an army of 40,000, supported by artillery and machine guns, and began to drive the infant Red Army units across the Don Steppe towards the Volga, just as Hitler's armies were to do a generation later. In July, Krasnov launched his first attempt to seize Tsaritsyn and the surrounding area and cut off the food artery to the Bolshevik north.

It was Krasnov's threat to Tsaritsyn that prompted Lenin to send Stalin south to make sure that the town did not fall and that the critical grain supplies from the Caucasus, on which the Red Army and the cities depended, could be maintained. On 22 July, a Military Council was established composed of Stalin, a young Bolshevik commander named Kliment Voroshilov and the local communist organizer, S. K. Minin. Stalin set about reorganizing the local military effort, but he distrusted the former Tsarist officers appointed by the head of the Red Army, Leon Trotsky. Stalin acted with complete ruthlessness, ordering the execution of men he regarded as incompetent or politically unreliable. He reported back to Moscow: 'I chase and swear at everyone who asks for it... You can rest assured that I will not spare anyone.' The first Cossack assault was turned back in August. Red Army military forces were reorganized as the Southern Front under overall command of the former Tsarist general, Pavel Sytin, who had to put up with Stalin's interference in everything he did. The town and the food supply were still not safe, however. In September 1918, Krasnov reorganized his Cossack Host into two armies: one of 20,000 men and 47 guns; a second with 25,000 men, 93 guns and 6 armoured trains. Behind them stood a reserve army of new recruits, composed of another 20,000.

It was this battle in late September 1918 that gave rise to the myth of Stalin as the military hero who saved the revolution – he 'took the reins of leadership into his own firm hands', wrote Voroshilov in *Pravda* a decade later. The 10th Army defending the town was not outnumbered, since there were about 40,000 men, 152 guns and 13 armoured trains in support, but the Cossacks were savage and experienced fighters. There was fierce fighting in the suburbs of the town while in the first week of October, Cossack forces reached the Volga south of the town and crossed to the far side of the river, behind the Soviet front. As the White soldiers pressed towards the city, Zhloba's 'Steel Division' of 15,000 men, disobeying military orders, answered Stalin's summons and marched 800 kilometres (500 miles) in sixteen days, falling on the rear of the Cossack army on the seventeenth day and saving Tsaritsyn from capture. By 25 October, with help from other revolutionary armies, the Cossacks were driven back across the River Don, just as the Soviet counter-offensive in the rear of the German 6th Army later on saved Stalingrad.

It is difficult to separate myth and reality in the differing accounts of the battle. By the time Voroshilov, now commissar for the army and navy and Stalin's close ally, wrote his eulogy to the dictator in 1929, few people would have dared to contradict him. Tsaritsyn became known as the 'Red Verdun' because it suited Bolshevik propaganda to have an apparently hard-won and symbolic victory. The evidence surrounding the arrival of the 'Steel Division', in the nick of time thanks to Stalin, is unreliable. Moreover, Trotsky's irritation at Stalin's interference with military orders led to his removal back to Moscow on 19 October, and in November Voroshilov was relieved of command. Later, in 1919, Tsaritsyn was captured by the Whites without serious threat to the survival of the revolution elsewhere. As with many battles, the story of the defence of Tsaritsyn in 1918 was used to serve political purposes quite independent of the battle itself. Stalin, Voroshilov and other men who had fought with them rose to political power and high command; Stalin never forgave Trotsky's characterization of Bolshevik front-line representatives as 'Party ignoramuses' and drove him from Russia a decade after Tsaritsyn. The irony is that Stalingrad was saved from German capture in 1942 only because Stalin at last recognized the considerable limits to his military genius and let the professional soldiers take the lead, once again in the nick of time.

96. SINK THE BISMARCK
23–27 May 1941

There were very few naval battles in the European theatre of the Second World War. The German navy proved too small and the Italian navy too unprepared for naval war. The Royal Navy was over-whelmingly more powerful than the navies of the European Axis states. Yet, remarkably, the small German force did pose a challenge. Alongside aircraft and submarines, the German navy had a number of major vessels designed as merchant raiders. Their task was to support the blockade of Britain by sinking poorly armed and poorly protected merchant convoys in the Atlantic Ocean. The most famous of them was the German battleship *Bismarck*.

Launched in Hamburg in February 1939, *Bismarck* was the pride of the new German fleet. In spring 1941, the naval commander-in-chief, Grand Admiral Erich Raeder, planned to send his small high-seas squadron out into the Atlantic to contribute to the air and sea blockade that was threatening to undermine Britain's war effort. It was a gamble. *Bismarck* was to have been accompanied by the new battleship *Tirpitz*, but it was still undergoing trials; the large battle cruisers *Gneisenau* and *Scharnhorst* were undergoing repair. In the end, *Bismarck* sailed for the ocean on 18 May 1941, accompanied only by the heavy cruiser *Prinz Eugen*. The commander of the force, Vice Admiral Günther Lütjens, was dubious about the possibility of success – and was no enthusiast for Hiter – but he understood the penalty for protesting.

Lütjens was right to be cautious. His departure had been revealed to the Royal Navy by Ultra decrypts and by agents in Norway and Sweden. A reconnaissance Spitfire soon spotted the battleship off the Norwegian coast at Bergen. A British heavy cruiser, HMS *Norfolk*, finally made radar contact on 23 May in the Denmark Strait between Iceland and Greenland. The British ship shadowed *Bismarck* until heavier Royal Navy vessels arrived the following day. The new battleship *Prince of Wales* and the battle cruiser *Hood*, commanded by Vice Admiral Lancelot Holland, prepared to engage. It was, on paper, an even contest, but *Bismarck*'s gunners were well trained. Soon after firing began at 6 a.m., an accurate shell detonated the ammunition store on *Hood*. The ship blew up at once and within three minutes had sunk, taking down all but three of the 1,418 men on board. *Prince of Wales* was damaged too, but Lütjens refused to pursue it since his orders were to avoid engagement with major enemy vessels. *Bismarck* had also sustained some damage: the forward radar was knocked out and the fuel tanks damaged. Forced to sail at 20 knots, the battleship made for port at Saint-Nazaire on the French west coast to undertake essential repairs.

Smaller British vessels tried to shadow *Bismarck* but contact was lost after the German ship took evasive action. It now seemed very likely that *Bismarck* would escape. Within hours there would be long-distance German air cover from France and the support of

German destroyers. Then, against the advice of his staff, Lütjens inexplicably sent a half-hour radio message to shore. This was long enough for the British to intercept the transmission and to fix the ship's new position, but the British battleship *King George V* miscalculated the route and lost contact. By chance a Catalina flying boat of RAF Coastal Command found *Bismarck* on the evening of 26 May, steaming off the Irish coast and within striking distance of safety in France. The only prospect left for stopping *Bismarck*'s escape was a lucky air strike. It happened that the Royal Navy aircraft carrier *Ark Royal* had made its way north from the Mediterranean on hearing of the German threat. The carrier was close enough to be able to send its Fairey Swordfish bi-planes, armed with Britain's only effective aerial torpedo. The aircraft looked old-fashioned by the standards of recent air combat, but it could operate well enough where there was no air opposition. One of the aircraft found and attacked the German battleship at 9 p.m., shortly before dusk. The *Bismarck*'s rudder and steering mechanism were damaged and the battleship shuddered to a crawl.

The hit was made in the nick of time, but it was enough. The following morning *King George V* and the battleship *Rodney* moved in for the kill. This time the battle was anything but even. Hit after hit rocked the German ship, then at 9 a.m. the bridge was hit and the command wiped out. At approximately 10.30 a.m. the destroyer HMS *Dorsetshire* sent three torpedoes towards the stricken vessel. At 10.39 the *Bismarck* sank, with 1,900 out of its 2,000 crew drowned. Recent exploration of the wreck, taken with testimony of the survivors, has raised the possibility that the ship was scuttled at the last moment, rather than despatched by Royal Navy torpedoes. The exact truth of those last few moments may never be known with certainty.

The *Bismarck* might well have survived to fight another day, though even after repairs, the risk of trying to penetrate into the Atlantic was considerable. In the end, everything was owed to the luck of one Fleet Air Arm aircraft finding the ship at the last moment and, in fading light, inflicting sufficient damage to prevent its escape. The destruction of the *Bismarck* also highlighted an important truth about naval warfare. After thousands of years, the ship's dominant position in battle was effectively ended by the advent of air power. Without effective air protection, naval vessels became sitting ducks. *Prince of Wales* escaped because the Germans had no aircraft carriers, but six months later it was sunk in a matter of minutes by Japanese naval bombers in the South China Sea. Air power did not have it all its own way – the carrier *Ark Royal* was crippled by a submarine a few months later and sank on its way to Gibraltar – but the tide had turned. *Bismarck* may have been stopped in the nick of time, but time was running out for old-fashioned battleships.

97. BATTLE OF MIDWAY
4 June 1942

It is difficult to think of any battle in the Pacific war, or indeed the whole of the Second World War, quite as decisive and significant as the Battle of Midway. And yet it was a naval battle fought without a gun being fired. It was decided by just ten bombs, a ratio of effort to outcome only exceeded by the two nuclear bombs three years later. Those ten bombs could so easily have gone astray. If Midway was against the odds in the conventional sense of an imbalance of forces, it was also against any reasonable bet that enough American aircraft would get through the wall of Japanese fighters to inflict terminal damage on all the enemy's aircraft carriers.

The background to the battle lay in the decision by the Japanese naval high command to exploit the stunning attack at Pearl Harbor on 7 December 1941 by threatening Midway Island, which was within striking distance of Hawaii, and luring what was left of the US Pacific Fleet to a decisive engagement. Once defeated, the Japanese assumed that the United States would accept a stalemate in the Pacific and allow the Japanese to build their new Asia-Pacific empire. Japanese naval planners began preparation in May 1942, under the codename 'MI'. The navy brought together an imposing force organized in five attack groups: a carrier force of four fleet carriers commanded by Vice Admiral Nagumo, which was at the heart of the Japanese plan; a large battleship fleet, including the flagship *Yamato* commanded by the naval commander-in-chief, Admiral Isoroku Yamamoto; a smaller force to seize and occupy Midway Island; a further diversionary force to capture some of the Aleutian Islands, off Alaska; and finally a screen of submarines to provide intelligence and to intercept American vessels.

The Japanese could not be confident that the US Pacific Fleet would accept battle, but they assumed that the loss of Midway would be too great a threat for the Americans to ignore. Japanese intelligence discounted the two American aircraft carriers it knew about because those were assumed to be somewhere in the southwest Pacific, guarding Australia. What they did not know was that US Naval Intelligence on Hawaii had broken enough of the Japanese naval code, JN-25, to be able to work out Japanese intentions. American uncertainty about the destination of the Japanese fleet was overcome by a clever ruse. A message was sent to Midway by regular radio traffic, which it was known the Japanese would intercept. When the message was relayed back to the Japanese naval command in code, it betrayed the codeword for Midway, confirming the island as the fleet's destination. The American commander, Admiral Frank Fletcher, decided to position the American fleet northwest of Midway, out of range of Japanese aircraft and submarines, to ambush the Japanese when they advanced on the island. The whole strategy rested on the presence of not two, but three American aircraft carriers, commanded by Rear Admiral Raymond 'Electric Brain' Spruance, nicknamed after his capacity for cool and rapid thinking under pressure. *Hornet* and *Enterprise* sailed north from the southwest Pacific, and were joined by *Yorktown*, quickly repaired at Pearl Harbor in time to join the battle.

As the Japanese fleet steamed towards Midway and the Aleutians, it was assumed that the American navy had no knowledge of the plan. On 3 June, an American Catalina flying boat spotted the Midway task force and reported back. The Japanese carrier task force was known to be further to the north, so Fletcher moved his force to be on the northern flank of Nagumo's ships as they moved towards Midway. On the morning of 4 June, a Japanese reconnaissance plane flew over the American fleet but failed to see it; other reconnaissance aircraft failed to take off, but Nagumo was quite confident that no American strike force was within reach. He ordered waves of carrier aircraft to pound the small American base on Midway Island. An American aircraft spotted the carriers, and bombers from Midway air base flew out to attack Nagumo's force. Most were shot down by the screen of waiting Mitsubishi Zero fighters. Then at 7.30 a.m. news finally came from a Japanese aircraft that there were American ships to the north, but no carriers. Nagumo hesitated. He had aircraft converting from torpedoes to bombs, and aircraft about to return from the Midway raids to rearm. At 8.20 a.m. he was warned that there might after all be one American carrier. He decided this was not a great threat and allowed his aircraft to land for rearming and refuelling. His carriers were now exceptionally vulnerable; all over the decks and below decks were aircraft with fuel lines, stacks of bombs and torpedoes and gun ammunition.

Fletcher and Spruance enjoyed remarkable good fortune. Nagumo's decision meant that most Japanese aircraft were dangerously immobile at just the point when the American carrier aircraft prepared to make their strike. The attack was nevertheless not easy, over open ocean with a small target to locate. Aircraft from *Hornet* took off on a no-torious 'flight to nowhere', with some having to ditch into the ocean after failing to find the enemy and running out of fuel. Torpedo bombers from the other two carriers struck Nagumo's fleet at around 9.30 a.m. They were shot to pieces by the circling Zeros – only six out of forty-one returned, and not a single torpedo hit. Everything rested on a group of fifty-four Dauntless dive-bombers circling high above, undetected by Japanese fighters. They dived out of the sun 'like a beautiful silver waterfall', as one survivor recalled. Their bombs were the margin between victory and defeat. Most failed to hit the target, but Nagumo's flagship *Akagi* was hit by three bombs and turned into a floating torch; *Kaga* was hit by four bombs and *Soryu* by three, both blazing out of control. Aircraft from the remaining Japanese carrier, *Hiryu*, managed to damage *Yorktown* (which was sunk by submarine three days later) but at 5 p.m. it, too, was struck by four bombs dropped by dive-bombers from *Enterprise*, and sank the following morning, with its commander, Admiral Yamaguchi, standing on deck, sword drawn, as it slipped beneath the waves.

The Battle of Midway had been decided by just ten bombs. Of course the outcome relied on sound intelligence, Nagumo's failure to take the American threat seriously, and the solid training of America's professional naval aviators, but the margin was slim indeed. Most bombs fell harmlessly into the sea. For Yamamoto, the outcome was disastrous, different in every respect from what had been expected. The Japanese navy never recovered. Japan built a further seven carriers, the United States a further twenty-three. Almost three-quarters of Japan's elite naval airmen were casualties. For the American Pacific Fleet, and for the American people, the improbable victory against an overwhelmingly larger force, thanks to just a handful of bombs, finally confirmed that old-fashioned big fleet engagement, battleship to battleship, was history. Midway was won entirely by aircraft.

98. BATTLE OF KURSK
5–13 July 1943

The battle for a large Soviet-held salient around the Russian city of Kursk in the long German–Soviet line in July 1943 is remembered chiefly for being the biggest tank battle in history. The decisive intervention of General Pavel Rotmistrov's 5th Guards Tank Army in the famous Battle of Prokhorovka on 12 July, it was claimed, saved the Red Army from imminent disaster at the end of a week of gruelling combat. Western historians' scepticism about this account has promoted a rival version of events. Hitler's decision to cancel the German offensive, they have argued, should instead be attributed to the timely invasion of southern Sicily by British and American forces, which began on 9 July at the height of the Battle of Kursk. Neither of these explanations withstands close examination. This was a nick of time that never was. Soviet victory came from careful planning, a sound defensive field and the massing of a surprising quantity of key reserves.

The battle was the result of a German attempt to stabilize the long front line after the disastrous retreat from Stalingrad, perhaps even to create the conditions, in summer campaigning weather, which the Germans preferred, for a more adventurous set of operations. The key was thought to be the Kursk salient that jutted out for 100 kilometres (60 miles) into the German line. Field Marshal Erich von Manstein drew up a plan codenamed 'Citadel', the purpose of which was to attack the neck of the salient from south and north with heavy armour and air forces in order to cut off the large Soviet forces bottled up in the bulge. He wanted to attack in April or May before the Red Army had time to dig in, but Hitler was more cautious, keen to await new tank supplies and to avoid any risk of a further disaster. In the end the delays postponed the opening of 'Citadel' until 5 July when over 750,000 soldiers, 2,450 tanks, 1,830 aircraft and 7,420 heavy artillery pieces were positioned north and south of the Kursk bulge.

The Soviet leadership had suffered from two years of wrong guesses about German intentions, from the invasion in June 1941 to the southern offensive towards Stalingrad in 1942. This time, thanks to better intelligence, much of it supplied from British Ultra intercepts of German messages, they guessed correctly. Stalin's deputy supreme commander, General Georgy Zhukov, organized a complex defensive field around the perimeter of the Kursk salient. There were six layers of defence, each one bristling with tank traps, artillery, batteries and machine-gun nests; 5,000 kilometres (3,000 miles) of trenches were dug in a criss-cross pattern, allowing the defenders to move easily from one firing position to another. Over 400,000 mines were laid, and streams were dammed so that water could be released around oncoming tanks. Fifty dummy airfields were built to attract enemy planes. Into this obstacle course Zhukov placed seven armies, a total of 1,336,000 men (and some women), 3,440 tanks and self-propelled guns, 19,100 artillery pieces and 2,170 aircraft. About 250 kilometres (150 miles) further back was the reserve Steppe Front commanded by General Ivan Konev with another 500,000 men and 1,400 tanks, ready to strike at the right moment. The battle for the Kursk salient was the largest set-piece battle of the Second World War. If Manstein had succeeded in cutting the salient, 40 per cent of Red Army manpower and 75 per cent of Soviet armour would have been trapped.

There followed weeks of waiting for the Germans to come. Hitler hesitated until he was confident that the armies had what they needed, including a small number of the new heavy Panther and Tiger tanks. For Soviet soldiers, the suspense was enervating. Finally a captured German soldier confessed that the morning of 5 July was the start date. The Red Army fired off a spoiling bombardment in the middle of the night, alarming German commanders, who briefly thought they were the victims of an unanticipated Soviet offensive. Things were again quiet until, at 4.30 a.m., Field Marshal Walter Model's 9th Panzer Army in the north and General Hermann Hoth's 4th Panzer Army in the south, supported by three armoured divisions of Army Detachment Kempf, plunged into the lines of fixed defences.

The battle was on an extraordinary scale, with thousands of guns, aircraft and tanks pulverizing the ground, tearing apart the woods and villages in their path. A pall of acrid smoke obscured much of the battlefield. Model's armoured divisions made very slow progress against determined opposition, facing the worst field of fire they had yet experienced. They moved 6 kilometres (4 miles) on the first day and a further 11 kilometres (7 miles) by 7 July, subjected to continuous attacks. The limit of the advance was reached two days later. In the south, Hoth had greater success because the defensive forces were weaker than further north. Spearheaded by the three notorious SS panzer divisions – *Totenkopf*, *Das Reich* and *Leibstandarte SS Adolf Hitler* – the southern assault penetrated 32 kilometres (20 miles) by 7 July with the aim of cutting the main road to Kursk. It was halted by a strong counter-attack. On 9 July, the tank divisions grouped for one more thrust but were held as they were in the north. Hoth ordered the tanks to move northeast, towards a small rail junction at Prokhorovka.

The Soviet account of Kursk needed a hero suitable for the regular propaganda that exalted the bravery of Soviet men and women in the face of fascist aggression. The hero of this battle was General Pavel Rotmistrov, commander of the 5th Guards Tank Army, held back with Konev's reserves. On 9 July, he was ordered to move forward to join the main battle and on 12 July, his tanks clashed with the approaching German panzer divisions in what was hailed as the greatest tank battle of the war. At the end of the day the German assault was blunted and, so it was claimed, over 700 tanks littered the battlefield, their burning hulks a testament to the bitterness of the conflict and the triumph of Rotmistrov's men. The legend, however, has been over-turned by modern research. There was only one German panzer division at Prokhorovka, the *Leibstandarte SS Adolf Hitler*, with around 100 tanks, faced by two Soviet Tank Corps with 421 tanks and self-propelled guns. Charging forward, the Soviet tanks fell into one of the tank traps built by their own side, where many were damaged or destroyed. At the end of the day, the German force had lost only 32 tanks, the Soviet side 259.

Nevertheless, the overturning of the myth of Prokhorovka has done little to undermine the broader story of Soviet success in blunting the power of the fifteen panzer divisions hurled at the Kursk lines. If the great tank battle is an invention, the defence held firm and inflicted heavy losses on the attacker. What did happen on 12 July was a massive counter-offensive codenamed Operation Kutuzov mounted against the northern wing of the German attack. Not suspecting that there were reserves available, the counter-attack stunned the German command. The following day, Hitler, already anxious about the invasion of Sicily, for which forces would have to be moved from the Eastern Front, cancelled Citadel and ordered Hoth back to the German starting lines. On 3 August, a second Soviet offensive using the reserve armies, Operation Rumyantsev, smashed into the southern German line. The unleashing of the reserves after a week of battle stopped the last German offensive in its tracks. No legend of last-minute reinforcement was needed to embellish a comprehensive victory. The gleeful debunking of the Prokhorovka story cannot conceal the reality of Soviet success.

99. BATTLE OF DIEN BIEN PHU
13 March – 7 May 1954

The first Vietnam War, between the communist Viet Minh and French colonial forces, was waged for almost ten years following Japanese defeat in 1945, and has been overshadowed by the subsequent conflict with the American-sponsored south. Yet it was a long and savage war that ended in a catastrophic defeat for the French in the valley of Dien Bien Phu in the far north of Vietnam. For the communist Viet Minh timing was everything. As the battle raged, so the major powers were trying to broker a peace conference. Victory for the Viet Minh would make independence difficult to deny. The French at Dien Bien Phu surrendered on 7 May, the day before the French foreign minister, Georges Bidault, stood up at Geneva to begin discussions about the future of Vietnam. The timing was not accidental. The Viet Minh knew that they had to end the battle in time if their victory was to weigh anything in the scales of the negotiations. Military success and political hopes rose or fell together.

The communist insurgency led by Ho Chi Minh dominated much of northern Vietnam by 1953, confining the French colonial forces to the defence of the Red River delta around Hanoi. In the summer of that year a new French commander, General Henri Navarre, took control of operations. Navarre was determined to hold the line in Vietnam and, if possible, impose a crushing defeat on Ho's growing army, which was being reinforced with Chinese advisers and equipment. The Navarre Plan (Operation Castor) was to establish a heavily defended encampment in the valley of Dien Bien Phu in northern Tonkin that would cut off Viet Minh infiltration into Laos and inflict heavy punishment on an enemy force thought to be only 10–15,000 strong. The base was set up from late November 1953 under command of Colonel Christian de la Croix de Castries and was manned by 10,800 French and colonial troops, including newly trained Vietnamese, and supported by a corps of non-combatant workers. The main defensive zone was established around the airstrip, with smaller redoubts a mile or so away. Each was given a female name: 'Isabelle', 'Ann Marie', 'Gabrielle' and 'Beatrice'; the main camp had five more, named, it was rumoured, after de Castries' mistresses.

The Viet Minh observed the French move and were determined to respond. The overall commander, General Vo Nguyen Giap, gathered four divisions of more than 50,000 soldiers and extensive supplies. By the time the French camp was besieged he had 100 artillery pieces, including 75-millimetre and 105-millimetre howitzers. The plan, encouraged by Chinese advisers, was to attack in a fierce wave assault on 25 January 1954, but Giap hesitated until all the preparations were complete. The valley was barren and the Viet Minh needed proper trenches and dugouts, while the artillery needed to be dug into the stony ground and protected from attack. Giap preferred the strategy of 'steady attack, steady advance' to the Chinese preference for an overwhelming storming operation. Just before the final offensive, commando groups of Viet Minh destroyed French aircraft at their bases in the delta, slowing down the airborne supply programme. By 13 March, Giap was ready and an artillery barrage began that wrecked the airstrip and churned up the French trenches and bunkers, smoth-ering soldiers under earth and rubble. 'Beatrice' was overrun on the first day, 'Ann Marie' and 'Gabrielle' two days later. French artillery could do so little that the artillery commander, Colonel Charles Piroth, committed suicide using a grenade clutched to his chest.

Conditions for both sides were appalling. The Viet Minh took high casualties, losing 4,000 dead by early April, while suffering from chronic shortages of food and ammunition. For the French and colonial defenders, conditions were even worse. Trenches filled with up to a metre of water and food rations had to be halved. For alcohol they relied on vinogel, a jelly-like wine concentrate to which water – a rapidly shrinking resource – had to be added. Hospital conditions were primitive and the number of wounded very high under the constant bombardment and sniper fire. By mid-April, there were only 2,400 fit combat troops left, although 4,300 had been parachuted in during the siege. Some soldiers and workers hid early in the battle in abandoned trenches, living off supply drops that fell outside the em-battled centre. In the end, the Rats of Nam Youm, as they were called, numbered 4,000.

Bit by bit, the garrison was worn down and metre by metre the Viet Minh tunnels and trenches drew closer. Giap called for a strategy of 'nibbling away' at the enemy instead of any further frontal assaults, but the onset of talks in Geneva in late April made a more concerted drive necessary. De Castries sent out urgent messages to the headquar-ters in Hanoi for reinforcement or American aircraft, but there was little to be done for such a remote area. The US government of Dwight D. Eisenhower considered the possibility of direct military help but did nothing before the end, which came in a sudden, fierce final battle launched on 1 May. One after another the defensive zones fell. De Castries toyed with the idea of breaking out – an operation unfortunately codenamed 'Albatross' – but in the end decided to stay with his men and fight to a standstill. On 7 May, his command bunker was captured and he was taken prisoner together with a further 10,000 French, Vietnamese and colonial personnel, most of them non-combatants or those who had opted not to fight. Some 3,500 French and colonial soldiers died in the siege; thousands more were wounded and died on the forced march to Viet Minh holding camps.

The defence of Dien Bien Phu was a gamble, whose odds were not understood by the French. The Viet Minh were not old-style anti-colonial rebels, but a nationalist army equipped with modern weaponry. This was the first time that an Asian force had defeated a European force in pitched battle. After the Geneva talks, a northern Democratic Republic of Vietnam was set up under Ho Chi Minh and a southern Vietnam under Ngo Dinh Diem. Giap's last offensive against the remnants of De Castries' garrison tipped the balance at Geneva against any solution short of partition and French withdrawal. The Second Vietnam War was still in the future.

100. BATTLE FOR THE FALKLANDS
21 May – 14 June 1982

Time mattered a great deal in the British operation to recapture the Falkland Islands (the Islas Malvinas in Spanish), the South Atlantic colony occupied by Argentine forces on 2 April 1982. The campaign had to be conducted quickly before international pressure for a diplomatic solution became decisive; it had to be carried out before the harsh winter weather made operations impossible; it had to be a swift campaign because men and equipment could not easily be replenished thousands of miles from the homeland. In the end, an operation could only be launched with any chance of success in a ten-day period at the end of May. Any longer delay and the men would have to return to land. Timing proved to be everything in the eventual British victory.

The Argentine invasion, codenamed Operation Rosario, was part of a long-running dispute between the two countries over sovereignty of the Falklands, South Georgia and the South Sandwich Islands. The issue was revived late in 1981 by the military government of Argentina led by General Leopoldo Galtieri. The object was to apply diplomatic pressure to compel Britain to abandon the territories and to prepare for a military showdown if negotiations stalled. In Buenos Aires, it was not clear how determined Britain might be to hold on to the Falklands and growing frustration with the onset of talks finally prompted the military junta on 26 March 1982 to order an invasion. The islands had a small Royal Marine force, but resistance was pointless as almost 3,000 Argentine troops disembarked at the capital, Port Stanley. That same evening the British cabinet decided to send a naval task force, complete with aircraft carriers and a body of troops, to the South Atlantic. Britain had not yet ruled out a diplomatic solution and many overseas observers assumed that the task force was no more than a show of strength. To invade distant islands in an inhospitable climate was, a United States navy spokesman claimed, 'a military impossibility'.

There followed weeks of shuttle diplomacy as the United Nations Secretary-General and the United States State Department tried to broker a deal between the two parties. Naval and air conflict had already begun, including the sinking of the Argentine troopship *General Belgrano* on 2 May. The critical issue for Britain was the withdrawal of the Argentine garrison on the Falklands, and by mid-May it was evident that the Argentine regime would not accept the condition. On 19 May, the cabinet of Margaret Thatcher, the British prime minister, agreed to the launch of Operation Sutton, the reconquest of the islands. Feints and false intelligence were used to persuade the Argentinian commander on the islands, Brigadier General Mario Menendez, that the British would try to land close to Port Stanley, which is where the bulk of the 10,000-strong Argentine army was dug in, facing south and east. Instead the British Task Force delivered the 3,000 men of 3 Commando Brigade, commanded by Brigadier Julian Thompson, together with thousands of tons of stores and equipment, to the western shore of East Falkland at San Carlos, 80 kilometres (50 miles) to the west of Port Stanley. The bridgehead was rapidly consolidated, helped by uncertainty among the Argentine high command about whether the San Carlos landing was only a diversion. Despite repeated attacks by the Argentine air force flying from the mainland, in one of which the storeship *Atlantic Conveyor* was hit and burnt out, the small contingent of 42 Harrier fighters inflicted substantial losses on enemy aircraft, most of which were kept back from the conflict in case of an air assault on Argentina itself.

Speed was essential for Operation Sutton because resupply was difficult and there was constant diplomatic activity to try to prevent further escalation. After a week ashore, there was pressure from London to begin the assault on Port Stanley, but Thompson was anxious to wait for further reinforcements (the 5th Infantry Brigade of 5,000 men was on its way) and was aware that on the British right flank there was an Argentine base at Goose Green/Darwin. On 28 May, 600 men of the 2 Battalion Parachute Regiment advanced to the base and after fierce fighting, in which their commander, Lieutenant Colonel Herbert 'H' Jones, was killed, over 900 Argentinian troops were taken prisoner. The British moved forward across the island to take Mount Kent, the highest point in the circle of mountains around the capital. The Argentine chiefs-of-staff realized that an attack was imminent but offered no immediate reinforcements to Menendez, who was becoming increasingly demoralized at the prospect of maintaining the Argentine occupation. The forces at his command were a mix of regular soldiers, commandos and conscript troops, whose capacity to withstand the harsh conditions of mud, rain and cold while facing Britain's regular soldiers was evidently limited. Instead of sending out units to delay or obstruct the British advance, he ordered his forces to high alert around the capital and waited on events.

By early June, the 5th Infantry Brigade had arrived and command of the whole of Operation Sutton was taken over by Major General Jeremy Moore of the Royal Marines. The new units were shipped to the south coast of East Falkland, where Argentine aircraft hit two vessels loaded with men, *Sir Galahad* and *Sir Tristram*, leaving fifty dead. The infantry were to march across the south of the island to attack Port Stanley from the southwest. On the night of 11 June, the 3 Commando Brigade moved forward to take the high ground around Stanley at Mount Longdon, Two Sisters and Mount Harriet. The defence was fierce, if brief. By the end, the Argentine garrison of around 5,000 fighting troops was encircled. At 4 p.m. on 13 June, in a snow storm, the British assault began. The Argentine marines dug in at Mount Tumbledown proved difficult to dislodge, but they were withdrawn by the following morning. British advance was methodical and by the morning had reached the outskirts of Port Stanley. The one remaining stronghold on Mount Sapper was about to be assaulted by 5th Brigade when a ceasefire was announced.

The options had become increasingly narrow for Menendez. Galtieri ordered him to continue to fight with everything he could, but his troops had already taken high casualties and the conscripts were now of poor fighting quality. In the afternoon of 14 June, Menendez met British officers to discuss surrender terms. After agreeing to remove the term 'unconditional surrender', the British insisted that Menendez accept their conditions. The surrender was finally signed at 9.15 p.m. Three days later Galtieri resigned as Argentina's president. Against all expectations, and in the face of almost universal pressure to accept further negotiations, the British task force had succeeded in overturning the Argentine occupation before the crisis of resupply or the weather undermined the whole operation. Timing had been critical on all fronts, military and international, and despite victory, the factors that might have turned Operation Sutton into a disaster were never far away.

The cost was high to both sides: 649 Argentine dead, 1,657 wounded; 255 British dead and 775 wounded. A total of 11,313 Argentine soldiers, airmen, sailors and support troops were taken prisoner. The Argentine air force and army lost twenty-five helicopters and seventy-four other aircraft, the British twenty-four helicopters and ten fighters. The British were compelled to keep a substantial garrison in the islands thereafter. Despite a United Nations resolution passed on 4 November 1982 calling on the two sides to resume negotiations, the Falkland Islands have remained under British sovereignty to the present day, while Argentina has never abrogated its claim for the return of the Malvinas to Argentine rule.

BIBLIOGRAPHY

The following books and articles were used to provide the quotations and data in the introduction:

Bennett, Matthew, 'The Crusaders' "Fighting March" Revisited', *War in History*, 8 (2001), pp. 1–18

Billington, James, *The Face of Russia: Anguish, Aspiration and Achievement in Russian Culture* (New York: TV Books, 1998)

Bourke, Joanna, *An Intimate History of Killing: Face-to-Face Killing in Twentieth-Century Warfare* (London: Granta Books, 1999)

Carman, John, 'Beyond the Western Way of War: Ancient Battlefields' in Carman, John, Harding, Anthony (eds), *Ancient Warfare* (Stroud: The History Press, 2009)

Crowley, Roger, *Constantinople: The Last Great Siege*, 1453 (London: Faber & Faber, 2005)

Dudziak, Mary L., *War-Time: An idea, its History, its Consequences* (New York: Oxford University Press, 2012)

Dunn, John, 'For God, Emperor and Country! The Evolution of Ethiopia's Nineteenth-Century Army', *War in History*, 1 (1994), pp. 278–99

Gillingham, John, *Richard the Lionheart* (London: Weidenfeld & Nicolson, 1978)

Goldsworthy, A. K., 'The Othismos, Myths and Heresies: The Nature of Hoplite Battle', *War in History*, 4 (1997), pp. 1–26

Haas, Jonathan, 'The Origins of War and Ethnic Violence' in Carman, John, Harding, Anthony (eds), *Ancient Warfare*, pp. 16–21

Jones, Michael, 'The Battle of Verneuil (17 August 1424): Towards a History of Courage', *War in History*, 9 (2002), pp. 375–411

Keegan, John, *The Face of Battle: A Study of Agincourt, Waterloo and the Somme*, 2nd edition, (London: Barrie & Jenkins, 1988)

Keeley, Lawrence, *War before Civilization: The Myth of the Peaceful Savage* (New York: Oxford University Press, 1996)

Kristiansen, Kristian, 'The Emergence of Warrior Aristocracies in Later European

Prehistory and their Long-term History' in Carman, Harding (eds), *Ancient Warfare*, pp. 175–88

Lorge, Peter, *The Asian Military Revolution: From Gunpowder to the Bomb* (Cambridge: Cambridge University Press, 2008)

Moore, Aaron, *Writing War: Soldiers Record the Japanese Empire* (Cambridge, MA: Harvard University Press, 2013)

Morgan, David, *The Mongols* (London: Basil Blackwell, 1986)

Ostrowski, Donald, 'Alexander Nevskii's "Battle on the Ice": The Creation of a Legend', *Russian History/Histoire Russe*, 33 (2006), pp. 289-312

Remarque, Erich Maria, *All Quiet on the Western Front* (London: Jonathan Cape, 1994)

Reynolds, David, *The Long Shadow: The Great War and the Twentieth Century* (London: Simon & Schuster, 2013)

Scarre, Christopher (ed), *Herodotus: The Histories* (London: Folio Society, 1992)

Schieder, Theodor, *Frederick the Great* (London: Longman, 2000)

Stephenson, Michael, *The Last Full Measure: How Soldiers Die in Battle* (London: Duckworth, 2013)

Wharton, William, *Shrapnel* (London: HarperCollins, 2013)

Wilson, Peter, 'German Women and War, 1500–1800', *War in History*, 3 (1996), pp. 127–60

Ziftu, Ismat, Karari: *The Sudanese Account of the Battle of Omdurman* (London: Frederick Warne, 1980)

The following books and articles were used for the Battle texts:

Allison, William T., *The Gulf War, 1990-91* (Basingstoke: Palgrave, 2012)

Ayton, Andrew, Preston, Philip, *The Battle of Crécy, 1346* (Woodbridge: Boydell Press, 2005)

Barr, Niall, *Pendulum of War: The Three Battles of Alamein* (London: Jonathan Cape, 2004)

Baur, Hans, *I Was Hitler's Pilot: The Memoirs of Hans Bauer* (Barnsley: Frontline Books, 2013)

Beeching, Jack, *The Galleys at Lepanto* (London: Hutchinson, 1982)

Bellamy, Chris, *Absolute War: Soviet Russia in the Second World War* (London: Macmillan, 2007)

Bercuson, David, Herwig, Holger, *Bismarck* (London: Hutchinson, 2002)

Bicheno, Hugh, *Crescent and Cross: The Battle of Lepanto 1571* (London: Cassell, 2003)

Black, Jeremy, *Waterloo: The Battle That Brought Down Napoleon* (London: Icon Books, 2010)

Blond, Georges, *The Marne: The Battle that Saved Paris and Changed the Course of the First World War* (London: Prion Books, 2002)

Boog, Horst et al., *Das Deutsche Reich und der Zweite Weltkrieg: Band 6: Der globale Krieg: Die Ausweitung zum Weltkrieg und der Wechsel der Initiative* (Stuttgart: Deutsche Verlags-Anstalt, 1990)

Bowlus, Charles, *The Battle of Lechfeld and its Aftermath*, August 955 (Aldershot: Ashgate, 2006)

Brooks, Richard, *Solferino: The Battle for Italy's Freedom* (Oxford: Osprey, 2009)

Caddick-Adams, Peter, *Monte Cassino: Ten Armies in Hell* (London: Preface Publishing, 2012)

Carey, Brian T., *Hannibal's Last Battle: Zama & the Fall of Carthage* (Barnsley: Pen & Sword, 2007)

Carman, J., Harding, A. (eds), *Ancient Warfare* (Stroud: History Press, 1999)

Carpenter, Stanley, *Military Leadership in the British Civil Wars 1642–1651* (London: Frank Cass, 2002)

Chandler, David, *Blenheim Preparation: The English Army on the March to the Danube* (Staplehurst, Kent: Spellmount, 2004)

Clot, André, *Suleiman the Magnificent* (London: Saqi Books, 2012)

Collier, Simon, Sater, William, *A History of Chile, 1808–1994* (Cambridge: Cambridge University Press, 1996)

Cooper, Bryan, *The Ironclads of Cambrai* (Barnsley: Pen & Sword, 2010)

Crompton, Samuel, *Tenochtitlan* (Philadelphia: Chelsea House, 2002)

Cruickshank, Charles, *Deception in World War II* (Oxford: Oxford University Press, 1981)

Dam, Raymond van, *Remembering Constantine at the Milvian Bridge* (Cambridge: Cambridge University Press, 2011)

David, Saul, *100 Days to Victory: How the Great War was Fought and Won* (London: Hodder & Stoughton, 2013)

David Saul, *Zulu: The Heroism and Tragedy of the Zulu War of 1879* (London: Penguin Viking, 2005)

Denton, Barry, *Cromwell's Soldiers: The Moulding of the New Model Army 1644–1645* (Huntingdon: Denton Dare Publishing, 2004)

Duffy, Seán, *Brian Boru and the Battle of Clontarf* (Dublin: Gill & Macmillan, 2013)

Edwardes, Michael, *The Battle of Plassey and the Conquest of Bengal* (London: Batsford, 1963)

Englund, Peter, *The Battle that Shook Europe: Poltava and the Birth of the Russian Empire* (London: I. B. Tauris, 2003)

Esdaile, Charles, *Napoleon's Wars: An International History* (London: Allen Lane, 2007)

Evans, Martin, Burton, Peter, Westaway, Michael, *Naseby: English Civil War – June 1945* (Barnsley: Leo Cooper, 2002)

Falkner, James, *Blenheim 1704: Marlborough's Greatest Victory* (Barnsley: Pen & Sword, 2004)

Fine, John V., *The Late Medieval Balkans* (Ann Arbor, MI: University of Michigan Press, 1992)

Fox, Robin L., *Alexander the Great* (London: Penguin, 2004)

France, John, *Western Warfare in the Age of the Crusades 1000–1300* (Ithaca, NY: Cornell University Press, 1999)

Freedman, Lawrence, *Strategy: A History* (Oxford: Oxford University Press, 2013)

Freedman, Lawrence, Gamba-Stonehouse, Virginia, *Signals of War: The Falklands Conflict of 1982* (London: Faber & Faber, 1990)

Freeman, Philip, *Julius Caesar* (New York: Simon & Schuster, 2008)

Friendly, Alfred, *The Dreadful Day: The Battle of Manzikert, 1071* (London: Hutchinson, 1981)

Galinsky, Karl, *Augustus* (Cambridge: CUP, 2012)

Garland, Robert, *Hannibal* (London: Bloomsbury, 2010)

Gat, Azar, *War in Human Civilization* (New York: Oxford University Press, 2006)

Gates, David, *The Napoleonic Wars, 1803–1815* (London: Arnold, 1997)

Gentles, Ian, *The New Model Army in England, Ireland and Scotland, 1645–1653* (Oxford: Blackwell, 1992)

Ginion, Eyal, 'Mobilizing the Ottoman Nation during the Balkan Wars (1912–1913)', War in History, 12 (2005), pp. 156–77

Gilliver, C. M., *The Roman Art of War* (Stroud: Tempus, 1999)

Glass, Stafford, *The Matabele War* (London: Longmans, 1968)

Grant, Michael, *Caesar* (London: Weidenfeld & Nicolson, 1974)

Grant, Michael, *Julius Caesar* (London: Weidenfeld & Nicolson, 1969)

Hall, John W., *Cambridge History of Japan. Volume 4: Early Modern Japan* (Cambridge: Cambridge University Press, 1997)

Hall, John W., Nagahara, Keiji, Yamamura, Kozo, *Japan before Tokugawa: Political Consolidation and Economic Growth 1500–1650* (Princeton, NJ: Princeton University Press, 1980)

Hellie, Richard, 'Alexander Nevskii's April 5, 1242 Battle on the Ice', *Russian History/ Histoire Russe*, 33 (2006), pp. 283–87

Herwig, Holger, *The First World War: Germany and Austria-Hungary 1914–1918* (London: Arnold, 1997)

Hill, Paul, *The Viking Wars of Alfred the Great* (Barnsley: Pen & Sword, 2008)

Hillgarth, J. N., *The Spanish Kingdoms 1250–1516* (Oxford: Oxford University Press, 1976)

Hollins, David, *Marengo 1800: Napoleon's Day of Fate* (Oxford: Osprey, 2000)

Horne, Alistair, *How Far from Austerlitz: Napoleon 1805–1815* (London: Macmillan, 1996)

Housley, Norman, *The Later Crusades 1274–1580* (Oxford: Oxford University Press, 1992)

Howard, Michael, *Strategic Deception in the Second World War* (London: Pimlico, 1992)

Hunefeldt, Christine, *A Brief History of Peru* (New York: Facts on File, 2004)

Jonas, Raymond, *The Battle of Adwa: African Victory in the Age of Empire* (Cambridge, MA: Harvard University Press, 2011)

Kelly, Christopher, *The End of Empire: Attila the Hun and the Fall of Rome* (New York: Norton, 2009)

Kitson, Frank, *Old Ironsides: The Military Biography of Oliver Cromwell* (London: Weidenfeld & Nicolson, 2004)

Krentz, Peter, *The Battle of Marathon* (New Haven: Yale University Press, 2010)

Kulikowski, Michael, *Rome's Gothic Wars from the Third Century to Alaric* (Cambridge: Cambridge University Press, 2007)

Lamb, Harold, *Suleiman the Magnificent: Sultan of the East* (London: Robert Hale, 1952)

Lawrence, Mark, Logevall, Fredrik (eds), *The First Vietnam War: Colonial Conflict and Cold War Crisis* (Cambridge, MA: Harvard UP, 2007)

Lincoln, W. Bruce, *Red Victory: A History of the Russian Civil War* (New York: Simon & Schuster, 1989)

Logevall, Fredrik, *Embers of War: The Fall of an Empire and the Making of America's Vietnam* (New York: Random House, 2012)

Lomax, Derek, *The Reconquest of Spain* (London: Longman, 1978)

Luckett, Richard, *White Generals: An Account of the White Movement in the Russian Civil War* (London: Longmans, 1971)

Lynch, John, *San Martín: Argentine Soldier, American Hero* (New Haven: Yale University Press, 2009)

Macfie, A. L., *The End of the Ottoman Empire 1908–1923* (Harlow: Longmans, 1998)

Mancaron, Charles, *Austerlitz: The Story of a Battle* (London: George Allen & Unwin, 1966)

Manstein, Erich von, *Verlorene Siege* (Bonn: Athenäum-Verlag, 1955)

Martin, Colin, Parker, Geoffrey, *The Spanish Armada* (London: Hamish Hamilton, 1988)

Martin, H. Desmond, *The Rise of Chingis Khan and his Conquest of North China* (Baltimore, MD: Johns Hopkins Press, 1950)

Mason, Philip, *The Birth of a Dilemma: The Conquest and Settlement of Rhodesia* (Oxford: Oxford University Press, 1958)

Mawdsley, Evan, *The Russian Civil War* (Edinburgh: Birlinn, 2000)

Mawdsley, Evan, *Thunder in the East: The Nazi-Soviet War 1941–1945* (London: Hodder Arnold, 2005)

McDonald, Joanna, *"We Shall Meet Again": The First Battle of Manassas* (Bull Run) (New York: Oxford University Press, 2000)

McKitterick, Rosamond, *Charlemagne: The Formation of a European Identity* (Cambridge: Cambridge University Press, 2008)

McNab, Chris, *Verdun, 1916* (Stroud: History Press, 2013)

McPherson, James, *Battle Cry of Freedom: The Civil War Era* (New York: Oxford University Press, 1988)

Megargee, Geoffrey, *Inside Hitler's High Command* (Lawrence, KA: University Press of Kansas, 2000)

Merriman, Roger B., *Suleiman the Magnificent, 1520–1566* (Cambridge, MA: Harvard University Press, 1944)

Moorehead, Caroline, *Dunant's Dream: War, Switzerland and the History of the Red Cross* (New York: Carroll & Graf, 1999)

Nicolle, David, *Crusader Warfare: Volume 1, Byzantium, Europe and the Struggle for the Holy Land 1050–1300 AD* (London: Continuum, 2007)

Nicolle, David, *Manzikert 1071: The Breaking of Byzantium* (Oxford: Osprey, 2013)

Nicolle, David, *Poitiers AD 732: Charles Martel Turns the Islamic Tide* (Oxford: Osprey, 2008)

O'Callaghan, Joseph, *The Gibraltar Crusade: Castile and the Battle for the Strait* (Philadelphia: University of Pennsylvania Press, 2011)

Oren, Michael, *Six Days of War: June 1967 and the Making of the Modern Middle East* (London: Allen Lane, 2002)

Osgood, Josiah, *Caesar's Legacy: Civil War and the Emergence of the Roman Empire* (Cambridge: CUP, 2006)

Overy, Richard, *The Battle of Britain*, 2nd ed (London: Penguin, 2010)

Overy, Richard, *Russia's War* (London: Penguin, 1997)

Parker, Geoffrey, *The Thirty Years' War* (London: Routledge & Kegan Paul, 1984)

Philbrick, Nathaniel, *The Last Stand: Custer, Sitting Bull and the Battle of the Little Big Horn* (London: Bodley Head, 2010)

Pike, Frederick, *The Modern History of Peru* (London: Weidenfeld & Nicolson, 1967)

Pleshakov, Constantine, *The Tsar's Last Armada: The Epic Voyage to the Battle of Tsushima* (New York: Basic Books, 2002)

Porch, Douglas, *Hitler's Mediterranean Gamble: The North African and the Mediterranean Campaigns in World War II* (London: Weidenfeld & Nicolson, 2004)

Rawson, Andrew, *Tet Offensive 1968* (Stroud: History Press, 2013)

Ray, John, *The Battle of Britain: Dowding and the First Victory* (London: Cassell, 2009)

Ready, Dee, *The Battle of Yorktown* (Mankato, Minnesota: Capstone Press, 2002)

Reid, Stuart, *Wolfe: The Career of General James Wolfe from Culloden to Quebec* (Staplehurst, Kent: Spellmount, 2000)

Roberts, Michael, *Gustavus Adolphus: A History of Sweden 1611–1632* (London: Longmans, 1958)

Runciman, Stephen, *A History of the First Bulgarian Empire* (London: G.Bell, 1930)

Sassoon, Siegfried, *The War Poems* (London: Faber & Faber, 1983)

Schom, Alan, *Trafalgar: Countdown to Battle 1803–1805* (London: Michael Joseph, 1990)

Sears, Stephen, *Gettysburg* (New York: Houghton Mifflin, 2003)

Sheffield, Gary, *The Somme* (London: Cassell, 2003)

Sholod, Barton, *Charlemagne in Spain: The Cultural Legacy of Roncesvalles* (Geneva: Droz, 1966)

Showalter, Dennis, *Tannenberg: Clash of Empires* (Dulles, VA: Potomac Books, 2004)

Showalter, Dennis, *The Wars of Frederick the Great* (London: Longman, 1997)

Showalter, Dennis, *The Wars of German Unification* (London: Arnold, 2004)

Sidnell, Philip, *Warhorse: Cavalry in Ancient Warfare* (London: Continuum, 2006)

Smyth, Alfred, *King Alfred the Great* (Oxford: Oxford University Press, 1995)

Speirs, Edward (ed), *Sudan: The Reconquest Reappraised* (London: Frank Cass, 1998)

Strachan, Hew, *The First World War: Volume I* (Oxford: Oxford University Press, 2001)

Strauss, Barry, *The Spartacus War* (London: Weidenfeld & Nicolson, 2009)

Symonds, Craig, *The Battle of Midway* (New York: Oxford University Press, 2011)

Tabraham, Chris, *Bannockburn 1314: Battle for a Nation* (Broxburn: Lomond Books, 2009)

Tonsetic, Robert, *1781: The Decisive Year of the Revolutionary War* (Oxford: Casemate, 2011)

Trigg, Jonathan, *Hastings 1066* (Stroud: History Press, 2012)

Turnbull, Stephen, *Samurai Invasion: Japan's Korean War 1592–98* (London: Cassell, 2002)

Underwood, Geoffrey, *Our Falklands War* (Liskeard: Maritime Books, 1983)

Vance, Eugene, *Reading the Song of Roland* (Englewood Cliffs, NJ: Prentice-Hall, 1970)

Viotti, Andrea, *Garibaldi: The revolutionary and his men* (Poole: Blandford Press, 1979)

Volkogonov, Dmitri, *Stalin: Triumph and Tragedy* (London: Weidenfeld & Nicolson, 1991)

Voroshilov, Kliment, *Stalin and the Red Army* (Moscow: Foreign Languages Publishing House, 1939)

Warlimont, Walter, *Inside Hitler's Headquarters, 1939–1945* (London: Weidenfeld & Nicolson, 1964)

Warren, Alan, *Singapore: Britain's Greatest Defeat* (London: Hambledon, 2002)

Wasti, Syed Tanvir, 'The 1912–13 Balkan Wars and the Siege of Edirne', Middle Eastern Studies, 40 (2004), pp. 59–78

Wheatcroft, Andrew, *Infidels: The Conflict between Christendom and Islam 638–2002* (New York: Penguin Viking, 2003)

White, David, *Bitter Ocean: The Battle of the Atlantic 1939–1945* (New York: Simon & Schuster, 2006)

White, John, *Cortés and the Downfall of the Aztec Empire* (London: Hamish Hamilton, 1971)

Whiting, Roger, *The Enterprise of England: The Spanish Armada* (Gloucester: Alan Sutton, 1988)

Wirtz, James J., *The Tet Offensive: Intelligence Failure in War* (Ithaca, NY: Cornell University Press, 1991)

Woodhouse, C. M., *The Battle of Navarino* (London: Hodder & Stoughton, 1965)

Zamoyski, Adam, *Warsaw 1920: Lenin's Failed Conquest of Europe* (London: HarperCollins, 2008)

INDEX

ACKNOWLEDGEMENTS

In writing the accounts of 100 battles, I have been indebted to the rich literature available on warfare.

I am also indebted to the following for advice when I needed it: Claudia Baldoli, Simon Barton, Stacey Hynd, Matt Rendle, Laura Rowe, Nick Terry and Martin Thomas. My thanks too to the editors at HarperCollins and in particular to Martin Redfern.

Picture credits

The publisher would like to thank the following for their kind permission to reproduce images:

Page 1 (top): Musee de la Marine, Paris, France/J.P. Zenobel/The Bridgeman Art Library; page 1 (bottom): Maciej Szczepanczyk; page 2 (top): jorisvo/Shutterstock; page 2 (bottom): Sayf al-Vâhidî; page 3 (top): Pictorial Press Ltd/Alamy; page 3 (bottom): Prisma Archivo/Alamy; page 4 (top left): Sovfoto/Universal Images Group/Getty; page 4 (bottom): The Art Archive/Alamy; page 5 (top): GL Archive/Alamy; page 5 (bottom): Paul Popper/Popperfoto/Getty; page 6 (top): Florilegius/Alamy; page 6 (bottom): Everett Collection Historical/Alamy; page 7 (top): Martin, Pierre-Denis/Private Collection/The Bridgeman Art Library; page 7 (bottom): Mary Evans Picture Library/Alamy; page 8 (top): Classic Image/Alamy; page 8 (middle): Ognyan Stefanov; page 8 (bottom): Keith Tarrier/Shutterstock; page 9 (top): U.S. Army; page 9 (bottom): Andrew Holt/Alamy; page 10 (top): Ralf Hettler/Getty; page 10 (bottom): The Bridgeman Art Library/Getty; page 11 (top): The Gallery Collection/Corbis; page 11 (bottom): De Agostini/Getty Images; page 12 (top): The Bridgeman Art Library/Getty; page 12 (bottom): Bettmann/Corbis; page 13 (top): Hulton Archive/Getty; page 13 (bottom): Hulton Archive/Getty; page 14 (top):

Adam Cuerden; page 14 (bottom): Imperial War Museum; page 15 (top): Universal Images Group/Getty; page 15 (bottom): De Agostini/Getty; page 16 (top): Hulton-Deutsch Collection/CORBIS; page 16 (middle): Smithsonian Institution/Corbis; page 16 (bottom): Richard Cooke/Alamy